TALK ABOUT A DREAM

TALK ABOUT A DREAM

THE ESSENTIAL INTERVIEWS OF BRUCE SPRINGSTEEN

Edited by Christopher Phillips
and Louis P. Masur

BLOOMSBURY PRESS
NEW YORK • LONDON • NEW DELHI • SYDNEY

Published by Bloomsbury Press, New York

All papers used by Bloomsbury Press are natural, recyclable products made from wood grown in well-managed forests. The manufacturing processes conform to the environmental regulations of the country of origin.

LIBRARY OF CONGRESS CATALOGING-IN-PUBLICATION DATA

Talk about a dream : the essential interviews of Bruce Springsteen / edited by Christopher Phillips and Louis P. Masur.—First U.S. edition.
pages cm
Includes index.
ISBN 978-1-62040-072-2
1. Springsteen, Bruce—Interviews. 2. Rock musicians—United States—Interviews. I. Phillips, Christopher (Christopher Blake), 1971–, editor. II. Masur, Louis P., editor. III. Springsteen, Bruce.
ML420.S77A5 2013
782.42166092—dc23
2013007766

First U.S. Edition 2013

1 3 5 7 9 10 8 6 4 2

Typeset by Westchester Book Group
Printed and bound in the U.S.A. by Thomson-Shore, Inc. Dexter, Michigan

For
Lucy, Ben, and Sophie

Contents

Introduction
Christopher Phillips and Louis P. Masur

"Rock 'n' roll is my life's blood"—Bruce Springsteen, 1977

BRUCE SPRINGSTEEN'S FIRST album, *Greetings from Asbury Park, N.J.*, appeared in January 1973. Shortly afterward he spoke to a reporter for the *Asbury Park Evening Press* who noted how "he mumbled in a characteristically sullen manner." Asked about his future, Bruce said, "It's a waste of time to think about it. I'd rather think about my music."

Forty years later, thanks to that focus on his art, Bruce Springsteen stands as one of the defining artists and public figures of his generation. Time and again his work has rhymed with the times, whether *Born to Run* (1975), *Born in the U.S.A.* (1984), *The Rising* (2002), or *Wrecking Ball* (2012). He has released 17 studio albums, performed before millions of fans worldwide in marathon shows that inspire and thrill, and has become a voice for everyday people struggling with circumstance. "My work has always been about judging the distance between American reality and the American dream," he told reporters in 2012.

Springsteen has taken that measure not only through his songs but also in dozens of interviews with print, radio, and television journalists. "Talk" is a crucial word in the Springsteen lexicon, and it appears time and again in song lyrics, whether "I talk the way I wanna talk" from

"Out in the Street," or "I learned how to make it talk" (his guitar, of course) from "Thunder Road," or "talk about a dream" from "Badlands." Bruce has been singing and talking about dreams his entire life—dreams of escape, community, love, and life itself. The music is well known and fully celebrated; the talk, however, has never before been collected. Bruce's interviews provide a running account of the artist's life—at least those aspects he is willing to discuss, and there are few subjects that he has not eventually addressed. The interviews are key sources for understanding what Springsteen was thinking and feeling at the time.

The interviews gathered here, many of them rare and including never-before transcribed radio and television interviews, provide a multidimensional portrait of an artist of international renown. They are essential to any attempt to understand Springsteen, his work, and his place in culture. In this volume he talks to us—directly and passionately.

For those who have heard Bruce talk about his work only recently, speaking with clarity and authority about his beliefs and experiences, it may come as a surprise that it took him a long time to become master of his own public voice, to teach himself to speak fully and intelligently, with bursts of deep insight and carefree humor. In 1974, Philadelphia DJ Ed Sciaky said to Bruce, "I know you don't like to talk too much about things." Indeed, Bruce often stuttered and stammered, deflecting any serious questions to joke and goof around. Typescripts do not always capture the meaning of early interviews because we can't hear the inflection of Bruce's voice, the way he swallows his words and tries to sound cool. He is fresh from the Shore, and he wants only to play music and save whatever talking he is going to do for the stage.

The fame that came with *Born to Run* didn't make him any more comfortable. Through the 1970s and 1980s Springsteen had an uneasy relationship with his celebrity. He mistrusted the considerable hype around him and despaired over "hustling for the record machine," as he phrased it in "Jungleland." But if his public voice remained restrained, his musical voice blossomed. His work began to move away from stories of youth and romance to a deeper inquiry into the struggles of survival and the everyday lives of working-class people. Musically, his composing became more taut—coiled songs that unleashed blows to head and heart. Onstage, Bruce spoke ever more openly about personal matters, such as his relationship with his father, and larger social issues such as the plight of Vietnam veterans.

The international success of *Born in the U.S.A.* in 1984 gave Bruce a truly massive public pulpit. He was drawn into discussing the meaning of his work when the president of the United States offered him up as example of the optimistic youth of America. Bruce, in turn, found a new voice, both in his music as well as in his interviews. Partly as a matter of "growin' up," partly a result of expanded horizons, Springsteen grew increasingly fluent in articulating his own vision, rather than allowing the Reagans of the world to do it for him. As his work brought him to the world stage, Springsteen's casual, cool-cat patois of the '70s fully gave way to meditative, carefully observed expression (with high-pitched laughter interspersed). By 1992, a journalist observed, "Springsteen has little small talk. His answers to questions are all long, often mazy and frequently beyond the reach of punctuation, but they are always answers and do betray the signs of having had some considerable thought expended on them."

He also took an inward, private turn. He married (and divorced and remarried) and became a father. He and the E Street Band separated, and the gap in interviews from the late '80s to the early '90s mirrors Bruce's own withdrawal, not from the music scene but from larger-than-life iconic status. By the time he reunited with the E Street Band and heeded a call to respond to 9/11, he was prepared for another act in a career in its third decade. Springsteen embraced and enlarged his place in American culture and accepted the challenge of being a voice of conscience and commitment without losing sight of the essential joy of rock 'n' roll played live and loud. A decade down the road, both his voice and his huge audience are steady.

Reading some of the most incisive interviews he has given over 40 years enables us to chart this development as a musician and as a public figure. These interviews offer insights into everything from the roots of his rock 'n' roll passion, the meaning of his songs, and his performance onstage, to his childhood memories, his intellectual and emotional awakenings, and his deepening political commitment. Bruce has not spoken with a single, unchanging voice. Through the interviews, we can hear his diction change as he morphs from a young punk on the streets (and boardwalks) to a chastened rocker facing the darkness of fame to a misunderstood, pumped-up symbol of America gone awry to a husband and father and activist who in late middle age sought to make America live up to its promises. Just as his music has changed, so has he, and only through these interviews can we come to understand Springsteen's various personas and his ever-evolving meaning.

BORN IN FREEHOLD, New Jersey, on September 23, 1949, Bruce Frederick Joseph Springsteen, descended from Dutch, Irish, and Italian stock, had a working-class upbringing. His father, Douglas, held a variety of jobs—as a factory worker in a rug mill, a bus driver, and even a prison guard for a spell. His mother, Adele, was employed as a legal secretary. Bruce's younger sisters, Virginia and Pamela, were born in 1950 and 1962 respectively.

Springsteen attended parochial school at St. Rose of Lima through eighth grade, from 1954 to 1963, and graduated from Freehold High School in 1967. By all accounts he was an outsider, a loner whom his teachers did not understand. "A screw-up, in a small town" is how he later described himself. While the vocabulary of religious training permeates his work (sin, redemption, salvation, promised land), the experience of parochial school left its marks. "I hated school," he recalled in 1978. "I had the big hate." Freehold High wasn't any better. Nearly 40 years after he graduated, he was given an award in absentia and sent along an acceptance speech: "My advice to teachers today is to keep your eyes on the ones who don't fit in. Those are the ones that can think out of the box. You'll never know where they'll be going."

Life wasn't much better at home. While Adele was nurturing and loving, Douglas was angry and bitter. Father and son often clashed. "I remember when I was a kid," Bruce recalls, "I always wondered what my old man was so mad about all the time." Many a night Bruce stormed out of the house, only to find his father waiting in the kitchen on his return. Thinking of his father's existence, Bruce said in 1981, "when I was real young I decided that if I was gonna have to live that way, I was gonna die."

The guitar saved him. He first became enamored at age seven after seeing Elvis Presley on the *Ed Sullivan Show*, but his hands were too small to play. When he was 13 or 14 he tried again. He bought a guitar for 18 dollars, and he rarely set it down. "Everything from then on revolved around music. Everything," he would recall. "I was someone who grew up in isolation, emotionally. That's how I learned to play the guitar. I played for eight hours a day in my room." Time and again "music saved me. From the beginning, my guitar was something I could go to . . . Once I found the guitar," he realized, "I had the key to the highway."

But Springsteen's embrace of rock 'n' roll did nothing to ease tensions at home. Onstage, before introducing his cover of the Animals' "It's My Life," he would tell a long story about screaming battles with his father, his mother trying to pull his father off him, his running once again out the door. "There were two things that were unpopular in my house," he realized. "One was me, the other one was my guitar." Bruce would eventually make peace with his father and appreciate the irony of Douglas attending his concerts where the decibels far exceeded anything ever heard at home.

All Bruce cared about was the music. It is all that has ever preoccupied him (other than, some might add, cars and girls). Being true to his art and his audience is a recurring theme through some 40 years of interviews. It accounts for the weeks spent in the studio, recording take after take, rewriting the lyrics, laying down tracks that would not be released because he thought they were not good enough. It accounts for his work as a bandleader, playing for decades with a group of friends— the E Street Band—and driving the unit until night after night it reached new heights. It accounts for live performances that stretch for three or more hours, never the same set twice, never routine but singular, never mechanical but creative. "The only thing that matters is your music," says Springsteen.

The Springsteen family moved to California in 1969, but Bruce remained in New Jersey and relocated to Asbury Park, where he pursued a rock 'n' roll career in bars and clubs. He developed his craft playing in bands such as the Castiles (1965–68) and then with Earth (1968), Child (1969), and Steel Mill (1970–71). After they disbanded, Bruce continued to perform with different combinations of friends. He played regularly at the clubs of Asbury Park, especially the Upstage from 1968 to 1971 as well as other venues such as the Student Prince and the Wonder Bar. In 1972, Bruce signed a management deal with Mike Appel and auditioned for John Hammond, who had signed Bob Dylan at Columbia Records.

Springsteen would have to shed the label of "new Dylan," which stuck not only from having been signed by Hammond (who said Bruce was farther along than Dylan was at the same age), but also from writing frenzied, funhouse lyrics that sounded like no one else's. Critics had been anointing musicians the next Dylan since 1966, when Dylan withdrew from the public eye, and Springsteen was the latest selection.

Signed, like Dylan, as a solo acoustic performer, he confounded expectations by showing up with a band for his first album. In summer 1973 he recorded his second album, *The Wild, the Innocent & the E Street Shuffle*. The effort received rave reviews including a notice in the *New York Times* that said "Springsteen has delivered another stone, howling, joyous monster of a record . . . Can you imagine what his third album will be like?" the reviewer asked.

That third album proved to be a horror—to Springsteen himself, at least. He felt pressure from Columbia Records to produce a hit; he felt pressure about being labeled the future of rock 'n' roll, an out-of-context line from a review by the critic Jon Landau (who would soon come to be Bruce's producer); he felt pressure from within, an artist determined to create music that transcended what he had done before. After spending six months recording the song "Born to Run," David Sancious (whose Jersey Shore address gave the band its name) and Ernest Carter left the group. A new keyboardist, Roy Bittan, and drummer, Max Weinberg, came onboard. Along with Clarence Clemons on saxophone, Danny Federici on organ, Steve Van Zandt on guitar, and Garry Tallent on bass, they would constitute the E Street Band.

He almost didn't want the third album to be released. "The tension making that record I could never describe," Bruce told one journalist in 1975. "It was killing, almost, it was inhuman. I hated it. I couldn't stand it. It was the worst, hardest, lousiest thing I ever had to do." But *Born to Run* made him a star. He appeared on the covers of both *Time* and *Newsweek* that fall, he played London for the first time, and he received stellar reviews. Writing in *Rolling Stone*, Greil Marcus called it "a magnificent album" and predicted "it should crack his career wide open."

But just as soon as the horizon seemed limitless, the heavens collapsed. A protracted lawsuit against his manager, Mike Appel, to regain control of his music kept him from recording. It took nearly a year for the suit to be settled. Bruce returned to the studio with dozens of songs and, in 1978, released *Darkness on the Edge of Town*. Three years between albums is an eternity in the recording industry. The new album was stark and inspiring, both angry and hopeful. Bruce told Peter Knobler, "on *Born to Run* there was the hope of the free ride. On *Darkness*, there ain't no free ride—you wanna ride, you gotta pay." These polarities of light and darkness, hope and despair, salvation and damnation permeate Springsteen's work and are a recurrent theme in the interviews.

Springsteen toured extensively behind *Darkness*, and some of that tour's performances are considered among the finest that he and the band have ever delivered. Once it ended, he was back in the studio, this time recording dozens of new songs. Bruce refused to compromise on the artistic process, and these interviews reveal a person who might give up a lot, but never control. "You make your record like it's the last record you'll ever make," he told Dave DiMartino. What emerged was a double album, *The River*, which traversed a range of emotion, from ebullient rockers to poignant ballads. The album reached number one on the charts and gave Springsteen his first top-ten hit with the song "Hungry Heart."

The *River* tour took Springsteen to Europe, and there he gained a new perspective on the United States and started thinking deeply about the American experience. Bruce had always told stories onstage. However much he squirmed when talking to a single interviewer, he had little difficulty staring into a darkened sold-out arena and offering fantasies and confessions. Sometimes he told long, whimsical tales such as when he introduced "The E Street Shuffle" in 1975 or "Growin' Up" in 1976. Sometimes, the stories took a more personal and serious tone. During the *River* tour, while introducing "Independence Day," he often admitted, "I grew up in a house where it seems nobody ever talked to each other." Bruce had to learn how to open up, and as he thought deeply about his upbringing he wondered "how things got to be the way they are today, how you end up a victim without even knowing it, and how people get old and just die after not having hardly a day's satisfaction or peace of mind in their lives."

Following the tour for *The River*, Springsteen started to see a psychiatrist. He found himself at home in Colts Neck writing a new group of songs. "I was interested in writing kind of smaller than I had been," he said. Although he originally intended to record the new songs with the band, he ultimately released his stark, home demo: *Nebraska* wound up a solo, largely acoustic album about American isolation, an album influenced by distinctive "outsider" American voices from Hank Williams and Flannery O'Connor to the dark, electronic proto-punk band Suicide. *Rolling Stone* called it "a violent, acid-etched portrait of a wounded America that fuels its machinery by consuming its people's dreams."

Nebraska also showed that Springsteen would follow his muse and not be governed by his rock star fame, by audience or record-label expectations. Ironically, while he was considering whether to record *Nebraska* material with his band, Bruce wound up laying down the first side of *Born in the U.S.A.*, an album that would take Bruce from mere stardom to a place in the rock firmament few ever achieve. *Born in the U.S.A.* would eventually sell more than twenty million copies, it would yield seven top-ten singles, and it would compel the artist to speak more publicly than before about the meaning of his work and his political views. There was no denying the massive popularity of the 1984 album and '84–'85 tour, which found Bruce and his E Street Band essentially conquering the world, playing massive stadiums from Europe to Japan.

After the *Born in the U.S.A.* juggernaut, Bruce says he "went through a very confusing time, a depression really . . . I began to reassess everything I'd gone through . . . I just felt overwhelmed by the whole thing. I felt dehumanized," he confided in 1992. Springsteen had faced deep changes. His oldest friend, Steve Van Zandt, left the band in 1984 (Nils Lofgren replaced him); he met the actress Julianne Phillips and married in May 1985 (they would separate three years later); he continued to seek help in therapy. Bruce released *Tunnel of Love*, a quiet album filled with reflective songs of love, loss, and loneliness, as much an antithesis to *Born in the U.S.A.* as *Nebraska* was to *The River*. In 1989, the E Street Band officially disbanded. Springsteen told James Henke, "I just kind of felt 'Bruced' out."

He continued to follow his muse and in 1992 released two albums, *Human Touch* and *Lucky Town*, and toured with a new group of musicians ("I thought it was time to play with other people"). He also did something that, as a 25-year-old, he would not have imagined: in 1990 he became a father. Bruce soon married Patti Scialfa, a Jersey girl who joined the E Street Band on the *Born in the U.S.A.* tour. Two more children would follow. The responsibilities of family and friendship, of coming to terms with his identity as a son, husband, and father, as a bandleader and as the "Boss," a nickname he always despised, are recurrent motifs in these interviews.

Entering the 1990s, Bruce was no longer the laconic punk of his twenties or the muscular superstar of his thirties. He was intent on dismantling his iconic stature and reclaiming his identity. "I thought I had to reintroduce myself as a songwriter," he told *Rolling Stone*. He also needed at the time to free himself from New Jersey; so he settled in Los Angeles where he could escape from being "a figment of your own imagination." Music was his life, it had saved him from his father's fate, it gave him a reason to live, and it was the only form of communication that mattered to him. In "Thunder Road," Bruce wrote that he had learned how to make his guitar talk. Now he had also learned how to communicate without the instrument. "The two best days of my life," he realized, "were the day I picked up the guitar and the day that I learned how to put it down."

Always attuned to the promise and perils of the American dream, Springsteen, in the '90s—in the aftermath of a six-week tour for Amnesty International in 1988 and the Los Angeles Riots of 1992—seemed even more keenly engaged in his work with the problems of social justice. "Streets of Philadelphia," about the ravages of AIDS, won an Academy Award in 1994 for Best Song. A few years later he wrote "American Skin (41 Shots)" in response to the police shooting of an unarmed immigrant in New York City. In 1995 he reunited in the studio with E Street Band members to record several new songs for a *Greatest Hits* compilation. One of them, "This Hard Land," revisited ground covered by the Woody Guthrie classic "This Land Is Your Land."

That same year, Bruce released *The Ghost of Tom Joad* and launched an extensive solo tour behind it. John Ford's classic film *The Grapes of Wrath* (more than the Steinbeck novel) had profoundly affected Springsteen, who admitted to having wept at the memorable final speech of Henry Fonda's character, Tom Joad. The stripped-down solo album was Bruce's attempt to examine "what the country feels like to me right now," and the pared-down solo performances "makes what you are about and what you are doing real clear." Bruce was always a folk artist and a rock artist, a soloist and a band leader, and through much of the '90s it was the folk voice that reemerged in his writing and performing.

Working together in the studio with the E Street Band in 1995 sowed the seeds for a reunion. They hadn't recorded together in nearly a decade. "One of the things I realized when I saw the guys," he told Neil Strauss, "was that we're like each others' arms and legs."

He also seemed ready to rediscover the pure joy of what he did best. "It's the greatest, greatest job in the world," he told Mark Hagen in 1999. "I still try to do it as well as I can and hopefully better than I have done it previously." That year, he was inducted into the Rock and Roll Hall of Fame; he simultaneously re-formed the E Street Band—including, as in '95, both Lofgren and Van Zandt—and began a reunion tour that celebrated "the power and the glory, the majesty, the mystery, the ministry of rock and roll!"

The events of September 11, 2001, propelled Bruce further into the public arena and perhaps to a deeper understanding of his place not only as a rock star but also as a citizen. Not long after 9/11 and *The Rising*, his first album of new studio material with the E Street Band since 1984, Springsteen shed his reluctance to engage overtly in politics. In an editorial published in the *New York Times* in August 2004 he announced that he would be part of a broad constituency of musicians who would devote themselves to Vote for Change, to get people to register and work "to change the direction of the government and change the current administration come November." The policies of the Bush administration felt like an assault on the working and middle classes, and Bruce felt the stakes had risen to a point where he could no longer stay out of politics: "I've tried to think long and hard about what it means to be an American," and this was the time, he felt, to fight for "the country we carry in our hearts." These interviews reveal Bruce's development as a citizen working to understand the meaning of America and taking measures to help refashion it.

. Since 2004, Springsteen has continued his activism and has campaigned for John Kerry and Barack Obama. He has encouraged fans from stage night after night to fight back against the erosion the American dream. In a series of albums (*Devils & Dust, Seeger Sessions, Magic, Working on a Dream*) he continued to write and perform folk and rock songs that inspire and entertain, that make the audience feel alive. "The greatest pop music," Bruce has observed, is a "music of liberation."

In February 2012, before a group of international journalists in Paris, Bruce spoke at length about music and politics. Now 62, Bruce was about to release a new album, *Wrecking Ball*, and embark on a world tour, but this time without Clarence Clemons, who had passed away in June 2011. A few years earlier, the band had lost Danny Federici. "Losing Clarence," Springsteen said, "is like losing the rain, or air." But while the ghosts of his bandmates can be heard in its grooves, Bruce was never one to look back: this new record was a driving and direct response to the state of our nation's post-financial crisis

Wrecking Ball was a call to arms; it sought to startle, inspire, incite, and enlist. It lifted listeners up and knocked them down. It was unlike anything Springsteen had done before, and yet it was familiar, part of his ongoing meditation on the meaning of America. It was an angry album, and, asked about it in Paris, Springsteen smiled and observed, "you can never go wrong pissed off in rock 'n' roll."

Bruce's interview performance before international journalists was a measure of how far he had come as a public figure. Speaking to so many outlets at once, he deftly used the media pulpit to sell his work, deliver his message, and win over new fans while gesturing appreciatively to his older ones.

Springsteen's talk matters profoundly; these interviews are essential to gaining insight into the person, the work, and the changing times. But we must take care not to mistake the musings of the artist for the art. ("Trust the art, be suspicious of the artist. He's generally untrustworthy," says Bruce.) Throughout these interviews, Springsteen provides substantial insight into his life and music at different moments. But he also reminds us that his job is not to speak but to shout. "I'm a lifetime musician," he declared at age 43. "I'm going to be playing music forever. I don't foresee a time when I would not be onstage somewhere, playing a guitar and playing it loud, with power and passion. I look forward to being 60 or 65 and doing that." On September 22, 2012, Springsteen and the E Street Band performed a *Wrecking Ball* concert before a sold-out crowd at MetLife Stadium in New Jersey. At midnight, he turned 63.

Barbara Schoenweis
The Asbury Park Evening Press,
February 9, 1973

Springsteen's first album, *Greetings from Asbury Park, N.J.*, was released January 5, 1973. A month later he spoke with his hometown paper. Twenty-three years old, Springsteen was already a veteran of the
Jersey Shore club scene. Some of the key themes to his early career
are already here: his anxiety over being part of a big company and
not having control, his insistence on playing good music, the comparisons to Bob Dylan, and his desire to be "honest" about what he is doing. Barbara Schoenweis notes that his songs "have an urgency that is
typical of his generation, and more so, of Bruce himself."

Springsteen Takes City Aloft

Music put Asbury Park on the map about 30 years ago when Frank
Sinatra asked "Is it Grenada I see or only Asbury Park?"

Well, it's back on the map again in a more contemporary version
with Bruce Springsteen's new LP for Columbia Records, *Greetings from
Asbury Park, N.J.* The jacket is a blow-up of a popular color postcard
found among the city's famous boardwalk's stands.

Bruce, who hails from Freehold and moved here when he was 18, has been singing and playing guitar in the area for nearly 10 of his 23 years, both on his own and with bands like Steel Mill. And now on his way to the top, he'll be stopping at the Sunshine Inn tomorrow night to perform for his loyal and local fans. Then it's off to California for six weeks where he'll be on bills with groups like the Beach Boys, Paul Butterfield, and others. He recently finished a week's gig at Max's Kansas City, New York, which he says was an unusual experience because the crowd really came to listen to him and his band.

On one of his rare stays at his apartment in Bradley Beach, he visited The Press to talk about what it's been like being pushed into the limelight in less than six weeks. Dressed in a tattered green leather jacket, jeans, a wrinkled shirt, and lace-up boots, he hardly looks like the picture of upcoming fame and fortune. He does not seem impressed, either, by the machinery that has put him where he is, only somewhat shaken up by it.

"There's a lot of confusion," he says, about how it's been since his friend and local manager "Tinker" (Carl West) introduced him to Mike Appel and Jim Cretecos in New York and how from there he met John Hammond who got him on the Columbia label.

"He's the same guy who introduced Billie Holiday, Aretha Franklin, and Bob Dylan," says Bruce. "The man knows his business."

"It's weird working for a big company, though," he mumbled in a characteristically sullen manner. "It was like pulling teeth to get me to sign. You're not your own man anymore. But you can always get up and walk away from it all. What can they do, sue me for my shoes? I ain't got nothin' else."

Of course, he admits, his attitude toward this whole new world changes each day with whether he's eaten and slept well.

"Some days you think when you start making a record, people drive you nuts," he says. "Somehow it all comes back to money. And then other days you meet some really great people and it seems all worth it and terrific."

On the way to where he is now, Bruce spent his time playing back street clubs and bars in the area for pin money, and made himself a respected but controversial reputation, because he believed in being honest with his audience and doing only music he thought was good.

"I broke up a lot of bands in my day," he admits with a wry grin, "because I'd get up there and start playing junk with them, and all of a sudden in the middle of it all, I'd just stop and say, 'What is this jive?'"

"All you can ask of a person is that he's honest about what he's doing. I hope I'll never change in that respect," he continues. "The world does not need another four-piece rock 'n' roll band, and the market needs less to be flooded with more junk."

When you ask Bruce what his music is all about (he wrote and arranged and plays all nine songs on his album), he tells you to listen to the record. When you ask him about his background, he tells you that he doesn't go in for a personality image, that it's his music that should stand or fall on its own.

His music style is not unlike Bob Dylan's in mood and sound, but it is also unique in the way he puts words and sounds together. His tunes are not melodic but they have a drive, an urgency that is typical of his generation, and more so, of Bruce himself. His lyrics go from poetic and highly intelligible to wanderings of a way-out mind or a bad trip.

Among the best songs on the album is "Lost in the Flood," a piece which marries the hypocrisy of the Vietnam War to the hypocrisy of our everyday lives. Bruce has a knack for bringing things to light in vivid images, some of which are drawn from local landmarks and the landmarks of his past.

The ragamuffin gunner is returning home like a hungry runaway.
He walks through the town all alone
He must be from the fort he hears the high school girls say.
His countryside's burnin' with wolfman fairies dressed in drag for
*   homicide*
The hit and run, plead sanctuary 'neath a holy stone they hide.
They're breakin' beams and crosses with a spastic's reelin' perfection
Nuns run bald through Vatican halls pregnant, pleadin' immaculate
*   conception.*
And everybody's wrecked on Main Street from drinking unholy
*   blood.*

And then there's what Bruce does admit to as his "nothing" songs:

Madman drummers bummers and Indians in the summer with a
teen-age diplomat. In the dumps with the mumps as the adolescent
pumps his way into his hat. With a bolder on my shoulder, feelin'
kinda older I tripped the merry-go-round. With this very unpleasing
sneezing and wheezing the calliope crashed to the ground.

He plays the acoustic, electric guitars, and bass as well as the harmonica on his album. He's a self-taught musician, who can read music "a little" and who started playing piano when his grandfather gave him one at age 14.

"It was one of the nicest things that ever happened to me," he says.

Bruce is backed up by a group of local musicians who, at this point, have no trade name. They are Vincent Lopez on drums, Clarence Clemons on sax and background vocals, Garry Tallent, bass, David Sancious, piano and organ. Harold Wheeler and Richard Davis fill in on piano and bass in a couple of songs.

What's different about Bruce's songs that made him catch the ears of the music world?

"Well, it's me," he says.

And about the future?

"It's a waste of time to think about it," he comments. "I'd rather think about my music."

Robert Hilburn
Melody Maker,
August 24, 1974

Like many critics, Robert Hilburn discovered Springsteen early on
and became an enthusiastic supporter. Music editor at the *Los Angeles
Times*, Hilburn made sure that LA audiences heard about the shows at
the Santa Monica Civic Auditorium and the Troubadour in July 1974
and were primed for a series of historic shows Bruce would perform at
the Roxy in October 1975. With his first two albums out, Bruce admits
"the writing is more difficult now." He was working on what would be
his make-or-break third album, and he was feeling the pressure. "You
have to let out more of yourself all the time. You strip off the first layer,
then the second, then the third. It gets harder because it's more personal."

"The writing is more difficult now," said Bruce Springsteen, the hot
new, much acclaimed American singer-songwriter, as he sat in his modest hotel room (he isn't booking suites yet) after a Santa Monica Civic
Auditorium [show] and tried to put his suddenly accelerating career
into perspective.

"I got a lot of things out in that first album. I let out an incredible amount of things at once—a million things in each song. They were written in half hour, 15 minute blasts. I don't know where they came from. A few of them I worked on for a week or so, but most of them were just jets, a real energy situation.

"I had all that stuff stored up for years because there was no outlet in the bars I had been playing because no-one's listening in a bar and if they are, you've got a low PA [system] and they can't hear the words anyway. So, the first album was a big outlet.

"On the second album, I started slowly to find out who I am and where I want to be. It was like coming out of the shadow of various influences and trying to be me," continued the 24-year-old who bears a startling facial resemblance to Bob Dylan on stage.

"You have to let out more of yourself all the time. You strip off the first layer, then the second, then the third. It gets harder because it's more personal."

Though Springsteen had received three standing ovations at the evening's concert, he was still vaguely displeased with the show. Because he was the opening act (for Dr. John), he had been limited to 45 minutes. Too short, he felt.

"It was like we didn't even play at all," he muttered in his slightly shy, hesitant way. "It reminded me of the time we toured with Chicago. We got introduced, walked on stage, blinked and that was it. It's hard to show an audience what the band is about in that little time."

But Springsteen had salvaged some of the evening for himself through his choice of an encore number. For most of the show, he and his five-piece band had given the audience uptempo tunes—songs bristling with the fire, energy, passion and sensualness of the New York and New Jersey streets of his youth.

For the encore, however, he played the slow, disarming "New York Serenade," a tune that detracted from rather than added to the strong energy level that had been building in the auditorium.

The applause was clearly less when he finished that song than it would have been if he had given the audience another boogie number. But Springsteen had known it would happen and, unlike many young performers eager for the strongest possible applause, he had done it anyway.

Springsteen is shooting for high stakes in rock and he knows there are no short cuts. By doing "New York Serenade," he was telling the audience and reminding himself that the song is just as much of his music as the uptempo numbers.

It's a combination the public ultimately is going to have to accept or reject so why not, he figured, lay it on the line now.

"I thought it was important to do that song," he said. "It completed the set for me. It might get more response to do a boom-boom thing and really rock the joint, but when I walked down the steps afterward I felt complete. Otherwise, I feel messed up.

"It's just being honest with the audience and with myself, I guess. You can't conform to the formula of always giving the audience what it wants or you're killing yourself and you're killing the audience.

"Because they don't really want it either. Just because they respond to something doesn't mean they want it. I think it has come to the point where they respond automatically to things they think they should respond to. You've got to give them more than that."

Springsteen, who began playing in rock bands around his native New Jersey while in his early teens, burst onto the national pop music scene in 1972 with an album (*Greetings from Asbury Park, N.J.*) that reminded you of Dylan because of its machine-gun barrage of surrealistic lyrics, such as these from "Blinded By the Light."

Some brimstone baritone anti-cyclone rolling stone preacher from the east.
He says, "Dethrone the Dictaphone, hit it in its funny bone. That's where they expect it the least."

Because the album stressed lyrics more than music (Columbia had originally encouraged him to simply record the songs with a guitar backing, but he insisted on using a band), Springsteen was immediately thrown into the folk-flavoured, singer-songwriter category where some began hailing him—along with John Prine, Elliott Murphy, Jackson Browne and Loudon Wainwright III—as the new Dylan. His second album, *The Wild, the Innocent & the E Street Shuffle*, made enormous strides towards giving Springsteen that separate identity.

Without sacrificing the surrealistic lyrics, both his themes—normally reflecting the innocence, wonder, frustrations, urgency of youth—were more disciplined and his musical backing bolder than in the first album.

In a song like "Sandy," Springsteen brings together several of his themes, set against the natural illusion/fantasy setting of an amusement park:

Sandy, the fireworks are hailing over little Eden tonight.
Forcing a light into all those stoney faces left stranded on this warm
   July . . .
And the boys from the casino dance with their shirts open like Latin
   lovers on the shore
Chasin' those silly New York virgins by the score . . .
Did you hear the cops finally busted Madame Marie
For telling fortunes better than they do . . .

What Springsteen does is compress a broad collection of scenes into song, leaving the listener to draw his own truths, realities. He, thus, provides a puzzle for his audience to assemble. Clues, rather than the answers.

"There's a certain understatement that is important to maintain," he explained—speaking slowly—a bit uncertain about how much an artist should reveal of himself.

"People don't want to see things in black and white," he continued. "Songs have to have possibilities. You have to let the audience search it out for themselves. You can't say, 'Here it is. This is exactly what I mean' and give it to them. You have to let them search."

Despite his reluctant, withdrawn manner off-stage, Springsteen brings a sense of drama with him on stage. It's not the staged theatrics of an Alice Cooper, but the strong sense of a powerful, charismatic performer. He has the same cold, intent, determined, uncompromising stance that Dylan brings on stage.

Wearing a white undershirt (not a T-shirt) and black pants that underscore the street roots of his music, Springsteen, also wearing dark glasses that make his music all the more mysterious, attacks the microphone with a sudden barrage of words, retreats like a prizefighter to a neutral corner as the band plays, then returns for another assault.

On the second number, he picks up an electric guitar and later, more in the style of Elvis than Dylan, points the neck to the ceiling and twists his way across stage. It was done more in the sense of relieving tension in his music than, as Elvis would have done, to elicit shrieks from female fans.

Springsteen's no sex symbol. He's more a challenger, a stimulator of thoughts and emotions.

Despite the many Dylan comparisons, it was Presley who first pushed Springsteen toward music. He remembers seeing Elvis on the old Ed Sullivan television show. Springsteen was just nine at the time, but asked his mother for a guitar. She got him the guitar but also made him take lessons which he hated so much he ended up discarding the guitar.

It wasn't until the Beatles arrived in 1964 that he picked up the guitar again. This time he taught himself how to play. Within six months he had formed his first band.

"Before that I didn't have any purpose. I tried to play football and baseball and all those things. I checked out all the alleys and just didn't fit. I was running through a maze. Music gave me something. It was a reason to live."

Over the next few years, Springsteen was in and out of several bands, eventually moving from school dances to bars, clubs and even a couple of cross-country tours. He played the Fillmore West in San Francisco when he was 18 and auditioned for Fillmore Records while on the coast but was turned down. He was signed by Columbia in 1972.

"I never got into being discouraged because I never got into hoping," he said with a laugh. "When I was a kid, I never got used to expecting success. I got used to failing.

"Once you do that, the rest is easy. It took a lot of pressure off. I just said, 'Hell, I'm a loser. I don't have to worry about anything.' I assumed immediately nothing was happening.

"But that's not the same," he said, pausing to emphasize the difference in concepts, "as giving up. You keep trying, but you don't count on things. It can be a strength. Because I know some people who sweat out winning so much it kills them. So in the end, they lose anyway. They win, but they lose."

He's now looking forward to recording his third album and expanding his band (it now includes organ, piano, saxophone, guitar, bass, drums) with more horns. Unlike most of his songwriting contemporaries, he prizes the music as much as the lyrics.

"You've got to work on the different levels," he said.

Ed Sciaky
WMMR,
November 3, 1974

Ed Sciaky, of WMMR Philadelphia, was one of the first disc jockeys to champion Springsteen; the impact of that support in what would become the career-long fan stronghold of Philly can't be overestimated. For this, one of their many on-air chats, Sciaky was surprised not only that Bruce actually showed up at the studio the day after a Tower Theater show, but that he also brought along several others members of the band. On the one hand, Springsteen isn't so much forthcoming in this setting; on the other, he's clearly relaxed and enjoying himself. With plenty of goofing around, he even does an on-air advertisement for Santori wine and ad-libs "you can pour it all over your face." More consequentially, Springsteen brought along a tape of "Born to Run," his new song that would be released the following summer. It is the studio recording's worldwide premiere. Asked how he likes hearing it on the radio, Bruce only responds, "Do I get to do another commercial."

I'm sure a lot of people would like to know the honest and true story of the actual history of you and the bands and so on. When

you started and all that stuff. Also I'll mention that you told me once you don't really like to do interviews.
It's the same old story.

That's why I really appreciate you coming down here today.
It's the same as everything else, every other kid, 13, pick up the guitar, scrub away on it. I had a succession of every sort of band you could imagine. Ten piece bands, three piece bands, power trios. Everything. We played down in Virginia a lot. That's where we made our living, between Virginia and New Jersey.

One day I was sitting on my porch and this guy said, Hey, come on up to New York and meet this guy. I said, Nah, I don't want to go to New York, I don't want to meet this guy. A week or so later he came by and said "I'm coming up tonight, it's a nice night." I was totally bored so I said okay and I got in the car and met Mike [Appel]. He said, "I want to be your manager." I said I'd think about it. I went away for about five months. I went to California.

How old were you at this time?
I don't know. Jesus, I must have been, this must have happened when I was about 22. Twenty-one or 22.

And how old are you now?
I'm 25 [*laughter in studio*].

Looking back on your youth, Bruce.
Good idea, let's look back on it.

You had a band called the Steel Mill. Was that the name at the time? Were there other names?
There were other names.

But you never made any records. Just kind of hung around the bars?
I did make one when I was about 16. I made it in Bricktown, New Jersey, in this country and western studio.

Was it released?
No. It was released to the extent that for $100 you get a hundred of them.

Do you have any left?
I have one that doesn't play very well.

What was the tune?
I don't know. I did that when I was about 16. That's about it.

[Sciaky asked about Springsteen's audition for John Hammond]
I had this guitar, this little guitar. Its neck was broke when I brought it up into the office. I was brought there by the guy that is my manager now and at the time I always took the attitude that nothing was going to come of anything because that's usually the way it always worked out. I had been playing down in Jersey in the bars for like nine years.

Wow, that long?
Yeah, and I heard some good bands down there. And, "Hey I'm going to bring down the manager to see you guys tonight" and you sit there until three in the morning. Anyhow, I went up there, and we went in and I introduced myself and met the guy and sat down. And my manager, he jumped up and started to give him this big hype already. I didn't play a note! I said, Oh no. So I played a few things. I played "Saint in the City," and he liked it. He was really enthusiastic about it, and we went in the studio with him and we did 13 or 14 songs on demo tape with him. And that was, like, the day that never comes. I felt like I was going to go outside and get hit by a car after that.

It was all over, right?
Yeah. That's what I figured. Yeah, that was a day.

[At some point, Bruce took over doing an on-air promotion for Akadama Wines.]
Santori Akadama. [*He reads note from Sciaky.*] "Feel free to ad lib." There are lots of ways you can enjoy Santori Akadama wine. Did you know that, Ed? You can drink it chilled. You can drink it on the rocks with ice and soda. You can pour it all over your face. Akadama red wine makes a fine sangria, it says right here. You can own one square of English earth, oh, wrong commercial. Akadama red wine and orange juice is one of the better ways to start the day. Goes great with apple juice, ginger ale, tonic water. . . .

That's all they have time for.
How am I doing, fellas?

That's all the time they paid for.
Must read, it says here at the bottom.

Read that.
These guys are gonna be mad. Akadama wines are imported . . . Oh, this part. And don't forget to pass the Akadema [*laughter*] . . . They spelled it wrong!

It is imported by Santori International. They used to be one of our sponsors. What better authority on wine than Bruce Springsteen to surprise us here. You've drunk a bottle of wine in your time, Bruce.
No, I hate wine. You don't like wine? Okay.

Believe it or not, Bruce is actually here. I didn't know if you were going to make it, Bruce. You didn't seem too enthusiastic last night about getting out today.
Yeah, it's hard to tell.

Well we are going to start off by playing the tune—you have not heard it yet on the radio.
No I haven't.

One called "Born to Run." Well, I've been waiting. I've had some calls on it, but just in case you came here today I thought I'd save it and play it. Go out into the hall and you can listen to it on the little radio—go ahead out there. All go out in the hall now. Now while Bruce can't hear me [*laughter*] . . . No, Bruce can hear me. Bruce I hope you are out there. He hasn't heard it on the radio. And there's a thing about hearing a song in the studio it sounds a lot different than when you get it onto your little transistor radio. Everyone knows that out on the beach at Asbury you've got to hear it on the radio and that's how you know how it sounds. So here it is, "Born to Run" on a small radio.
[*Song plays*]

"Born to Run," Bruce Springsteen. I like it. How do you like it, Bruce?
Do I get to do another commercial?

No, not yet. So what have you been doing with yourself, Bruce? Making a new record?
Yeah, yeah, make another album. Working on my band, working with my band. Trying to make it better. That's about it. Going to Texas after tonight. I guess we go to Texas tomorrow.

How you going? You going to fly?
In the magic bus.

You going in the magic bus huh? They got a spiffy green bus, I've got to say it's real nice.
Sort of *Exorcist* green.

How long do you think it will take you to drive to Texas?
I don't know.

When's your gig?
I don't know that either.

You don't know where you're going, but you know where you're coming from, I guess. We have Max [Weinberg] and Roy [Bittan] with us here. And Garry [Tallent] also. Max and Roy, the new guys on the block. Say hello. [*Shouts of hello*]
That's Max, and that's Roy [*laughter*].

Max is a drummer, and Roy is a piano player. I was telling you that people were concerned about what was happening with you and the band, and I can tell them that everything is working out fine including your new violin player.
That's Suki. The guy who does the engineering on the album, on our albums, Louis Lahav, that's his wife. And she's a girl, she did all the voices on "Sandy." She sings all the background on "Sandy" on the *Wild, the Innocent* album. She's been playing with us for two, three weeks. It sounded nice.

Come on in, Garry. Garry is one of the old guys. He's been around for a while. All sorts of folks here today. We've talked, not here on the air, a lot about what Bruce is into and how long it's taken for Bruce to break out nationally and it's gotta happen soon.
Why, why.

You don't care too much, huh.
Uh, you know.

You're pretty mellow about it, I guess. But the people who are enthusiastic about you really want it to go real big so everybody will know about you. Do you want everybody to know about you, Bruce?
I don't think about it that much, about that aspect of it. What happens now is when you are doing gigs like last night, which is really nice, really nice gig, the audience was a great audience. And we just came from Boston where we got a nice reception up there too. But we actually haven't ever been in the Midwest at all. I don't think the records get played out there at all. You can't concern yourself about too many of those kinds of things. Business is tough enough. You can't get the music straight, can't get it clear enough.

Do you have time to write still? You play an awful lot.
Now we do "Jungleland," that's a new song. We do "She's the One," that's a new song. "A Love So Fine," that's a new song.

Which used to be something else.
I've got about six other things that we're gonna work on. So there's time. It manifests itself when it does.

[*Sciaky asks about other songs Springsteen performs.*]
We pick up different things. We do different songs all the time. We've been doing a Crystals song.

"And Then He Kissed Me."
What else have we been doing? "Spanish Harlem" we've been doing.

"Spanish Harlem" is real good, real good. I half expected you to go into "Rosalita" right after that, but it wasn't the right place for it.
Well next time you run up and cue me [*laughter*].

Bruce Springsteen is here and the phones are just jammed.
In New Jersey the number is Bigelow 8.

Please pledge your money so that this struggling rock star can go on to Texas. Have you heard this one, this is a tune called ["If I Was the Priest"].
That's not what it's called.

What is it called?
It has no name. This song I wrote, we did it about four years ago, we did it in the Prince, we did this in the Student Prince, which is a bar we used to play down in Jersey. I wrote it about four years ago. Thought I'd burned every copy. Somebody got a hold of it.

What we are talking about is it is on the new Allan Clarke album, it's only available in England.
But there's one part that's great, when the harmonies come in he does these great Hollies harmonies.

They call it "If I Were the Priest"? You ever going to do that tune?
No, I wrote it four years ago and we used to play it in the bar. No, we're not going to do that one.

But just the fact that this one popped up.
The harmonies are great. I love the harmonies he put on that.

There must be a whole raft of old material that you wrote that we never heard.
Yeah, most of it I burn. It's things that aren't really indicative of where I want to be or where I'm trying to go. I think the only stuff they send around now is the material on the two albums.

Have you had anybody else record any of these tunes? Did I hear about Bowie recording something?
Supposedly. I haven't heard it yet. Supposedly he did "Saint in the City" and "Growin' Up." The Hollies did "Sandy." I heard that the other day.

Where do you put your songwriting as opposed to your performing?
It's all in one. It's all connected. I don't like to separate it. I don't really

like to think of myself as a songwriter or just as a performer. Whatever. I don't know. That's a weird question, Ed.

I think it is part of it. Obviously your material reflects who you are. Your performing is really important to why people have come to appreciate you so much.
What it does, in performance, things crystallize. To know what I am trying to do and what the band is you have to see it. It's hard to have a complete understanding just off the record.

What about when somebody else does your tune?
It's hard which is why not too many people have done any of the songs at all. Because they are like fairly personalized numbers and it is hard for people to get a reasonable approach to take towards it. There's not a whole lot of approaches that can be had towards the songs.

But a lot of them stand up by themselves. It's hard to think of them without thinking of you. But I'm sure if somebody else tried to do "Saint in the City" they could do it, because it is a good song.
For some reason I always imagined Joe Cocker doing "Spirit in the Night." When I wrote the song I had his kind of voice in mind which is something that I rarely do.

Give us a little bit of Cocker doing it, how would you imagine that?
I wouldn't imagine it.

Going to play an old tune here. What is this tune, "The Fever"?
What is this? It's an old demo tape that you got. I don't know where. It's something we did a couple years ago, a little after the first album. It was done as a demo for other artists. It was done in one take.

Who played on this?
Who played on it: Me. Danny, Clarence, "Mad Dog" Vini [Lopez], Garry.

And Mad Dog sings the backup.
Mad Dog sings the backup.

I want to thank you for coming down, because I know you don't like to talk too much about things.
It's nice down here. It's been a town where the band has got a lot of incredible support from Philadelphia. Because we are still really scuffling to make it work. And it's getting better and getting better. And Philadelphia was the first town that really responded.

You better make another record, because this one is getting worn out.

"The Lost Interviews," 1975

The following interviews date to 1975, both pre- and post-*Born to Run*. Little is known about their provenance; unearthed by *Backstreets* magazine in the '90s, they were professionally recorded, conducted by European journalists (likely for promotion, as Springsteen would cross the ocean for the first time that fall), and stored in a record company vault. They are remarkably personal and revealing— speaking with a Swedish interviewer, Springsteen takes great care in describing his background and his concerns for a foreign audience. Having just completed *Born to Run,* Springsteen confesses, "The tension making that record I could never describe. It was killing, almost, it was inhuman. I hated it. I couldn't stand it. It was the worst, hardest, lousiest thing I ever had to do." Excerpts from the interviews appeared originally in *Backstreets* magazines #57 and #58, Winter 1997 and Spring 1998.

Tell us a little bit about Asbury Park, and E Street, because that's one thing we don't know anything about.
I guess you must have coastal canals? Boardwalks, fast wheels driving

around? That's what it is. It's a small, sort of has-been resort town, where mostly older people go and people that ain't got enough money to go burn gas and go farther south to a bigger resort town, they stop there. It's okay, it's nice, I liked it, I lived there for quite a while. E Street, that's just a street . . . [it's] where my piano player, who played with me on the first two albums, named Davey Sancious, that's the street he lived on. We just took the name of the street for the name of the band.

What sort of music did you listen to when you grew up and started to play in small bands?
At the time I listened to whatever was on AM radio. There was no FM, of course. Is there FM in Sweden? There is? Well, at that time there was no FM radio, but the radio had some good music on it. In the early '60s, when I started playing . . . Elvis was big then, the Ronettes, all the [Phil] Spector stuff, and the girl groups from New York, which is a big part of my background. The Ronettes, the Shirelles, the Crystals, the Chiffons, who put out a lot of great music at the time. And then the big English thing happened, the Beatles and all that stuff, and the Stones, Manfred Mann . . .

AM radio was fine right up until about 1967 when FM came in and started to play long cuts, and you could see the disappearance of the really good three-minute single. So the music that got me was what was on AM from 1959 to 1965. And then later on I got into the early '50s. They had that big San Francisco thing which went down over here; I never got too involved in that. My roots were sort of formed by then: Roy Orbison, the great English singles bands, the girl groups from New York. Chuck Berry, of course—your classics.

You were quite young when you started. Where did you play?
Everywhere. High school dances, bars, weddings. I can remember staying up all night learning "Moon River" because the bride requested it—"Moon River!" [*laughs*] We didn't play any of that stuff at the time, but we needed the bucks, right?

First thing I ever did was in a trailer camp, out in the country. It was the fall, with trailer camp people. Ain't got no trailer camps in Sweden? Motor homes, like you pull them with your car. You know America, everybody's moving all over all the damn time. Trailer camps . . . you pull 'em and you park 'em. And there's a certain trailer camp type of person, right? We played there, and it was us and this other country music band who had an accordion, a bass guitar, a guitar player, and a little girl who stood on a stool and sang into one of these big RCA/Victor microphones, like in them old Shirley Temple movies . . . And we came out and we did "Twist and Shout" and Ray Charles songs and Chuck Berry songs. And the people went nuts . . . and man, we played for like eight hours that day. I remember starting at noon and we played until like eight or nine, when we had to stop. That was one of the first gigs I ever did.

So I was doing everything. I played for the fireman's ball, where they didn't know what kind of band they were hiring, and we'd get there and just blow everybody's mind. The fireman's ball, played for the Boy Scouts once, did every kind of gig. High school dances, clubs, anything, we did it. Played in the mental institutions, for the patients—everything.

Where did you get your musicians? Was it all people that you knew growing up?
This guy Miami Steve is a guy that I knew since I was about 15. Steve had his own band, I had my own band. I just got him in the band a few months ago, but he'd been in all my bands except for this one. So it was good to get him back in. So I've known him a long time; Garry, I've known Garry for about five years now, I guess, and he's been in other bands with me. Danny I've known for six or seven years. They're all people I've known. Clarence I met about three or four years ago. Most of them local boys, except for Max and Roy. Roy's from Long Island, and Max is from North Jersey—which is not considered local [*laughs*]. Local is your town, maybe ten miles out. North Jersey is a whole other scene from where I live—it's industrial, more like New York.

With that very strong local feeling, you must be interested in the same things and have the same sort of associations and jokes and everything like that.
Well, no, not really; everybody's sort of different. Everybody's been through different things, different ages, different experiences. But there's a real strong vibe there, because everybody realizes we've got a really good thing going. And they're all good guys, very easygoing nice guys,

and it's a very smooth-running thing right now. So yeah, to a degree, everybody knows New Jersey—when you got your local boys with you, you've got a thing you just can't buy. I wouldn't trade these guys for nobody. First of all because they all are great musicians, and there's that extra thing.

Like me and Steve do that rap in "E Street Shuffle," and that's what it was like. We sat at that table in that club at three in the morning, and we dreamed and dreamed the day would come when we could make some records. That was number one. I've known Steve since he was about 15, and since then it's been the same thing—that's all we ever talked about. All we ever wanted to do was make a record. And we'd say, what's the matter with us? We're as good as those guys, we're as good as those guys, how come we ain't got a record deal? What's going on?

And it's funny, because the other day we were riding somewhere, like coming down here, and everybody was so excited: there we were, playing on the [radio]. We used to trudge around in this old van, me and Steve riding up and down the East Coast, riding to Virginia and Atlanta, all these different towns, just scrubbing away, and that damn van was breaking down all the time . . . and now here we were on the air. And I said "Steve." And he said "Yeah!" And I said, "This is it! Remember all those towns, we'd be riding in the van saying 'when this happens, when this happens . . .'"—and I never stopped to think that *it was happening*. And him either. But it's something that I'd never take for granted, not for a second. Like last night with that crowd in that hall, I'd never take that for granted. For every night like last night, there were a hundred other nights that we played in these little bars in Jersey, and there was nobody there.

What did your family and schoolteachers think about you in the early years, playing guitar in bars?
Oh, they hated it. My mother—you know, your mother's your mother. And she tries to be cool with you and let you do your thing. My father, he hated it, couldn't stand it, wanted me to stop. Always was down on it. Wanted me to be a lawyer, some kind of heavy thing—a doctor. Guaranteed income. But I was a stubborn and strong kid, did what I wanted to do and just figured I could do it. Eventually they moved away, and before they knew it, it was happening.

You've talk about influences; how influenced are you, as you see it yourself, by rhythm & blues and Latin American songs?

I would say that I'm the kind of guy that whatever goes in my ear I digest. But I'm not a big looker; I don't go around looking for it. I'm not a big record collector, I'm not real familiar with the old R&B artists. But whatever I hear I digest very quickly, and it comes right back out the way I want it to. All the Stax stuff and Atlantic stuff, I'm very into that. Wilson Pickett, Sam Cooke, Sam and Dave, Eddie Floyd, the MGs, Steve Cropper . . . yeah, the band has moments when it's based a lot on those rhythm & blues bands, especially in the way I use the band. If you see Otis Redding in Monterey Pop, the way he uses his band; the way James Brown uses his band. Because most of your better bandleaders have all been your soul bandleaders.

Because the white guys always tend to be a little too sloppy, too lazy; they think it's part of the act to be not together or something, I don't know. The best bandleaders of the last ten, twenty years, from what I've listened to, have been your soul bandleaders. They whip them bands into shape. I tend to use my band that way. I'm doing different things, but in that tradition . . . Ain't nobody does it better than them soul artists. Like Sam and Dave, James Brown. James Brown is an idol, man . . . he spits, and those guys do somersaults. It's incredible.

You don't write what you could call ordinary love songs; it's more about life, and you could read the lyrics without listening to the music and you'd get some sort of picture about life.

That's what some people say. [When] I write the songs, I write them to stand up as *song* lyrics. You're supposed to listen to the song and hear the lyrics. You're not supposed to read the lyrics, because they're *song* lyrics. They go to a song, you know? That's the idea. I'm a songwriter, I'm not a poetry man. That's what I concern myself with. They describe whatever I write into them: just what I know about, what I grew up with.

Could you talk a little bit, from an autobiographical standpoint, about your background?

A screw-up, in a small town. I ran away a mess of times, and to New York all the time and stayed there, and played in the Café Wha? down in the West Village, banged around down there for a few years. Met some people and my parents moved away and I stayed around here and I just kept playing. I just played and hung around. Went to school, to high school, that's about it. That's the capsule version.

What do you think about getting so much coverage right now? Critics really respond to your music.
I don't know. I guess it's good. It's nice—okay, it's dynamite. But I don't get hooked up in it or involved in it, because papers are just papers. I don't know how much they influence people; we get a lot of coverage, we get a lot of reviews, but all I know is I still make $115 a week, I still live in New Jersey. The main thing is I'm glad I've got a good band, and I can have jobs to play and some things to do, and I get to travel around. I don't know anything about the press, and what's going on with them.

But, I mean, suddenly you are recognized.
Well, I don't know if it's real sudden. Two years ago when I recorded my first album it was a big deal, then it cooled out and the record company cooled out on us and didn't want to promote our second album. Then they decided they *did* want to promote the second album. Then we played in New York, and I hadn't played in New York in a while, and the band had changed a lot. I don't know, it's like I'm getting better.

Why didn't they want to promote the second album?
A million reasons, a million reasons that were like no reason at all. I guess somebody didn't believe in it, didn't think it was right. It was business. See, in the end, it doesn't matter. That's the funny thing people don't realize, is that, all right, so you don't get promoted, and this doesn't happen and that doesn't happen, but in the end it doesn't matter. If you've got the music and you've got *something*—the music *and*—then that's it. If you're going to win, you're going to win. No matter what. Say the second album didn't get promoted, which it didn't at first. But it came out, and it got a lot of good reviews in the press, so they couldn't keep it down. There weren't any ads, but it was written about all the time. So I don't necessarily even believe in ads. I hate all those ads—I haven't seen an ad of mine that I like. It's unnecessary. They hype you, and they don't have to. When they're dealing with a certain type of artist, there shouldn't be any need for that whole hype

attitude. If you're dealing with certain people who can't play [*laughs*], you *better* hype 'em because they ain't gonna make it! But if you're just dealing with people who are in control, who are good, then it's not necessary because the music speaks for itself. That's why it's unnecessary even for me to talk about any of this stuff, because the music speaks for itself. There's nothing I can possibly say that could add or give any insight to it.

Where did you learn to write songs and lyrics?
I never learned. You don't learn any of that stuff. I don't know about learnin'. I don't believe in learnin' [*laughs*]. You just do it, that's all. I can do it. I mean, I learned how to write in first grade, but besides that . . . I can do it. I woke up one day and started to write some songs when I was, I don't know, 13 or 14 years old. At first they were pretty lousy. And I just kept writing and writing. It's not something you can learn, you just do it.

How much personal experience went into your songs?
I don't know, it's all based on that. There ain't a word or a note played that didn't come from something that happened to me somewhere long the line. It depends on how literally you want to take the whole situation, but it's all based on personal experience directly or indirectly. You change it around—you change the names to protect the innocent [*laughs*], stuff like that.

Can you give me any examples? I like "4th of July, Asbury Park." What kind of personal experience inspired that?
Well, I live in Asbury Park! I've lived there for a while now. I live like a block from the boardwalk. Before I was doing anything—okay, the past two years I've been busy, the past year and a half. But before that, I wasn't doing anything. I scraped up gigs here and there, and I had a lot of free time. At night that's what you do: you hang out down there. And you meet people, and you see things, and that was it. I don't want to say "there was this girl, there was this and that," you know.

Let's put it this way: what does Asbury Park mean for people who were growing up in New Jersey or in the neighborhood where you grew up?
Doesn't mean a thing. It's just a dumpy town. It doesn't mean anything.

But it's probably a meeting-place for people, isn't it?
There's the boardwalk, people are always attracted to the bright lights, and the rides, the games and, yeah, a lot of people down there. It's where the kids go, it's where we all go at night. I used to go there a lot more than I do now; I've hardly been there this summer at all.

How about New York City? You've written a lot about it, how do you see the difference between the two?
New York City, for me, was a place where I could be myself. It was real tough down in Asbury; being like 16 or 15, you come to the city, step out of the bus, and you're somebody else. Or you're who you are. It was escape, a good escape. From my parents, and the kids and everything, from the whole scene. And I come to New York and it's overwhelming. When you're there, without a thing to do, no money but a few bucks, and you step out of that bus, it's just an overwhelming thing. I just dug the feeling of it.

And you put that into your music, like "Does That Bus Stop on 82nd Street?"
I wrote that on the bus!

And "New York City Serenade." How did you come to that song?
Part of it had been sitting around for about a year, a verse or two, and then that song just came together pretty quick, in a day or so. A lot of the songs did like that. These are things that just mean a lot to me. This is my life, and the songs are usually parts of my life that I want to remember. Even though they're born, probably, out of the parts of my life that I'd most like to forget. The moments I write down are the ones that I want to remember. That's confusing, maybe.

So growing up in Asbury Park, but near the city . . .
You've got a little more room. That was one thing I was fortunate to have, when I was a kid, there was always the option of splitting to the city, I could come into New York, and when it got too much for me I could go back. There were a lot of cats that just didn't have that particular option. So I sort of was able to choose the best of both worlds. Which is why I can write optimistically about a lot of tough subjects. I can write about how good it is to be in the city in the summer, while a lot of people get trapped in there. I always had the option: I could run

there to get away from here, and I could run here to get away from there.

You're going to prepare another album now, what's that going to be like?
I write a lot during recording, I get those blasts of energy. Some new songs. We've been performing one or two of them, but I change my mind in the course of recording so much and I write so much new stuff that I couldn't even say. Some new musicians, so it should be good, should be interesting.

Let's talk more about the songs. Tell me about "Kitty's Back."
It's a strip-tease number, that's what that is. A follow-up to the David Rose Orchestra [*laughs*]. It's a strange song. Sort of big band-y. I like it because it communicates the heat. You get the heat. That's why I want to add a trumpet player to the band, because a trumpet communicates incredible heat. And that's what I want. Different instruments have different temperatures. Depending on the guy that's playing it, too, but a trumpet has just got that great Latin heat that I like. And "Kitty's Back" does that too.

Do you use different instruments to express certain feelings? I think that's done very well in "New York City Serenade," which starts very slowly and becomes more and more . . .
Every time I do that number we do it a little differently. I like to do that number when we play. That's like, *forever*. It gets that beat, it gets that groove going. It just goes on forever, it's one of those songs that hooks up with a rhythm and goes on and on into the night. That song's really special to me. I don't know why—it's hard to talk about. I really can't explain it. You have to see us perform it.

I saw you at Central Park.
I don't think we did that number at Central Park.

You did "Jungleland."
Yeah, that's a new song. But you have to see us perform "New York City" to really know. Because the whole rhythm of the whole street thing runs right through that song. And there are so many little battles going on inside it, yet it all works together.

What about "Rosalita"?
Just wrote it in one day. It's a rocker. It's a dance song. It's all there in the song, there's really nothing I could say. I could relate it to my own personal experience but I don't really want to.

Could you at least explain what's in the song? The content?
It's just about a guy. Like when I was a kid, I had this one girl, and her mother—it's the same old thing, it happens every day: the hassles with the parents and stuff. And I had a court injunction put against me when I was 17 or 16 or something. That I couldn't go near this girl because I was—I don't know what the hell I was, but they did that. It was a thing where her mother disliked me a lot and went to the trouble of calling the cops on me if I came around. Had a court thing go down where I couldn't see her. So I guess that's what "Rosie" is about. At night you walk by the house but you wouldn't go up to it, or you'd run up the driveway and stand under the window, and say, "Hey!"

What about "E Street Shuffle"?
That's what it's about, it's just about people, kids I know. It's just a place. Our piano player lives there, lives on that street. It's just a place. "Incident on 57th Street" is the same thing. They're all about the same thing: decisions, escapes, the way various people cope with them. There's never any solutions, there's never any answers, because there's never any in real life.

Are you pessimistic?
I don't think so, I think I'm real optimistic. There just aren't any real solutions. There's a lot of false answers and false solutions, but there's not any real ones. That's why the songs, they go on forever. They don't begin and they don't end, because that's the way life is. It's just day-to-day, moments, incidents. It's not like, *and then he died.* There's not stuff like that. It always goes on. Goes on and on and on. All the songs should just fade out, as a matter of fact—should never end.

How are you coping, and what's your idea of coping, with mass media?
What do you mean, like interviews and stuff?

Interviews, radio, television. In my opinion there are two ways: you either try to stay somewhat of a mysterious personality, or you go out and be on the Mike Douglas show or anything.

Well, I'm not doing any TV, and I don't want to do any TV. We get all these TV offers, but what do you want to go on TV for? It's too easy. Radio, I don't go on the radio too much. I try not to do anything like that too much. For me, I don't think it's necessary. All that's necessary is to go out on stage and do what I do. I do interviews once in a while, usually only if I have to. Only sometimes you're in the mood, you get somebody you like, and it's like, okay, let's talk. Because I never really have anything in particular to add to the album. That's about how I'm coping with it.

So when Johnny Carson calls you tomorrow? A lot of people would say, "I'm glad that you called me—I've been waiting for your call."

It depends. If you're trying to break into that area of the market or something, then it's important. But I was never into this big, quick I'm-gonna-do-everything-I-can-to-get-out-there routine, because I don't think it's important. I don't think the matter of time it takes is important. People say it won't last, if it looks like things are going good. It's funny, because we didn't do things in the most expedient way, or the fastest way; but the only way for me to do it was the way I wanted to do it, and in the end it's worked out best. All them kids came down there last night, and it's a good thing—it's a thing between me and them, and that's what it is. And that's weird. It's a thing between me and the kids with no particular channels, just direct. That's the way we've been running it.

And you are strongly addressing yourself to kids. All the other people try and sell to the older market, too, to sell as much as they can. Without denying that you are trying to sell as much as you can, you set out for giving it to the kids specifically.

That depends on what you think kids are. It's just that when I think of an audience, that's what I think of. I guess there's older people, I don't know, I guess there's some people in their 30s or 30 years old there, but it's not like I'm thinking of the whole age situation. People come to see you—it's "the kids." "The kids" come to see you. I don't play to any particular crowd.

I was wondering, maybe you are arousing this very involved reaction of an audience not alone by your music, which is a great part of it of course, but also by the fact you're a man of your own. You're not out there in these shells where all these other fuckers are, you are in the theater. So you're not so much related to people they don't like too much, with dollar signs in your eyes. Your integrity is there, and people are aware of that and like you for that.

We had a chance to go on big tours. And I always try things, so I tried it once. Went on that big Chicago tour, and it didn't work out: it was bad, it was bad for me. After that I realized. I knew the way we should have done it even before then, but I figured with people saying, "Do it, do it," I thought okay, I'll try that. If it works, good. And when I say "if it works," what I mean is if it works band-to-audience. I don't mean if we sell a lot of records. But it is all connected: if it works band-to-audience, then you'll sell a lot of records. See, that's what people forget. I read this thing in the *Times* where this guy said something about bad management, that we didn't go out and try for new audiences. Which was totally wrong. What he should have said is that we didn't go out and try for new audiences *in the accepted way* that bands go out and try for new audiences. We didn't get on a tour with the Who and play in front of 10 million thousand people or nothing. What we did was we went to a place where we were not known, and we played in a club for 20 or 30 people. And then two months later we came back and we played for 50 people. Two months later we came back again, to the same town, and we played for about 100 people. And two months later we came back and the place was full. Two or three months after that we came back and played a theater, and we just about sold out. And then two months later we'd come back and sell out one or two shows at the theater, and that's the way we did it. In almost every town, every place we went. In all the major cities that's the way we did it. I went to Boston five or six times before I ever sold out a club. We played to ten people. I went to Philadelphia five or six times before we ever sold out a club. It goes on and on. So we did try for new audiences, but we did it our way.

I thought of it last night, seeing these people being so enthusiastic, I was thinking of the times when a band could be huge without having made an album, just by the sheer potential of people making music on a stage.

I've based the whole thing around this: if my band plays the best, if I do the best I can, and if I legitimately should be doing this and I have the ability to do what I'm trying to do, well then everything else is going to follow suit and work out. That's the only kind of thing I ever concentrated on. Only two things that were important. Number one, making sure the band is playing the best it could at all times. Number two, making sure the band is being presented correctly, so that it could *be able to* play the best that it could. You play a half hour opening for Black Oak Arkansas, it don't matter if you're kings of the world, you ain't gonna be presented right to show how you can play. We've done that, I did a gig like that, and I learned right away. So we stopped, and we didn't go second on any bills anymore. Most of the time we didn't play with anyone else at all. We decided we were going to go into these towns on our own and play to whoever came. And we would, and we'd go to a school and maybe two or three hundred kids would show up, and the next time we went back the place was half full, and the next time it was sold out. Word-of-mouth. All the hype in the world is nothing compared to a kid telling another kid, "Man, you should've seen that!" Because a kid listens to his buddy. He don't listen to the papers! He looks, and he reads, but he doesn't believe. But if his buddy comes up and says these guys were great, he'll check it out. He'll go to the show. And that's the thing we've worked on, what made us keep going, even back when things weren't going so well, when we weren't getting promoted by Columbia—who I don't want to say nasty things against, since they're being so great now—when all we did was just go out there and play and play and play. And the kids did it, man, the kids themselves. A kid told another kid, word-of-mouth, they'd call up radio stations. The papers may get a few critics down there, or a few kids, but in general the kids don't go unless they know it's going to be good. They can't afford to spend the bucks for curiosity's sake. It was the audience that did it, and that came back, and that's the way we did it. And it was good, because it established a certain type of relationship between me and the band and the crowd. It was the kind of thing where there was no mass success, but there was this very intense thing. At concerts, the kids would go *crazy*, they would go nuts, you know? Because there was this intense exchange going on between us and the crowd. And now it seems—and I'll believe it when I see it—but it seems like it's going better [*laughs*]. I don't put too much faith in anything, I don't care what it looks like. It *seems* like it's going better. And I know if I did it any other way I don't think it would be, and I would not have the same relationship I do with the crowd, which is what the people are coming for.

So you did it on your own.
Me and Mike [Appel]. People say, you know, bad management—and in the traditional sense it might have been. He didn't put me on tour with the Who, because I wouldn't go! He wouldn't put me on this other tour, because I wouldn't go there. So from a traditional view it might seem like bad management, but Mike knew the way I was about what I do, which is that I do it my way, a certain way. When I worked other jobs, I painted somebody's house green when they wanted it green. But when I do this, I felt it was something I wanted to do my way, all the way. Or else I don't do it. We're not going to do gigs to go out and play 40 minutes, it's a waste of time.

Do you have the impression that you took your record company on your bandwagon, rather than the other way around, as it usually is? They'd have to follow you now if you've created this momentum.
Initially, there was big hype when I first came out, with Clive and stuff.

Is that story true, by the way, about you reading the Scaduto book on Dylan, and by that, going to John Hammond?
It wasn't *by* that. I'd read the book, or I'd been reading the book, and I happened to be involved with Mike. I went in to Mike and Mike said we've got this appointment with John Hammond! So then we went up there. So yeah, it is . . . but it was just a freaky thing. There was a whole series of events at that time that were happening to me almost exactly how they happened to Dylan when he first started, and it was just co-incidence. I met Hammond, then I went and played the Gaslight, and a lot of those little clubs, and it was by myself, I had no band. So anyway, Clive did a big hype, which probably as he looks back on it was a mistake. I mean the way it was done. I think I read somewhere he thinks it was a mistake himself—in his books he says it. Anyway, the big hype came out, and then for a long time I was thought of as like a Clive project that bombed. I sold 20,000 records or something. Even though the band was consistently getting good press, and Mike was always shoving it back to Columbia, when the record sales ain't there, they can ignore it. So when the second album came out I had an argument with the A&R department. They didn't think it was good, I thought it was good; they didn't want to release it, I wanted to release it; eventually they did release the album, and it got pretty good reviews and did pretty well.

So meanwhile, all this time the albums are selling every week, but at the record company at that time, well, there were a lot of inner conflicts between us and them. There were a lot of people there who were really pulling for us, but the people who had the big say at the time were not too involved with my project. I think Billy Joel was happening then, somebody was happening then. So, I don't know if they figured we'd disappear and go away or what. But we kept going out there and kept playing. See, to bet against us was to make a bad bet, because the guys, we had nothing else to do! You were dealing with desperate faces—we *had* to go out there every night, we had to do that. And it was great, it was something we lived to do. This was our chance, and there was no turning around. I wasn't going to stop and go back and fix TVs; there was nothing else I could do, so this was it for me. So they were dealing with something that would not stop. Could not stop. If you can stop, in this music-type thing, well then you *should* stop.

Finally, a year went by, and *Wild and Innocent* started to sell quite a few records, and then several major things happened. [Irwin Segelstein's] kid—was the president of CBS records—came to see us at a show. Freaked out, went back and was bugging his old man: "What's the matter with you?" and on and on. And the Jon Landau article came out at the same time. And all of a sudden the tide turned. It just went over the hump where it became too much to ignore anymore. They finally wised up to this. And things started to come around, and I started the new album, and it went on and on. In the end—and I've always worked on this principle—you go to somebody, and you've got a deal on their terms. You're in their ballpark playing their game. I always found it's better if you make them come to you. Then they're in your neighborhood, playing your game. To a degree, you can call the shots. In our situation, we just played and played—those guys, they're the most consistent band, they play good every night, I mean, *real* good every night. Even on a bad night, they're still good [*laughs*].

It was a good night last night!
Last night was a good night. It wasn't a great night, but it felt real good. It's that kind of band that comes out, man, and always during the night they're doing something . . . So that's what we did every night: played and played, over and over. So finally what happened was the company came to us and said, "Hey, let's get together," and when they finally did, that's when it started to work out. And now, they're all like bonzo over the whole thing. It's like, "Whatever you want, whatever you want." And

they've been doing an incredible job, like down here they did a fantastic job. Columbia is a company that, if they want to, it's incredible what they can do. They can do anything. And this is the way it should be. We just wanted to team up and make it work out. In most acts' case, it's like: pull here, give, take; they've got to pull something out of the act, then the act's got to pull something out of the company. And I think a lot of people didn't understand my reasoning on some things.

They might not have understood that you were not scared of not making it. I think many bands give in to what a record company wants, or a manager, because they figure, well, if we fail, it's not our fault. You have to be pretty strong, and that must be part of the reason for your success: you are obviously that strong. To think, "I can do it. And if I can't do it, I have at least tried on my own terms, and that makes me happy enough."
And there's also a certain way you have to legitimately care about what you're doing, intensely. I mean, it has to be one of your only forces, and you have to legitimately *not* care about really making it. I couldn't have cared less. I had my band, I was out there, I was making more money than I'd ever made before, maybe 150 bucks a week; I had my own house, it was a step up in the world. I was happy, everybody was happy, and we cared intensely about what we were doing. And in a way, we did not care about breaking into the big mainstream. The only thing that matters is your music. And if that's right, then things come around. But that's got to be it, that's got to be what you care about. You've got to have your priorities in order.

So they were dealing with a situation like that, like I was in no big sweat to make it. And they said, "Well, if you don't do this, this ain't gonna happen"; and I said, "I don't care!" They were dealing with an attitude that they couldn't deal with. That was the key to keeping my sanity and the band's sanity. If we're sweating about whether or not we were going to sell 300,000 records next time out, then we ain't gonna. Anybody caring about that kind of stuff shouldn't do it. It *shouldn't* sell.

That's hard to handle sometimes for people who are concerned with another aspect of the business. They think you are not in line with what they are doing. If you're not a very prolific thinker, you don't come up with the idea that an artist shouldn't be concerned about what you think he should be concerned about.

When we were playing in bars it was the same way. We were playing in the bars, and the band was playing great. Five or six years ago—there's a videotape of our band at the Student Prince. Somebody found it the other day, a videotape of us at this club in Asbury Park, at the Student Prince. Me, Steve, Davey, Garry, Mad Dog, all of us doing our thing. And Max saw it the other day. I said, "Max, how's that sound, don't we sound really good?" [*laughs*]. The band was playing the same way back then, five years ago. Six years ago. We were going on in them bars with the same feeling as last night. Surroundings change, but that's all superficial stuff. You go out there with what's inside you; you close your eyes and you could be anywhere. So where you are doesn't matter.

Did you change in the way you expose yourself onstage, from a small club to last night? I saw you last year at the Troubadour and I saw you last night, and in my opinion there are certain differences.
Well, at the Troubadour, with the band you saw last year? That was not a good show from what I remember. Mostly because it takes you a set or two to settle into a club, I've found. Even at the Bottom Line that happened to us.

But when you can see someone's eyes, when you can see every little movement, even muscle movement, that's a different way of acting. You're acting for 200 people or 3,000. I think I've seen a different way of acting. Last year you were, to me, more menacing, more mean. That didn't happen last night. You were sometimes menacing, but not all of the time. I remember last year, girls started crying, and shouting in the middle of the song—they couldn't handle it, they couldn't wait until it was over to let it go. Applause is a way of relieving tension, it's not only appreciation, it's a relief of tension when there's a good artist there that can build it up. People last year couldn't wait for that—they had to start yelling and shouting. You came out with the sunglasses, moving mainly in one spot but with the tension of wanting to break out of it. Now you're moving about, you're going across the whole stage, but then you gave this impression that you could do it, but you were forced by some magic force to stay there, and you were wrestling with your body.
There's two kinds of sets that the band plays, even to this day. At the Troubadour, I was involved with wrestling with the situation, which I

was probably not enjoying at the time. So this would cause this particular thing. It was the same with the first night at the Bottom Line, I was very involved with wrestling with what I was trying to do. I was realizing that it was not quite coming off. With the Troubadour set—once every so many gigs, sometimes you go out there and you've really got to fight with it to make a go of it; sometimes you go out and it just falls out like nothing. That's when you tend to be looser. In comparison to the Troubadour, last night was like the "loose" set, where everybody's feeling good.

At the Troubadour, it was like the artist struggling with his art; other times it's the artist _performing_ his art.
Yeah, that's it. That's the difference. At the Troubadour it really was a struggle to come through.

I got this weird impression last night sometimes of watching _West Side Story_, and seeing George Chakiris there.
That's interesting, I never saw that.

You never saw that film?
No.

Oh, well, it was the same kind of . . . well, it's the feel in your lyrics of the East Side of New York, down-and-out people. Because of the dancing, it's a very stylized movie. But the music wasn't really bad, and the movie has the same kind of effect that you try to do with your lines, and it works well on many occasions. Everything coming together, you know: a bridge, a line change, falling on the ground, freeze.
We're trying to do a whole mess of things at once. We're trying to do a real structured thing, but keep it real loose at the same time. The structure is like the frame on a picture, where the picture is constantly moving. So some nights it depends on how you are that night, how you're feeling and how creative you are at any given moment. So it can vary a lot, it can vary a little night to night, it can not vary, it can do anything. Because there are certain set things we use as a skeleton for the set, and we try to let whatever happens happen around that.

It's interesting how you can bring across so much charisma using all the old themes in show business, like the Laurel and Hardy theme: Clarence, the big guy with the hat, and you're the little guy, doing what you do.
Yeah [*laughs*].

And it always works again. But you do it with rock music, which is quite new, to do it that perfectly: choreography, humor . . .
That's because those things are all very real to begin with, the first time they were done. They're like situations that happen, day to day. You see it on the street, those people are everywhere.

Did you at any one moment in the development of your career come to realize that you have charisma? You're a very charismatic artist.
Nah, I don't think about that stuff.

Are you ever aware of that? I mean, it's obvious, I think it's hard to evade.
I don't know. Before I go on—I'm very tense all the time before I go on. I got put in a weird situation for a lot of years; I got put in the situation for three years—and I'll probably do this the rest of my life—where you got to go out every night. Probably a situation that other artists don't have: you got to go out and prove yourself. Because I got so bombarded with all that stuff in the beginning, all that hype, I was put in a situation where I had to go out and prove myself. Night after night. It's hard to do. And the longer you have to do it, the harder it gets. And for a while I thought it was that hype that made me feel like that, but then a few days ago, three or four days ago, I realized that that's never what it was at all, that it was always me. And I think that's what it is. I don't know if it's fate or what it is, but I go out there every night feeling that way: "Tonight, I gotta prove myself." It never was to anybody, it was always to myself. And it's funny, I just realized that the other night. It's a weird thing.

It might have to do with being brought up Roman Catholic. Where God will see you, everything you do—under your blankets—God will see you, and you will be punished. That brings a certain frame of mind that's not really good. There are some Roman Catholics,

including myself, who come to realize only later why they are so damn ambitious. They want to prove everything. I presume, or I guess I read somewhere, that you are from a middle class family, or lower middle class. And these people really want you to get somewhere. You said to someone that you phoned your mother saying you had a contract and she said, "Did you change your name?" I could really feel that, imagine my mother saying the same thing. All these years, through religion, through this lower middle class family, they push you and they bring about a huge guilt. And I think it's from the guilt complex that you think you have to prove yourself. As you were nobody all your life. And it's hard to come to realize that—and when—you are anybody. Maybe that's what you really want.

Yeah, it was really a mind-blower.

And maybe it's not good to realize that!

Yeah, you have to deal with that too, all the time. You start to find out more about yourself, which changes what you do. But that's what it's all about. You can't do one thing forever; there are things that change your work, I guess. It's interesting because I started to read a lot about it, read reviews about the way different people see you onstage, and I started to wonder, yeah, why am I acting like that? And what is this thing that is driving me to be out there like that? Why do I do this every night? Why do I take myself to the exhaustion point, and if I don't, why do I feel terrible about it? It was the whole thing with the three-hour sets: I had to take myself to a point where I couldn't stand up, where I felt sick, where I absolutely knew that I couldn't do anything else. I had to do this every night. I still do. I did it last night. And the fact that the audience is there and coming along with you is incidental [*laughs*]. It's like a second thought. In the end I realized that they were an excuse for me to be out there, and in reality what I was really doing out there I could do to an empty hall. Almost. They provide a certain . . . you know. Of course I never did think I was out there for the audience, I always knew I was out there for me, but I really didn't know the darker side of being out there for you. There's a light side of it, and a dark side. You're out there for you, you think to have fun, and play, but you're also out there for *you* to prove yourself to yourself, to beat yourself down as far as you can go and see how much you can take. So there's two sides to it every night. And it's funny, I also realized that there's a certain amount of illusion at work onstage too, no matter how easy it looks, it's always a certain amount of struggle, always a struggle going on underneath. Sometimes the struggle is closer to the surface and it's more visible—like at the Troubadour or the first set at the Bottom Line—you can see it. You can see it on my face; I don't think I smiled once during the first set at the Bottom Line, and I know I didn't smile at all at the Troubadour, because it was too close—it was so close to the surface, it affects you physically.

That was the menacing part of it: it was like a death-rattle for yourself.
So that's the hardest, when it has captured you. That means I'm not in control, it is in control of me and I'm in the middle of this battle with this thing. Last night, it's always there, but maybe I have an edge on it. And it goes up and down during the set. You can see it come out. Last night I had an edge on it, like I was on top of it, but it's always there. What it is is the potential for failure is always there. That's what's exciting about it, especially when you get to the point where you're a big winner [*laughs*].

It's the same thing you said before, but now you're approaching it from the other side, the same thing as trying to prove yourself, looked at from the other side.
Big winners are big losers. It's like that. When you're at Las Vegas and you're a big winner, and you've got all this money in front of you, then all it takes is *that* to be a big loser. So I've found now that I'm more tense before I go on. Last night for the first time since I don't remember when, I was real tense. I was uptight, almost. I was scared, I think. I might not have been scared, but I was close to being scared. Which I haven't been in years.

So you like that?
I like it and I don't. The whole thing of winning is also an illusion. People yelling don't mean you won. I'm the only guy who knows, I think, if I made it that night. This is totally from my viewpoint. Other people, like John Rockwell, for one, his favorite set at the Bottom Line was the first set. He's one of those guys who just sat there and just enjoyed watching the incredible struggle onstage. He came up to me and said the second set was fantastic, it was like clockwork, it was more ex-

citing, it was tighter, it got everybody going more, but I liked the first set better. Because I was able to sit there and watch a guy struggling with his thing. He liked that. And I was! The first set I was fighting like a madman with that stuff. Other people, they'd rather get off and groove along with it. So it depends. It's something that you would not want to see every night. There were other people who were disappointed, like Paul Nelson, who came down and was disappointed in the first set. He came back Sunday, and he said it in his article, the set Sunday night was like the perfect set: the band was in control, and that's a beautiful sight in itself. When everything is working right with our band, it's smooth. It's like the finest machine you've ever seen. It's something. And the other way, that's the darker side. Which comes out more on the record than on anything else. That's a very hard record to play live, the new record. Because the situation I was in at the time, on that record, that comes out more. For me it does anyway.

I can hear that in some lines, the tension.
The tension making that record I could never describe. It was killing, almost, it was inhuman. I hated it. I couldn't stand it. It was the worst, hardest, lousiest thing I ever had to do.

Were there pressures outside yourself?
Once again, you would tend to say yes, but I've come to decide that, no. I know myself enough to where I know that in a way I didn't care if it was late, I didn't care if the record company didn't like it or what. For me to say, yeah, it was the tensions put on me by the press, or by the record company . . . I would tend to say that's what made the record so hard for me.

You had to prove yourself against yourself. There was no audience at all that could relieve you by being receptive and getting you back three times. You were the yardstick.
And with myself I'm never satisfied. I push myself hard all the time. I really don't know why. Like the thought of doing an intermission never, ever crossed my mind. Not until someone said that the Allman Brothers did one [*laughs*], not until today, or yesterday. It never crossed my mind. I *never* did an intermission in my life. I figured, what do you need an intermission for? If it's going perfect, if the band is running like it should run, it should be just a long, long set. And I just thought

about it, I just thought about it this morning. What would happen if we did this? We could actually do more. If we did an intermission, we could play more songs! Do more! But I was never into this logical approach. The idea was that was the human way to do it. And I'm not into that [laughs]. I was into this other way. Anybody can do it that way, I don't want to do it that way. Which in a way is self-defeating.

And the same thing went for the album. The album couldn't be easy. It just could not be easy, and it wasn't. It was the hardest thing. You don't know. I was going to cry over it so many nights. Really, I actually did. The other day I was in this hotel in New York, the Holiday Inn, I was there for the whole summer, and this little room, not even the size of this room, was like the worst room in the world. That was the worst room they had. The mirror was crooked. It wouldn't go straight for nothin'. The sucker was as crooked as could be, it just hung crooked. Couldn't get it to hang right. It just blew my mind after a certain amount of time. The other day this drove me nuts. It was the album that mirror became—it was crooked, it just wouldn't hang right! Karen was with me. She was going nuts. She went crazy several nights. I'd be in the studio eight hours, come home at five, and she was going crazy. Because she had come from Texas, didn't know anybody, didn't know any place to go, she just sat in the Holiday Inn all summer, in this one room, and she went nuts. So it went on and on, night after night. The album was beating me to death, then I had this relationship going on that was murder. It was the heaviest. I told her I could understand exactly how she felt; she was in this hotel room for hours and was seeing me only at night, early in the morning and at night. She didn't know anybody else, so of course she'd get mad at me, even if she understood what was going on. So that got insane, the whole thing, it was really like freak-out time.

Then, even as we got towards the end, the end of the album lasted for like two or three weeks! It was going to be over for weeks—the next day it would be over, for weeks and weeks. I'd be gone for two days from the Holiday Inn, and I'd come back and all she'd say was, "Is it over?" [laughs]. I'd say no! No, it ain't over. I'd go back out, and I'd be gone for another two days; I'd come back and I'd say this is it, got one more song we're gonna mix, I'll come back and everything'll be fine. "Is it over?" and I'd have to say no, it is not over. And this went on and on.

Finally I spent three or four days at the studio, 'round the clock. The last morning. I had a gig in Providence, Rhode Island, that night; that morning I was singing "She's the One" at the same time I was mixing "Jungleland" in another studio downstairs; at the same time I was in another studio, rehearsing the band for the gig that night. That's the truth. I almost died. There's a picture of it, this girl Barbara [Pyle] took a picture of it, and it's the scariest thing I've ever seen. You have to see the band. It should be on the cover of that album. Scariest thing ever. You ain't never seen faces like that in your life. She may have it. Because if she has it, it's something to see. You ain't never seen more messed-up, beat-down—we were there for four days, and every single minute is in everybody's face. The light comes through the window, it's like ten in the morning, we've been up for days. We got a gig that night, we're rehearsing, and what's worse is, I can't even sing! Because I've been singing, trying to sing all these songs, and I've got to sing that night. The picture just captures that moment. And then, we didn't get it done, even that day. I went home, "Is it over?"—we're leaving the hotel, we're packed—"Is it over?" I said no, it isn't over. I could've cried. I could've died when we didn't get it done. We walked out of that studio and I wanted to kill somebody. And then you had to deal with that.

Like me, if things don't happen right away in the studio, people get weird. I get real weird. People would walk out, they couldn't talk any more. Not because they were uptight at anybody, they just couldn't talk. Like Landau, I'll never forget it: he was incredible, he made it the whole way, but the last day, we were doing the last song, and he walked out. Not mad, you gotta understand. Not mad, not uptight; it was not an uptight walk-out. He just drifted out the door. He went home. He says, "I sat there and realized there was nothing I could do, and if anything was going to happen that you guys were going to do it." And we sat there at that board mixing "She's the One." I think I was asleep, I think I slept most of the time. I know the engineer was awake, I know Mike was awake. Mike is a great guy—he's always awake [*laughs*]. But you've got to dig that that is where it was at some times on this record: you were great if you were awake! Because a lot of people were asleep, passed out. It was an ordeal.

What do you think of it now that it's finished?
The record? Oh, I like the record. I hated it for the first few times I heard it, I wasn't going to release it. I called Philby up about it, I was

going to throw it out! I went nuts. I went crazy. But they were all really pro putting it out. People legitimately liked the record, which I couldn't fathom at the time, because I hated it so much.

Do you have a definite favorite off the album?
I like "Born to Run." That's always been my favorite. Just because it was something I executed the way I sort of wanted to.

Now you're going to be famous. You are famous.
I don't know, I ain't famous yet.

Oh yeah, I think so. I mean, it hasn't materialized in your personal life yet, but that will happen. What are your thoughts about that?
I don't have any thoughts about it. I don't know what's possible, what ain't possible. I just do what feels right at the moment. I know what feels right and I know what don't. And that's the way I always worked. I never planned anything. I never thought, in three years it'll work out.

Last night we were walking out on the streets; in three years you won't be able to do that. You see that happen to people.
I can't imagine it happening to me. Not where I can't walk out on the street and stuff. I can't imagine that happening. I ain't into daydreaming about being big and famous and stuff like that. Not to say that you don't think about it, because everybody thinks about it, but I think about it now the same way I thought about it when me and Stevie were riding in this dumpy old van in Richmond, Virginia, about six years ago. It's something that's impossible to try to come to terms with before you're there.

But knowing something about how things go in this business, you might say I more or less know where this is leading me. And I might not be very pleased with it. So let's stop it here or there to keep it together for myself so I can handle it. It might get out of hand.

My situation is that when things start happening that I don't like, when I find things starting to slip out of control as far as presenting myself and my band the way I want to, that's when I stop. We got this gig we were supposed to do in two days. I knew it was going to be a lousy gig; Karen knew it was going to be a lousy gig; we're not going to do the gig. So we stop it. And that's the way I work. We may do another hall a few miles away, and it's a nice hall. And we'll charge only a buck to get in, so that people will come. Maybe we'll do that. When I find it slipping from my control, that's when I say wait, stop, Mike, come here, let's not do this, let's do this. And that's the governor on the whole thing, that I'm very conscious of it running away with me. I've never been into that, I've always been into directing myself and me riding it where I want to, me on the back telling it where I want to go. I know myself, and I know I'm the kind of person that can keep it that way. I'm not too worried about it.

Ray Coleman
Melody Maker,
November 15, 1975

In anticipation of Springsteen's first-ever performance in London, *Melody Maker* produced an 80-page extravaganza under the title "Smash Hit Springsteen." The issue included an interview conducted in Los Angeles by Ray Coleman, who would become editor of *Melody Maker*. Asked whether he saw himself as the future of rock 'n' roll, as Jon Landau famously wrote in the *Real Paper*, Springsteen responds, "Hey, gimme a break with that stuff, will you? It's nuts. It's crazy. Who could take that seriously?"

Do you feel a big responsibility now as opposed to one year ago? You are now "a star." Do you feel this affecting you?
No. No. I don't feel any different. That stuff—it's a bunch of jive. The only responsibility you have is to remain true to yourself, true to what you do. If you do that I think you'll do all right, you know. It's harder to do as it goes along because all of a sudden you're something that money can be made with, you know? Then you gotta watch out,

because people are gonna want you to do things you don't wanna do . . .

Like this interview?
[*Laughs*] Nah—I wanted to do this interview . . .

But this interview might not be happening right now had you not been a big property to Columbia Records . . .
What's the difference? You know, records or no records, some place in the world I'm gonna play. It's like if it wasn't here, if it wasn't in Los Angeles, it'd be back in Asbury Park, because that's what I do. It's my life, you know? And ah—this interview today, this interview is just not particularly symbolic of anything.

You don't feel caught up in any machine?
Well . . . [*Long silence*].

Star-making machine?
In a way, yes. I don't know how they can make somebody a star, because not all of the machinery is as tough. It's not necessarily a bad thing; it is very often a stupid and foolish thing, the way it's used sometimes.

What they'll do is hurt you trying to help you, you know? I can't be put in a position of having to dig out of somebody's idea of what I am. For years now, first I was Dylan, digging my way from under that, right? Then I was like something else—the Future! I dig out from under that. So that's the position I've been put in.

But I've sorta come to accept it, even though I resent it very much. Because all I've ever done is write my songs and play with my band. I've tried to keep tabs on what people are doing, promotion-wise, and there's been a lot of ads that I've pulled out of the press, just in time.

By the time you pull the ads, it's too late, you're like in the press, everybody picks it up, whatever was in the ad, you know? I'm a lot more than just words on paper, you know?

You can't jive the kid in the street, no matter what everybody says. He don't care what's on the radio, don't care what somebody is saying. The kid on the street, I think, sees what's jive. These kids in that audience, living the whole thing, dying with the whole thing, you know—

that's what it's all about. Like, the kids knew all the songs, and they liked the band.

But disregarding the publicity that's happened for you in the last year, which has built up to a peak this very week, the fans also seem to regard you as rather important in that you're very fresh, your music isn't really a copy of anyone else's even though it has its roots in the '60s rock. Do you agree that they seem ready to accept a new giant star and you're there, right now, ready to be plucked off the tree? Are your new fans waiting to erect a new statue?
No, I don't think the kids think like that. Every kid relates to you on his own personal level, you know, like what you mean to him specifically. I think if they find something in you, if something helps him out, something that clears something out for him. I think it's as simple as that.

I don't think there's any basis in it. People are ready? People are always ready, you know? Something comes along and it's what they like. As far as big symbols or big beat, big stars or something, I don't know. It's not exactly me.

I can't see myself big or a star kind of guy. I mean, ah, not in the normal sense or in the original sense. Maybe . . . I don't know. I mean, I gotta good band. I've got some of the greatest guys in the world, I think, guys who will go anywhere, do anything.

They've worked for no money for years, they've seen the sights, played every kind of place you can imagine. I've seen situations that are unbelievable. And they come out and they play like it's life or death. Because it's important to them. This is the reason to live.

It ain't a job and it ain't business, you know. If you approach it like that you might as well get a real job or something! It's my whole life. First time I ever feel any good is when I'm playing and I have a good time. It's everything to me, and it's the same thing to those guys.

Do you feel the audiences are different now? You're attracting different audiences from those you were attracting, say, a year ago?
The response to the band has always been very, very good. That's why it's a joke, you know, all the jive. That's where it came from, man, the kids. Response from the audience has always been great.

We never sold a lot of records, maybe because you couldn't get the whole story from the records we did earlier, but whenever we played it was like—instant! Wherever we go we'd always feel a part of all those kids—sometimes 10, 20, 30, 40 and 100, sometimes we sell out. We vary.

They knew it all. They knew your whole, knew all your songs, all the words and they were like they were just right THERE, into it as much as us. On stage you know, that's the situation, man. So it's funny. Like, in reality, a lot of things haven't changed that much.

What do you want of an audience? Do you want them to bounce off from?

Ideally, the kind of audience that comes to do it with you. The hardest audience is opening night. Maybe a few people can get into it but most disregard all the stuff, don't believe in anything, or half of what they see.

You can not get a sense of the city on the first show. Because these people flip and they all got in free, and the people flew in from other places outside of LA. The kids don't get in till the next night. That one was fantastic and the audiences were great, great audiences.

Having "taken" Los Angeles, do you regard this as a turning point, a milestone, in your career?

I'm doing the best I can right now, you know, that's all. Like, I worked really great in Los Angeles but in general I think that if the concerts open the door for me to come back again—that's what it's about. Outside of that, you know—just sing every night, you know. Do a show, just go out to play, best I can.

Has the fame of this last year affected your writing in any way? Do you find it more difficult to write now?

No, the writings are crazy. I don't know about it at all. It just comes and goes, and I write almost strictly when I have to.

When you started playing, leading a band, in New Jersey, did you set off thinking: "I want to be a superstar? I want to be the new Elvis Presley?"

When I started I wanted to play rhythm guitar in a local band. Like, sit back there, play a rhythm guitar. Just wanna play rhythm! And like— stand back! I didn't wanna sing, just get a nice band and play rhythm.

But I found out I had a little more sense than I thought, I found out that I just knew more about it than other guys that were in the band.

So I slowly just became the leader, you know, and that's pretty much how we became a band.

You know, you always say: "Oh, I wanna be famous and I'll make the box office someday," but it's bad—you don't have to think about it.

I'll go out there [*points as if to stage*]. I mean, right THERE is all that matters, because if you ain't delivering now, you know, there's no excuse, there's no reason, no matter what you feel. Hell, no matter how tough it is, you gotta do it, then and now. So, I never thought too much about it at the time.

How much is *Born to Run* autobiographical?
Oh I don't know . . . it's hard to say. I don't really write like that. I write overall feelings of things, you know, mixed in with lots of different shades of the same reality—I don't know if that makes any sense! It's, like, just varying shades of the same things, like some of it is on an immediate, very physical level of experience, the other is on a more emotional level.

How do you write songs? Do you discipline yourself and say I'm going to write some music today?
I just sit down and f—around for a couple of hours. Usually something comes up. I sit down and I work on the song, and I sit down and work on it some more, then some more and some more, and maybe I've got to discipline myself.

How far do you want the popularity to go?
To tell you the truth, I just don't know. I don't know what the hell's going on. I don't ever want it to get in the way of what I'm doing first of all, you know? I don't ever plan to let it water down anything that I'm doing.

It's OK as long as it stays out of the way, and HELPS. For as far as it helps that's as far as I want it to go. Otherwise it's me freaked out, so why bother with the whole thing? I get upset by it sometimes, you know—I just don't wanna go and get lost in a bunch of stuff that don't mean nothing to me.

How much does your current popularity affect your movement, day by day?
I got the kind of face that gets recognised! I look like, you know, Mr. Face-in-the-crowd, that's me! Only place I get recognised if I go out is

in a club, but in general the most that happens is somebody comes up and says "Hi."

But it doesn't prevent you from walking around?
Oh no, no.

Would you resent it if it did?
I guess so. It's just that I don't wanna get into that aspect of it. I ain't into, like, riding around in limousines—a DRAG, you know! I wouldn't dig it if I couldn't do what I wanna do. Can't go any place, you know, can't do nothing—I mean, that's not what people like doing, that's not reality.

This is a business, man, it's like dope or something. You get what they want sometimes, but, like, feeling is a dope in the form of money, in the form of limousines, in the form of different stuff, you know? So it makes it so easy, man.

You know, all of a sudden: "Hey, man, it's comfortable back here! Why didn't they TELL me it was like this? Wow, this is NICE!" It's like: "Yeah, wow, where are we going? [*Slumps in a chair as if in back of a limousine.*] We're going to play a 20,000 seater dance? Yeah, DRIVE me down there. Italy!"

If you don't watch out I think that can happen and—like, I just ain't into getting hooked on that kinda stuff.

What would you do if you were terrifically rich?
I'd spend a lot of money or something! If I was rich? If I made a LOT of money, you mean? Let me think. Phew! Get my mother to quit working. My father to quit working. My mother's been working since she was 18—she's 50 now. It's too LONG to work. Right off, that's about all I can think . . . maybe get an apartment in New York.

You're very fond of stressing in your act your links with New Jersey; you mention that a lot in your talking. Why is this? Do you constantly want to remind yourself of where you're from originally and your roots, or do you want the audience to know you're a city person?
I'm not really a city person. Jersey is a sort of boardwalk town. It ain't like New York. I've been to New York a lot, but I want people to understand what I am, where I'm from, you know. Get a clear picture of me.

Like the main reason I put it on that first album (as the title) was because they were pushing for this big New York thing—this, this big town. I said "wait, you guys are nuts or something. I'm from Asbury Park, New Jersey. Can you dig it? NEW JERSEY."

I wasn't too cool. I said, I want this on the album cover. They fought and fought, but we finally got it put on. And it's a part of my thing, it's like—I'm from New Jersey! It's important for people to get a clear picture of me.

Your songs are full of jagged edges but not much talk of love. Do you consider yourself a romantic? Emotional?
Oh yeah, yeah. I guess that's me.

Do you ever cry?
Sure, yeah, sure. Hey, I'm not telling you THAT, man!

You're often moved and touched by events that happen close to you?
No, I ain't that kind of guy. I guess I'm more of a romantic guy. I don't run around too much. I kinda keep to myself. As a writer it's where you're from. You know, if you grow up in a slum, you just want it like that. You didn't show, like, that kind of emotion. To show too much was not the thing to do in those days, I guess. I sort of keep to myself as far as I can.

Do you drive a Chevrolet, the car which figures frequently in your lyrics?
I used to drive a truck, a heavy truck. Got an old Chevy now.

Do you drive alone?
Yeah, pretty much. I don't like a bunch of people yelling in my ear, you know. I can't stand kids in the back seat, man—they start yelling in my bad ear!

Once I'd got this little kid sitting in the car and he said, "Wah—take me for a ride," and he started going nuts. Just wanna like stay by myself, you know, or have a girlfriend.

And do you like privacy? Is that important to you, to be on your own? Do you need solitude?
Yeah, I like friends, but I'm pretty much by myself out there, most of the time. My father was always like that. Lived with my father for

20 years. Never once saw a friend come over to the house. Not one time.

Do you have a good atmosphere within your band?
We don't have a bad atmosphere. If you have a bad atmosphere you're gonna come out and think "this guy is a fool!" You've gotta think, "this guy's the greatest," and the only way you can think that is if he is. He's human. Everybody's human, and everybody screws up sometimes.

But in general the guys in this band are some of the greatest guys in the world. You'll never meet nicer people. And you've gotta have that feeling, man, to get that unity, to get that full-out thing: "I believe in this guy, this guy is real."

Do you get nervous before an act?
Occasionally. Not too much.

Do you drink? Do you smoke?
No.

Go to concerts?
No, not much.

Parties?
No.

What do you think about the music industry?
I don't think about anything too much. I don't think about industry. I just don't wanna know. I'm wary now. I know what I want. I don't wanna be sidetracked with any industry concerns. It's not my deal, it's not the deal I got going. As long as it can be used to the good, that's all that matters to me.

What would you do if you were not a musician? Any ideas what you might have done?
I wouldn't have done anything. Probably done something crazy. Maybe robbed stores or something! That always appealed to me, robbing things. If I wasn't a musician . . . the thing is—in life you've gotta keep yourself bare, you've gotta keep yourself trimmed down. Can't start collecting a lot of junk.

I throw out almost everything I ever own. I don't believe in collecting anything. The least you have to lose the better you are, because the more chances you'll take. The more you've got, the worse off you get, because it comes harder.

You start to worry about this, so you've got to keep yourself trimmed down. Some guys I see sometimes—it's a tragic situation, they'll do anything, they've got nothing to lose. Like, they start to get fat, get messed up, do something wrong, and it's a mistake.

It's like, you gotta watch out—that's the way it's gotta be to get control. All of a sudden you get kids, get them jobs and houses and mortgages and bills, all of a sudden, Jesus Christ, if they don't work they're going to lose this, they're gonna lose their car, they're gonna lose their house, they're gonna lose their kid, they're gonna lose their money, they're gonna lose their self-respect, they're gonna lose EVERY-THING.

That's how America imprisons everybody. It's like a confining, society-type trip. Because they imprison you with all these damned goods, you know.

And if you can get these things, if you can get things that you want but still manage to run free when you have to, burst free, you know—then you're a winner, because having nothing—well, that's no way, you know, but having everything and being afraid of losing it, being afraid, scared to death of taking a chance of blowing it, that's just as bad.

Do you believe that music, especially rock, should just be a sound or should it represent something? Should it just be a release or should it provoke thought from its audience?
It should be everything. For me it always was. Made me think about myself. I was provoked to think by Elvis Presley. He provoked thought in me, you know, made me think "Where am I at?" Dylan, Elvis Presley, Eddie Cochran—these guys provoke thought in me.

They give you a little spark; it's fun, it's life—rock and roll. Other music just didn't have it. It socked you in the face: "One for the money, two for the show," you know, "three to get ready!" That was IT.

Are you politically minded?
No.

You don't think, for instance, of government decisions? Don't study world events particularly?
No.

How do you view the prospect that you might in the foreseeable future play the Forum in Los Angeles, and Madison Square Garden, New York, each with 20,000 fans? This could happen and you wouldn't have communication with an audience that you have always enjoyed in smaller places. How do you feel about those giant arenas?
It's beyond a physical thing. It's something else. If you work yourself up to a certain intensity where you can actually project to that many people . . . it's very, very difficult. I don't know if it's possible. If I thought I could do in a big place what I do in a theatre with three or four thousand . . . I'll have to see.

   If I couldn't, I just wouldn't do it. I gotta realise that maybe there's a lot of people wanting to see me, but you just can't compromise on your thing. You can't say, "Well, I ain't gonna do as well, but to hell," because I'm out here basically for myself, because I have to be fair to myself as well, you know?

Do you ever dress up, wear a suit?
I like a suit but I don't look right in a suit. I put a suit on, my face just don't go with the suit, man! You know. My face—I just ain't got a suit face. It's too bumpy. Weird.

When you go on stage in clothes very casual, probably similar to something that you're wearing now, are you conscious of what you're going on stage in?
Yeah, sure. I think I'll wear this shirt, and these shoes. You go on stage and you feel good and right. I'm just gonna present myself as what I am, which is—basically, I'm dealing with basic people, and situations, and survival situations.

You've not conceived "dressing-down" to contrast with the band? For instance, Miami Steve [guitarist] dresses up.
I would like to wear a suit sometimes, now I think about it. For a while I didn't wear jeans—I wore pants, other kinds of, like ah, you know,

trousers, or whatever you call them. But I never really dressed up. Mostly because it's hard to stretch, hard to sorta relax, hard to work.

It's like when you're all dressed up and it's . . . yeah, I'd like a suit, maybe, someday. Just for the hell of it. Like, those guys dress up, why don't I?

You wear a hat and sometimes throw one around in your act, but you didn't have it here in Los Angeles. Why?
No, I cut my hair short, and it didn't fit right. Yeah, I used to have long hair a few weeks ago, and I cut it off. Hat just didn't fit right anymore, so I didn't wear it.

Do you like seeing your picture in the paper?
No.

Why not?
I don't like pictures. I don't like video tapes. It ain't a natural thing. It's weird, very weird.

Do you read articles about yourself and the band?
Sometimes.

If they're critical, how do you feel?
There was a piece I read and the only thing that upsets me is the guy, whoever wrote it, couldn't hear what was on the album. To me that was upsetting. Because I know what's on there, because I died on the damn thing graduating! Like, everything I got is on there. I BELIEVE that record.

It sorta upset me that he couldn't hear what was on it. He was, like, complaining about it being repetitious. That's a dumb comment, you know. It's like, so what? That ain't the point of the record, you know, and even if it is it doesn't matter.

I hooked into this one thing, wrote basically about the same thing, for a large part of the record. I dealt with this one thing. It was like a whole. The hardest thing I ever did in my life. I bled dry on that thing, groaning, conked out on the floor, half-dead on the street at six in the morning on the corner, you know, trying to walk uptown, trying to make it to my hotel room.

I was staying for two months on it. And people lost themselves doing it. Conditions were so extreme. So I know what's on that record, you know, and I stand by that record with my LIFE! I just believed in the damn thing, you know, 100 percent. So if somebody can't hear it, I can't help it. It's my silver machine, or something

Who's your best friend? Do you have one? Or just a lot of acquaintances?
I got some friends. The guys in the band are my friends. I got a girl-friend. That's who I am with most.

Do you plan to marry? Have children?
No, I can't do that, that's for sure.

Why?
I couldn't bring up kids. I couldn't handle it. I mean, it's too heavy, it's too much. A kid—like, you better be ready for them. I'm so far off of that track, I'm so far out of line, that it would be disastrous. I don't understand it. I just don't see why people get married. It's so strange. I guess it's a nice track, but not for me.

The spectre of Bob Dylan has been raised so many times you must be quite fed up with hearing his name in relation to your own career. But could you say how you view him?
Dylan is great. A good rock 'n' roller. "Like A Rolling Stone"—great song.

At any point did you model yourself or any segment of your career on his?
No, I'm not really into stuff like that. When he was big I was too young. I was 15, you know. In '65 I was 15 years old, so I never got into it. I realised real quick that you got to be yourself. If you ain't yourself, then what are you? You're some crazy image, and it don't make sense. I like Elvis, I like a lot of people. My first love! He was great.

What was the first record you can remember that gripped you?
"Wooly Bully." I can't even remember how big I was. First record I ever bought, I think, was "Jailhouse Rock." I always worshipped Phil Spector. About 1963 I was 13. I didn't start playing until I was 14, I remember digging all the songs but remember that I had to go back as I started

really getting into it, go back, dig out all the old singles and stuff and see what I'd missed.

The only stuff I caught was the English explosion, man, like the Beatles. That was when I was 16, 17, 14, and 15. That's when that happened. I was into it. Manfred Mann, man, I was nuts about those guys. Paul Jones was one of my favourites, and I dug the Animals, the Stones, I dug the Searchers, I dug, of course, the Beatles.

Do you consider yourself the future of rock 'n' roll, as you have been described?

Hey, gimme a break with that stuff, will you? It's nuts, it's crazy. Who could take that seriously? The guy was sorta saying I wasn't just like a mixture of past influences, that I was like doing my own thing. CBS took this, promoted it real heavy, and I was like "SENSATIONAL!" Cheap thrill time!

You know, it was a big mistake on their part. They probably don't realise it, they probably think they're right and I'm nuts, you know. But it was a very big mistake, and I would like to strangle the guy who thought that up if I ever get hold of him.

Because the idea of taking that quote and blowing that thing up like that, that's a bunch of jive. The future ain't any damned thing. Who was gonna swallow that? This is me. Who the hell wants to read stuff like that?

Just like suicide tactics. Crazy, crazy, crazy stuff to do. You wanna kill somebody off? It's like I said earlier—you gotta fight out from underneath something all the time. Who CARES, anyway? A kid in his chair—he couldn't give a damn what the future is or anything!

You know, he DON'T CARE about that kind of stuff, don't even pay attention to, it's just business like what it amounts to is, Jon Landau [one of the producers on the *Born to Run* LP] wrote a great article—with his heart—and on that level it was very, very encouraging to me.

At the time we weren't doing so good, and it helped me out with the record company. But what they did with it was, like, a cheap publicity trick, and I resent it very much, that they used that quote.

I guess good intentions were intended but it was a D-R-A-G, the whole episode was a big drag for me, and still is. I mean, who wants to come out on stage and be the future every night? Not me.

You know, let somebody else, let the guy who thought up using it in the ad, come out and do it! You know? See how he likes it. It was like another big, big mistake, right up there with the New Dylan thing. Same calibre.

Taking a wide view of the rock scene before you came into it with any strength with albums, do you think rock needed you, or someone, to revitalise the music scene?
I don't think about it. I've lived on a pretty personal basis. It's as simple as that, you know. I don't know why anybody needs it. People always moan and moan—rock this, rock that, and everybody's all saying: hey, that's supposed to be cool.

To say everything stinks is supposed to be right. Well, it's affected the musicians, I'm sure it has. I never felt that way. I always felt it was always very real. I know what it did to me, and it still does. I know when it happens to be right, and when I put it on a record, I go NUTS! You know, I love it.

It's a reason to live, helps people out. Now a lot of the new music hasn't done that. In fact, you know, it's like . . . I don't know why, I wish I knew why. It just hasn't done that.

You mean heavy rock?
Yeah, I could do with hearing some good new stuff. The Move had a single out once which was great, great song, and there are good records that still come out, but a lot of them get lost in the shuffle. A lot of them don't get a chance. That should have been a hit single, that song, on the radio, all over the country.

But it didn't. And, you know, so many good musicians are just trying to make it happen, just trying to make it through to the next day.

Your manager has to approach things more professionally than you, with more business consciousness than perhaps you do—he has to take a financial view of things. How is your relationship with him in that respect? If he wants for you massive commercial success is there any situation here when you'll say to him: "I'll go no further than that because I don't like it"?
Sure there is. I gotta watch out with that stuff. There's not going to be an easy way out for anybody just hanging round here, you know. I think everybody realizes that and anybody who doesn't realize it that's working with us will soon realise it, you know. Because it's not going to get easier. It's gonna get harder, 'cos it gets harder on me.

Robert Duncan
Creem,
January 1976

Founded in 1969 and based in Detroit, *Creem* billed itself as "America's Only Rock 'n Roll Magazine." Edited by Lester Bangs, who became one of the premier rock critics of the 1970s, the magazine also featured the early writing of such notable critics as Dave Marsh, Greil Marcus, and Robert Duncan, who wrote this feature. Referring back to the recording of *Born to Run*, Springsteen says, "that was the most horrible period of my life." Telling his "crooked mirror" story about the making of the album (see "The Lost Interviews"), Springsteen also tells Duncan, "I thought [*Born to Run*] was the worst piece of garbage I'd ever heard. I told Columbia I wouldn't release it. I told 'em I'd just go down to the Bottom Line gig and do all the new songs and make it a live album."

Understand. New Jersey has no baseball or football teams and half of it stinks. It used to be that if you were from Jersey and you came over to New York—by that I mean Manhattan, naturally; Queens certainly doesn't count—you didn't admit you were from Jersey. No, if there was one thing we New Yorkers could get together on it was Jersey: not a one

TALK ABOUT A DREAM 71

of us would've given a second thought to blowing the joint off the face of the universe like the infected pimple that it was . . . *Was*, I say. My God, how times change. I mean, I stopped going to the Academy of Music on 14th Street because the average patron there was a Jerseyite—you know, loud or nodded out or smelly or in any way obnoxious. But now, just like the guys down the hall from me who pretend that they're *black* and jive and shuffle about the building all day, I—a New York chauvinist if ever there was one—wonder why my mother wasn't considerate enough to have gone to Jersey to borne me. And when folks ask, *these* days, if I have any interest in impressing them, I say: "Me? Hey, I'm from *Jersey*, man!" Because—may Fiorello LaGuardia rest in peace—it's finally and unmistakably *hip* to be from the "armpit of the nation," that newly venerable State of New Jersey . . .

But, of course, I don't try to fool these guys, these authentic specimens, and besides, they probably have ways of checking . . .

"I was born in Sheboygan," I tell Bruce Springsteen, Miami Steve Van Zandt and company, who unanimously fall over in their seats laughing, having just discussed the drag scene that had gone down in Wisconsin—they think it was "some place like Sheboygan probably." And they're still laughing while this chick journalist who is accompanying the band and who lives in England "but originally came from Jersey"—I bet, *bitch!*—asks me with a singular ridiculing distaste, "Exactly how do you spell that . . . She-boy-gan?" Well, all I know is God wasn't shittin'! The last shall be the first, *indeed!* And I begin to counterattack.

"Sure, I know," Springsteen readily admits. "When I was 18 and playing in this place in California in this bar band these people would come up to us and say, 'Hey, I really dig you guys! Where do ya come from?' And I'd say, 'New Jersey.' And they'd just go 'Yecch! Ecch!'" So he knows, huh. I suggest to Springsteen that he probably should get some sort of public service citation from the Governor (if this one's not in jail yet) for finally making Jersey—I choose my next word carefully so as not to flatter my uppity tormentors—"tolerable." But Bruce doesn't detect my thinly veiled sarcasm, mulls the point over for a moment, stroking his grizzly chin, and says, "I ain't got nothin' from nobody in Jersey. I mean, when I'm home I walk up and down the boardwalk all day and not one person—well, sometimes one—stops and says, 'Hi!' or 'Hey, I know you!'" Then the lights go on behind this Jersey punk's eyes—which he averts from mine, shyly, because we've just recently met—and he tells me whimsically, but only half-jokingly, "What I think I'm gonna do is get on all the clothes I'm wearing on the album, you know, and get it just right. And hold my guitar, out here, this way, just so . . . And maybe I'll even get ol' Clarence and lean on him just so . . . Do the whole cover thing . . . Maybe *then* people'll notice." And for the first time since the show several hours earlier Springsteen laughs in his wheezing kind of chortle-through-the-nose way and looks directly at me. The ice is broken.

As the waitress passes, my new buddy (can a guy from New York really call a guy from Jersey his "buddy"? I am drunk) and I decide that more beer is in order. While it is only Springsteen's second of the evening, the record company man asks protectively of his Next Big Thing, "You sure you should have another, Bruce?" In mortal fear that I may lose a drinking partner, I insist that Springsteen try the famous local brand. Over the protestations of the company man, Springsteen instructs the waitress, "O.K., yeah. Give me one of them." He points to my empty. "But I won't know the difference," he says to me. "I don't really drink beer." Doesn't drink beer? I remark to myself suspiciously. And when he confirms the stories that he doesn't take drugs either . . . well, frankly, it *bothers* me. Somehow, in terms of the tradition which he is carrying on, it makes Springsteen, the would-be new Rock 'n' Roll Rebel King, somewhat inauthentic.

I must deal with this contradiction. Sitting across from him in this sleazy downtown Detroit jock bar, once owned by the ex-football star turned TV personality Alex Karras, this place that is absolutely a drinker's hangout, I assess the Phenomenon's offstage persona, seeking the flaws. The clothing immediately stands out. In place of the studded black leather jacket, which Springsteen expropriated from James Dean for stage use, is a much more stylish, tapered sport coat of reddish leather. In place of the sneakers, which the record company has established as some sort of trademark, is a pair of brand new shiny highheeled boots. Aha! This street kid stuff is just so much showmanship as I had suspected! Beside me, Miami Steve, who has a much more recognizably Jersey accent as well, looks more the part than Springsteen (or "Da Boss," as he calls him), having shed his onstage pimp costume to deck himself out entirely in black leather. Disillusionment is setting in. Then I listen to the conversation.

Springsteen is speaking in what appears to be his natural voice, breathy, gritty with a black cadence. He and Miami are talking about their old buddies on E Street (yes, there is such a place) and if those guys could see them now. As Bruce has been warming up with the beer which he so rarely indulges in, Steve has been warming up with these miniature bottles of rosé. Now they're talking quite seriously about the boardwalk at Asbury Park and the pinball machines. Miami Steve has made the seemingly logical proposal to Bruce that if the pinball people can make an "Elton John–Pinball Wizard" table, why shouldn't there be a "Bruce Springsteen–Born to Run" table as well. Bruce explains to him with a similar forthrightness and logic, "Ya see, these guys wanna make *bucks* . . . You gotta be *famous*." (Little did the two kids quietly turning over their dream world, determining what is and what will be, realize that around the next corner lurked *Time* and *Newsweek* covers. Little did they dream of Springsteen's unprecedented ascension to nationwide fame.) Then they started to tease their record company guys, New York City rats both, about a recent trip to Asbury Park. Bruce mockingly relates the incident wherein one of the guys joined him on Asbury Park's infamous "Rock 'n' Roll Ride." "It goes around and round," he explains. "And up and down, in and out"—he accelerates with the ride—"and this and that way and-all-over-the-place! Wow!" He laughs. The company guy owns up, "Yeah, I was screwed up for two whole days afterwards." Tapered red leather sports coat? That's just the way they dress up in Jersey for a Saturday night. Listening to Springsteen, it becomes readily apparent that he's for real, that if he's no longer one of them, at least he's *from* them, those kids he writes about, and deeply rooted in the steamy, frenetic landscape of Asbury Park, New Jersey. And while the Next Big Punk/Street Poet/Rock 'n' Roller hype may have put his current album at the top of the charts, it certainly isn't disseminated by him and seems to have caused Springsteen enough pain with the pleasure.

We're talking about the recording of *Born to Run*. Abruptly, Bruce shifts gears and stomps on the pedal. He leans across the table willfully to within inches of my face. Everyone else at the table is shut out. His eyes are ablaze. "That was the most horrible period of my life . . . *the most horrible period of my life*," he states, shaking his head slowly back and forth and sweeping his hand unequivocally across everything. And when I ask him why, he grabs the Columbia press packet from in front of his publicist and holds it up beside his face. Across the top is Jon Landau's famous quote, "I saw the rock 'n' roll future and its name is Springsteen." Bugging eyes rivet me. Then impulsively, frustratedly,

Springsteen bites the packet and rips it with his teeth, finally tearing it in half with his hands and throwing it to the floor. "THAT!" he barks savagely in answer to my question.

"Let me tell ya," he continues more quietly, but no less intensely. "I had this *horrible* pressure in the studio and for the whole last part of the record I was living in this certain Inn in New York over west. [The place is, in fact, notorious and has been raided more than once for gambling and prostitution.] And the room there had this . . ." He sizes something up. "It had this crooked mirror. And every day, before I'd go over to the studio I'd straighten out this crooked mirror . . . And every day when I'd come home, that mirror was *crooked* again. Every time. That crooked mirror . . . it just couldn't stay straight . . . So I'm in there with this crooked mirror and after about a week the room started to look like Nagasaki *anyway* . . ." He pauses suspended in his gesture that indicates the room and then launches in again. ". . . junk *all over* the place. And *then* one day this chick I was with one night in Texas calls up and says she's in Jersey and she doesn't have any place to stay and she's *freakin' out!* And so finally I say, 'O.K. You can stay here.' So every day I'd go into the studio and there was *that* and then I'd come home and there'd be this crooked mirror and . . . this crazy chick, you see." And he has to laugh as each Chinese box of his story gives way to another absurd package.

But as Springsteen goes on, elaborating on how every day of recording was *supposed* to be the last, brief sessions stretching on into weeks, and how *everybody* was "getting crazy," he gets serious again. "One night," he tells me, towards the end of the record, "I was sittin' there at the piano in the studio, tryin' to get down the last cut, 'She's the One,' and Landau's in the booth and we've been at it for hours and hours. I just lean my head down on the piano. It just won't come. And everybody's tryin' to tell me how to do it—they were all there to *help* me and they were really tryin'—and Landau's sayin' this and that and freakin' out . . . and then, all of a sudden, everyone looks around and Landau has just disappeared, just walked off into the night—night, it was like *six a.m.*—couldn't take it. He was smart to go home and get some sleep. The whole thing was like that. And when I got home around ten in the morning to the room with the crooked mirror, this chick she says to me—she says it every night when I come home—" and Springsteen's voice softens, " 'Is it finished?' and I say, 'No.' And I could've cried . . . I almost cried . . ." Springsteen goes further away for a moment.

". . . Well, maybe I did cry a little . . ." And then snaps back. ". . . I almost cried."

The "crazy chick" is now his near-longtime girlfriend, Karen Darvin. And the record? "After it was finished? I *hated* it! I couldn't stand to listen to it. I thought it was the worst piece of garbage I'd ever heard. I told Columbia I wouldn't release it. I told 'em I'd just go down to the Bottom Line gig and do all the new songs and make it a live album." Of course, Columbia prevailed upon him to release the record, and while it did rise to the top of the charts and while Bruce can now laugh and say of the album these several months later, "I like it," he also assures firmly: "Never again!"

But you mustn't believe him. First of all, he's from Jersey. Second: just listen to the care that went into *Born to Run* and you try to figure out how he can retreat from that. Third: he has this limitless energy and is driven by a sincere desire to give an audience everything that they could have hoped for in a performance because "You cannot take that audience lightly." Unless he gets thoroughly corrupted by corporate economic policy and/or his own publicity, this guy will never just put out "product"—live or in the studio—he's too honest.

Miami Steve is making sure that the barmaid tells Alex Karras that "Miami says hello," as we're all swept out of the bar. One record company guy has gone ahead to get the car, and, as we emerge onto the street, he pulls up. Everybody is piling in when Springsteen announces, "Nahh, I don't want to drive. I'm gonna walk back." And he expands his chest to take in a lungful of the dubiously nutritional Detroit air. In drunken mimicry, I do the same . . . and damned if it don't feel good! I tap on my chest and shout to Springsteen, "H2O! H2O!" And he responds at first with a sheepish grin, unsure of my comic intentions, but a little drunk himself, echoes "Right! H2O!" And despite the protests of the company chaperones, the Next Big Thing and I set off into the murky Motown night, oblivious to danger and also oblivious to the fact that I'm not at all sure of the direction of the hotel, though I'm a certifiably good guesser.

Springsteen has his harp out and is stepping jauntily in time to his own unaccompanied version of "Not Fade Away," singing between his honks in a quiet sinuous wheeze. (If they ain't drowned out, Jersey cats can get hopelessly corny.) A block into our perilous journey, Springsteen realizes that the company guys are following slowly behind us in the car. He motions them on. When they stay put, he steps up to the

car and good-naturedly tells them to "Get outta here!" We walk on.
Another block. The car remains on our trail. Suddenly, Springsteen
pivots and races head-on at the slow-moving car, bounding solidly onto
the hood in his high-heeled boots, and then stomping and skidding his
way onto the roof where in mock-frenzy attack he jumps up and down
repeatedly. "Hey! You're gonna wreck the goddamned rented car, Bruce!"
some Nervous Nellie within shouts out. "Nahhh!" Springsteen coun-
termands as he finishes his assault and leaps back to the pavement. The
car scoots off.

I laugh. It's the kind of wanton nonsense that I expect from Rock 'n'
Roll Kings. He chortles in his nose and withdraws back into the harp
and "Not Fade Away." But fade away he does. Back at the hotel (amazingly enough) he makes a gracious, if perfunctory, gesture to invite us
all in, but when we get off the elevator at the sixth floor it's clear that
he's heading towards his room—swaying, actually—and sleep and that
everyone else should go elsewhere. Aww! Those Jersey punks could
never take it! I think as I careen off to whatever I can find. But in a more
rational moment, I realize that mere mortals must sleep.

Dave Herman
syndicated radio interview on
King Biscuit Flower Hour,
July 9, 1978

Dave Herman was one of the earliest and most influential FM radio rock 'n' roll disc jockeys, first at WMMR in Philadelphia (along with Ed Sciaky) and then WNEW in New York. In 1975, he resisted playing Springsteen because he was turned off by all the hype, but after seeing him live that August at the Bottom Line, he became an impassioned fan. Promoting his brand new *Darkness on the Edge of Town*, Bruce talks about his reaction to the *Born to Run* phenomenon, about his relationship with Jon Landau, about the members of the band, and the new album: "I like it, which is always a hard thing to do."

A few weeks ago, we went to San Diego where the band was performing on their current tour, for a rare radio interview with Bruce Springsteen. Bruce had been somewhat of a recluse during the last three years and we were eager to find out what he had been up to.

Bruce, there seems to be quite a change going on with you. I mean, for one, you've never given interviews before and now suddenly you're quite agreeable to talking. What's up?

I didn't want an instant replay of my *Born to Run* release, and so I initially thought, well, I'm not going to do any interviews right now. I'm not going to, I'm going to lay low and let the record come out and stuff. And I just realized a lot of things had changed since '75 I guess, since 1975 and slowly like you said over the last month or so, I took a different attitude towards, towards I guess promoting your record.

That's what a boy's band does, I guess.
Which is something' that like, it was something that like, what? Promote my record? I can't do that.

Did you think it was kind of like selling your own stuff, like calling the promoting as almost like selling, maybe?
Yeah, well it is, that's what you do. That's what you do. I chased very aggressively after what I was trying to get in the studio, and I worked real, real hard on it and, and I believe in it a lot. And for some reason I guess it dawned on me that it was silly to, like, do that. I mean, the records aren't going to like sprout legs and walk out stores and jump on the people's record players and say "listen to me."

There's a lot of records out there.
I said, here it is, I worked a year on this thing and I put everything I had into it. Now I want it to get out there, I want it to get heard. I want to get as many people listening to it as possible. An audience is something, you don't inherit an audience, and they don't run over to your door and knock on your door and sit in your lap. You got to, I think you got to go out and you got to say, here's what I think, I believe this, and give people a chance to hear it and make up their minds. I was a little wary first of all, of . . . I was afraid of the *Born to Run* thing.

By that, you mean all the publicity and all the press and all the . . .
Yeah, what I mean is I didn't have it in perspective. I didn't know what had frightened me about that and what had not. And so I bunched everything into something that I just called, like, the *Born to Run* experience or whatever it was.

Have you been able to separate from that, what it was that frightened you then?
Since then, what frightened me about it was I started to play, to get as

much, say, control of my life as I could, and that's what I felt slipping away and that's what scared me. And I was real naïve about it at the time. We'd blown through three or four years of playing, we had albums out. And the money came in, the money went out. And I was doing what I always wanted to do with my life, I was travelling around, and I I felt really good. And then what happens is, once you become what is known as a capital generator, something that makes money . . .

For lots of other people.
Right, all of a sudden it's a different ballgame and a different ballpark and you better get wise to it or else you're going to get stomped on.

You mean that you become not only Bruce Springsteen the person, but Bruce Springsteen the product.
Well, the whole thing, it's like, to ignore that fact is just stupid and it's just what it is: it's not real. And I spent a lot of time ignoring that. For quite a while, not even intentional because it didn't connect to me that way. It was like I was living out my rock 'n' roll dream there.

Fantasy . . .
And it was something that once I had gotten that position of all a sudden, hey look, there's more money than we can spend. What happens is, then come the distractions. Hey, do you want this, do you want that. Hey, you can have this. Do you want a car? Do you want a limousine? Whatever. All the standard distractions that . . .

Things that happen when you get to be rich and famous . . .
. . . come down the line to take your mind off of, to distract you from what is real and from your initial motivations, the things you started out for. But I always had it in my head, I always knew that, I always knew what I was doing there. Because I knew that when I was losing, I knew that it was slipping away. Like, I knew why I started, and I knew it was slipping away, and I got scared by it.

Well I want to get something specific from you. What is it, what is it you wanted to do when you started?
It's easy. A lot of people wander, wander through their lives. You're bouncing off walls, you're bouncing off people, you're bouncing off different

jobs. And you end up 55 and you never found something that you wanted to do.

Sounds like "Racing in the Street."
And you're down the tubes. And when I was 13 or 14, I found something that was like a key to a little door that said there's more to it than this. There's like . . . there's just more to this than living that way.

So is that when you decided you wanted to get into rock and roll, when you were 13, 14 and heard these records?
Well, originally I was nine and I saw my mother was an Elvis Presley fan and she had him on the TV and she used to listen to him on the radio, like every morning in my house. Come down before you go to school. My mother's cooking up the breakfast, got the radio on top of the refrigerator, tuned to the AM station ever since I could remember. And there was something connected then but I was a little young to, I didn't have the discipline to stick with it or something. And when I was 13, the English thing happened, the Beatles and the Animals and the Stones, that really kicked it off for me. I said, that looks like something that's good to get into. And the point was once again to have some say in the way you're going to live and the way you're going to do the thing you're going to do. And for the first time in a long time, it was during the *Born to Run* thing that I felt that slipping away. I felt the old gas pedal stuck to the floor, in a runaway car.

People were running you and you weren't running your life.
Yeah, and it was like I was lucky enough to realize it and grind it to a halt, and it was a moment where I guess I assessed my strengths and my weaknesses. And I'm glad it happened. I'm like, I don't . . . I ain't got one regret about, about one second of the past three years. Because I learned a lot from it.

So, *Darkness on the Edge of Town* is a whole new beginning for you. It's a whole change, it's just a whole new beginning because you've got a whole new perspective on yourself and your life.
It's a continuation, actually, and I think it's in the record, stuff you can hear. You can hear it on the record, I hope. And it was just something where I just learned a lot of stuff the hard way.

Would it be right for me to say, because what I'm getting from you is that the album, *Darkness*, even though it's your fourth album, that you feel emotionally attached to it and you have a lot of yourself invested in it, more than even the first three? That it's a real important step in your life, this record. I'm kind of picking that up from you. And it brings me around to talking about certain things about the making of *Darkness on the Edge of Town* and some of the stuff on it. First thing that I'm wondering about is how did you and Jon Landau first get together? Jon co-produced the album with you.
I met Jon in Boston at a place called Charlie's Place. I think it was in Harvard Square, it's not there anymore. He came down, I remember I was standing outside, I think it was in the wintertime, I was standing out there freezing cold. And he had written a review of *The Wild, the Innocent* now and they had it in the window I guess to get people to come in or something. And I watched it, I mean I read it. He walked up to me as I was reading it and said, I wrote that, this is Jon Landau. I said, how you doing? And he came in and saw the show.

That's the review that had the famous line . . .
Nah, that's not the famous line.

That's not the famous, that's not the "future" line?
No, no, which is the funny thing about that line, it's like . . .

Let me say the line for the benefit of the people listening. The line we're talking about, the famous line that they used in ads and stuff. Jon Landau's line. "I saw the future of rock and roll and its name is Bruce Springsteen."
It was like, the funny thing about that line . . . I don't know, I guess most people didn't read the article that it came from. And if they did, if they had read the article it was not saying exactly what it seemed to say when it was used in the ad. And I believe it was only run in one ad but it was picked up so fast, because as soon as I saw it I said, uh oh, this looks like trouble to me. It was good intentions intended, but it was like a kiss of death sort of. And the article, actually, which is the article he wrote at the time, that means a lot to me, is that he saw a show and was writing about it. And I think what he was actually saying was that the music that we were playing, me and the band, was a compilation of a lot of things, not just past influences and present but also . . .

Your own.
Future. Yeah, I think that was the intention of the line but it was like, I guess somebody at the ad department was, like, this is it! And it went out.

Advertising people are always looking for little catch phrases.
Oh yeah, yeah, I guess that's their job.

Anyway, he came up to you and said, "I wrote the article."
And I said, hey how you doing, come in. Sat down and we played, and then I didn't see him, and he was sick for a while, and he went in the hospital. And we made *Born to Run*, me and Mike Appel and produced it. And I sent him a tape when he was in the hospital and I called him. I think I called him on the phone and he said, "Gee whiz, first time I heard you, it just sounded like a bunch of noise, but after I listened to it for a while, I could hear what was going on there." So we came back to New York and we got together and I was having problems creatively in the studio. I was just having a hard time making records. It was a long time between *The Wild, the Innocent* and *Born to Run*. I don't know if people remember it was like two years, I think. So I was having a hard time making records. We were all a bunch of amateurs, you know, basically. Even still, there's not that much experience between us. And we came across some problems that we couldn't solve and I talked to Jon and he had some answers. And he was just . . . I saw him as being another key to me being able to go on and do what I want to do. And eventually he came in and co-produced *Born to Run*. He was a big open, he opened a lot of doors for me. Because he was different than me and he was someone who had been exposed to different things than I had. When I grew up, it was like we used to joke around—say when my school was put down, I was like what are you, some kind of smart guy? And his school was put down, it was like what are you some kind of hick, some kind of dummy? So he exposed me to things that I hadn't, that I hadn't been exposed to before.

So you started hanging around a lot together, going to the movies, just hanging out.
Oh yeah, sure. I spent a lot of time with him. Well then we made the record and I spent a lot of time with him, I don't know, I guess for six, seven, eight months. Anyway, I spent quite a bit of time then. And

then he came in and broke down a lot of the barriers to some of the problems we were having.

Could you be more specific, like, what, like a problem . . .
There was a million little things. Like the right piano, the right, the right studio.

And arrangements, and sound, and getting the sound that you wanted.
Sound: I knew what sound I wanted, I was having some difficulty getting it. Trying to get something that is a non-physical thing, you're trying to make it physical. You're trying to make it real.

You've got something in your head and you're trying to get it to vinyl.
So I knew what I wanted and that was how I knew I wasn't getting it. I knew I was having a problem. And he just said, well, we could use a better studio, we could use a better this, we could use different things, certain technical problems. And then, and then also he'd just have different perceptions of things, like, try this tone on the guitar. Various small things that when it all came together was a big contribution to put the thing over the hill.

Is that one of the reasons why it took so much time?
Born to Run, it didn't take that long, actually. *Born to Run,* the album was recorded in about four months.

I think the first release date on *Darkness on the Edge of Town* was somewhere around . . .
Around two years ago.

October '77, I think. Columbia wanted it out for Christmas I think and we finally got it a year and a half later or something like that.
Yeah, it all was . . . well, I had an idea and I was just going after it and I don't think there's a . . . if you can go in and do it in two weeks, great. And if you go in and it takes a year, it takes six months, it's your own shirt. So you might as well do what you want to do.

And you feel real good about the way this one has come out, I take it.
Yeah, I like it. I like it, which is always a hard thing to do. It's hard to . . . I mean, there's a lot of things that I'd do differently and I hear differently now, but in general, I think it's an honest record and that's basically what I was trying to make.

I think it's a great record, for whatever that's worth.
Well, that's good.

But part of the reason that it took so long, I'm told, and cost so much money is that you did a lot more songs than you needed for an album. There are ten songs on _Darkness_, ten?
Yeah, there was about 30 songs we did.

You did about 30.
We did not finish, but we, like, started. Some we have, some of them are finished. And some of them found their ways to other places. "Fire," Robert Gordon did; "Because the Night," Patti [Smith] did. And there was about, it was about 30 songs or 30 ideas that we recorded in the studio.

So which track was the hardest one to get down on the album?
Um, let me think.

What about "Badlands"?
I guess, maybe, maybe so. Maybe so. It was hard to sing.

It was hard to what?
It was hard to sing.

To sing?
Yeah because what happens is that I sit down when I write, I play the music because I usually write the music first and then I think, oh brother, now I got to write words to go with this.

The melody you just kind of start hearing.
Like with "Badlands," I had the word. I had "Badlands." And then I had chord changes and we got in the studio and we laid the track down. And I had a vague outline and I'd go home, I'd play the tape and I'd write the words. But I wouldn't do it out loud, I'd write them in my

head. So I go in the studio and I'd try to sing it. And I'd realize that what I had written was, like . . . it was hard to breathe and sing it all at once. So that was hard to sing. Some of the new songs were physically harder to play than some of the other ones. "Born to Run" was like that too though, because that's sort of the way that I do it.

I gotta talk to you about the band. Find out how you met these guys and your relationship with them. And all because, the E Street Band is so much a part of Bruce Springsteen and the whole record and the show, it's such a great rock 'n' roll band. We'll talk about Danny first. Danny Federici is now the oldest member of the band, right? How did you guys get together?
Yeah. How did I meet him? I met him, I remember I was in a place called the Upstage in Asbury Park. He was in a band that was, I believe they were pretty hot at the time, I believe that the name of the band was the Moment of Truth, him and Vini "Mad Dog" [Lopez]. And I met Mad Dog, he came up to me, his head shaved bald. He'd been in jail or something, and he said, listen, I just got out of jail but I got this band and we need a guitar player and you want to play? And at the time, I said sure.

What were you doing at the time?
I was freelancing on the guitar, sort of. I'd quit school and I was just, just playing. And I was making money at this club Upstage, called Upstage. I'd make anywhere from five to 25 dollars a night by just jammin'.

They wanted you to join their band, I mean, Danny and Mad Dog?
Yeah. I met Danny, I remember he's in a leather jacket, had his hair slicked back and I think he had his wife with him. And I met him and I didn't remember because she had on a blonde wig and the next time I met them both I guess she had dark hair. And that was at the first rehearsal. And it was me, and it was Danny and it was Vini and who played the bass, this fella called Little Vinnie [Roslin]. Fella was a smaller version of Vini.

Were you the singer in the band?
Yeah, at the time I was singing and playing.

And when did Garry show up?
Garry was funny, because like the first night I walked into this club, I was from 20 miles inland. I was from Freehold. And this place, this place was on the shore. And very strict town lines and county lines. It was very strict, very different lifestyles every 10 or 20 miles.

I know, I've lived in Asbury Park for 10 years so I know if like you're from Neptune, it means you're not from Asbury Park and if you're inland you're from another country.
Exactly, exactly. And I was, I had played north more on the coast like up around Red Bank and Sea Bright where there was the beach clubs and there was more jobs there, it was tough to break in. And if you were from Freehold, Freehold was like, I don't know what they thought . . .

Farmers.
Yeah, it was like that. And Asbury, that was funny. Asbury was the only beach greaser town, it was not like a collegiate beach town at all. It was like Newark by the Sea.

Working-class people . . . Newark by the Sea, that's great.
That's sort of was what it was like. And I went up to this club and I started to play the first night, and this guy pulls a chair out, sits it right in the middle of the dance floor, sits down on it and started giving me what I perceived as dirty looks. And it was Garry. I didn't talk to him for quite a while after that. I assumed for one reason or another we weren't going to get along. And eventually, we got together, not for quite a while later. Garry didn't start playing with me 'til nineteen sixty . . . no, maybe, 1971 or '70, somewhere in there. And 'cause Steve, Miami Steve played bass before then. He played bass. I was in a four-piece band. It was me, Danny, Mad Dog and when this fella Little Vinnie left, Steve played bass guitar.

Wait a minute, now, I thought you got together with Miami Steve around '75. I thought that when you did the Bottom Line, you introduced him as a new member of the band.
See, the thing is all these people have gone in and out.

Alright, the revolving door.
What happened was we had a band, like, Steve, Steve was in my band, but it was a ways before the record when I had no band. I

was just at home writing songs. We toured down south and stuff. So at the time of *Greetings from Asbury Park* there was no formal band.

Is Miami Steve on *Greetings from Asbury Park*?
He is. I can't tell, I shouldn't tell you where.

Why not?
He might be mad at me.

You know where though.
It's funny. But like, see, we had a band. Steve was a bass player. We split up and Steve played with the Dovells and the Belmonts. I mean, Dion. It wasn't the Belmonts at the time. And he worked construction for a couple of years. But he actually didn't get in to the E Street Band I guess until after the *Born to Run* album . . .

Was completed?
Right.

How 'bout Roy? Now, when'd you get together with Roy? Roy Bittan, piano, god I mean the way he's playing on this tour and the sound of that piano, it's really beautiful. It's gorgeous.
I put an ad in *The Village Voice* for a drummer and piano player and I auditioned 60 guys—thirty drummers and 30 piano players up at Studio Instrument Rentals in New York—and that's where I got Roy and Max. That's where I found Roy and Max.

Max said he showed up with one little snare drum and a little . . . Max just told me this this afternoon, he said guys came before him and they had big drum kits and he said, gee . . . He said he was playing in the Broadway, in the pit of *Godspell*, I think, and he said he came up and he had two or three little drums with him and other guys were showing up with these big drum kits. And you worked him out on his little drums there and then you said to him—this is what he told me just at the pool this afternoon—he said, "I never thought I'd get the job but Bruce finally said, listen if you want the job you can have it, it pays 75 dollars a week."
Oh, oh, oh, god.

And he said, I'll take it.
It's true. What happened is we, at the time, that's what we were all making. And when was this, this was right before *Born to Run* at the time.

Just a struggling band.
Seventy-five dollars a week. And he came up, he just had the right feel. And there was a lot of guys coming in with the bigger drum sets and I knew.

And what about C. C. Clarence. Where'd you find the Big Man?
I was playing in Asbury Park, in another club called the Student Prince. And it was me and Steven and Garry and Davey Sancious and Vini Lopez and one night, this guy walked in and I'd heard about him. I'd heard about him in the area because I'd been looking for a saxophone player.

He had a rep.
For a long time. And everyone was always talking about Clarence Clemons. And he walked in and he said, can I sit in? And we said sure, nobody's going to say no and they got up. And we played this one song and I said this is the guy who I've been looking' for all my life. This is the guy I've been looking for all my life. And ever since then we stuck together.

And that's the E Street Band.
Yeah, that's everybody.

Seeing the guys in the band today and being with you now and all, it all seems to me that you're having a terrific time, I mean working. That you're all just up and together and there seems to be even on stage a lot of really . . . a lot of *fun*, that's what I'm saying. It looks like as if you're all having a lot of fun, which is of course the best way for it to look. Is the tour really going that well, are you having a lot of fun or . . .
Yeah, it has been real good. It's been the best tour we've ever done.

You had quite a show in Phoenix the other night. I wasn't there but I heard about some real craziness. What happened?
It was pretty wild. Some little girl, actually it was three, front row there was about I guess 10- or 15-year-old girls and the place was going

pretty crazy. There was just a lot going on. And this little girl jumped up on stage and kissed me so hard it almost knocked out my front tooth. I thought she was going to . . . it's like we fell back, fell back on the stage and everybody started screaming and running around and kids got up on stage and danced. It was just a lot of, it was funny.

Is that scary when it happens? Or is it just part of the fun and the madness of it all?
Oh, it's like, it's not scary. It's like, you can always feel the situation out when you're on stage. People come down to shows, it's an excited crowd, but it's not mean.

They're just real turned on. Happy.
It's just a blowout.

Which is what you wanted, just a big party, a big blowout . . .
It should be fun and it was great, that was a great show. That was one of the best shows we ever did.

As long as we're talking about tour stories, you've got to tell me the one about the sign on the Sunset Strip. In Los Angeles they have gigantic billboards advertising records. There are 20, 30 of them right on Sunset Boulevard, on the strip. What was that like?
It was just real ugly looking.

Tell them what the sign was.
It was just a sign, it was like an advertisement. They put up, like, those big advertisements, they paint your face real big and out of shape. Your nose is big enough, they made it 10 feet long and like it was just funny. It was just the ugliest thing I've ever seen.

It was just a big picture of you?
Oh no, it was words and stuff, too. So I said, OK guys, we're going to hit the sign. We're going to get some paint and we're going to hit the sign. I don't know if we were a little drunk or what was going on, but we came back home and I said tonight's the night. It was two or three in the morning and I said whoever wants to go and hit the sign come on, we're going to go now. So we all—Clarence says he wants to go. It was me and him, Garry and some of the guys from the crew and the road manager,

we all went down there. We had bought all these cans of spray paint. And we went down there, and the building was wide open and it was vacant. It was real strange. And the elevator was working and everything.

You had to get way up to the top where the sign was, right?
Yeah, well, the sign was like six stories up and then up on a frame. Some of the guys went up the fire escape, they didn't know the elevator was working and we went up and we walked up, we figured there was going to be a locked door or something. The elevator opened up, we went up a flight of stairs and there we were out on the roof and there it was. It was just big and bright. So we all went up there, we climbed up there. There was a ladder that climbed up to the sign. We just got out the paint and started to work on the thing. And then we wrote "Prove It All Night" and I wanted to get, I wanted to write E Street, the band's name up there, so Clarence says, well, get on my shoulders. So I got on his shoulders and we're like six stories up, five stories up and I'm saying, Clarence, you tired yet? He says no, I got you, Boss, I got you. Clarence—I'd do a letter—you tired yet? He'd say no, no, I got you, I got you . . . I looked back and it was nothing but the pavement. But it was fun to do.

How'd "The Boss" name get started?
I don't know. I never—that started with people who worked for me.

I thought Clarence might've started it.
Nah, it was not meant like The Boss, capital B. It was meant like the boss, where's my dough this week? It was sort of like that and it was sort of friendly . . . I guess it was from the band it was sort of just a thing, just a term among friends. And it's funny, because I never really liked it. I still—I never really liked it.

Well you may not like it, but you're not going to lose it. It's just a term of affection. Bruce, do you have like any kind of life that is totally divorced from music? Do you have anything when you're not working or, I mean like you're not recording, you're not on the road . . . do you do anything that's got nothing to do with rock 'n' roll?
No, just . . . I don't think I do. Trying to think.

Your friends are all in . . .
I've had girlfriends. In general, I've got one friend that's not really involved in the music business and he owns a motorcycle shop in Westwood . . . Town and Country Cycle. And there's a little plug there I guess, his name is Matty. And I guess he's my only friend that doesn't work for me, or is not involved in some other way. He's been a real source of inspiration and friendship. Like, he's interested in playing and I'm interested in his motorcycles and stuff.

So you really are a prisoner of rock 'n' roll?
I don't know if I am . . . I don't know.

I get from you, again a thing I get often is you like really care a great deal about your fans and people who love your music. I mean, you really feel close to them.
It's a shame that seems to be such a big deal or something.

I agree, but it is. It's unusual.
When I'm on stage, I'm almost—I'm half in the audience and I'm half on stage. And it's really more of a one-on-one level. Like I see the crowd as a crowd but I also see them as like a one-on-one. If I see somebody getting in any trouble down there, if the crowd's getting too excited, you've got a responsibility, that's all. It's no big deal.

Earlier, in the beginning of the interview, you said that when you were nine and then 13 and 14 and you realized it was music that you wanted to do and that's what you're doing with your life, did you also at one point somewhere along the way figure and think about being, quote, a rock 'n' roll star, unquote?
Uh, I guess if you think about it, it depends what that word, what it means to you. Being a "star" or something is too associated with, I think, the trap. For me, that word has always been associated with the trappings of the music business. And I really, I'd rather not see the day when I can't be able to get down in the crowd or something. I hope that day don't ever come. It means you can hire 10 people to kiss your butt 10 times a day maybe.

What it means, I think, let me give you some meaning. What it means is that you're really adored or idolized. It means that just a lot of people, huge crowds of people, just get to love you for the, for the joy and the music and the entertainment and the pleasure that you bring them. Can you accept that definition of it?

What they like is the music and the shows. I guess I have a certain aversion to it as everybody does. Like most people, they have a reaction and mine has always been to reach out and then when I reach out then the next thing I want to do is I want to pull back. It was sort of like this with *Darkness*. I got to pull back, I got to pull in tight. I got to, I got to keep to myself. And then I said, what am I doing? I worked hard on this record. I want to reach out, I want to go after it, a bigger audience. And I think you go through periods of reaching out and pulling back and reaching out and pulling back. There's always a conflict, there's a basic conflict there. There's a lot of paradoxes—I think that's the right word, yeah—that you have to learn to live with, because they're not going to go away. The main thing is to cut down on the distance as much as possible, which is something that I've been interested a lot in lately. It's just to get as close as possible to the audience. It's when the whole concept of . . . like, the people come and they're at the show. Well, they're not *at* the show, they're in the show. I'm not only in the show, I'm *at* the show. It's very . . . it's a cooperative thing, I'm not explaining it very well.

I think I know what you mean, that it doesn't all rest on one person, that it's part of a whole event that happens. But you're the catalyst. You're the person that's making it all happen in that theater, in that arena.

Yeah, I'm trying to figure out a way to explain this because a couple of people have asked me this same question.

Maybe it's best not to try to explain it?

It's like I said. There's a lot of contradictions and paradoxes that you have to sort out in certain ways. It's like the more popular you become, the farther people have to sit away to see you. And then, but yet, then you're reaching more people in a way. And it's like these are things that they go against each other but they're like they're both real and what are you going to do? You got to . . .

And these are the problems that you're going to have to solve for yourself more and more as time goes on.
And you got to work it out somehow. And I see myself in a particular way. I think I was lucky to find something that meant as much to me as young as I was, and I just wish that luck on everybody.

I'll tell you, the thing that you found that means so much to you just means a lot to more people than you can imagine. Thanks a lot, Bruce.

Dave DiMartino,
October 1980

Dave DiMartino spoke with Springsteen while on tour to promote *The River*, which wasn't yet available in stores. They discuss the "paradox" of material on the new double album: "sometimes you write about things as they are," Bruce explains, "and sometimes you write about them as they should be, as they could be . . . And that's basically what I wanted to do. And you can't say no to either thing." DiMartino covers a great deal of territory, from the nickname "The Boss," to Gary U.S. Bonds, to bootlegs. Springsteen talks about forgetting the words to "Born to Run" on opening night and says about performing live, "I don't gauge the show by the audience reaction, I don't gauge the show by the review in the paper the next day. I know when I get on the bus to go to the next town. I know if I can go to sleep easy that night." An edited version of this interview appeared in *Creem* in January 1981; later in the '80s, *Backstreets* ran the complete Q&A.

At the appropriate hour of quarter to three in the morning, manager Jon Landau asks DiMartino, "No more than a half-hour, OK?" But the prob-

lem is not DiMartino, but Bruce, who is in the mood to talk. The interview runs easily to an hour, despite the fact the band has a show in Chicago in less than 18 hours.

With The River *still not in stores, Bruce focuses not so much on the new songs themselves, but on the process of making the record, his own perception of how he works in creating an LP and his own expectations of himself. Bruce is humorous and at times complex in responding to provocative questions from DiMartino, who he is meeting for the first time.*

They [the crew] all call you the boss?
Well, the thing I have with this "Boss" is funny, because it came from people like that, who work around you. And then, somebody started to do it on the radio. I hate being called "Boss" [*laughs*]. I just do. Always did from the beginning. I hate bosses. I hate being called the boss. It just started from all the people around me, then by somebody on the radio and once that happens, everybody said "Hey Boss," and I'd say, "No. Bruce. BRUCE." I always hated that. I always hated being called "Boss."

I have lots of relatives in Jersey, Seaside Heights and Point Pleasant. It's a pretty interesting place for somebody to grow up.
Yeah, it's pretty strange. It's real "away," you know? It's like an hour from New York, but it might as well be ten million miles, because when I was growing up, I think I wasn't in New York once until I was sixteen, except maybe once when my parents took me to see the circus. And New York was just so far away! It's funny, because when we first came out, everyone tagged us as being a New York band, which we never really were. We were down there from Jersey, which was very, very different. It's like my sister. She went to New York last year, and said "Hey, I went to New York and we couldn't find Fifth Avenue, so we went home" [*laughs*]. It was like you just didn't go to New York. It was a million miles away. I remember, you didn't talk about it, you didn't think about it. It was all very, very local. That's the way those little towns and stuff are, you just never get out.

I remember we'd go to Seaside Heights when we were 14 and 15 years old. It was a good place to pick up girls.
Yeah. Asbury was where you'd go if you didn't have the gas to get to Seaside Heights. That was a whole other thing.

Bob Seger told us he saw you in LA and you were going through the same problems finishing *The River* that he had with *Against the Wind*, that you were pulling your hair out. What made you decide you had the right songs? Last we heard, you pulled a tune off it.

Well, from the beginning I had an idea of what I felt the record should be. And I don't think, I'm not interested in going in the studio and [*pauses*], I don't want to just take up space on the shelf, or worry that if you don't have something out every six months, or even a year, that people are going to forget about you. I was never interested in approaching it that way. We never have from the beginning. I have a feeling about the best I can do at a particular time, and that's what I wanted to do. I don't come out until I feel that, and that's what I've done. Because there's so many records coming out, there's so much stuff on the shelves, why put out something that you don't feel is what it should be, or that you feel—and I don't believe in tomorrows—that "Oh, I'll put the other half out six months from now." You don't know what's gonna be happening six months from now. You may be dead, you just don't know. It's like from the very beginning, I just never believed in doing things that way. You make your record like it's the last record you'll ever make. You go out and play at night. I don't think if I don't play good tonight, I'll play good tomorrow. I don't think that if I didn't play good tonight, that, well, I played good last night. It's like there's no tomorrows and there's no yesterdays. There's only right now.

You gotta prove it all night, right?

Well that's the thing with the kids. Like if a kid buys a ticket, he comes in, tonight is his night. Tonight is the night for you and him, you and him are not gonna have this night again. And if you don't take it as seriously as he's taking it, I mean, this is his dough, he worked for it all week, money's tough now and there's a certain thing . . . I just think you gotta lay it all on the line when you go out there and then I feel good afterwards. That's the only way I feel right and it's the same thing with the record.

How do you feel about *The River* now that it's finished? Are you 100 percent satisfied with it?

Oh, you're never like that, you're never 100 percent satisfied, because you're thinking about all the wrong stuff you did. You always think you could've played that one other song, like tonight. When we started this tour, we said, "OK. We're not gonna play 'Quarter to Three.' We played that the whole last tour and we're not gonna play it this tour." And sure enough, we get backstage [tonight] and this is the first time we had to come out again one more time, and it's like, "What are we gonna play? 'Quarter to Three'!" So that was probably the swan song of that.

You have to admit that as high as expectations were when you produced *Darkness*, **the expectations for this new album were considerably higher. Do you think you were a little sensitive or paranoid about the final version of this LP?**
No, because nobody's expectations are higher than your own. You do what you can do and that's the way it stands. People have their expectations and I try to live up to a certain thing I feel myself. And I know I have strict ideals about the way we do things, the way the band does things, so outside forces, they play a secondary role. Like, I know when I've done all I can do after a show and I know when I've done all I can do when I make a record. And you know when it could be better—like there was something wrong with the stage or you couldn't quite say what you wanted to say. But, you know, people's expectations are gonna be what they're gonna be; in the end, you're gonna disappoint everybody anyway [*laughs*].

OK, but if I were you, I know I'd have been scared. With *No Nukes*, **the talk about you as the highlight, the viable screen commodity, all building up to the long-awaited LP. All I know is I'd be happy as hell to be out on the road and not have to deal with all that.**
Yeah, well that's the reality, like you're hit with the reality every night. All the outer stuff, it's like, what's to be frightened of? That somebody's not gonna like it? That's just not that much, you know?

On opening night in Ann Arbor you had to stop on occasion because the band hadn't learned the new songs completely.
Well Ann Arbor, that was a wild show, because I came out and we started playing and we went into "Born to Run," which I'd just listened to in the dressing room like ten times.

To try and remember the words?

Yeah, and I went up to the mike and I couldn't remember the words, and I was up there and said, "Oh shit. I don't know these words." And I thought, "Not only do I not know these, I don't know any of the others." This was all taking place within about five seconds. "What the hell am I gonna do?" I mean, you can't stop. And then out in the audience I hear "In the day we sweat it . . ." and it was GREAT. And then it was fine. That was an amazing audience.

But how do you feel about that? You seem to be one of the only performers that the audience truly loves. Not to flatter you, but it seems like you probably haven't been up against an audience that wasn't totally familiar with you and hadn't memorized the lyrics of all your songs. Do you ever wish you were facing an audience as a complete unknown?

I opened for Black Oak Arkansas. I opened for Brownsville Station and I opened for Sha Na Na. I'm 31 and I've been playing in bars since I was 15, and I've faced a lot of audiences that don't give a shit that you're onstage. And if you're calling percentages, we've had only 2 to 5 percent nights like tonight against 95 percent in the 10 to 15 years we've been playing when, let me tell you, that did not happen. That does not happen, and it keeps you from ever getting spoiled, because you know what it's like when nobody gives a damn when you come out there. It keeps you in certain places, it stays with you. There are no free rides. When we first started playing, I'd go to every show expecting nobody to come, and I'd go onstage expecting nobody to give me anything for free. And that's the way you have to play. If you don't play like that, pack your guitar up, throw it in the trashcan, go home, fix televisions, do some other line of work, you know? Do something where that's the way you feel about it. And the night I stop thinking that way, that's the night I won't do it no more, because that's just the bottom line. I don't gauge the show by the audience reaction; I don't gauge the show by the review in the paper the next day. I know what I did when I'm done, I know how I feel, and I know if I'm comfortable when I get on the bus to go to the next town. I know if I feel good and I know if I feel bad. I know if I can go to sleep easy that night. That's the way that we judge it and that's the way that we run it. And if we didn't, that noise that you were hearing, that would not be happening in the first place.

Do you ever worry about that? Do you think that might not happen in the future, that you might not give your all?
No. I'm not that kind of person. I don't have any fear about that because, I guess, I have other things that are much more frightening that keep me from falling into that.

What's it like these days getting recognized?
People don't recognize me that much. They don't. If you go around humming "Badlands" or something [*laughs*], they might. People just don't look for you. They recognize you outside the show, but it just doesn't happen otherwise. I mean, back home, if I go around a bar or something on a Saturday afternoon, forget it.

Do you still do that?
Yeah I do that. I mean that's what you do when you go home, there's nothing else to do when you go home. But if you do that in the bars back home, most of the time people do recognize you so they don't bother you. It depends. It just doesn't happen to the point where it really bothers you or something. It just doesn't happen.

Do you get approached frequently to produce other artists or appear on their records? I know you just worked with Gary U.S. Bonds.
Some bands, yeah. Some people ask me, but I can't go in there and do things the way I do my own records, I just wouldn't feel right doing it. I wouldn't feel right, behind them, you know. And plus, I am not a producer. I've always felt that essentially I'm a playing musician, that's what I've done the longest. I'm a playing musician. I go out on the road and play, we do live rock 'n' roll shows and everybody has a good time. And then on the side, after that, I write the songs and make albums, but I feel most like myself when I'm playing, when we're doing shows.

Dave Marsh's book was obviously a great success. What are you feelings about it?
Yeah, that was terrific, that was really exciting. You know, we didn't put an album out for that whole year and then came the book, and kids would come up with it and say "Hey, sign the book." It was really just a nice thing for everybody.

The guys in the band, you've all been friends for years and all that. When Marsh's book came out there was a big deal about you, the picture on the cover of you smiling, did the guys come up to you and say "Oh, come on Bruce. We all know you're just a little shit."
No [*laughs*]. It's like you don't think that much about it. Most of the people I'm with have been my friends for a long time, in my band, and they're all in the book. I mean, since I was 16 I've known Steve. You just sit there and look at the book and there's all those things happening, but you just accept those things happening.

With your success you've created a familiar "Springsteen sound." When you hear new artists that seem to imitate your sound, do you think about what you've created?
No, I never have those particular feelings. Myself, I've been influenced by so much music. Even on the new album there's some Johnny and the Hurricanes kind of stuff. I don't think about it.

How did your involvement with Gary U.S. Bonds come about?
We met in a bar right by my house and we just started talking. He's just a great guy with a great voice. He's just got this voice, and there's only one of this voice. The stuff on his records didn't have that sound. That sound was him, that was his voice, and when he sings, that's what he sounds like. There was a situation because of the nature of the music business where there was so many people. What happened was that the music business changed from where there were writers and singers and producers. Now a kid comes up and he's got to do everything. Well, that's no good, because people don't do everything good. That's why there are so many bad albums, because people don't do everything good. Maybe someone's a hell of a producer, maybe some kid is a hell of a songwriter or a great singer, or maybe some kid ain't a good singer and songwriter. They're sort of forced by the way the thing is based now to attempt to do all these things. They think they should. In the '60s, what happened was you had all these tremendous people out there, these great singers particularly, who were popular back then, who were just stopped, run over, you know. In a flash, 20 years old. Now, they just don't fit in, they don't fit the structure of the music business. Who is their audience? Gary was like that. Gary's a great singer, but it's hard now. It's hard to get people to pay attention.

Do you wonder what your records might sound like if you didn't produce yourself?
Our method now is a very personal way of recording, where somebody coming in from the outside would have a difficult time. We wrote and recorded about 48 songs [for *The River*] and at one time I thought they were all gonna be on [*laughs*]. And somebody sitting there seeing four albums being recorded, well, you gotta be in it for life, you know? To just have the patience and the perseverance. And we recorded that stuff real fast, there was not a lot of overdubbing, not a lot of takes even. We just recorded so much stuff.

What was the major criteria for the completion of the album, the selection of songs?
I'd say the main thing was trying to focus on exactly what I wanted on the album, and what I wanted to do with characters. Like on *Darkness*, that stopped at a certain point. Well, what happens now? I don't feel different every six months, it takes a while. What I wanted to do, and what I hoped was working out was those little four-song albums they tried to put out for a while, I don't know if they're gonna keep doing it or not, those "Nu Disks" [10" EPs like *Black Market Clash*, circa 1979] or whatever you call 'em. I wanted to, from time to time, release those with all the stuff that's in the can and all the stuff that for one reason or another didn't make it on. I wanted to put those out in between albums so that it was a different kind of thing. I don't think they're gonna make those anymore.

How did you end up on [Lou Reed's] *Street Hassle*?
He called me up in the studio, it was funny. We were at the Record Plant; I hadn't really met him and I liked his stuff, I always really liked it. He called me up and said "I've got this part," and it was related to "Born to Run," I guess, in some way, and said "Come on upstairs," and he had these words, and I went upstairs . . .

And you read them.
Yeah, and so I did it once, no, I think I did it twice, and he just picked one and I was real happy.

Did you enjoy the No Nukes shows?
That was great. That was one of the favorite shows that we ever did. I liked working with all those different people. What happened was

when we first started, the way we got to playing by ourselves was inadvertent. We never meant to do shows by ourselves. But we couldn't get on any other tours. People will tell you today, if you're a new band, you can't get on other tours, people won't take you out. And if you're good, then forget about it. You're never gonna make it out. So, at the time, we were doing pick-up shows for absolutely anybody that would put us on. But it got to a point where just nobody would put us on, we couldn't get any shows. So we started playing clubs by ourselves. Then eventually the shows started getting longer and developed into what it is. But the thing about the Nukes show was we only played an hour; and it was fun [*laughs*], because you could go like a runaway train in an hour. We could come off and dance around the block after that, so it was funny. And I wanted to do something with that, and it was just one of the best things. I felt real good about it.

I was told you plan to be on tour until next summer.
Because I want to play in the summertime this year. I just miss doing that, I miss travelling around and playing in the summertime. We haven't done that in a while. We're gonna do this tour, and then it stops for Christmas a little while, and then we go to Canada, and then the South and then overseas. I want to do that because we've never been overseas, we've only been overseas for four shows, and that was in 1975. We've only done two shows in England and that was the kind of shows that, well, one was the kind of show that, when I think back upon it, was the kind of show that I don't want our shows to go. That was the worst, and that was when I was real down.

Talking about moods, I thought that the *Wild, the Innocent* LP had a real happy mood to it across the whole record. *Born to Run* was a mixed bag, but one of the reasons I especially liked *Darkness* was its consistency of mood. It ultimately seemed very depressing, especially "Racing in the Street." Are there any kind of moods on the new LP that you can put your finger on?
Well, it's different. When I did *Darkness*, I was very focused on one particular idea, one particular feeling that I wanted to do. In the show there are all sorts of things, there's a wide range of emotion.

But when I listen to *Darkness*, I wanna go slit my wrists.
Yeah. Like you say, that's my favorite record, *Darkness*, so this time one of the things that I felt was on *Darkness*, I didn't make room for certain [*pauses*] things, you know. Because I just couldn't understand how you could feel so good and so bad at the same time. And it was very confusing to me. "Sherry Darling" was gonna be on *Darkness*, "Independence Day" was a song that was gonna be on *Darkness*, and the song I wrote right after *Darkness* was "Point Blank" which takes that thing to its furthest. Because at the time, I remember because Jon asked me, and I said "Jon, I just can't see all this different stuff being on it because it's gonna be too confusing for people," and he said "No, it's not gonna be too confusing for people," and I said, "Well, I guess it's gonna be too confusing for me." It just is that way for me right now, for some reason.

I was surprised that there weren't any razor blades attached to the LP.
Yeah, well it wasn't meant to be that way. After *Born to Run* and all that stuff, I felt that was just the way it was. And so when I did this album, I tried to accept the fact that, you know, the world is a paradox, and that's the way it is. And the only thing you can do with a paradox is live with it. I wanted to do that this time out; I wanted to live with particularly conflicting emotions, because I always personally, in a funny kind of way, lean toward the *Darkness* kind of material. When I didn't put the album out in '79, it was because I didn't feel that that was there, I felt that that was missing and I didn't feel that that was right. And even when the band says "Why isn't this on it, why isn't that on it," what do you say, "Gee. I don't know"? It was something where I just got a bigger picture of it, I felt, what things are, of the way things work, and I tried to just learn to be able to live with that. I mean, how can you live when sometimes things are so beautiful, and I know it sounds corny but . . .

So I'm gonna listen to *The River* and I'm gonna feel that paradox you're talking about?
I think so. In the end, I think that's the emotion. What I wanted was just the paradox of those things.

Did a lot of the time spent in deciding what tracks went on the LP work to this whole approach of balance? Does the paradox correspond to the way you personally feel?

Well there's the thing where a lot of stuff just ROCKS, and that was the main thing. There's a lot of idealistic stuff on there, there's a lot of stuff that, hey, you can listen to it and laugh at it or whatever, some of it is very idealist, and I wanted that all on there. At first, I wasn't gonna put it all on there, but sometimes I just feel those things. Sometimes when I'm playing . . . like life just ain't this good, you know? And it just ain't. And it may never ever be. But that doesn't make those emotions not real. Because they are real and they happen. And that stuff happens onstage a lot, when people sing some of the songs it's like a community thing that happens that don't happen in the street. You go out on the street and it's just a dream. Hey, that's the way it's supposed to be. And a lot of songs we do now, they're just dreams, but they're based on an emotion that's very real, and they're always being possibilities. To say no to that stuff is wrong, to say no to it is wrong and to give yourself to it is a lie. To give yourself over is an illusion. On the album I was interested in, I saw it as romantic. It's a romantic record and to me, romantic is when you see realities and when you understand the realities, but you also see the possibilities. And sometimes you write about things as they are, and sometimes you write about them as they should be, as they could be, maybe, you know? And that's basically what I wanted to do. And you can't say no to either thing. If you say no, you're cheating yourself out of feelings that are important and should be a part of you.

Do you have a girlfriend now? Do you find yourself lacking the time for strong relationships like that and does it affect your material?

That always affects you, and I've always had a girlfriend, same one now that I've been going out with for a couple of years, and that always affects a lot of things. The band, some of the guys are in their 30s, some are in their early 20s, and I realize that you think different then, you don't think the same way you did when you were 20, and I try to, stay in tune to that fact. And the music I write has, I think, those extra 10 years in there. And there's other guys who do other things, younger things, and they say that, you know? And on this record, it was funny, some of the guys got married, some . . . it was just a sense of the conflict everybody feels; you want to be a part of it. You want to walk down the street and feel that you're a part of all those people. There's a combination with some people where you're drawn to being with them, while at the same time you're horrified by them, repulsed by them, scared by them. That was the other thing I hoped I was gonna be able to get in the record, that you have both of those feelings and they're both real and they're both honest and that's the way it is.

I'm sure you agree that while there's "x" amount of words and "x" amount of melodies, the combination of both is unlimited, as are the effects. One of the strong points of *Darkness*, I thought, was the conflict of moods between both.
It was different, yeah. At the end of *Darkness*, the guy ends up feeling very isolated.

There are parallels between that character's feeling and your own life, starting out as a happy guy with happy music that suddenly ends up on the cover of tons of magazines. How much of that music is about a character and how much is about yourself?
Every guy that writes a song is writing about himself, in the most general way I'm talking, like it comes outta you. Why did it come out of you? And all the facts are changed, you think up a lot of stuff and some stuff is real, I don't know. I had a funny . . . New Jersey was funny. It was very insulated. I grew up playing in bars since I was 15 and I always liked my job. I liked going down to that club, and if I made $35 a week or whatever, it didn't matter because I liked the job I was doing and I was enjoying it. I was lucky enough that from when I was very young, I was able to make my living at it. And it went along and, I mean, I never knew anyone who made a record, I never knew anyone who knew anyone who even knew anyone in the professional music business [*laughs*]. We didn't even brush up against people like that back then, you were away from it. You weren't there. And that's the way it was—same bunch of guys, same town. And when I got out more, well, things changed. You get older and things change. I mean, I liked my job.

Do the guys in the band miss going out and playing?
That's the way it is. People miss it, but, believe it or not, I'm going as fast as I can [*laughs*].

Is that really true?
I was burning up man, let me tell you, I ain't kidding you [*laughs*]. The

stuff is really . . . like we didn't do a whole lot of takes of each song. I don't think there's a song on there that went any more than ten takes, and most of them were done under five. The only overdubbing is vocal overdubbing, and that's not on everything. Most of the stuff we recorded very fast, and when you get a chance to listen to it, we recorded it in a big room and we got a real hard drum sound. Of them all, I think it's the album that most captures what happens when we play. But it's the kind of thing where I don't know if I'll ever make records fast, because I don't see the point in making them fast.

Well, there's a view in the rock world that you should go in and bang them out as it's more spontaneous that way. Would you say *The River* is spontaneous?
It is very spontaneous. Spontaneity, number one, is not made by fastness. Elvis, I believe, did like 30 takes of "Hound Dog," and you can put THAT thing on. The idea is to sound spontaneous. I mean it's to be spontaneous, but it's like these records come out that were done real fast and they sound like they were done real fast. If I thought I could've made a better record in half the time, that's exactly what I would've done. Because, I would've rather been out playing. It's the kinda thing where, I mean, I know what I'm listening to when I hear it played back, and I just had particular guidelines. And one thing, it's not a musically put together record. I mean, the performances were fast. I think the thing that takes the most time is the thinking, the conceptual thing. It takes a certain amount of time for me to think about exactly what it is I wanna do, and then I gotta wait until I finally realize that I've actually done it. You know, we made the Gary U.S. Bonds thing real fast, and a lot of the things on this were made very fast. It's just the ALBUM that took a long time.

Why did you change your opinion about bootlegs?
I felt that there was a point there where, when it first started, a lot of bootlegs were made by fans, there was more of a connection. But it became, there was a point where there were just so many. Just so many that it was big business. It was made by people who, you know, they didn't care what the quality was. It just got to the point where I'd walk in and see a price tag of $30 on a record of mine that, to me, really sounded bad, and I just thought it was a rip. I thought I was getting ripped, I wrote the music, the songs—it all came out of me! And I felt it was a rip, and the people who were doing it had warehouses full of

records and were just sitting back, getting fat, rushing and putting out anything and getting 30 fucking dollars for it. And I just got really mad about it at one point.

Are you ever gonna come out with some of this live stuff? I've got some that I like just because I'm a fan.
I don't know. I have a hard time listening to them, because I always hear the bad things. I guess the main thing is that I just want to make a live record. The plan was to do a live one after this one.

Some of the stuff is great like the CBS take of "Santa Claus" and the Greg Kihn song "Rendezvous." Why did you give that away? Did it sound too much like a *Born to Run* song?
That song I wrote in about five minutes before a rehearsal one day. We played it on tour and we liked it, and I liked him because I liked the way he did "For You" on that early album, and we just had it around and I told him "Hey, we got this song that we're not recording now." That's mainly how some of those songs got out. I just wrote them fast.

I remember you playing tunes like "Independence Day," "The Ties That Bind" and "Point Blank" two years ago. Were those written for *Darkness* but just didn't fit your concept?
The reason they got thrown out was because of this thing I was telling you about, the way I felt about the *Darkness* album. I don't know, that's just the way I felt about them at the time.

Are you your own worst critic?
I think you certainly should be. That's the way you have to be. You have to be most severe with yourself.

Do you anticipate a large critical backlash after being on top for so long?
That stuff happens all the time, besides, that's happened to me already, I've lived that already. And it's the kind of thing that just happens; people write good things and then they don't. The first time I went through that it was confusing for me, it was disheartening. I guess I felt that I knew what I wanted to do and what I was about. The same old story when I was 25 when that first happened and I'd been playing for 10 years. Now I'm 31, so I went through that. When you first come up

and people start writing about you, you're just not used to it. It's just strange. There were a lot of things that brought me real down at the time, and there were a lot of things that brought me real up. I was very susceptible to being immediately emotionally affected by something like that at the time. But I went through it, I saw it happen, I saw how it happens. I was younger and I was much more insecure. I hadn't put the time in that we've put in since then, and seen some of the things that happened since then happen. I've seen all sides of the music thing, and now, whatever happens is only gonna be a shadow of that moment. So if a lot of people wrote a lot of good stuff and then they wrote a lot of bad stuff, whatever happens, it happens. You have a concern about it, because I spent a long time and put a lot into doing a record. Same old story, anybody who says it ain't a heartbreaker, it ain't true [*laughs*]. But that's the way things are, and I'm at a point now where I got a better perspective on a lot of those things.

Any changes in the future?
No, I don't see changing the particular way that I do that thing right now, because . . .

You're happy.
Yeah. Because if I felt that if I was just sitting there and squeezing the life out of the music, I wouldn't do it. But that's not what happens, that's not what we do. The physical act is not what takes the time, I mean, this was our fifth album. We rented the studio. We knew how to make a record. As fast or slow as we wanted to, you know? The physical thing is not the story, it's how you feel inside about it, and that don't run on any clock, just how you feel inside. Just where you are today and what your record is gonna be saying out there, and what the people that buy that record are going to feel and get from it. I had an idea, and I wasn't going to go half way with it, wasn't no point in it. Like I said, I don't trust no tomorrows on that kind of thing. And I'd rather do the time—and the time is no fun to do—because if I didn't do the time there, I couldn't walk out there on that stage. We're going to be playing a lot of shows, and we're going to be out there for a real long time. And when I go out there at night, I just like to feel like myself, like I've done what I have to do. And when I play those songs onstage, I know those songs, I know what went into them and I know where I stand. And people will and people will not like it, but I know that it's real. I know that it's there.

Dave Marsh
Musician,
February 1981

Springsteen's double album *The River* was released in October 1980 and went to number one on the charts. It also generated his first top-ten single in "Hungry Heart." No one was better situated to engage Springsteen in a lengthy, revealing conversation than Dave Marsh, Bruce's biographer. *Born to Run: The Bruce Springsteen Story,* appeared in 1979 and established the genre of serious rock biographies. Marsh conducted the interview at a motel in Arizona, staying up until dawn discussing musical influences and themes in Springsteen's work, specific tracks on *The River,* as well as the tensions between recording and performing live. "Usually two weeks after we're out on the road, I cannot listen to my record anymore," Bruce admits. *The River* was an exception.

A year ago, taking a respite from recording to play two nights of the M.U.S.E. anti-nuke concerts, Bruce Springsteen pared his normal three hour show down to a more everyday 90 minutes. The result was pandemonium just this side of Beatle-mania. Following the biggest stars in American soft rock to the Madison Square Garden stage, Springsteen and the E Street Band upstaged everyone, including the issue itself. The air in the hall that night was one of fanaticism and conversion, as though Springsteen were a rock 'n' roll evangelist and the Garden his tabernacle.

It's easy to imagine that Springsteen was just a pro rising to an occasion which included a camera crew and a recording truck, not to mention a backstage full of peers. What's harder to explain, unless you've seen him onstage before a crowd that might not include so much as a weekly newspaper reviewer, is that the M.U.S.E. shows were just a fragment of what he usually does. "After those shows went over so great, I just figured that that's what we'd be doing on this tour," remembers E Street guitarist Steve Van Zandt. "Just 90 minutes, a couple of ballads, and we make people as crazy as you can, like the old days. We can do that. But not Bruce. What we ended up doing was just adding that 90 minutes to the show we always did."

By late October, when the E Streeters hit L.A. for four shows at the 15,000 seat Sports Arena, they were playing four-and-one-half-hour shows, five nights a week. Going on at 8:30, they'd break at 10, and return a half hour later to play until 12:45—or 1:00 or 1:15. And they weren't playing the ebb-and-flow show offered by most bands who play so long. We're talking about four hours of ensemble rock and roll here, in which even the ballads are attacked more strenuously than most modal jams. Yet Jon Landau, his manager, said one night, "I think Bruce might actually play *longer*, except that the band just gets worn out." True enough, drummer Max Weinberg often spends intermission taping bleeding fingers, and the others are spared such medicaments only because their instruments are less physically demanding.

Generally, Springsteen did 32 or 33 songs, including 17 or 18 from *The River*, a half dozen from *Darkness on the Edge of Town*, five from *Born to Run*, the perennial setcloser "Rosalita" from *The Wild, the Innocent & the E Street Shuffle*, plus "Fire" and "Because the Night" from his seemingly bottomless supply of unrecorded hits. And, of course, the Mitch Ryder medley which was the highlight of the *No Nukes* LP.

But the show has that shape only on nights when Springsteen hasn't declared a special occasion, which is a rare night in itself. On Halloween, the second night in L.A., he cooked up a version of "Haunted House," the old Jumpin' Gene Simmons hit, at soundcheck, and opened the set with it—after appearing from a coffin and being chased around the stage by ghoul-robed roadies during the guitar break.

On Saturday, Bruce added an acoustic guitar and accordion version of "The Price You Pay" and debuted "Fade Away," the one song from *The River* he'd avoided. On Monday night, with Bob Dylan in the house for a *second* night (he'd come with Jim Keltner on Thursday, and been impressed), Springsteen put "The Price You Pay" back in and dedicated it to his "inspiration." Plus a lengthy version of "Growin' Up," from his first album. On both nights, he ended with encores with Jackson Browne, dueting on "Sweet Little Sixteen." On neither night did the inclusion of the additional songs mean the removal of any of the others.

"Yeah, but you really missed it in St. Paul," said Van Zandt. "He turned around and called 'Midnight Hour,' and we all just about fainted. Funky [bassist Garry Tallent] didn't even believe we were doing it until about the second chorus." The band had not rehearsed the song, and it's unlikely that the E Street Band's present lineup had ever played it before in its five years together. But even the musicians thought that it sounded great.

The expansiveness and elasticity of Springsteen's show is a conundrum, because arena rock is in all other hands the surest route to formula. One of the most miserable summers of my existence was spent watching 15 Rolling Stones shows in 1975. By the fifth, I was fighting to stay awake; by the tenth I'd stopped fighting, a circumstance I ascribed to the band's senility until it occurred to me that no one was meant to look at more than one or maybe two of their damn fiestas.

That's rock and roll for tourists. Springsteen plays for the natives. Although he would probably put it more idealistically, he's really just never lost the consciousness of a bar band musician, who knows that a good part of the house may be seeing all three sets. And like a bar band veteran, he refuses to resort to gimmicks. Marc Brickman's lighting is the best in rock, but it's based on relatively simple theatrical gels and an authoritative sense of timing with follow spots; any funk band in the Midwest might have a more elaborate *concept*, but nobody with lasers achieves such an effective result. (Brickman has a computer along on this tour, but only, he told me, because "if you can figure out a way to program Bruce's show, you can figure a way to make it work for anything." Most nights, Brickman and soundman Bruce Jackson might as well throw their set lists away.)

But what reveals Springsteen bar band roots more than anything is his sense of intimacy with the crowds. One night during this tour, someone told me, he actually announced from the stage, "If the guy I met at the airport yesterday is here, please come to the stage at the break. I've got something for you," which is about as close to sock hop mentality as you could ask. At his show in Phoenix, during "Rosalita," Bruce made one of his patented leaps to the speakers at the side of the stage. But this time he missed.

The crowd just kept on cheering, but back at the soundboard where Jackson and I were sitting, the tension was thick. Bruce might do anything, but this was weird; the band was holding the chord, and the chords of "Rosalita" are not meant to be held for five seconds, much less fifteen.

It's a good long drop from the speakers, two feet high, to the floor, a good eight or nine feet away. All there was between Bruce and the hard concrete floor was the band's monitor mixing board, but as he tumbled down, roadie Bob Werner reached out and broke the fall. (He sprained his wrist in the process.)

Neither the band nor the crowd could see any of this. The next thing any of us knew, the guitar appeared, tossed atop the speakers. Then a pair of hands and at last, Springsteen's head, with his silly-faced-little-boy grin. He shook his head, pulled himself the rest of the way up, and strapped on his guitar, went back into action as if nothing had occurred.

This moment is presumably on film—there was a crew shooting a commercial that night—though from what angle I cannot say. But what the incident proclaims, more than anything, even Bruce's sense of spontaneity, is his sense of event. The cardinal rule of his shows is that something *always* happens. It's not only, as he says in the interview below, that he's prepared for whatever happens. Somehow, he always makes sure that something does occur. I've seen at least 100 shows in the past six or seven years. The worst of them was fascinating, but maybe the most awesome have been the times when, after four or five nights of hell raising action, he manages to make it different again. This guy does not know the meaning of anticlimax.

But there's the bright side. There are darker ones. In Los Angeles, where ticket scalping is legal, front row seats for this extravaganza were going for $180, $200, $250. And fans wrote Bruce to complain, not just that tickets were being scalped, but that the best ones were. It's an old story, and most bands would let it slide, but Bruce took a stand.

Each night in L.A., he gave the crowd the name of the state legislator, and a radio station, who'd agreed to campaign to change the scalping law in California. This might qualify as a gesture—although the night after Landau got a pre-show phone call from a "ticket agent" suggesting that Bruce "do what he does, and I'll do what I do, so why don't he just lay off," he made the announcement *three* times—but he's also hired investigators to get to the bottom of the mess, with intentions of turning the information over to the proper authorities, if any hard evidence can be turned up.

And this reflects the spirit in which Springsteen played M.U.S.E. Although he was one of only two musicians at the benefit who did not make a political statement in the concert program (the other was Tom Petty), Springsteen upstaged the issue only accidentally. He felt that particular problem to his marrow; "Roulette," the song he wrote right after Three Mile Island, is the scariest piece of music he's ever done, for my money more frightening than even the last lines of "Stolen Car," and unmistakably based on the event. (Not to mention Del Shannon's paranoic "Stranger in Town.") There is more to come.

The River itself feels like a farewell to innocence. As Springsteen notes in the interview below, the innocent characters on this album are anachronisms. Their time is gone. That guy lying by the side of the road in "Wreck on the Highway" is not only the guy in "Cadillac Ranch" and "Ramrod," he is also Spanish Johnny, the original man-child hero of *The Wild, the Innocent & the E Street Shuffle*.

The River is, I think, Bruce Springsteen's best album for this very reason. It sums up seven years of work, and it does not shy away from the errors of his career thus far, nor does it disown them. He remains a romantic and a bit of a juvenile, after all this, for who but a romantic juvenile could conceive of a purposeless car thief as a genuine figure of tragedy? But he is also capable now of tying together his hopes and fears—the most joyous of songs are awash with brutal undercurrents.

The River wasn't the record anyone would have predicted Bruce Springsteen would make. Epics aren't anticipated (although they might be the subject of certain fervent hopes.) But if *The River* was unpredictable, the album that will follow it is almost unimaginable. And not only because the society that shaped Springsteen's most beloved characters and the musical tradition he cherishes is now crumbling.

Among other things, *The River* is a Number One record. "Hungry Heart" looks likely to be his first Top Ten single. Things change when that happens, and we have not yet seen the rock and roller who is strong enough to withstand those changes. It would be naïve to expect Bruce Springsteen to be any different.

Yet Bruce Springsteen's career is all about naïve faith. Who else could have survived The New Dylan, The Future of Rock and Roll, The Hype, The Boss? And emerged not only successful, but respected. It's easy to play cynical rock journalist and suppose the worst—no one else has exactly cruised through success—but the fact is, Bruce Springsteen is the only human I have ever met who cannot sell out. He doesn't have a price, because the things he wants are quite literally beyond price. You don't have to believe me. Just wait and see. As Miami Steve says, "For the first time, I can really imagine rock and roll at 40."

The interview below took place at the Fiesta Motel in Tempe, Arizona, on Nov. 6th, from about 3:30 AM until dawn. (The time frame is typical.) Bruce had just completed a show at Arizona State University, and in a strange way, what I'll remember about that night isn't talking with him or even the fall off the speakers but the lines he sang just after the fall, that climactic verse of "Rosalita":

> *Tell your daddy this is his last chance*
> *If he wants his daughter to have some fun*
> *Because my brand new record, Rosie*
> *Just came in at Number one*

He won't forget, either.

Here you are, *The River* is a Number One album, the single is a hit, you're playing great shows in the biggest halls, and selling them out. In a sense, a lot of goals you must have had are now achieved. What goals are left?

Doing it is the goal. It's not to play some big place, or for a record to be Number One. Doing it is the end—not the means. That's the point. So the point is: What's next? Some more of this.

But bigness—that is no end. That as an end, is meaningless, essentially. It's good, 'cause you can reach a lotta people, and that's the idea.

The idea was just to go out and to reach people. And after tonight, you go out and you reach more people, and then the night after that, you do that again.

One of the things that *The River* and also the show, its length and certain of the things you say between songs, are about is seeing more possibilities, more opportunities for things to do.
Yeah. There's an immense amount, and I'm just starting to get some idea about what I want to do. Because we've been in a situation, always, until recently, there's been a lot of instability in everybody's life. The band's and mine. It dates back to the very beginning, from the bars on up to even after we were successful. Then there was the lawsuit.

And then there's the way we work, which is: We're *slow*. And in the studio, I'm slow. I take a long time. That means you spend a lotta money in the studio. Not only do you spend a lotta money, you don't make any money, because you're out of the stream of things. It's like you can never get ahead, because as soon as you get ahead, you stop for two years and you go back to where you were.

Is that slowness as frustrating for you as it is for everybody else?
I'm lucky, because I'm in there, I'm seeing it every step of the way. I would assume that if you didn't know what was going on, and you cared about it, it would be frustrating. With me, it was not frustrating.

You know, we started to work [on the album] and I had a certain idea at the beginning. And at the end, that was the idea that came out on the record. It took a very long time, all the coloring and stuff, there was a lot of decisions and songs to be written. Right up until the very last two weeks, when I rewrote the last two verses to "Point Blank." "Drive All Night" was done just the week before that. Those songs didn't exist, in the form that they're on the record, until the last few weeks we were in the studio. So there's stuff happening all the time. But we get into that little bit of a cycle, which hopefully we'll be able to break—maybe, I don't know.

In a lot of ways, *The River* feels like the end of a cycle. Certain ideas that began with the second and third albums have matured and a lot of the contrasts and contradictions have been—not resolved—but they've been heightened.

On this album, I just said, "I don't understand these things. I don't see where all these things fit. I don't see how all these things can work together." It was because I was always focusing in on some small thing; when I stepped back, they made a sense of their own. It was just a situation of living with all those contradiction. And that's what happens. There's never any resolution. You have moments of clarity, things become clear to you that you didn't understand before. But there's never any making ends meet or finding any time of longstanding peace of mind about something.

That's sort of like "Wreck on the Highway," where, for the first time in your songs, you've got the nightmare and the dream in a package.
That was a funny song. I wrote that song real fast, in one night. We came in and played a few takes of it and that's pretty much what's on the album, I think. That's an automatic song, a song that you don't really think about, or work on. You just look back and it sorta surprises you.

On this record, it also feels like you're relying a lot more on your instincts, the sort of things that happen on stage.
Yeah, that's what happens the most to make the record different. A lot of it is real instinctive. "Hungry Heart" I wrote in a half hour, or ten minutes, real fast. All the rockers—"Crush on You," "You Can Look," "Ramrod"—were all written very quickly, from what I can remember. "Wreck on the Highway" was; "Stolen Car" was. Most of the songs were, sit down and write 'em. There weren't any songs where I worked— "Point Blank" I did, but actually those last two verses I wrote pretty quickly. "The River" took awhile. I had the verses, I never had any chorus, and I didn't have no title for a long time.

But you always had the basic arrangement?
No, on that song, I had these verses, and I was fooling around with the music. What gave me the idea for the title was a Hank Williams song, I think it's "My Bucket's Got a Hole in It," where he goes down to the river to jump in and kill himself, and he can't because it dried up. So I was just sitting there one night, thinking, and I just thought about this song, "My Bucket's Got a Hole in It," and that's where I got the chorus. [Actually, he's referring to "Long Gone, Lonesome Blues"—D.M.]

I love that old country music. All during the last tour that's what I listened to a whole lot—I listened to Hank Williams. I went back and dug up all his first sessions, the gospel kind of stuff that he did. That and the first real Johnny Cash record with "Give My Love to Rose," "I Walk the Line," "Hey Porter," "Six Foot High and Risin'," "I Don't Like It But I Guess Things Happen That Way." That and the rockabilly.

There was a certain something in all that stuff that just seemed to fit in with things that I was thinking about, or worrying about. Especially the Hank Williams stuff. He always has all that conflict, he always has that real religious side, and the honky tonkin', all that side. There's a great song, "Settin' the Woods on Fire." That thing is outrageous. That's "Ramrod," that had some of that in it. And "Cadillac Ranch."

Earlier, you said that "Ramrod" was one of the saddest things you'd written. Why?
[*Laughs*] Well, it's so anachronistic, you know. The character—it's impossible, what he wants to do. One of the ideas of it, when I wrote it, it was sort of like a partner to "Cadillac Ranch" and a few things, it's got that old big engine sound. That song is a goddam *gas* guzzler [*laughing*]. And that was the sound I wanted, that big, rumbling, big engine sound. And this guy, he's there, but he's really *not* there no more. He's the guy in "Wreck on the Highway"—either guy, actually. But he's also the guy, in the end, who says, "I'll give you the word, now, sugar, we'll go ramroddin' forevermore." I don't know; that's a real sad line to me, sometimes.

If you believe it, you mean.
Yeah, but it's a funny kinda thing. I love it when we play that song on stage. It's just a happy song, a celebration of all that stuff that's gonna be gone—is gone already, almost.

I threw that song ten million times off the record. Ten million times I threw it off *Darkness* and I threw it off this one, too. Because I thought it was wrong.

You mentioned something similar about "Out in the Street," that it was too much of a fantasy to possibly believe it.
I was just wary of it at that time, I guess for some of the same reasons. It always seemed anachronistic, and at the time, I was demanding of all the songs that they be able to translate. All the characters, they're part of my past, they're part of the future and they're part of the present. And I guess there was a certain frightening aspect to seeing one that wasn't part of the future. He was part of the past.

To me, that was the conflict of that particular song. I loved it, we used to play it all the time. And there was that confusion too. Well, if I love playing the damn thing so much, why the hell don't I want to put it on the record?

I guess I always made sure that the characters always had that foot planted up ahead somewhere. Not just the one back there. That's what makes 'em viable, or real, today. But I also knew a lotta people who were exactly like this. So I said, well, that's OK. There was just a point where I said, that's OK, to a lot of things where I previously would not have said so.

I gained a certain freedom, in making the two record set, because I could let all those people out, that usually I'd put away. Most of the time, they'd end up being my favorite songs, and probably some of my best songs, you know.

You mean the kind of songs that would show up on stage, but not on record? [*"Fire," "Because the Night," "Sherry Darling"*]
Yeah. I'm the kind of person, I think a lot about everything. Nothin' I can do about it. It's like, I'm a thinkin' fool. That's a big part of me. Now, the other part is, I can get onstage and cut that off and be super-instinctive. To be a good live performer, you have to be instinctive. It's like, to walk in the jungle, or to do anything where there's a certain tightrope wire aspect you need to be instinctive. And you have to be comfortable at it also.

Like tonight, I was falling on my head. I wasn't *worryin'* about it. I just went, it just happened [*laughs*]. You just think, what happens next? When I was gonna jump on that speaker, I couldn't worry about whether I was gonna make it or not. You can't. You just gotta do it. And if you do, you do, and if you don't, you don't, and then something else happens. That's the point of the live performance.

Now, when I get into the studio, both things operate. When we perform on this record, I feel that we have that thing going that we've got live. To me, we're not rockin' that stuff better live than a lot of it is on the record. I can still listen to it. Usually, two weeks after we're out on the road, I cannot listen to my record anymore. 'Cause as soon as I hear some crappy tape off the board, it sounds ten times better than what we spent all that time doing in the studio. This is the very first album that I've been able to go back and put on to play, and it sounds good to me.

But in the studio, I'm conceptual. I have a self-consciousness. And there's a point where I often would try to stop that. "No, that's bad. Look at these great records, and I betcha they didn't think about it like this, or think about it this long." You realize that it doesn't matter. That's unimportant, it's ridiculous. I got into a situation where I just said, "Hey, this is what I do, and these are my assets and these are my burdens." I got comfortable with myself being that kind of person.

But only after going to extremes. *Darkness* is the least spontaneous of your records.
That's right. And it's funny because "Darkness on the Edge of Town," that cut is live in the studio. "Streets of Fire" is live in the studio, essentially. "Factory" is live. It's not a question of how you actually do it. The idea is to *sound* spontaneous, not be spontaneous.

So at this point, I just got settled into accepting certain things that I've always been uncomfortable with. I stopped setting limits and definitions—which I always threw out anyway, but which I'd always feel guilty about. Spending a long time in the studio, I stopped feeling bad about that. I said, that's me, that's what I do. I work slow, and I work slow for a reason: To get the results that I want.

When you try to define what makes a good rock and roll record, or what is rock and roll, everyone has their own personal definition. But when you put limits on it, you're just throwing stuff away.

Isn't one of your definitions that it's limitless?
I think it is. That's my definition, I guess. Hey, you can go out in the street and do the twist and that's rock and roll. It's the moment, it's all things [*laughs*]. It's funny, to me, it just is.

You know, my music utilizes things from the past, because that's what the past is for. It's to learn from. It's not to limit you, you shouldn't be limited by it, which I guess was one of my fears on "Ramrod." I don't want to make a record like they made in the '50s or the '60s or the '70s. I want to make a record like today, that's right now.

To do that, I go back, back further all the time. Back into Hank Williams, back into Jimmie Rodgers. Because the human thing in those records, that should be at least the heart of it. The human thing that's in those records is just beautiful and awesome. I put on that Hank Williams and Jimmie Rodgers stuff and Wow! What inspiration!

It's got that beauty and the purity. The same thing with a lot of the great '50s records, and the early rockabilly. I went back and dug up all the early rockabilly stuff because . . . what mysterious people they were.

There's this song, "Jungle Rock" by Hank Mizell. *Where is Hank Mizell?* What happened to him? What a mysterious person, what a ghost. And you put that thing on and you can see him. You can see him standing in some little studio, way back when, and just singing that song. No reason [*laughs*]. Nothing gonna come out of it. Didn't sell. That wasn't no Number One record, and he wasn't playin' no big arena after it, either.

But what a moment, what a mythic moment, what a mystery. Those records are filled with mystery; they're shrouded with mystery. Like these wild men came out from somewhere, and man, they were so *alive*. The joy and the abandon. Inspirational, inspirational records, those records.

You mentioned earlier that when you went into the arenas that you were worried about losing certain things.
I was afraid maybe it would screw up the range of artistic expression that the band had. Because of the lack of silence. A couple things happened. Number one, it's a rock and roll show. People are gonna scream their heads off whenever they feel like it. That's fine—happens in theatres, happens in clubs [*laughs*]. Doesn't matter where the hell it is, happens every place, and that's part of it, you know.

On this tour, it's been really amazing, because we've been doing all those real quiet songs. And we've been able to do 'em. And then we've been able to rock real hard and get that thing happening from the audience. I think part of the difference is that the demands that are made on the audience now are much heavier, much heavier on the audience that sees us now than on the last tour.

But the moment you begin to depend on audience reaction, you're doing the wrong thing. You're doin' it wrong, it's a mistake, it's not right. You can't allow yourself, no matter what, to depend on them. I put that mike out to the crowd, you have a certain faith that somebody's gonna yell somethin' back. Some nights it's louder than other nights and some nights they do, and some songs they don't. But that's the idea. I think when you begin to expect a reaction, it's a mistake. You gotta have your thing completely together—boom! right there with you. That's what makes nights special and what makes nights different from other nights.

On the other hand, the only way to do a really perfect show is to involve that audience. Maybe an audience only gets lazy if the performer doesn't somehow keep it on its toes.
I'm out there for a good time and to be inspired at night, and to play with my band and to rock those songs as hard as we can rock 'em. I think that you can have some of the best nights under the very roughest conditions. A lotta times, at Max's or some of the clubs down in Jersey, they'd be sittin' on their hands or nobody wants to dance, and the adversity is a positive motivation.

The only concern is that what's being done is being done the way it should be done. The rest you don't have control over. But I think that our audience is the best audience in the world. The amount of freedom that I get from the crowd is really a lot.

The way the stage show is organized is that the first half is about work and struggling; the second half is about joy, release, transcending a lot of those things in the first half. Is that conscious?
I knew that I wanted a certain feeling for the first set. That's sorta the way it stacks up.

What you rarely get a sense of around rock bands is work, especially rock and roll as a job of work. Yet around this band, you can't miss it.
That's at the heart of the whole thing. There's a beauty in work and I love it, all different kinds of work. That's what I consider it. This is my job, and that's my work. And I work my ass off, you know.

In Los Angeles one night, when you introduced "Factory," you made a distinction between two different kinds of work. Do you remember it?
There's people that get a chance to do the kind of work that changes the world, and make things really different. And then there's the kind that just keeps the world from falling apart. And that was the kind that my dad always did. 'Cause we were always together as a family, and we grew up in a . . . good situation, where we had what we needed. And there was a lot of sacrifice on his part and my mother's part for that to happen . . .

The River has a lot of those sorts of workers—the people in "Jackson Cage," the guy in "The River" itself.
I never knew anybody who was unhappy with their job and was happy with their life. It's your sense of purpose. Now, some people can find it elsewhere. Some people can work a job and find it some place else.

Like the character in "Racing in the Street"?
Yeah. But I don't know if that's lasting. But people do, they find ways.

Or else . . . ?
[*Long pause*] Or else they join the Ku Klux Klan or something. That's where it can take you, you know. It can take you to a lot of strange places.

Introducing "Factory" on a different night, you spoke about your father having been real angry, and then, after awhile, not being angry anymore. "He was just silent." Are *you* still angry?
I don't know. I don't know. I don't know if I know myself that well. I think I know myself a lot but I'm not sure [*laughs*]. It's impossible not to be [angry] when you see the state of things and look around. You have to be, somewhat.

Tonight, you were saying on stage that you found the election terrifying. That seems to go hand in hand with playing the M.U.S.E. benefits, and striking back at ticket scalpers in L.A. You wouldn't have done those things two year ago, I don't think. Are you finding social outlets for that anger now?
That's true. It's just a whole values thing. Take the ticket thing. It's a hustle. And a hustle has become . . . respected. In a lot of quarters—on a street level, dope pushers—it's a respectable thing, to hustle somebody. I mean, how many times in the Watergate thing did people say about Nixon, "Well, he just wasn't smart enough to get away with it." Like his only mistake was that he didn't get away with it. And there's a certain point where people have become cynical, where the hustle, that's the American way. I think it's just turned upside down in a real bad way. I think it should lose its respect.

Do you feel that way about nuclear energy?
It's just the whole thing, it's the *whole* thing. It's terrible, it's horrible. Somewhere along the way, the idea, which I think was initially to get

some fair transaction between people, went out the window. And what came in was, the most you can get [*laughs*]. The most you can get and the least you can give. That's why cars are the way they are today. It's just an erosion of all the things that were true and right about the original idea.

But that isn't something that was on your mind much until the *Darkness* album?
Up to then, I didn't think about too many things. In *Greetings from Asbury Park*, I did. And then I went off a little bit, and sort of round-about came back to it.

I guess it just started after *Born to Run* somehow. I had all that time off, and I spent a lotta time home. We were off for three years, and home for a long time. It came out of a local kind of thing—what my old friends were doing, what my relatives were doing. How things were affecting them, and what their lives were like. And what my life was like.

Did you have a sense that no one else was telling that story?
I didn't see it too much, except in the English stuff. Things were being addressed that way in that stuff.

You mean, for instance, the Clash?
Yeah, all that kind of stuff. I liked it, I always liked that stuff. But there wasn't too much stuff in America happening. It just seemed to me that's the story. But there was a crucial level of things missing, and it is today still. Maybe it's just me getting older and seeing things more as they are.

On *Darkness*, the character's response is to isolate himself from any community, and try to beat the system on his own. The various characters on *The River* are much more living in the mainstream of society.
That guy at the end of *Darkness* has reached a point where you just have to strip yourself of everything, to get yourself together. For a minute, sometimes, you just have to get rid of everything, just to get yourself together inside, be able to push everything away. And I think that's what happened at the end of the record.

And then there was the thing where the guy comes back.

And *The River* is what he sees?
Yeah, these are his feelings, it's pretty much there, and in the shows, it's there now, too, I guess. I hate to get too literal about it, because I can never explain it as well as when I wrote about it. I hate to limit it. I look back at *Darkness* or the other records, and there were other things going on that I never knew were going on.

Do you like *Born to Run* and *Darkness* better now?
Not particularly. On *Darkness*, I like the ideas, I'm not crazy about the performances. We play all those songs ten times better live. But I like the idea. *Born to Run*, I like the performances and the sound. Sometimes, it sounds funny.

Young and innocent?
Yeah, yeah. Same thing with *The Wild and the Innocent*. I have a hard time listening to any of those records. Certain things on each record I can listen to: "Racing in the Street," "Backstreets," "Prove It All Night," "Darkness on the Edge of Town." But not a lot, because either the performance doesn't sound right to me, or the ideas sound like a long time ago.

Do you remember when you threw the birthday cake into the crowd, at the second M.U.S.E. concert?
[*Laughs*] Oh yeah. That was a wild night.

You'd just turned 30 that night, and didn't seem to be overjoyed by it. But a couple weeks ago in Cleveland, I was kidding Danny about turning 30, and said, "Oh yeah, we're 30 now, can't do what we used to do." You said, real quick, "That's not true." What happened in that year? Was that significant, turning 30?
I don't remember. It just made me wanna do more things. I think, as a matter of fact, when we were in the studio, that was the thing that was big. I didn't feel we were going too slow for what we were doing. But I felt that I wanted to be quicker just to have more time. I wanted to be touring, for one thing. I wanted to be touring *right now*.

But by the time you finish this tour, you'll be crowding 32. Then, if you're right and it's just gonna take a year or so to make a record,

you'll be 33 or 34 by the time you get out again. Can you still have the stamina to do the kind of show you feel the need to do?
Who knows? I'm sure it'll be a different type of show. It's impossible to tell and a waste of time guessin'.

When I was in the studio and wanted to play, it wasn't the way I felt in a physical kind of way, it was what I felt mentally. I was excited about the record and I wanted to play those songs live. I wanted to get out there and travel around the world with people who were my friends. And see every place and play just as hard as we could play, every place in the world. Just get into things, see things, see what happens.

Like in "Badlands"?
That's it. That's the idea. I want to see what happens, what's next. All I knew when I was in the studio, sometimes, was that I felt great that day. And I was wishing I was somewhere strange, playing. I guess that's the thing I love doing the most. And it's the thing that makes me feel most alert and alive.

You look awful before a show, and then those hours up there, which exhaust everyone else, refresh you.
I always look terrible before the show. That's when I feel worst. And after the show it's like a million bucks. Simple as that. You feel a little tired but you *never* feel better. Nothing makes me feel as good as those hours between when you walk offstage, until I go to bed. That's the hours that I live for. As feelings go, that's ten on a scale of ten. I just feel like talking to people, going out back and meeting those kids, doing any damn thing. Most times I just come back and eat and lay down and feel good. Most people, I don't think, get to feel that good, doing whatever they do.

You can't get that in the studio?
Sometimes, but it's different. You get wired for two or three days or a week or so and then sometimes, you feel real low. I never feel as low, playing, as I do in the studio.

You know, I just knew that's what I wanted to do—go all over and play. See people and go all over the world. I want to see what all those people are like. I want to meet people from all different countries and stuff.

You've always liked to have a certain mobility, a certain freedom of movement. Can you still walk down the street?

Oh sure, sure. It depends on where you go. Usually . . . you can do anything you want to do. The idea that you can't walk down the street is in people's minds. You can walk down any street, any time. What you gonna be afraid of, someone coming up to you? In general, it's not that different than it ever was, except you meet people you ordinarily might not meet—you meet some strangers and you talk to 'em for a little while.

The other night I went out, I went driving, we were in Denver. Got a car and went out, drove all around. Went to the movies by myself, walked in, got my popcorn. This guy comes up to me, real nice guy. He says, "Listen, you want to sit with me and my sister?" I said, "All right." So we watch the movie [*laughs*]. It was great, too, because it was that Woody Allen movie [*Stardust Memories*], the guy's slammin' to his fans. And I'm sittin' there and this poor kid says, "Jesus, I don't know what to say to ya. Is this the way it is? Is this how you feel?" I said, "No, I don't feel like that so much." And he had the amazing courage to come up to me at the end of the movie, and ask if I'd go to his home and meet his mother and father. I said, "What time is it?" It was 11 o'clock, so I said, "Well OK."

So I go home with him; he lives out in some suburb. So we get over to the house and here's his mother and father, laying out on the couch, watching TV and reading the paper. He brings me in and says, "Hey I got Bruce Springsteen here." And they don't believe him. So he pulls me over, and he says, "This is Bruce Springsteen." "Aw, g'wan," they say. So he runs in his room and brings out an album and he holds it up to my face. And his mother says [*breathlessly*] "Ohh *yeah*!" She starts yelling "Yeah," she starts screaming.

And for two hours I was in this kid's house, talking with these people, they were really nice, they cooked me up all this food, watermelon, and the guy gave me a ride home a few hours later.

I felt so good that night. Because here are these strange people I didn't know, they take you in their house, treat you fantastic and this kid was real nice, they were real nice. That is something that can happen to me that can't happen to most people. And when it does happen, it's fantastic. You get somebody's whole life in three hours. You get their parents, you get their sister, you get their family life, in three hours. And I went back to that hotel and felt really good because I thought, "*Wow [almost whispering*], what a thing to be able to do. What an experience to be able to have, to be able to step into some stranger's life."

And that's what I thought about in the studio. I thought about going out and meeting people I don't know. Going to France and Germany and Japan, and meeting Japanese people and French people and German people. Meeting them and seeing what they think, and being able to go over there with something. To go over there with a pocketful of ideas or to go over there with just something, to be able to take something over. And boom! To do it.

But you can't do one without the other. I couldn't do it if I hadn't spent time in the studio, knowing what I saw and what I felt right now.

Because then you wouldn't have that pocketful of ideas?
Then, if you don't have that, stay home or something. If you have some ideas to exchange, that's what it's about. That's at the heart of it. I just wouldn't go out and tour unless I had that. There wouldn't be a reason.

The reason is you have some idea you wanna say. You have an idea about things, an opinion, a feeling about the way things are or the way things could be. You wanna go out and tell people about it. You wanna tell people, well, if everybody did this or if people thought this, maybe it would be better.

When we play the long show, that's because it gives the whole picture. And if you aren't given the whole picture, you're not gonna get the whole picture. We play the first part . . . that first part is about those things that you said it was about. That's the foundation, without that the rest couldn't happen. Wouldn't be no second half without the first half; couldn't be all them other things, without those things. Without that foundation of the hard things, and the struggling things, the work things. That's the heart, that's what it comes down to.

And then on top of that, there's the living, the things that surround that. That's why the show's so long. "You wanna leave out 'Stolen Car'?" No, that's a little part of the puzzle. "You wanna leave this out?" No that's a little part of the puzzle. And at the end, if you want, you can look back and see . . . just a point of view really. You see somebody's idea, the way somebody sees things. And you know somebody.

People go to that show, they know me. They know a lotta me, as much as I know that part of myself. That's why, when I meet 'em on the street, they know you already. And you can know them, too. Because of their response.

Even these days, it's still not very far from the dressing room to the stage for you, is it?
I don't know if it is. I don't know if it should be. I don't know for sure how different the thing is or how it's perceived. Except a lot of the music is real idealistic, and I guess like anybody else, you don't live up to it all the time. You just don't. That's the challenge. You got to walk it like you talk it. That's the idea. That's the line. I guess that's pretty much what it's about.

Roger Scott and Patrick Humphries
Hot Press,
November 2, 1984

A few months into the *Born in the U.S.A.* tour, Springsteen spoke with Ireland's *Hot Press* after a show in Hartford. Asked about the danger of success, he admits, "well it's a funny thing. One of the problems is that the audience and the performer have got to leave some room for each other, to be human." Humphries would co-write 1985's *Springsteen: Blinded by the Light,* a significant compendium (now out of print) for collectors and fans; this interview displays Scott's depth of knowledge, from the Vietnam draft to hopping the wall at Graceland to the outtake "Murder Incorporated."

The bets were on: Following David Bowie's foray into "Serious Moonlight" in 1983, *the* rock event of 1984 had to be the Jacksons' *Victory* tour. On the face of it, there was no competition. Michael Jackson had become the '80s' brightest star, with *Thriller* shattering all known records and this was the tour on which that new status would reap ultimate dividends. But when it came to it, the Jacksons' "Victory" proved to be a hollow one—exorbitant ticket prices and extravagant fantasies do not compensate for musical paucity.

In stark contrast, it was a scrawny 35-year-old from New Jersey who gave rock 'n' roll a roaring voice in 1984. Bruce Springsteen had done it before, of course; those who witnessed him on the 1980/81 *River* tour came away converted by Springsteen's zealous rock 'n' roll revivalist shows. But even the diehard must have wondered if he could still pack a punch. Three years away is, after all, a long time in rock 'n' roll.

The omens on his seventh album, *Born in the U.S.A.*, were promising— Bruce Springsteen was back doing what he did best, rocking his heart out! Yet at the core of the new album, beneath the exuberance of such classic rockers as "Darlington County," "No Surrender" and "Glory Days" was a note of caution, with Springsteen coming to terms with his love of rock 'n' roll, and the fact that he's reached his mid-30s. Surely those legendary four-hour shows were now a part of rock history? No one could keep up that intensity. But with fervor and reckless abandon, Springsteen proved such speculation premature. His 1984 tour opened in St. Paul, Minnesota, on June 29 with a marathon 4½-hour, 30-song show. Bruce Springsteen was back, Jack!

In conversation, the voice sounds husky, like too many cigarettes in too many roadside bars, like too many tequila chasers chasing something long forgotten. It couldn't be further from the truth. Bruce Springsteen is the essence of the puritanical rock star.

In a world where "excess" is almost written into the contract, Springsteen is an unlikely rock hero. He doesn't smoke, drinks beer only in moderation, and only seems to come alive in performance, or when carving out a new album in the studio. He'd be too good to be true, if it wasn't for the immensely moving quality of his music.

Springsteen's restraint is carried over into his recording. During his 12 years with CBS, he has only released seven official albums. (The dedication of his fans in obtaining bootlegs is legendary. Along with Dylan and Bowie, Springsteen is rock's most widely bootlegged artist. It's an ironic barometer, but one which testifies Springsteen's stature in rock legend.) It is only really in performance that Springsteen indulges in excess—in the positive sense of screaming, soaring shows, which stretch into four-hour celebrations of life, youth, of maturity—and of rock 'n' roll itself.

A Springsteen show is a virtual potted history of rock music, alongside his own classic rockers like "Born to Run" and "Rosalita," he'll slot in songs by Creedence Clearwater Revival, Jimmy Cliff, the Beatles, Jerry Lee Lewis, Chuck Berry and Elvis Presley—the sort of sounds that allowed Bruce Frederick Springsteen to escape the confines of Freehold, New Jersey, except that now it's *him* up on stage pouring his heart out in concert, Springsteen puts *everything* into the performance, nothing and no one is spared.

The afternoon before the show there's none of the usual rock 'n' roll excesses. Springsteen can be seen diligently pacing every aisle of the auditorium, ensuring that the sound quality is right for everyone, not just those with enough money to blow on seats right up front.

That fine attention to detail, that *caring* separates Springsteen from the legions of Spinal Tappers ploughing 'round the rock circuit with one eye on the clock and the other on the house percentage! It's a quality that's been in abundant evidence since Bruce Springsteen emerged in the early 1970s.

There was a brash exuberance to his debut *Greetings from Asbury Park* in 1973. With verbose enthusiasm, Springsteen crammed everything into his debut like it was his last chance. *Born to Run* in 1975 was an album of epic panache, Springsteen elevating the street suss characters of his first two albums into heroes of the American Dream, arriving at their rock 'n' roll goal in burned-out Chevys.

By *Darkness on the Edge of Town* in 1978, the dream had turned sour, and the album's 10 songs dealt in the darkness of disillusionment and despair. There was a reconciliation of sorts on the double *River* of 1980, with hearty rockers like "Sherry Darling" and "Ramrod" nestling next to bleak ballads such as "The River" and "Independence Day." But the stark, acoustic detour through *Nebraska* (1982) left no doubts about Springsteen's resolute artistic integrity. He would not tailor his output to suit the demands of the marketplace. Uncompromisingly bleak, *Nebraska* was totally solo, a collection of folk tales dwelling on those crushed by the weight of Reagonomics, stylistically similar to earlier efforts by Woody Guthrie, Hank Williams and Robert Johnson.

With his seventh album, *Born in the U.S.A.* (1984), Springsteen managed to fuse the disparate elements of his career most successfully: the exuberance can be found on such cocky rockers as "Darlington County" and "Working on the Highway," the somber introspection finds a place on "Downbound Train" and "My Hometown." The 12-track album was arrived at after a two-year recording stint, which meant sifting through around 100 songs to arrive at the final dozen.

Born in the U.S.A. was such a defiantly rock 'n' roll album, the reviews were surprisingly favourable. But its success and that of the two singles—

"Dancing in the Dark" and "Cover Me"—saw the 35-year-old blue collar rocker back at the top. And with Springsteen back on the road, some sort of honesty and merit infuses the bloated and avaricious caricature rock music too often seems to have become. Springsteen was a month into his first American tour in three years when Roger Scott talked to him in Hartford, Connecticut. It was the first time that Springsteen had spoken to a member of the European press in over three years. The intervening years had produced *Nebraska* and *Born in the U.S.A.* had seen video become another spoke in the rock 'n' roll wheel. Springsteen was pensive and attentive during the interview, attaching the same sort of care to conversation, as he does to recording.

What did you do after *The River* tour when you came off the road?
Clarence got married, a couple of weeks after we got off the road. So we went to his wedding, and I was the best man. We came back to New Jersey, and very shortly after that, I started to write the *Nebraska* songs. That was the fall and early winter, and I think I recorded those right around New Year, in a couple of days. And that was about it. Not much happened. We went into the studio a couple of times, and I attempted to record some of those songs with the band, but it just didn't work out, didn't sound as good, but we did end up recording about half of the *Born in the U.S.A.* album. Those two records were always kinda intermingled—I have some *Nebraska*-like demos of "Born in the U.S.A." "Downbound Train" y'know? Then we decided that we were gonna put the *Nebraska* album out, the demos that I'd made at my house . . .

I know you'd read the Woody Guthrie's biography [*Woody Guthrie: A Life* by Joe Klein] and were doing a couple of his songs on the *River* tour. Was that an influence?
No, it was just basically that was the way that they sounded best. The songs had a lot of detail so that, when the band started to wail away into it, the characters got lost. Like "Johnny 99"—I thought, "oh, that'd be great if we could do a rock version." But when you did that, the song disappeared. A lot of its content was in its style, in the treatment of it. It needed that really kinda austere, echoey sound, just one guitar—one guy telling his story. That's what made the record work, the sound of real conversation . . . like you were meeting different people, and they just told you what had happened to them, or what was happening to them. So you kinda walked for a little bit in somebody else's shoes.

Where did all the desperate people on that record come from?
I dunno. That's just what I was writing at the time, that's what I was interested in writing about. I don't know where songs come from really, myself. I just had a certain *tone* in mind, which I felt was the tone of what it was like when I was a kid growing up. And at the same time it felt like the tone of what the country was like at that time. That was kinda the heart that I was drawing from.

Leading on from *The River*, which was full of these sharply contrasting songs, these wild celebrations alongside these hopeless people.
On *Born in the U.S.A.* I kinda combined the two things. On *The River* I'd have a song like this and a song like that because I didn't know how to combine it . . . By the time I'd got to the *Born in the U.S.A.* album, I kinda combined those two things, like "Darlington County," even "Glory Days," uh, "Dancing in the Dark." I did a little bit on *The River*, like "Cadillac Ranch"—that was the way I was dealing with different types of material. I hadn't figured out a way to synthesise it into one song, y'know. I knew it was all part of the same picture, which is why *The River* was a double album.

"Born in the U.S.A.", I see as an indictment of America's treatment of Vietnam Veterans, and you've played shows for Vietnam Vets. I wondered—looking back—if you feel at all guilty about dodging the draft when you see these guys?
No, no. At the time, I had no political standpoint whatsoever when I was 18, and neither did any of my friends, and the whole draft thing was a pure street thing—you don't wanna go! And you didn't want to go because you'd seen other people go and not come back! The first drummer in a band [of mine] called the Castiles, he enlisted, and he came back in his uniform, and it was all, "Here I go, goin' to Vietnam"— laughin' and jokin' about it. And he went, and he was killed. There were a lot of guys from my neighborhood, guys in bands—one of the best lead singers went, and he was missing in action—so it got to be kinda a street thing. When I was 17 or 18, I didn't even know where Vietnam was. We just knew we didn't wanna go and *die*! It wasn't until later in the '70s there was this kind of awareness of the type of war it was, what it meant—the way it was felt to be a subversion of all the true American ideals. It twisted the country inside out.

I saw you at Meadowlands, and you did "Johnny Bye-Bye" on the anniversary of Elvis' death [August 16, 1977] and you said— almost like it was to yourself—that it was maybe dangerous to have all your dreams come true. Is it—because yours have?

Well, you know, a little bit of mine has—the whole thing of when I was 15 I wanted to play the guitar, I wanted to have a band, I wanted to travel. I wanted to be good, as good as I could be at that job. I wanted to be good at doing something that was useful to other people, and to myself. You know, I think that's the biggest reward of the whole thing—you make a lot of dough, you know, and that's great, that's fun, uh, but the feeling that you go out there at night, you play some role in people's lives, whether it's just a night out, a dance, a good time, or maybe you make someone think a little bit different about themselves, or about the way they live, which is what rock 'n' roll music did for me. The interaction with the community is the real reward— that's where I get the most satisfaction, and just doin' it well . . . I'm proud of the way that we play, the kind of band that I've got now. It's been a long time putting it together, we're all 10 years down the road . . . and it's something I got a lot of pride in right now. So when we walk out on stage, your pride is on the line, and, you know, you don't wanna let yourself down. And you don't want to let down the people who come and see you.

There are dangers attached to success, though, aren't there? I mean all my heroes let me down eventually.

Well it's a funny thing. One of the problems is that the audience and the performer have got to leave some room for each other, to be human. Or else they don't deserve each other, in a funny kinda way . . . I think the position that you get put in is unrealistic to begin with. Basically, you're just somebody who plays the guitar, and you do that good, and that's great, that's nice. If you do your job well, and people like it, and admire you for it, or respect you for it, that's a plus. But the rest of the time, you're scramblin' around in the dark like everyone else is. The idealising of performers or politicians doesn't seem to make much sense—it's based on an image, and an image is always, basically, limiting. That doesn't mean it's necessarily false, it's just not complete. I don't know, does that answer your question [*laughs*] 'cos I trailed off there.

It's that inspiration that you felt, when you saw Elvis . . .

The thing is, the inspiration comes from the music. The performer, he's the guy that's doing the music, but he's not the thing. The thing itself is in the music—that's where the spirit of the thing is. The performer is kind of what the music is coming through, but I guess what I feel is that Elvis . . . they got disillusioned. Well I don't feel personally that Elvis let anybody down. I don't think he owed anything to anybody. As it was, he did more for most people than they'll ever have done for them in their lives. The trouble that he ran into, well, it's hard to keep your head above the water. But sometimes it's not right for people to judge.

What would you have said to him that time you climbed over the wall of Graceland, if he'd been in and answered the door?

[*Laughs*] I don't know, I wasn't thinkin' about *that*. I saw the light in the window. I was with Steve, Little Steven, and this taxi cab driver, who was telling me not to go 'cos there were big dogs over there who'd bite! But I saw the light, and I just had to go, so I climbed over the wall and ran all the way up the driveway—this was about 3 or 4 a.m.—and I got to the door [*laughs*] and the guards came out. I said "Gee, I'm a musician, had my picture on the cover of *Time*!" He just looked at me like I was a lunatic and said "Elvis isn't here and you gotta go."

How does it feel coming up to 35?

I feel good, feel better than I've ever felt before. I'm kinda at peace with the whole thing. I don't think about it that much. I thought about it . . . I think I turned 30 when I was 27 [*laughs*] and thought a lot about it then. After a while, it got to be not so important as you might think. I deal with it in songs a little bit, and that's fun. It just doesn't seem relevant to me.

Tell me how you make records now. It's obviously changed a lot since the agonies that surrounded *Born to Run*. I understand these days, a lot of it's live?

Yeah, that's the way we made the *Born in the U.S.A.* record. It takes a long time making the records—but what I take a long time doing is not the recording, it's in the conceptualizing of the record, where I'll write three or four songs, and the fifth one I'll keep. I'll do that for quite a while. Generally we just go in, and we'll spend a night—"Born in the U.S.A.," that's live, that's a second take. "Darlington County" is all live—

only two takes of that song. None of those songs are over five or six takes, and they're all live vocals, with the exception, I think, of "Dancing in the Dark," we overdubbed that voice. But it's basically the band plays good, and we can go in, and once you do more than five or six takes, it doesn't get any better!

I usually don't teach the band the songs until we're in the studio, until we're about to record. Then I show 'em the chords real quick, so that they *can't* learn how to play it, 'cos the minute they start learnin' to play it, they start figurin' out parts and they get self-conscious. But the first two takes when they're learnin' it, they're worried about just hangin' on. So they're playing right at the edge, and they're playing very intuitively, which is in general how our best stuff happens right now.

When do you conceptualize all this? Does it spring from one song, or does it gradually appear as you're doing the songs?
I don't really know how it's gonna come out until the end. I have an idea sometimes of a tune that I want, or a feeling, and I'll go in that direction. That I usually come up with somehow, but never the way I think I'm gonna come up with it! . . . I never made a record that's come out the way I thought it was gonna come out. A record is like anything else, if it's a real creation, it has a life of its own. You have to respect that fact, that there comes a point where it's gonna go where it's gonna go. To try and control it is to try and limit it. It's like with a child. When a kid gets to a certain point, it's his own life, and you gotta give him room.

When you did the "Dancing in the Dark" video, and the 12″, was that you being pressured? Did you not want to seem like some reactionary old rock 'n' roller?
[*Laughs*] No I was interested in it. We did a video for *Nebraska*, an "Atlantic City" video which I liked. I wasn't in it! So people said, "Oh you gotta do one that you're *in*!" So we tried one for "Dancing in the Dark." But the thing I didn't like about that was that it was lip-synched (mimed), which is not what I'm interested in doing, 'cos I think the best thing that our band does is address the moment, and we go for some authentic emotion. That gets all sort of knocked out of whack when you're singin' to something that was recorded a long time ago . . .

The main thing with my songs right now is that I write them to be complete things, and they're filled with a lot of geographical detail and a lot of detail about what people are wearing, where they live. You get a lot of detail in most of the songs, and the thing about a video is that you only really have a few choices about what you can do. You can either do a live thing, which is something that we've done before, like "Rosalita"—which is fine, because you record the moment—or you can illustrate the story which generally comes out stupid! Because if you're singin' about a house, then you show a house, then you're messing up. You're robbing people of their imaginations. Everybody sees a different house! Like on "My Father's House" from *Nebraska* everybody would see a different house, a different field—they all have those things inside 'em which are their own. Music is meant to be evocative, it is meant to evoke emotion. To individualize personal emotion in the listener. So either you illustrate the story, which limits it, or you relay another story in something that is already telling a story. Which doesn't make sense, because if you did it right the first time, why are you going to do it again? That's the video dilemma as I see it, and those are the questions I'm trying to address when I look at that particular medium, which I don't have any answers for right now. I'm not really interested in making an ad for my record. I am interested in video, it is very powerful. In this country, the video audience starts about six or seven years old, and its most intense audience is between six and sixteen.

Little kids, seven or eight, come up to me 'cos they've seen the "Dancing in the Dark" video. And those people can't go to shows, they're too young, they have no visual access to rock 'n' roll music. Those are the kids that are glued to MTV . . . Every house I go in, the kids are glued to it, they know all the bands. So there is a completely different audience out there—I think it puts the responsibility of what you're putting on the air to kids that young . . . There's a cartoonish thing that the videos employ. I was down at the beach, this little kid called Mike who was about eight came up to me and said you want me to show you my "Dancing in the Dark" moves? [*Laughs*] So I said okay.

When I was over here for the Meadowlands shows, I drove through Freehold [New Jersey, where Springsteen was born] and it looked like such a dump, so incredibly boring. Was that the problem?
It's just such a small town, a small, narrow-minded town, no different probably from any other provincial town. Um, it was very conservative. There was a time in the late '60s when I couldn't walk down the street 'cos of the way I looked. It was just very stagnating. There were some factories, some farms and stuff, that if you didn't go to college

you ended up in. there really wasn't that much, you know, there wasn't that much.

It seems to me important for you to keep that bar band mentality, the way the Beatles did in Hamburg, playing totally different sets every night.
I really do that to keep it interesting for myself, y'know? The minute we play the set the same two nights in a row, or even a piece of the set the same—the whole thing that our band is about, is lessening the distance, as much as possible, the distance between the performer and the audience. Distance—on stage—is kinda your own worst enemy. At least it is for us. So I wanna stay very deep down in the material, to stay involved with it, and the best way to do that is to change it a lot, so things don't get stale, so you don't run the same routines night after night.

We have certain things that we do, but the show changes quite a bit. Mainly, it keeps the band sharp, it's more entertaining for the crowd, 'cos we do have a lot of fans who come two or three nights if you're in a town that long, so they get to hear all different songs they like. And we get to go through something different onstage at night, so it keeps it from getting boring, and it keeps you involved down there, *in* the music, which is where you have to be to get the emotion out of it that we want.

That line from "No Surrender": *"We learned more from a three minute record than we ever learned in school"* **is so perfect. Was that written about you and Miami Steve [aka Little Steven]?**
Not really. It just kinda came out one night. I was sitting around my house . . . A song like that, or "Backstreets" or "Bobby Jean," are just basic songs about friendship, which me and Steve—we've been best friends since we were like 16, so anytime I wrote one of those, I had to be drawing on our relationship I guess to a certain degree. They're just songs about people passin' through, the rites of passage together.

Legend has it that there's another album called *Murder Incorporated* raring to go. Is there anything to that?
No. There's a *song* called "Murder Incorporated."

Who do you rely upon to criticize your work, if anybody?
Well, Jon [Landau, Springsteen's manager], he does that quite a bit. He'll say you're doing this too much, he helps me focus sometimes. If I

have a song I'm stuck on, sometimes I'll play him part of it, he'll give me an idea. Jon, I guess, the band—you know, an arrangement idea— and I'm pretty harsh with the stuff myself. I have a feeling when I'm doing my best. Which is why we take a long time doing the records, 'cos a lot of times, I don't think I'm doing my best [*laughs*].

Do you enjoy making records now?
Oh yeah. It's a different job. It's not the same job as performing. They're really two different jobs entirely, with very little to do with each other, which is why you have people who make really good records and don't perform well, and people who perform well and don't make good records. I don't think they're really connected. I like it because it forces you to come up with good ideas, and expand the area that you're working in. What happens to those people now? What happens to your characters? What happens to *you*? It's reflective in that sense—at once it's reflective, and it's also forward looking. That's a good thing. We'll get off the road, which is a very physical experience, very tied in to the moment, not particularly reflective. Then you get off, and you do a record that is more of a . . . it's not quite as immediate, you can expand a little bit I guess.

You've got a nice house now, a pool. Is there danger of cutting yourself off?
I feel that the night you look into your audience, and you don't see yourself, and the night the audience looks at you, and they don't see themselves, that's when it's all over, you know? I think to do it really well, and to do it right, you've got to be down in there in some fashion. I don't feel it's a thing about where you live, or if you're rich or if you're poor, or what your particular politics are. I feel that you have to have that emotional connection, to the people that you're singing to, and about, I don't feel that people "sold out." I don't think Elvis sold out when he lived in Graceland—people never sold out by *buying* something, it wasn't ever something they bought. It was something they *thought* that changed . . . My audience, I always hoped, would be all sorts of people, rich, and poor, middle class people. I don't feel like I'm singing to any one group of people. I don't want to put up those sort of walls—that's not really what our band is about.

I don't live that much differently than I did, I still live in New Jersey, I still go down and play in the clubs, still see people that I always saw.

In that sense it hasn't changed that much. I got a nice house, I got a couple different cars, but for the most part, those things, if they're not distractions . . . The main thing, the things that always meant the most to me was the performing and the playing, feeling that connection, feeling I was right down in there. To me, that's the important thing, maintaining that connection, and how people lose that I'm not exactly sure. Maybe it's your values changing . . . I was never much of a cynic myself. We just come out, play as hard as we can, the best we can every night, *all* night!

AFTER THE SHOW, after the interview, with one mighty bound Springsteen was free! It was long gone midnight. The auditorium was empty, Hartford was quieter than a broken amplifier. The wind rattled the trees giving the first hint of autumn. The chance of a meal at the hotel was as unlikely as a Reagan insight. It meant a solitary walk through those mean streets (down which, of course, a man must walk alone). In the distance, the yellow light of the diner shone like a beacon. Lines from songs floated like fallen leaves. Dodging between the trees, a stocky figure hove into view; it was all so like a line from one of his songs (so *this* is what he does after a show!) "Hey Roger, how ya doing'?" "Fine, Bruce, how are you?" "Good. Good. Gonna eat?"

A sandwich shared, coffee drunk, like figures in an Edward Hopper painting, like soldiers on a winter's night . . . Somewhere over New England, dawn was breaking. Springsteen shivered, "Time to be movin' on." In the best outlaw tradition, he walked off into the night—alone. The fans had long gone, now wrapped in each other's arms, coiled in memory. For once, they had all been together. The man responsible for creating that community, responsible for creating the vinyl memories they would share until the next time, walked off into the bitter pre-dawn wind . . . So what *can* a poor boy do, 'cept sing for a rock 'n' roll band?

Chet Flippo
Musician,
November 1984

With Bruce Mania well under way, *Born in the U.S.A.* having burst out
of the gate in June and riding the top of the charts in July, *Musician* provides another in-depth talk with Springsteen, who describes his intent: "I wanted the record to feel like what life felt like. You know, not
romantic and not some sort of big heroic thing. I just wanted to feel like
an everyday, "Darlington County" kind of thing . . . Wanted to make it
feel like you meet somebody. The *Nebraska* stuff was like that: you
meet somebody and you walk a little while in their shoes and see what
their life is like. And then what does that mean to you?" Much of the
interview is spent talking about his songwriting, including its increasingly adult bent. In discussing both *Nebraska* and his new #1 album,
Bruce spoke about making his characters "grow up": "You got to.
Everybody has to. It was something I wanted to do right after *Born to
Run.* I was thinking about it then. I said, Well, how old am I? I'm this old,
so I wanna address that in some fashion. Address it as it is and I didn't
see that that was done a whole lot [in rock lyrics]."

In a year when both political parties are fighting to see which can most reclaim the American flag and its attendant values as its own, how odd to see a rock 'n' roller predate them. Bruce Springsteen, as evidenced by *Born in the U.S.A.*'s introspective, even homey slice of American-life sagas has created a curious but very real rock audience that might unknowingly have more in common with Cotton Mather than with Judas Priest, with Woody Guthrie than with Prince. Springsteen's shows, his music and his attitudes share with his audiences a sort of New Puritanism, a sense of a quasi-religious manifest destiny, and a fundamentalist acceptance of life and its troubles, along with the faith that true belief will bring a better way. When Springsteen ends his shows with a cry to "let freedom ring—that's what we're here for, even if we have to fight for it every day" there are no scoffers in his rock 'n' roll flock, only true believers.

Springsteen has the power and the touch. In many ways, he resembles the television evangelists riding the crest of a rebirth of religious fervor in this country. Unlike Jerry Falwell, though, Springsteen's message is that true salvation lies in a rock 'n' roll way of life. Articulating that was not easy; it seems to be an intuitive way of knowledge. How unusual it is to hear 20,000 rock fans cheer a performer's rap on why you should love your street and your hometown and your state and your country. Bruce talks more about family values than Reagan does. Yet none of this suggests jingoism so much as a pure yearning for a return to solid values. Of course any value is better than no value, as demagogues and hucksters have always known. Any shyster can flourish in a moral vacuum, and in the past rock 'n' roll has never gotten gold medals for presenting either wholesome role models or messages to young people. So what is *this* all about?

Part of Bruce Springsteen's current level of success must be attributed to his talent as an entertainer, and the absence of any real hard-edged competition. Even so, the oft-hesitant *New York Times* has flatly proclaimed Springsteen the "best rock performer ever." And there is no denying the fanatical intensity he brings to a show, the evangelical zeal of the true believer. Springsteen is the hardest-working white man in show business. His appeal transcends traditional rock 'n' roll parameters, though. He's selling something unique among rock superstars: a self-evident faith. And in the performance, he manages to project a R&R greatest hits collage: a bit of Buddy Holly's innocence, some of the dark sensuality of Elvis, a bit of Bob Seger's blue collar integrity, and the exuberance and abandon of a Mitch Ryder.

That charisma is as strong offstage. I caught up with Springsteen at shows in Detroit and New Jersey and found the backstage atmosphere unusual for rock. No hysteria of any sort, no cocker-spaniel bed-wetting exuberance. The feeling was rather like being in a busy ant colony at work. (The parallel to the Crusades shall go unmentioned.) People around Bruce don't want reflected glamour so much as approval. The Springsteen work ethic is clearly palpable. MTV may offer its viewers a lost weekend with Van Halen—for Bruce, it's the chance to be a roadie.

Bruce does not behave like a star either. When he met me in his dressing room in Detroit after a show, his manner was that of an accomplice, a confidant, a comrade. For someone who seldom grants interviews, he was forthright, to the point, and funny. When I told him that he finally had a big enough constituency to either run for the Senate or start his own church, he laughed it off: "Naw, Clarence is gonna do that." That breezy Jersey Shore camaraderie does not disguise a manner that is so simple and direct that it's almost misleading. This is a man who clearly has thought out his position in the scheme of things and has some things to say about it.

Aren't you offering uplifting rock 'n' roll? Isn't there a moral lesson involved with all that you do?
Yeah, I guess. The one thing that bothered me about the *Born to Run* record was that when it was initially criticized people thought it was a record about escape. To me, there was an aspect of that, but I always felt it was more about searching. After that, that's what I tried with *Darkness on the Edge of Town* and *The River* and *Nebraska*. It was like: How real are these things in people's everyday lives? How important are they? I don't know exactly what I'd call it, but I know that most of my records after *Born to Run* were somehow a reaction to the *Born to Run* album. To my own experience of it, which was really wild, it was really a big moment in my life. Now, "Born to Run," the song, means a lot more to me than it did then. I can sing it tonight and feel like it breathes in all those extra years. It's been, like—I wrote it ten years ago now. But it still feels really real. Very real, for me. It's one of the most emotional moments of the night. I can see all of those people and that song to them is like—that's their song, man. It's almost as much the

audience's as it is mine. I like it when the lights are up because you can see so much from people's faces. That's what it's about. But I like doing the old songs now, because I really feel they let the years in, they don't feel limiting. Like, I hear part of *Nebraska* in "Born to Run" now.

Is *Born in the U.S.A.* primarily about, as it suggests, blue-collar patriotic values and rock 'n' roll realism?
That was the direction I was going in. It was kind of hard to get there because I was just learning the importance of certain types of detail, which I began to get a handle on, I think, in *Darkness on the Edge of Town*. And "Stolen Car" and "Wreck on the Highway," which was kind of country-music-influenced stuff. I wanted the record to feel like what life felt like. You know, not romantic and not some sort of big heroic thing. Like in "Glory Days," it sounds like you're just talking to somebody; that's what I wanted to do. Wanted to make it feel like you meet somebody. The *Nebraska* stuff was like that: you meet somebody and you walk a little while in their shoes and see what their life is like. And then what does that mean to you? That's kind of the direction my writing's going in and in general it's just the thing I end up finding most satisfying. Just saying what somebody had to say and not making a big deal out of it.

Do you feel that you have real, believable characters now that people your songs?
That's the hardest thing to do, the very hardest. When I wrote the *Nebraska* stuff, there were songs that I really didn't get, because I didn't get the people. I had all the detail, but if you don't have that underlying emotional connection that connects the details together, then you don't have anything. There were songs that didn't get onto *Nebraska* because they didn't say anything in the end. They had no meaning. That's the trickiest thing to do and that was my only test of songs: is this believable? Is this real? Do I know this person? I was real lucky because I wrote almost all the *Nebraska* songs in about two months. Which is really fast for me. I just locked in and it was really different for me. I stayed in my house. I just worked all the time. Sat at a table or with the guitar. It was exciting because I realized that this was different from stuff I'd done before and I didn't know what it was. But with songs like "Highway Patrolman" and the "Nebraska" song itself, writing like that, I was real happy with it. It just felt real. I didn't know I was gonna do that, but I knew I was going somewhere in that direction.

Are those songs a reaction to what is happening in America? To American values?

I don't know. I think that what happened during the '70s was that, first of all, the hustle became legitimized. First through Watergate. That was a real hurting thing, in that the cheater, the hustler, the dope pusher on the street—that was legitimization for him. It was: you can do it, just don't get caught. Someone will ask, what did you do wrong? And you'll say, I got caught. In a funny kind of way, *Born to Run* was a spiritual record in dealing with values. And then *Nebraska* was about the breakdown of all those values, of all those things. It was kind of about a spiritual crisis, in which man is left lost. It's like he has nothing left to tie him into society anymore. He's isolated from the government. Isolated from his job. Isolated from his family. And, in something like "Highway Patrolman," isolated from his friends. That's what the record is all about. That happens in this country, don't you see, all the time. You see it on the news. And it seems to be a part of modern society. I don't know what anybody can do about it. There is a lot of that happening. When you get to the point where nothing makes sense. Where you don't feel connected to your family, where you don't feel any real connection to your friends. You just feel that alone thing, that loneness. That's the beginning of the end. It's like you start existing outside of all those things. So *Born to Run* and *Nebraska* were kind of at opposite poles. I think *Born in the U.S.A.* kind of casts a suspicious eye on a lot of things. That's the idea. These are not the same people anymore and it's not the same situation. These are survivors and I guess that's the bottom line. That's what a lot of those characters are saying in "Glory Days" or "Darlington County" or "Working on the Highway." It certainly is not as innocent anymore. But, like I said, it's ten years down the line now.

So you and your characters are facing adulthood?

That's kind of where I'm at right now. I wanted to make the characters grow up. You got to. Everybody has to. It was something I wanted to do right after *Born to Run*. I was thinking about it then. I said, Well, how old am I? I'm this old, so I wanna address that in some fashion. Address it as it is and I didn't see that that was done a whole lot [in rock lyrics]. To me it seemed like, hey, it's just life, you know. It's nothin' but life. Let's get it in there. I wrote "Racing in the Street" kind of about that. See I love all those Beach Boys songs. I love "Don't Worry, Baby."

If I hear that thing in the right mood, forget it. I go over the edge, you know? But I said: How does it feel for you right now? So I wrote "Racing in the Street" and that felt good. As I get older I write about me, I guess, and what I see happening around me and my family. So that's *Born in the U.S.A. Born to Run* was the beginning of that and it's funny because I always felt that was my birthday album. All of a sudden, *bang!* Something happened, something crystallized and you don't even know what. And now what are you gonna do? That's the big question. You have an audience; you have a relationship with that audience; it's just as real as any relationship with that audience; it's just as real as any relationship you have with your friends. It's funny. I wrote "Born to Run" in 1974 and now it's 1984 and you can kind of see that something happened along the way. That's a good feeling.

How do your rock values apply to your audience? What can you tell them of what you've learned?

I think it's different for every performer. I don't think it's any one thing anymore. You really can't tell people what to hold onto—you can only tell your story. Whether it's to tell it to just one person or to a bunch of people. There's nothing more satisfying to me than coming in and playing really hard . . . and watching people—watching their faces. And then going home and feeling real tired at the end of the day but knowing that something happened. So, I don't know about the question of what rock 'n' roll means to anyone. I think every individual has got to answer that question for themselves at this point. I don't think there ever was anyone with an answer. It's like the difference between Jerry Lee and Elvis. At the time, they were both great. It's just that you've got to take it for what it is and see if you can make something out of it. Some people, they don't even hear it. It just goes over their heads or something. So I don't think you can really generalize.

So, is your music just about girls and cars?

That's what everybody is saying. I always like those reviews. It's funny, because I remember that when I was about 24 and I said, "I don't want to write about girls and cars anymore." Then I realized, "Hey! That's what Chuck Berry wrote about!" So, it wasn't my idea. It was a genre thing. Like detective movies. I used to compare it to spaghetti westerns.

Or morality plays, maybe?
Yeah. It's probably less like that now than it was at one time. But I was always very interested in keeping a continuity in the whole thing. Part of it for me was the John Ford westerns, where I studied how he did it, how he carried it off. And then I got into this writer, William Price Fox, who wrote *Dixiana Moon* and a lot of short stories. He's just great with detail. In "Open All Night" I remember he had some short story that inspired me. I forgot what it was. But I was just interested in maintaining a real line through the thing. If you look just beneath the immediate surface, it's usually right there. So I like the girls and cars idea.

But you consciously write images.
Oh yeah, I always loved the movies. And, after all, music is evocative. That's the beauty of it. Which is also the danger of video. The tools can be great there and obviously it can be used real well. But it can also be used badly because it's an inanimate thing in and of itself. The thing about a good song is it evocative power. What does it evoke in the listener?

A song like "Mansion on the Hill"—it's different to everybody. It's in people's lives, in that sense. That's what I always want my songs to do: to kind of just pan out and be very cinematic. The *Nebraska* record had that cinematic quality, where you get in there and you get the feel of life. Just some of the grit and some of the beauty. I was thinking in a way of *To Kill a Mockingbird*, because in that movie there was a child's eye view. And *Night of the Hunter* also had that—I'm not sure if surrealistic is the right view. But that was poetic when the little girl was running through the woods. I was thinking of scenes like that.

What about your relationship with video, from "Atlantic City" filmed without you in it to "Dancing in the Dark"?
Well, when I did the *Nebraska* record they didn't want it. I really didn't have anything to do with the "Atlantic City" video. The only direction I gave was to say that it should be kind of gritty-looking and it should have no images that matched up to the images in the song. I was really happy with it. I liked the way it came out. "Dancing in the Dark" was Brian DePalma. That was interesting, working with him. I really haven't gotten into video as of yet. We did that one around the time we were

starting the tour and putting together the show. And that is the center of what we do. That has to be right. I look forward to getting into video, to see what can be done with it.

What about reactions to the Blaster Mix of "Dancing in the Dark"?
People kind of get a rigid view of certain things. That mix was an experimental thing initially. I heard one on the radio and I said, "Man, that sounds like fun! Let's do one of those." And so we got it to [producer] Arthur Baker and he was great, he was tremendous. I had a good time with it. He did the whole thing. His overdubs were kind of connected to my songs. He would put something that sounded like a glock [glockenspiel] or a twangy guitar. When I heard it I just thought it was fun. This was kind of wild, man, this guy, he's got an unchained imagination. I thought the stuff was real creative. You've gotta do different things and try stuff. I figured that a lot of people would like it and that the people that didn't like it would get over it. My audience is not that fragile, you know. They can take it. I'm just into seeing some different things. I could easily go out and do just what I did before. But now we're playing outdoors on this tour, which I hadn't done before. And we did the blaster thing and the video thing. I want to learn it myself. I want to just step out and see what works. If something doesn't work and if something does, great. In ten years, I've built up a relationship with my audience.

To the point where they would support a quasi-commercial risk such as *Nebraska*?
Yeah! It was really well-supported by my audience, which was real satisfying and in tune. So, I say, hey let's do some things, get in there. I can't stand in one place. You've got to take some chances.

What about fans' expectations? Especially the assumption that you've inherited the rock 'n' roll crown.
I don't think you can ever think about that. I certainly would never think that. All those people were my heroes at some point or another. I still love Dylan, love the Stones. I kind of look at what I do in a couple of different ways. One is that it's my job and it's something I like doing and I do it the best that I can. Obviously I'm aware of people's expectations and you gotta wrestle with that. But at the same time you gotta say, I write songs and we got a band, and that's who you are, you know?

I don't think you can carry that kind of thing around with you. I just want to do what I can do. At different times, I allowed myself to live under those types of pressures, of expectations.

I think that the audience and the performer must allow each other room to be human and to make mistakes. If not, then they don't deserve each other. That's what I wanted our band to be like. When I'm onstage I always feel, "What would I want to see if I was the guy in the fifth row?" I'm watching it and being up there and doing it all at the same time. I still feel like such a big fan myself of all music.

What happened with Steve Van Zandt?
It was real emotional, him going, and I'll certainly miss him. But he had to. He had written a lot of real good songs; he had something to say and he has for quite a while. And it was time he stepped out and did what he had to do. But I talk to him all the time. Nils [Lofgren] I'd known on and off. Me and Nils auditioned the same night at the Fillmore West in 1969. When the situation came up, I had spent some time with him and knew that he thought and felt about music and rock 'n' roll the way that I did. So that was kind of it. We never auditioned anybody or anything. He really brought an emotional thing to the band. At this point I think that the band is the only thing that counts. It's the emotional commitment you gotta have to get on that stage.

Are you going to vote this year?
I'm not registered yet. I think I am going to register and vote my conscience. I don't know that much about politics. I guess my politics are in my songs, whatever they may be. My basic attitude is people-oriented, you know. Kind of like human politics. I feel that I can do my best by making songs. Make some difference in that way.

You have no perfume or beer companies or anybody sponsoring your tour. Would you ever?
We get approached by corporations. It's just not something that struck me as the thing that I wanted to do. Independence is nice. That's why I started this. For the independence. I'm telling my story out there. I'm not telling somebody else's. I'm saying what I want to say. That's the only thing I'm selling. I had a few small jobs before I started playing, but when I picked up that guitar, that was when I could walk down my own path. That's just the way I like it. It's a lucky feeling, you know,

because how many people get to set their own standards and kind of run their own circus?

You're doing the Rolling Stones' "Street Fighting Man" as an encore. Is that a political statement?
I don't know. I like that one line in the song, "What can a poor boy do but play for a rock 'n' roll band?" It's one of the greatest rock 'n' roll lines of all time. It just seemed right for me to do it. It's just fun. In that spot of the night it just fits in there. It's just so driving, man. After "Born to Run," we got to go up. That's the trick. 'Cause it's hard to find songs for our encore. You gotta go up and then you gotta go up again. It has tremendous chord changes, that song.

Is this another tour that lasts forever?
Well, it's just the way we've always done it. It's partly because the records take a while and by the time we get out, you want to go everyplace. But that was the original idea: this is a traveling band. You gotta bring it to people. Up real close, as close as you can get. That's what I like to do. 'Cause if you want it for yourself, you gotta want it for everybody, 'cause it's all connected. In the end it's all part of the same thing. Which is why Elvis' message was so profound. It reaches everybody, everywhere. Doesn't matter where or what the problems are or what the government is like. It bypasses those things. It's a heart to heart. It's a human thing. That's why they should go out. Somebody comes out, they shout and yell, they have a great night, it's a rock 'n' roll show. It makes a difference, makes them think about something different. If I walk out on stage and I feel it, there's a moment there that can't be recaptured. This is the night that they meet you and you meet them, head on. That chance only comes once. One time. And you gotta take advantage of it. Some nights, like tonight in that Detroit medley, you can hear the scream and that captures the entire night. That's what I came to do. That's all I wanted to say.

James Henke
Rolling Stone,
August 6, 1992

The *Born in the U.S.A.* tour ended in October 1985, and Springsteen felt "Bruced out." In rapid succession he made changes in his life. In 1985 he wed Julianne Phillips, a marriage that lasted only several years. He recorded 1987's *Tunnel of Love* largely on his own, and though he reconvened the E Street Band for touring in 1988, he officially disbanded the group the following year. In 1990 he became a father, and in 1991 he married Patti Scialfa. In 1992, when James Henke, a prominent music critic and later head of exhibitions at the Rock and Roll Hall of Fame, conducted this interview, Springsteen had just released two albums, *Human Touch* and *Lucky Town*. Of his numerous interviews with *Rolling Stone* over the years, this was arguably the most crucial upon its publication, as Bruce discussed breaking up the E Street Band, moving from New Jersey to Los Angeles, and, most revealing, entering therapy: "That was really valuable. I crashed into myself and saw a lot of myself as I really was. And I questioned all my motivations. Why am I writing what I'm writing? Why am I saying what I'm saying? . . . I questioned everything I'd ever done, and it was good."

"In the crystal ball, I see romance, I see adventure, I see financial reward. I see those albums, man I see them going back up the charts. I see them rising past that old Def Leppard, past that Kriss Kross. I see them all the way up past 'Weird Al' Yankovic, even . . . Wait a minute. We're slipping. We're slipping down them charts. We're going down, down, out of sight, into the darkness . . ."

It was June 5th, and as Bruce Springsteen was performing "Glory Days" near the end of a live radio broadcast from a Los Angeles sound stage, he finally offered his commentary on the much-publicized failure of his latest albums—*Human Touch* and *Lucky Town*—to dominate the charts in the same way that some of their predecessors had. Thankfully, Springsteen demonstrated that while he may have lost a little of his commercial clout, he hasn't lost his sense of humor.

The show, in front of about 250 invited guests and radio contest winners, was a "dress rehearsal" meant to introduce his new band— keyboardist Roy Bittan, guitarist Shane Fontayne, bassist Tommy Sims, drummer Zachary Alford, singer-guitarist Crystal Taliefero and vocalists Bobby King, Gia Ciambotti, Carol Dennis, Cleo Kennedy and Angel Rogers—and to stir up excitement for his summer tour of the States. He succeeded on both counts. The concert proved that even without the E Street Band, Springsteen is still a masterful performer; in fact, his new band rocks harder, and musically it challenges him more than his previous group. And he still has more than a few loyal fans: The day after the radio broadcast, he sold out eleven shows at New Jersey's Brendan Byrne Arena (more than 200,000 tickets) in just two and a half hours.

Even so, it has been an unusually trying season for Springsteen. Though *Human Touch* and *Lucky Town* entered the charts at Numbers Two and Three, respectively, they quickly slipped and eventually dropped out of the Top Forty. On top of that, some segments of the media seemed to be reaping pleasure from Springsteen's relative lack of success (and indeed, it is relative: Each of the albums has sold more than 1.5 million copies). One magazine, *Entertainment Weekly*, even put Springsteen on its cover with the headline WHAT EVER HAPPENED TO BRUCE?

But things could be worse, as Springsteen well knows. For the past several years, he has been waging a far tougher battle—trying to repair what had become a badly damaged personal life. "I was real *good* at music," he says, "and real *bad* at everything else."

Onstage, of course, Springsteen could do it all; offstage, it was a different story. Something of a loner by nature, he had difficulty maintaining any kind of long-term relationship. Even as he was preaching about "community" during his *Born in the U.S.A.* tour, he himself was keeping his distance from just about everyone. And when he wasn't working, he wasn't happy.

When he hit the road in 1988 to support his *Tunnel of Love* album, the cracks in Springsteen's personal life were beginning to show. His marriage to actress Julianne Phillips had begun to deteriorate, and thanks to the tabloids, it soon became public knowledge that he was seeing E Street Band singer Patti Scialfa. When he got off the road in late 1988 after playing a series of shows for Amnesty International, Springsteen hit rock bottom.

Gradually, he began to regain control of his life. He went into therapy. He got divorced from Phillips and eventually married Scialfa. He parted ways with the E Street Band. He left New Jersey and moved to Los Angeles. And with Scialfa, he fathered two children: Evan James, who's almost two, and Jessica Rae, who was born last New Year's Eve.

Springsteen's personal trials are documented on *Human Touch*; his victory over those trials is the subject of *Lucky Town*. The jury is still out on whether his U.S. tour, which kicks off on July 23rd in New Jersey, will resuscitate those albums. But there's no question that Springsteen himself is the happiest he's been in a long time. Over the course of three lengthy interviews in Los Angeles and New York—the first in-depth interviews he's done since 1986—he outlined in great detail what he calls "the biggest struggle of my life," and he addressed a variety of other subjects, ranging from rap music to the presidential race.

The music scene has changed a lot since you last released an album. Where do you see yourself fitting in these days?
I never kind of fit in, in a funny kind of way. In the '70s the music I wrote was sort of romantic, and there was lots of innocence in it, and it certainly didn't feel like it was a part of that particular time. And in the '80s, I was writing and singing about what I felt was happening to the people I was seeing around me or what direction I saw the country going in. and that really wasn't in step with the times, either.

Well, given the response to your music then, I think you fit in pretty well during the '80s.
Well, we were *popular*, but that's not the same thing. All I try to do is to write music that feels meaningful to me, that has commitment and

passion behind it. And I guess I feel that if what I'm writing about is real, and if there's emotion, then hey, there'll be somebody who wants to hear it. I don't know if it's a big audience or a smaller audience than I've had. But that's never been my primary interest. I've had a kind of story I've been telling, and I'm really only in the middle of it.

At the same time, your new albums haven't fared as well on the charts as most people expected, and you've had to endure some sniping from the media. How do you feel about that?
I try not to get involved in it. It does seem to be out there in the air, for everybody and anybody, but I don't take it that personally. I mean, if you spend any time in Los Angeles, you see that a lot: "Great, you're a tremendous success—now *fail!*"

There's a media game that's played out there, and I guess it sells newspapers and magazines. But it's not central to who I am or what I do. You make your music, then you try to find whatever audience is out there for it.

Do you think that a teenager who's into rap or heavy metal would be interested in your new albums?
I don't know. And I don't know if you can generalize like that. I think some yes and some no. All I can do is put my music out there. I can't contrive something that doesn't feel honest. I don't write demographically. I don't write a song to reach these people or those people.

Of course, I'm interested in having a young audience. I'm interested in whoever's interested in what I'm doing. And what I have to say is "This is how I've grown up. Maybe this will have some value. These are the places I've been, and these are the things I've learned."

But I want to sing about who I am now. I want to get up onstage and sing with all of the 42 years that are in me. When I was young, I always said I didn't want to end up being 45 or 50 and pretending I was 15 or 16 or 20. That just didn't interest me. I'm a lifetime musician; I'm going to be playing music forever. I don't foresee a time when I would not be onstage somewhere, playing a guitar and playing it loud, with power and passion. I look forward to being 60 or 65 and doing that.

For the first time in about twenty years you're embarking on a tour without the E Street Band. What led to your decision to get rid of them?
At the end of the *Born in the U.S.A.* tour and after we made the live album, I felt like it was the end of the first part of my journey. And then, for the *Tunnel of Love* tour, I switched the band around quite a bit. I switched where people had stood for fifteen years, just trying to give it a different twist.

But you can get to a place where you start to replay the ritual, and nostalgia creeps in, and I decided it was time to mix it up. I just had to cut it loose a bit so I could have something new to bring to the table. I wanted to get rid of some of the old expectations. People were coming to my shows expecting to hear "Born to Run" or stuff that I wrote fifteen or twenty years ago. And I wanted to get to a spot where if people came to the show, there'd be a feeling of like, well, it's not going to be this, it's going to be something else.

Did you call each of the guys to give them the news?
Oh, sure, yeah. Initially, some people were surprised, some people were not so surprised. I'm sure some people were angry, and other people weren't angry. But as time passed, everything came around to a really nice place. I mean, I wasn't the guy writing the check every month. Suddenly, I was just Bruce, and some of the friendships started coming forward a little bit. And it was interesting, because we hadn't had that kind of relationship. We had all been working together for so long that we didn't really have a relationship outside of the work environment.

You mentioned the *Born in the U.S.A.* tour as marking the end of one phase of your career. How did the enormousness of that album and tour affect your life?
I really enjoyed the success of *Born in the U.S.A.*, but by the end of that whole thing, I just kind of felt "Bruced" out. I was like "Whoa, enough of that." You end up creating this sort of icon, and eventually it oppresses you.

What specifically are you referring to?
Well, for example, the whole image that had been created—and that I'm sure I promoted—it really always felt like "Hey, that's not me." I

mean, the macho thing, that was just never me. It might be a little more of me than I think, but when I was a kid, I was a real gentle child, and I was more in touch with those sorts of things.

It's funny, you know, what you create, but in the end, I think, the only thing you can do is destroy it. So when I wrote *Tunnel of Love*, I thought I had to reintroduce myself as a songwriter, in a very noniconic role. And it was a relief. And then I got to a place where I had to sit some more of that stuff down, and part of it was coming out here to L.A. and making some music with some different people and seeing what that's about and living in a different place for a while.

How's it been out here, compared with New Jersey?
Los Angeles provides a lot of anonymity. You're not like the big fish in the small pond. People wave to you and say hi, but you're pretty much left to go your own way. Me in New Jersey, on the other hand, was like Santa Claus at the North Pole [*laughs*].

What do you mean?
Hmm, how can I put it? It's like you're a bit of a figment of a lot of other people's imaginations. And that always takes some sorting out. But it's even worse when you see yourself as a figment of your own imagination. And in the last three or four years, that's something I've really freed myself from.

I think what happened was that when I was young, I had this idea of playing out my life like it was some movie, writing the script and making all the pieces fit. And I really did that for a long time. But you can get enslaved by your own myth or your own image, for the lack of a better word. And it's bad enough having other people seeing you that way, but seeing yourself that way is really bad. It's pathetic. And I got to a place, when Patti and I hooked up, where I said I got to stop writing this story. It doesn't work.

And that's when I realized I needed a change, and I like the West. I like the geography. Los Angeles is a funny city. Thirty minutes and you're in the mountains, where for 100 miles there's one store. Or you're in the desert, where for 500 miles there's five towns.

So Patti and I came out here and put the house together and had the babies and . . . the thing is, I'd really missed a big part of my life. The only way I could describe it is that being successful in one area is illusory. People think because you're so good at one particular thing, you're good at many things. And that's almost always not the case. You're good at that particular thing, and the danger is that that particular thing allows you the indulgence to remove yourself from the rest of your life. And as time passed, I realized that I was using my job well in many ways, but there was a fashion in which I was also abusing it. And—this began in my early thirties—I really knew that something was wrong.

That was about ten years ago?
Yeah, it started after I got back from the *River* tour. I'd had more success than I'd ever thought I'd have. We'd played around the world and I thought, like, "Wow, this is it." And I decided, "Okay, I want to have a house." And I started to look for a house.

I looked for two years. Couldn't find one. I've probably been in every house in the state of New Jersey—twice. Never bought a house. Figured I just couldn't find one that I liked. And then I realized that it ain't that I can't *find* one, I couldn't *buy* one. I can find one, but I can't buy one. Damn! *Why is that?*

And I stared to pursue why that was. Why did I only feel good on the road? Why were all my characters in my songs in cars? I mean, when I was in my early twenties, I was always sort of like "Hey, what I can put in this suitcase, that guitar case, that bus—that's all I need, now and forever." And I really believed it. And really lived it. Lived it for a long time.

In a *Rolling Stone* cover story from 1978, Dave Marsh wrote that you were so devoted to music that it was impossible to imagine you being married or having kids or a house . . .
A lot of people have said that same thing. But then something started ticking. It didn't feel right. It was depressing. It was like "This is a joke. I've come a long way, and there's some dark joke here at the end."

I didn't want to be one of those guys who can write music and tell stories and have an effect on people's lives, and maybe on society in some fashion, but not be able to get into his own self. But that was pretty much my story.

I tend to be an isolationist by nature. And it's not about money or where you live or how you live. It's about psychology. My dad was certainly the same way. You don't need a ton of dough and walls around your house to be isolated. I know plenty of people who are isolated with a six-pack of beer and a television set. But that was a big part of my nature.

Then music came along, and I latched onto it as a way to combat that part of myself. It was a way that I could talk to people. It provided me with a means of communication, a means of placing myself in a social context—which I had a tendency not to want to do.

And music did those things but in an abstract fashion, ultimately. It did them for the guy with the guitar, but the guy without the guitar was pretty much the same as he had been.

Now I see that two of the best days of my life were the day I picked up the guitar and the day that I learned how to put it down. Somebody said, "Man, how did you play for so long?" I said: "That's the easy part. It's the stopping that's hard."

When did you learn to put the guitar down?

Pretty recently. I had locked into what was pretty much a hectic obsession, which gave me enormous focus and energy and fire to burn, because it was coming out of pure fear and self-loathing and self-hatred. I'd get onstage and it was hard for me to stop. That's why my shows were so long. They weren't long because I had an idea or a plan that they should be that long. I couldn't stop until I felt burnt, period. Thoroughly burnt.

It's funny, because the results of the show or the music might have been positive for other people, but there was an element of it that was abusive for me. Basically, it was my drug. And so I started to follow the thread of weaning myself.

For a long time, I had been able to ignore it. When you're 19 and you're in a truck and you're crossing the country back and forth, and then you're 25 and you're on tour with the band—that just fit my personality completely. That's why I was able to be good at it. But then I reached an age where I began to miss my real life—or to even know that there was another life to be lived. I mean, it was almost a surprise. First you think you are living it. You got a variety of different girlfriends, and then, "Gee, sorry, gotta go now." It was like the Groucho Marx routine—it's funny, 'cause it runs in my family a little bit, and we get into this: "Hello, I came to say I'd like to stay, but I really must be going." And that was me.

What was it that woke you up to the fact that you were missing something or had a problem?

Unhappiness. And other things, like my relationships. They always ended poorly; I didn't really know how to have a relationship with a woman. Also, I wondered how can I have this much money and not spend it? Up until the '80s, I really didn't have any money. When we started the *River* tour, I had about twenty grand, I think. So, really, around 1983 was the first time I had some money in the bank. But I couldn't spend it, I couldn't have any fun. So a lot of things started to not feel logical. I realized there was some aberrational behavior going on here. And I didn't feel that good. Once out of the touring context, and out of the context of my work, I felt lost.

Did you ever go to a therapist or seek help like that?
Oh, yeah. I mean, I got really down. Really bad off for a while. And what happened was, all my rock & roll answers had fizzled out. I realized that my central idea—which, at a young age, was attacking music with a really religious type of intensity—was okay to a point. But there was a point where it turns in on itself. And you start to go down that dark path, and there is a distortion of even the best of things. And I reached a point where I felt my life was distorted. I love my music, and I wanted to just take it for what it was. I didn't want to try to distort it into being my entire life. Because that's a lie. It's not true. It's not your entire life. It never can be.

And I realized my real life is waiting to be lived. All the love and the hope and the sorrow and sadness—that's all over there, waiting to be lived. And I could ignore it and push it aside or I could say yes to it. But to say yes to part of it is to say yes to all of it. That's why people say no to all of it. Whether it's drugs or whatever. That's why people say no: I'll skip the happiness as long as I don't have to feel the pain.

So I decided to work on it. I worked hard on it. And basically, you have to start to open up to who you are. I certainly wasn't the person I thought I was. This was around the time of *Born in the U.S.A.* And I bought this big house in New Jersey, which was really quite a thing for me to do. It was a place I used to run by all the time. It was a big house, and I said, "Hey, this is a rich man's house." And I think the toughest thing was that it was in a town where I'd been spit on when I was a kid.

This was in Rumson?
Yeah. When I was 16 or 17 my band, from Freehold, was booked in a beach club. And we engendered some real hostile reaction. I guess we looked kind of—we had on phony snakeskin vests and had long hair.

There's a picture of me in the Castiles, that's what it was. And I can remember being onstage, with guys literally spitting on it. This was before it was fashionable, when it kind of meant what it really meant.

So it was a funny decision, but I bought this house, and at first I really began to enjoy it, but then along came the *Born in the U.S.A.* tour, and I was off down the road again. I had a good time, and I began to try to figure out things. I was trying to find out how to make some of these connections, but once again it was sort of abstract, like how to integrate the band into some idea of community in the places we passed through.

It was during this time that you met Julianne?
Yeah, we met about halfway through that tour. And we got married. And it was tough. I didn't really know how to be a husband. She was a terrific person, but I just didn't know how to do it.

Was the marriage part of your whole effort to make connections, to deal with that part of your life?
Yeah, yeah. I really needed something, and I was giving it a shot. Anybody who's been through a divorce can tell you what that's about. It's difficult, hard, and painful for everybody involved. But I sort of went on.

Then Patti and I got together, on the *Tunnel of Love* tour, and I began to find my way around again. But after we came off the road in 1988, I had a bad year right away. I got home, and I wasn't very helpful to anyone.

You were still living in Rumson?
Yeah, and then we lived in New York for a while. That wasn't for me, on account of growing up in a small town and being used to having cars and all that stuff.

I'd made a lot of plans, but when we got home, I just kind of spun off for a while. I just got lost. That lasted for about a year.

What kinds of things did you do?
The best way I can say it is that I wasn't doing what I said I was going to do. Somewhere between realization and actualization, I slipped in between the cracks. I was in a lot of fear. And I was just holding out. I

made life generally unpleasant. And so at some point Patti and I just said, "Hell, let's go out to L.A."

I've always felt a little lighter out here. I've had a house in the Hollywood Hills since the early '80s, and I'd come out here three, four months out of the year. I always remember feeling just a little lighter, like I was carrying less. So Patti and I came out here, and things started to get better. And then the baby came along, and that was fantastic. That was just the greatest thing.

Had you wanted to have a baby in the past?
I know there were a lot of things in the paper about Juli and me and that the issue of having a baby was what caused us to break up. Well, that just wasn't true. That's a lie.

But it was something you wanted to do—have a family—or was it something you were afraid of?
Well, yeah [*pause*], I was *afraid*. But I was afraid of this whole thing. That's what this was about. I had made my music everything. I was real *good* at music and real *bad* at everything else.

Was Patti the person who really helped you get through all of this?
Yeah. She had a very sure eye for all of my bullshit. She recognized it. She was able to call me on it. I had become a master manipulator. You know, "Oh, I'm going out of the house for a little while, and I'm going down . . ." I always had a way of moving off, moving away, moving back and creating distance. I avoided closeness, and I wouldn't lay my cards on the table. I had many ways of doing that particular dance, and I thought they were pretty sophisticated. But maybe they weren't. I was just doing what came naturally. And then when I hit the stage, it was just the opposite. I would throw myself forward, but it was okay because it was brief. Hey, that's why they call them one-night stands. It's like you're there, then *bang!* You're gone. I went out in '85 and talked a lot about community, but I wasn't a part of any community.

So when I got back to New York after the Amnesty tour in '88, I was kind of wandering and lost, and it was Patti's patience and her understanding that got me through. She's a real friend, and we have a real great friendship. And finally I said I've got to start dealing with this, I've got to take some baby steps.

What were some of those baby steps?
The best thing I did was I got into therapy. That was really valuable. I crashed into myself and saw a lot of myself as I really was. And I questioned all my motivations. Why am I writing what I'm writing? Why am I saying what I'm saying? Do I mean it? Am I bullshitting? Am I just trying to be the most popular guy in town? Do I need to be liked that much? I questioned everything I'd ever done, and it was good. You should do that. And then you realize there is no single motivation to anything. You're doing it for all those reasons.

So I went through a real intense period of self-examination. I knew I had to sit in my room for eight hours a day with a guitar to learn how to play it, and now I had to put in that kind of time just to find my place again.

Were you writing any songs during that period?
At first, I had nothing to say. Throughout '88 and '89, every time I sat down to write, I was just sort of rehashing. I didn't have a new song to sing, I just ended up rehashing *Tunnel of Love*, except not as good. And it was all just down and nihilistic. It's funny, because I think people probably associate my music with a lot of positives. But it's like I really drift into that other thing—I think there's been a lot of desperate fun in my songs.

Then I remembered that Roy [Bittan] had some tracks that he'd play to me on occasion. So I called him and said, "Come on over, maybe I'll try to write to some of your tracks." So he had the music to "Roll of the Dice," and I came up with the idea for that, and I went home and wrote the song. It was really about what I was trying to do: I was trying to get up the nerve to take a chance.

And then Roy and I started working together pretty steadily. I had a little studio in my garage, and I came up with "Real World." What I started to do were little writing exercises. I tried to write something that was soul oriented. Or I'd play around with existing pop structures. And that's kind of how I did the *Human Touch* record. A lot of it is generic, in a certain sense.

We worked for about a year, and at the end I tried to put it together. Some albums come out full-blown: *Tunnel of Love*, *Nebraska*, *Lucky Town*—they just came out all at once. *Human Touch* was definitely something that I struggled to put together. It was like a job. I'd work at it every day. But at the end, I felt like it was good, but it was about me trying to get to a place. It sort of chronicled the post–*Tunnel of Love* period. So when we finished it, I just sat on it for a couple of months.

Then I wrote the song "Living Proof," and when I wrote that, I said: "Yeah, that's what I'm trying to say. That's how I feel." And that was a big moment, because I landed hard in the present, and that was where I wanted to be. I'd spent a lot of my life writing about my past, real and imagined, in some fashion. But with *Lucky Town*, I felt like that's where I am. This is who I am. This is what I have to say. These are the stories I have to tell. This is what's important in my life right now. And I wrote and recorded the whole record in three weeks in my house.

Did you ever think about not releasing *Human Touch*?
Yeah, except that every time I listened to it, I liked it. Also, I wanted to put out a lot of music, because I didn't want to be dependent on my old songs when I went out to tour. I wanted to have a good body of work to draw from when I hit the stage.

And then I realized that the two albums together kind of tell one story. There's *Tunnel of Love*, then there's what happened in between, which is *Human Touch*, then there's *Lucky Town*. And basically I said: Well, hey—Guns n' Roses! They put out two albums, maybe I'll try it!

There's a perception out there—and a couple of the reviews of the albums mentioned it—that you've sealed yourself off from reality, living in a big house in L.A. and so forth. Yet based on what you're saying, I assume you'd say the truth is quite the opposite.
Those are the clichés, and people have come to buy the clichés in rock music. You know, like it's somehow much more acceptable to be addicted to heroin than to, say, hang out with jet-setters. But you know, it's the old story. People don't know what you're doing unless they're walking in your shoes a bit.

Some of your fans seem to think along the same lines, that by moving to L.A. and buying a $14 million house, you've let them down or betrayed them.
I kept my promises. I didn't get burned out. I didn't waste myself. I didn't die. I didn't throw away my musical values. Hey, I've dug in my heels on all those things. And my music has been, for the most part, a positive, liberating, living, uplifting thing. And along the way I've made a lot of money, and I bought a big house. And I love it. Love it. It's

great. It's beautiful, really beautiful. And in some ways, it's my first real home. I have pictures of my family there. And there's a place where I make music, and a place for babies, and it's like a dream.

I still love New Jersey. We go back all the time. I've been looking at a farm there that I might buy. I'd like my kids to have that, too. But I came out here, and I just felt like the guy who was born in the U.S.A. had left the bandanna behind, you know?

I've struggled with a lot of things over the past two, three years, and it's been real rewarding. I've been very, very happy, truly the happiest I've ever been in my whole life. And it's not that one-dimensional idea of "happy." It's accepting a lot of death and sorrow and mortality. It's putting the script down and letting the chips fall where they may.

What's been the toughest thing about being a father?
Engagement. Engagement. Engagement. You're afraid to love something so much, you're afraid to be that in love. Because a world of fear leaps upon you, particularly in the world that we live in. But then you realize: "Oh, I see, to love something so much, as much as I love Patti and my kids, you've got to be able to accept and live with that world of fear, that world of doubt, of the future. And you've got to give it all today and not hold back." And that was my specialty; my specialty was keeping my distance so that if I lost something, it wouldn't hurt that much. And you can do that, but you're never going to have anything.

It's funny, because the night my little boy was born, it was amazing. I've played onstage for hundreds of thousands of people, and I've felt my own spirit really rise some nights. But when he came out, I had this feeling of a kind of love that I hadn't experienced before. And the minute I felt it, it was terrifying. It was like "Wow, I see. This love is here to be had and to be felt and experienced? To everybody, on a daily basis?" And I knew why you run, because it's very frightening. But it's also a window into another world. And it's the world that I want to live in right now.

Has having kids changed the way you look at your own parents?
It was amazing, actually, how much it did change. I'm closer to my folks now, and I think they feel closer to me. My pa, particularly. There must have been something about my own impending fatherhood that made him feel moved to address our relationship. I was kind of surprised; it came out of the blue.

He was never a big verbalizer, and I kind of talked to him through my songs. Not the best way to do that, you know. But I knew he heard them. And then, before Evan was born, we ended up talking about a lot of things I wasn't sure that we'd ever actually address. It was probably one of the nicest gifts of my life. And it made my own impending fatherhood very rich and more resonant. It's funny, because children are very powerful, they affect everything. And the baby wasn't even born yet, but he was affecting the way people felt and the way they spoke to each other, the way they treated each other.

You said the song "Pony Boy" was one that your mother used to sing to you.
My grandmother sang it to me when I was young. I made up a lot of the words for the verses; I'm sure there are real words, but I'm not sure they're the ones I used. It was the song that I used to sing to my little boy when he was still inside of Patti. And when he came out, he knew it. It's funny. And it used to work like magic. He'd be crying, and I'd sing it, and he'd stop on a dime. Amazing.

You and Patti had a big wedding, didn't you?
It wasn't that big, about 80 or 90 people. It was at the house, and it was a great day. You get to say out loud all the things that bring you to that place. I'm now a believer in all the rituals and things. I think they're really valuable. And I know that getting married deepened our relationship. For a long time, I didn't put a lot of faith in those things, but I've come to feel that they are important. Like, I miss going to church. I'd like to, but I don't know where to go. I don't buy into all the dogmatic aspects, but I like the idea of people coming together for some sort of spiritual enrichment or enlightenment or even just to say hi once a week.

The fact that the country is spiritually bankrupt is something you've mentioned in connection with the riots in Los Angeles.
We're kind of reaping what's been sown, in a very sad fashion. I mean, the legacy we're leaving our kids right now is a legacy of dread. That's a big part of what growing up in America is about right now: dread, fear, mistrust, blind hatred. We're being worn down to the point where who you are, what you think, what you believe, where you stand, what you feel in your soul means nothing on a given day. Instead, it's "What do you look like? Where are you from?" That's frightening.

I remember in the early '80s, I went back to the neighborhood where I put together my first band. It was always a mixed neighborhood, and I was with a friend of mine, and we got out of the car and were just walking around for about 20 minutes. And when I got back to the car, there were a bunch of older black men and younger guys, and they got all around the car and said, "What are you doing?" I said, "Well, I lived here for about four or five years," and I just basically said what we were doing there. And they said: "No, what are you doing in our neighborhood? When we go to your neighborhood, we get stopped for just walking down the streets. People want to know what we're doing in *your* neighborhood. So what are you doing in *our* neighborhood?" And it was pretty tense.

The riots broke out right after our second interview session. It was pretty frightening being in L.A. then.
It really felt like the wall was coming down. On Thursday [the day after the riots began], we were down in Hollywood rehearsing, and people were scared. People were really scared. And then you were just, like, sad or angry.

At the end of the '60s, there was a famous commission that Lyndon Johnson put together, and they said it would take a massive, sustained effort by the government and by the people to make life better in the inner cities. And all the things they started back then were dismantled in the last decade. And a lot of brutal signals were sent, which created a real climate for intolerance. And people picked up on it and ran with the ball. The rise of the right and of the radical right-wing groups is not accidental. David Duke—it's embarrassing.

So we've been going backward. And we didn't just come up short in our efforts to do anything about this, we came up bankrupt.

We're selling our future away, and I don't think anybody really believes that whoever is elected in the coming election is going to seriously address the issues in some meaningful fashion.

On the one hand there seems to be a tremendous sense of disillusionment in this country. Yet on the other hand, it seems like George Bush could be reelected.
I think so, too—but not on my vote. People have been flirting with the outside candidates, but that's all I think it is. When they go put their money down, though, it always winds up being with someone in the

mainstream. And the frustrating thing is, you know it's not going to work.

Do any of the candidates appeal to you?
What Jerry Brown is saying is true—all that stuff is true. And I liked Jesse Jackson when he ran last time around. But I guess there hasn't really been anyone who can bring these ideas to life, who can make people believe that there's some other way.

America is a conservative country, it really is. I think that's one thing the past ten years have shown. But I don't know if people are really organized, and I don't think there's a figure out there who's been able to embody the things that are eating away at the soul of the nation at large.

I mean, the political system has really broken down. We've abandoned a gigantic part of the population—we've just left them for dead. But we're gonna have to pay the piper some day. But you worry about the life of your own children, and people live in such a state of dread that it affects the overall spiritual life of the nation as a whole. I mean, I live great, and plenty of people do, but it affects you internally in some fashion, and it just eats away at whatever sort of spirituality you pursue.

Do you see any cause for optimism?
Well, somebody's going to have to address these issues. I don't think they can go unaddressed forever. I believe that the people won't stand for it, ultimately. Maybe we're not at that point yet. But at some point, the cost of not addressing these things is just going to be too high.

A lot of people have pointed out that rappers have addressed a lot of these issues. What kind of music do you listen to?
I like Sir Mix-a-Lot. I like Queen Latifah; I like her a lot. I also like Social Distortion. I think *Somewhere Between Heaven and Hell* is a great record, a great rock & roll album. "Born to Lose" is great stuff. I like Faith No More. I like Live; I think that guy [Edward Kowalczyk] is a really good singer. I like a song on the Peter Case record, "Beyond the Blues." Really good song.

How do you keep up with what's happening musically?
Every three or four months I'll just wander through Tower Records and buy, like, 50 things, and I get in my car and just pop things in and out. I'm a big curiosity buyer. Sometimes I get something just because of the cover. And then I also watch TV. On Sundays, I'll flick on *120 Minutes* and just see who's doing what.

Mike Appel, your former manager, has contributed to a new book [*Down Thunder Road: The Making of Bruce Springsteen*] that essentially claims that your current manager, Jon Landau, stole you out from under him.
Well, that's a shame, you know, because what happened was Mike and I had kind of reached a place where our relationship had kind of bumped up against its limitations. We were a dead-end street. And Jon came in, and he had a pretty sophisticated point of view, and he had an idea how to solve some very fundamental problems, like how to record and where to record.

   But Mike kind of turned Jon into this monster, maybe as a way of not turning me into one. It's a classic thing: Who wants to blame themselves for something that went wrong? Nobody does. It's tough to say, "Maybe I fucked it up." But the truth is, if it hadn't been Jon, it would have been somebody else—or nobody else, but I would have gone my own way. Jon didn't say, "Hey, let's do what I want to do." He said, "I'm here to help you do what you're going to do." And that's what he's done since the day we met.

Two other people who used to work with you, ex-roadies, sued a few years ago, charging that you hadn't paid them overtime, among other things. What was your reaction to that?
It was disappointing. I worked with these two people for a long time, and I thought I'd really done the right thing. And when they left, it was handshakes and hugs all around, you know. And then about a year later, *bang!*

   I think that if you asked the majority of people who had worked with me how they felt about the experience, they'd say they'd been treated really well. But it only takes one disgruntled or unhappy person, and that's what everyone wants to hear; the drum starts getting beat. But outside of all that—the bullshit aspect of it—if you spend a long time with someone and there's a very fundamental misunderstanding, well, you feel bad about it.

You recently appeared on *Saturday Night Live*. It was the first time you ever performed on TV. How did you like it?
It felt very intense. You rehearse two or three times before you go on, but when we actually did it, it was like "Okay, you've got three new songs, you got to give it up." It was different, but I really enjoyed it. I mean, I must not have been on TV for all this time for some reason, but now that I've done it, it's like "Gee, why didn't I do this before?" There must have been some reason. And I certainly think that I'm going to begin using television more in some fashion. I think it's in the cards for me at this point, to find a way to reach people who might be interested in what I'm saying, what I'm singing about.

I believe in this music as much as anything I've ever written. I think it's the real deal. I feel like I'm at the peak of my creative powers right now. I think that in my work I'm presenting a complexity of ideas that I've been struggling to get to in the past. And it took me ten years of hard work outside of the music to get to this place. Real hard work. But when I got here, I didn't find bitterness and disillusionment. I found friendship and hope and faith in myself and a sense of purpose and passion. And it feels good. I feel like that great Sam and Dave song, "Born Again." I feel like a new man.

Neil Strauss
Guitar World,
October 1995

Critic Neil Strauss catches Springsteen in the aftermath of the phe-
nomenal success of his single "Streets of Philadelphia" and his first
reunion with the E Street Band to record several new songs for a
Greatest Hits album. In retrospect, that January '95 studio session
was a turning point for Springsteen's career as the new century approached; here, Springsteen lays out a vision for the future that would
prove accurate: "I don't think I'd want to have to choose between the
band and the solo stuff. I'd like to have both. One of the things I realized when I saw the guys was that we're like each other's arms and
legs."

You can tell a lot about a musician by how he or she arrives at an interview. Some come with a manager, others with a publicist. Some come
with bodyguards, others with a retinue of hangers-on. Bruce Springsteen came to this interview alone. He drove himself from his home in
Rumson, New Jersey, to the Sony Studios in Manhattan in his black
Ford Explorer, and he arrived early. Sitting in solitude with his back to
the door in a darkened conference room, a mass of flannel and denim

and glinting silver-cross earring, he didn't need much prodding to be talked into heading to a nearby bar for drinks and atmosphere.

Springsteen entered the 1990s on shaky ground. He fired his long-time back-up group, the E Street Band, bought a $14 million spread in Beverly Hills, divorced his first wife, model Julianne Phillips, and married a member of his backing band, Patti Scialfa. Since then, his career has been the subject of hot debate. What is his relevance in the Nineties? Does his solo work hold up to his recordings with the E Street Band? Is he losing touch with his audience?

But in the past year, Springsteen ended the debate. He recorded his most successful solo song ever, "Streets of Philadelphia," earning himself a shelf full of Grammys and an Academy Award, and re-formed the E Street Band to record new songs for his *Greatest Hits* album, which debuted at Number One on the charts. On Labor Day weekend, he will perform at the opening ceremony for the Rock and Roll Hall of Fame museum in Cleveland, an institution he will no doubt be inducted into when he is eligible in two years.

In a rough cut of a documentary now being put together from 23 hours of film that were shot while the revived E Street Band was recording the new songs last winter, the reunion seemed like an easy one. Three days after Springsteen called the band, they were in the studio, stretching what was supposed to be a two-day process into one which took a full week. In one scene that doesn't seem created for the camera, the band gives its saxophonist, Clarence Clemons, a cake on his birthday and he gushes, "This is the best present a person could have for his birthday, being among you guys."

The documentary also shows the recording of "Secret Garden," a song that Springsteen originally wrote for his upcoming solo album. Here, he demonstrates the E Street's democratic approach when he hands out torn-up pieces of paper so that the band can anonymously vote for or against the inclusion of string arrangements. (The strings lost.)

Springsteen takes his interviews as seriously as he takes his music. During the two-hour discussion, he stared intently across the table, face still except for battling eyes, body solid and immobile except for constantly fidgeting hands, and set about answering each question as meaningfully as he could. Giving the waitress a 200 percent tip for his beer and a shot of tequila, he pulled up a chair at a table next to the jukebox in a dark corner of the bar and began talking.

What does it mean to you to have a "greatest hits" album?
It's interesting because when I started out making music, I wasn't fundamentally interested in having a big hit right away. I was into writing music that was going to thread its way into people's lives. I was interested in becoming a part of people's lives, and having some usefulness—that would be the best word. I would imagine that a lot of people that end up going into the arts or film or music were at some point told by somebody that they were useless. Everyone has felt that. So I know one of the main motivations for me was to try to be useful, and then, of course, there were all those other pop dreams of the Cadillac or the girls. All the stuff that comes with it was there, but sort of on the periphery. In some way I was trying to find a fundamental purpose for my own existence. And basically trying to enter people's lives in that fashion and hopefully maintain that relationship over a lifetime, or at least as long as I felt I had something useful to say. That was why we took so long between records. We made a lot of music. There are albums and albums of stuff sitting in the can. But I just didn't feel that they were that useful. That was the way I measured the records I put out.

Instead of doing a *Greatest Hits* album, did you ever consider just putting out what you thought were your most "useful" songs?
That would be so personal. It might be more interesting and maybe fun to write about, but the song selection for the *Greatest Hits* was pretty much Jon's [Landau, Springsteen's manager] idea. We didn't try to get into a "best of," because everybody's got their own ideas. Basically it was the songs that came out as singles. The only exception is "Thunder Road," but it seemed central. I like the classic idea of hits—it was sort of like *50,000,000 Elvis Fans Can't Be Wrong*. That was what we were thinking when we put it out. The album was supposed to be fun, something that you could vacuum the rug to if you wanted to. I think part of the reason we put the record out was that I wanted to introduce my music to younger fans, who for 12 bucks could get a pretty good overview of what I've done for years. And for my older fans, I wanted to say, "This still means something to me now, you still mean something to me now." It was just kind of a way of reaffirming the relationship I've built up with my audience over the past 25 years, which outside of my family is the most important relationship in my life.

Did you include the "Murder Incorporated" outtake for them?

A lot of fans have asked for outtakes, and I have so many sitting around. It might be fun at some point to throw together some sort of collection of stuff like my attempts at other genres—from the bubble-gum sort of thing to more pop-oriented material to the British Invasion things. We used to go in the studio and say, "Tonight is Beatles night," and we'd put things together that had all these influences either just for fun or because we thought they were going to work out at the time. In the end, I would generally opt for things that had my own voice in them the most. But a lot of the other stuff was fun, and at some point it might be a blast for some of the fans to hear.

Before you ever started releasing records, you were known more as a guitarist than a songwriter. Do you ever think about stepping out as a guitarist again?

I was always the guitar player in the band. But I reached a point in the early '70s where I said, "There are so many good guitarists, but there are not a lot of people who have their own songwriting voice." And I really focused on that. Then the label wanted a folk album, because I was really signed as a folk artist by John Hammond, who didn't know that I ever had a band.

Ultimately, my guitar playing came to be about fitting in with the ensemble. Then Clarence came along with his saxophone. He's sort of a force of nature, so if I wanted to hear a solo, I let him do it. I put a lot of my guitar playing in the rear, but at this point I'd like to bring it back to the front. As a matter of fact, I played with the Blasters the other night, and it was really fun. I was back to being just a blues guitarist; I used to play the blues all the time.

One of these days I'd like to toy around with making a record that's centered around loud guitars and me playing more. At some point I sort of opted out of the jam thing and got more into the solo being in service of the song. I'd like to do something where I've got to really play, you know. Now I feel like I'm at a place where I can do anything and I want to do it all. I like a lot of different types of music and musical styles and I want to use all those influences.

The best thing about being at this place in your career is you can be more relaxed about it. I think it's more like your job now, and you're just going out and trying new things that are hopefully interesting for both you and your fans.

You mentioned earlier that while "Thunder Road" wasn't a hit, or even a single, you included it on the *Greatest Hits* album because it seemed central to your work. Why do you think that's so?

I'm not sure what that song has. We played it the other night at the Sony studio, when we were taping a European show, and it just felt all-inclusive. It may be something about trying to seize a particular moment in your life and realizing you have to make very fundamental and basic decisions that you know will alter your life and how you live it. It's a funny song because it simultaneously contains both dreaming and disillusionment.

That's similar to what Melissa Etheridge was saying when she introduced "Thunder Road" on *MTV Unplugged*. It was just before you came on stage and she said, "If anyone can make you dream, it's Bruce Springsteen."

You know, you write your music and you never know where the seeds that you sow are going to fall. Melissa Etheridge comes out of the Midwest, and she comes out of the gay bars, and I like that that's where some of my influence falls. I think that a big part of what my songs are about is being who you are, and trying to create the world you want to live in. Generally, I think people use songs as a way to order their lives in a world that feels so out of order. It's a way of centering themselves and grounding themselves in a set of values, a sense of things they can go back and touch base with.

I'm basically a traditionalist, and I like the whole idea of a rock and roll lineage. I always saw myself as the kid who stepped up out of the front row and onto the stage—who would carry the guitar for a while, and then pass on the rock and roll flame. And you take it as far as you can and write your own map for people to follow a bit. You try to not make the mistakes that people who came before you made, and in some fashion you reset some of the rules of the game if you can.

So that was my idea about what I was here to do. I wasn't interested in immediate success or how much each particular record sold. I was interested in becoming a part of people's lives and, hopefully, growing up with them—growing up together.

I came from a small town where I grew up on popular music. The subversiveness of Top 40 music can't be overestimated. I grew up on music that was popular; I sat in my bedroom and wrote the Top 20 down religiously every Wednesday night, cheering for my heroes and hissing the villains of the day. So I wanted to play in that arena. I believed that it was a place where you could find both the strengths and the limitations of your work, who you are and who you are not. And I thought it was a worthwhile thing to risk. There was an element of risk in it because you're very exposed, you're very much under the magnifying glass, and it can be relentless and brutal. The town I grew up in was very divided—racially and class-wise—yet there were songs that united everyone at some point, like the great Motown music.

It's funny because today's alternative rock is a reaction against the experiences of music you had growing up. These new bands don't want to carry the flame, they want to stamp it out. Yet you've said in the past how much you like alternative music, and you played with Soul Asylum in New York.
Look at a band like Nirvana. They reset the rules of the game. They changed everything, they opened a vein of freedom that didn't exist previously. Kurt Cobain did something very similar to what Dylan did in the '60s, which was to sound different and get on the radio. He proved that a guitarist could sound different and still be heard. So Cobain reset a lot of very fundamental rules, and that type of artist is very few and far between.

A similar thing happened with a lot of early rap, which was a return of the rawness of the '50s records. It changed the conventional ideas of how drums should sound, how guitars should sound, how a singer should sound—even whether you have to sing at all. Those are things that keep the music moving forward.

With regard to alternative music, I sometimes think about the overall corporateness of everything and how that affects your thought processes. How do you find a place of your own when you're constantly being bombarded with so much frigging information that you really and truthfully don't need? What you see on TV is not a mirror image of most people's daily existence. Your chances of having a violent altercation are relatively small, unless you watch television, in which case you'll be brutalized every day.

And I think that what people are feeling is other people's fingerprints on their minds. And that seems to be a real strong and vital subject currently running through a lot of alternative music. I feel it myself. And, hey, there needs to be a voice against that sort of co-option of your own thinking space. What are your memories? What are your ideas? Everything is prepackaged and sold to you as desirable or seductive in some fashion. So how do you find out who you are, create your own world, find your own self? That's the business of rock music in the '90s.

A word that is often used to describe—and praise—you is "real." What do you think that means?
I'm not sure what it means. I'm not sure if it's the right word. Maybe "grounded" is a better way to put it. When I separated from the E Street Band, there was tremendous feedback from the fans. Some were hurt because, I think, among the values expressed in my music are loyalty, friendship, and remembering the past. So at some point, the question becomes, "How do you stay true to those values and yet grow up and become your own man?" And I think I've done pretty well threading my way through that sort of thing. I certainly haven't done it perfectly, but, of course, it ain't over yet.

I think every fan creates an image of you in his or her head that may not be totally accurate. I think that the pressure to be grounded—and for fans to feel like you're speaking to them—is good. That's what I want to do. But you also want to make the music you want to make, live the life that the road you're traveling on leads you to, and live with the contradictions that are a part of finding a large audience and having success in the world that you live in.

Was "Blood Brothers" [a new song on the *Greatest Hits* album] a reexamination of what the E Street Band meant to you, and why you fired them?
"Blood Brothers" was about trying to understand the meaning of friendship as you grow older. I guess I wrote it the night before I went in the studio with the band, and I was trying to sort out what I was doing and what those relationships meant to me now and what those types of friendships mean as a person moves through life.

Basically, I guess I always felt that relationships are the bonds that keep you from slipping into the abyss of self-destruction. Without those things, that abyss feels a lot closer—like it's on your heels. I think your own nihilism feels a lot closer without someone to grab you by the arm and pull you back and say, "Hey, come on, you're having a bad day." So with that song I was trying to sort out the role that those deep friendships played in my life. We all grew up together from the time we were kids, and people got married and divorced and had babies and went through their addictions and out the other side, and we drove each other crazy.

Did it feel immediately right to be back with the band again?
We hadn't worked together in eight years and really hadn't recorded together in 10. In the meantime, I did a lot of solo stuff, which I found satisfying. But I don't think I'd want to choose between the band and the solo stuff. I'd like to have both. One of the things I realized when I saw the guys was that we're like each other's arms and legs.

Maybe that's because it wasn't a band that was set up as a democracy, like maybe the Rolling Stones are, and on the other hand it wasn't purely people I'd hired as a backing band. It was somewhere in the middle. I wanted something that felt like mine, I wanted people I felt close to, I wanted the best of both worlds: creative control and people with whom I could collaborate emotionally, who felt connected to the music and the things I was writing about.

When you sing, "I don't know why I made this call/Or if any of this matters anymore after all," are you referring to calling up and firing each band member?
No, because all the guys in the band got along pretty well. I mean, we had our moments, and everybody drove everybody else nuts sometimes. But people pretty much like each other.

You have to understand, there were guys in that band that I met when we were 19 and living in Asbury Park, New Jersey. We were together for 20 years. It's very unusual to be sitting in the same room at 39 with people you met when you were 19, and it bred a certain sort of dedication. It came with a certain sense of purpose. There's also an intimacy that occurs after hundreds and hundreds of nights on stage that is very unique. I'm not sure what I would compare it to. Imagine finding a group of people and doing the same thing together for 25 or 35 years, from the time you were just out of high school. It's an amazing thing. And it's a gift that life doesn't often afford. Without sounding too hokey about it, it was pretty easy to call everybody up.

I've been luckier than most in being able to sustain those types of relationships. Over the years that we weren't working together, we had various conversations, some contentious. Some people were hurt, some were angry. But I love all the guys in the band. When we decided to record some new songs, I think I called the guys on a Thursday and we were all together on the following Monday or Tuesday, just happy to see one another.

We're probably going to do some more recording. I have some things that I'm going to record in the next couple of weeks, on my own, and see if I can finish up this solo record I've been working on. If it's good, I'll release it. If not, I'll throw it out. Then I'll see what the guys are doing and maybe cut some songs with them and see where that goes.

Did you write "Streets of Philadelphia" specifically for the movie *Philadelphia*?
Yes. That song was kind of a collaboration with [director] Jonathan Demme. He called me up and mentioned he needed a song and told me a little bit about the picture. The message of the song was something I've dealt with in the past, but I'm not sure I would have written it had he not asked me for it.

That period of collaboration is something that drew me back towards the E Street Band. The response from the song was pretty intense. It's funny, because when I wrote it, I wasn't even sure that I captured what I wanted to get. There were very few instruments, it's a very short song, it's very linear, there's not a lot of musical development. I thought it would sound good over the images that he sent me, but I didn't know if it would stand on its own. You just can't tell with these things. It made me think about other stuff I've chosen not to release over the years. In hindsight, I wish I hadn't been as rigid as I've been about what I would put out.

On the other hand, you did sue the English label Dare for trying to release your early material.
Right. On the other hand, there's a reason I don't put out the stuff that I don't put out—I don't think it's good or focused enough. You try to have some control over your releases, although you really don't, of course, because most of the stuff ends up bootlegged anyway. But the Dare thing was different because they were attempting to put it out as an actual legal release and they simply didn't have the right to do that. I don't have any strong feelings about the material one way or another. There were some good things and some stinkers on that tape, and some day I'd like to get some of it out. But your editing is part of your aesthetic process.

Certainly, I go back and realize that there are many outtakes that should have been released at different times. I still wish I'd put more records out, and maybe I could have. But I made records very purposefully, with very specific ideas of them being about and representing certain things. That probably caused me to be overly cautious about what I released and what I didn't. I certainly feel a lot more freedom now.

For many musicians, having children changes the way they write songs and experience the world. Is that true for you?
When you have your children, basically the best thing, the nicest thing, you can do for them is to slip into their time, into the way that they experience the world and the way that they experience the day. And that can be hard to do if you're a restless, anxious, nervous person, and also if you're someone who has always asked people to step into your world. Once you have kids, you realize that's hard to do.

By the time I had kids, I'd burned out on the idea of living internally, for my own excitement. I just had to give up that type of control. I think at some point you realize that you don't need that as much as you thought you did. You feel more centered and safer with kids and marriage, which gives you a lot more emotional flexibility and allows you to go along with other people's lives. For me it's still a struggle sometimes. I think I've been a good dad, but it calls for an entirely different set of responses than those that I've used for the past 30 years.

Are you worried that your success will keep your kids from having the same kind of experiences you had as a child?
It will change their experience tremendously from what my experience as a child was. A friend of mine, Van Dyke Parks, who worked on one of my records, came in the studio one day, and we got into this discussion about how I was concerned about my children growing up differently than I did. And in retrospect I felt that a lot of things about the way that I grew up were good, because I struggled and had the opportunity to make something from not a whole lot. He said, "Well, you give your kids the best and the world takes care of the rest." And I think that's what every parent tries to do. And also not to put them in any circumstances where the distortions of the experience are too overwhelming, or too unusual, and then just protect them as best as possible.

Before you ever married, you wrote a number of songs about characters that had wives and kids.
Yeah, I was probably testing it out.

Do you feel that you portrayed those relationships accurately before you had even experienced them?
Well, there were a lot of different types of portrayal. I guess the songs that come to mind when you talk about it would probably be "The River," "I Wanna Marry You," which is just a guy standing on the corner fantasizing, and "Stolen Car." I stayed away from that subject for a long time. I didn't write about relationships, probably because I didn't know much about 'em and I wasn't very good at 'em, and also it was a subject in pop music that had been written about so much and I wasn't interested in writing just your classic sort of pop love songs. Later on when I did write about them, I tended to write about them with all the real complications that they involve. I tried to write a more realistic sort of love song, like "Brilliant Disguise" or any of the stuff from *Tunnel of Love* or *Lucky Town* record. I just wanted something that felt grounded in the kind of tension and compromise that these things really involve.

What kind of advice would you give the young Bruce Springsteen now?
I would tell him to approach his job like, on one hand, it's the most serious thing in the world and, on the other hand, as if it's only rock and roll. You have to keep both of those things in your head at the same time, simultaneously. I still believe you have the possibility of influencing people's lives in some fashion, and at the same time it's only entertainment and you want to get people up and dancing. I think I took it very seriously. I don't regret doing so, but I think that I would have been a bit easier on myself as I went along and I would have been less self-punishing at different times if I'd remembered that it was only rock and roll. Being a little bit worried about it can be dangerous. It's a minefield, it's dangerous for your inner self and also for whatever your ideas and values are that you want to sing about.

You drift down your different self-destructive roads at different times and hopefully you have the type of bonds that pull you back out of the abyss and say, "Hey, wait a minute." When I was 25, I was in London and there were posters of me everywhere in this theater that were making me want to puke. I was disgusted at what I'd become, and then someone in the band would say, "Hey, do you believe we're in London, England, and we're going to play tonight and somebody's going to pay us for it?" So I was lucky. I had good friends and a good support network that assisted me along the way. In retrospect, I look back on those times now and they were just funny, you know. But there was good cause for worry because I'd read the maps of the people that came before me and I was interested in being something different, and accomplishing something slightly different.

And what advice would the young Bruce Springsteen give you?
Louder guitars.

Bob Costas
Columbia Radio Hour,
November 1995

Though reinvigorated by working again with the E Street Band, by the fall Springsteen was about to embark on what would become a year-and-a-half-long solo trek. Just prior to the start of the acoustic tour for *The Ghost of Tom Joad,* Springsteen spoke at length with broadcaster Bob Costas. Only a portion of the 90-minute interview aired. Delving into the inspirations behind his stark new record, Bruce was excited about returning to what he was when he started out playing Max's Kansas City by himself. "In a funny way," he tells Costas, "it's a throw-back to what that was. But it's something I haven't really done before; it's something I've wanted to do for a long time."

I'd made a record, or part of a record, last year, that I didn't finish, and I worked on it quite a bit and I listened to it . . . maybe before last Christmastime or something, and I said, "Gee, you know, it's not quite right." And I worked with the band on the *Greatest Hits* record. There's something about the band that always has sort of drawn me outside of myself to write more about the world outside, I suppose. I think I wrote "The Ghost of Tom Joad" originally as a rock song for the E

Street Band, thinking I might use it as one of the extra songs on the *Greatest Hits* record. And for one reason or another that didn't happen, but it kind of set me in that direction a little bit. And I had this song "Straight Time," which is on this record. And I had that for about a year or so, and I liked its basic feeling. And as I was working at that time—you follow where your voice is, you don't particularly choose where your voice is at any given moment. At this particular time in my work life it seemed like my voice is where this record ended up. It was more of a folk voice. That seemed to be something that was just saying, "Hey, work over here." I didn't sit down and plan to particularly make this type of record or not. Parts of it presented itself to me, and then you sort of follow it along.

Tom Joad is of course, from John Steinbeck's novel *The Grapes of Wrath*, but it's clear that your inspiration for this comes more from the John Ford film. Not just for this track, but the whole album has a cinematic feel. I know you're a fan of John Ford.
Yeah, that picture I guess I saw in the late '70s and it had a really deep effect on me. I think I'd read some John Steinbeck, probably earlier than that, in high school, and there was something about the film that sort of crystallized the story for me. And it always stayed with me after that; there was something in that picture that always resonated throughout almost all of my other work. It was just an image that popped out as I was sitting around on the couch messing around with the guitar.

Do you remember the first time that you watched Henry Fonda give that speech at the end?
Oh yeah, I cried. That was a very powerful speech for me. I think to some degree the things you write are a conversation with yourself . . . I think that's probably what that song was to me, it was a conversation I was having with myself. Not about, "Oh, brother, where art thou?" or "Where is this in the world today?" It was just, "Where is it in me?" I think you gotta start with that question. If you can get people to ask that question, then the song's done its job.

You've often come to the theme of a person in difficult circumstances trying to find some nobility, some dignity in those circumstances, maybe not in a dramatic way that everyone can see, but in

some small way that would have a redemptive power for that person. And in these cuts, I find a little bit of that, but also a lot of resignation on the part of these characters that maybe they're just not even gonna find that little bit of dignity.
Well, I guess I sort of see there's a little bit of it out there. I don't really start from any political point of view—no conscious one. I suppose everybody carries their politics innately and emotionally in their psychology in some fashion. But I think that's what's been happening. I think that the American idea of equal opportunity, obviously it hasn't been realized. And I think what's worse, every study that's come out about the division of wealth in society over the past 10 or 15 years has shown that the middle class has been getting smaller and people have been getting farther and farther apart. I think that while it's something that hasn't led to, say, riots, it leads to diminished hopes, diminished expectations, diminished possibilities. And so that feeling . . . like I said I don't sit down and start from any particular conscious point of view, but I think that feeling of the way things feel to me right now, that colors the stories and the characters' lives on the record.

Like we said earlier, "The Ghost of Tom Joad" is based much more on the movie, or draws its inspiration much more from the movie than from the book. And you think about the movie and this whole family making its way out west in this little rickety car, and nothing about their circumstances is nurturing. Nothing should give them reason to be optimistic. And they're trying to forge some sense of community among themselves and find something that's real that can help them transcend these circumstances. And that theme shows up in a lot of your work through the years, doesn't it?
I guess. See, my folks, in 1969, I was 19, my folks went west. They went to California to start a new life. It was my mom, my dad and my little sister, I think they had saved $3000. And I remember I stayed in New Jersey because I'd gotten very involved with the band, and I guess that'd become my family at that point in time, and it was also where I could make a living. I went out to California, I tried to make a living, and I couldn't get a job. I couldn't get a job where somebody'd pay me to play. And back home I had two or three clubs where I could come up with 100, 125, or a 150 bucks a week, which was enough to survive on. I was sleeping with six other guys in an apartment, and everybody's chipping in a few bucks for rent. But my folks went in '69, they

had three grand, they slept two nights in the car and one night in a motel, and that was what they did. They drove into California, they didn't know anybody. I had a girlfriend who was one of the first sort of hippies in the area, she was the only person anyone knew who'd ever been to San Francisco [*laughs*], and she sent 'em to Sausalito, which was this sort of hipsters' enclave at the time . . .

Was she sure to wear a pretty flower in her hair?
[*Laughs*] So my folks pull straight from New Jersey into Sausalito, where of course, they realize very quickly that they don't belong there. And my mother claims they pulled into a gas station and asked the attendant, "Hey, where do people like us live?" [*laughs*] And somebody said, "Oh, you live on the peninsula." That's her story. So they started a whole new life out there. They did well, but they struggled pretty hard.

I went out there—there was a time when I'd never been on an airplane, until I made a record, nobody could afford an airplane ticket. To get to see them about once every year or so, me and a buddy of mine, we'd drive across the country, go three days straight, we'd save—whatever, a 100 bucks . . . and drive straight through. I went to California. I did some auditioning, but I realized really quickly that I wasn't gonna be able to live out there . . . you know, there were just a lot of musicians, and while it was a much bigger music scene, I was a nobody. I realized very quickly that while someone might let you play, they're not gonna pay you. So I stayed about two months, and I realized I was gonna have to be living off my folks, and I didn't want to do that, so I went back to New Jersey. And I don't know if that's had something to do with part of what I've written about. Maybe it's some of my own experience and some of just, that's the American story. The American story is transience and the idea of "over the rise." Less [so] now, I suppose, but I think it's some ingrained part of not just the American spirit, but human spirit in general. My characters have always been on the move going someplace, searching for something—whether it's a better life or running from something with the idea that somehow moving will make you better, it'll heal you inside.

This may not be the exact quote, but you said something like this once: "I was 24 years old, I was sitting at home in New Jersey asking myself the question 'Is love real?' and if people have followed my characters through all the years, they can find a common

thread with them and they see that 'Lucky Town' is where those characters wind up." That's what it was at the time you made that statement. **Is "The Ghost of Tom Joad" where those characters wind up or where their thoughts wind up now, or is it more a nod of recognition at a path that all of us could conceivably take if we make the wrong choices or if our circumstances aren't so lucky?**

I guess I don't like to use the idea of "wind up." I guess you don't "wind up" till it's over [*laughs*]. There's a lot of different things, questions, I tried to work through in my work over the years. The idea of "is love real," yeah, I think it is, but it's hard to find. And it can be hard to find evidence of it.

I'd written [almost] all of this record, and I was in my library one night and pulled a book out called *Journey to Nowhere*, which was a book I'd bought years before and I hadn't read. The text is by a fellow named Dale Maharidge, and there are some really great photos by a fellow named Michael Williamson. And basically what they did, they went out on the road and they rode the trains from, I think, St. Louis to Oregon, and documented a lot of what had been happening to a group of Americans in the latter half of the '80s—the people that the trickle-down economy never trickled down to. It's a book that makes very real, puts real faces on what it's like if you slip through those cracks. I was very frightened, I remember I read it all in one night and I closed it—my God, you never know what tomorrow brings. It strikes some sort of fear: what if you couldn't take care of your family, what if you had to leave them, what if you couldn't be home with your sons and your daughters, what if you couldn't pay for their health care, couldn't provide them with the health care that they need? What if that was your kids? I know how deadly important my job is to me. What if I didn't have that job? Or what if I couldn't do that job after I did it for 20 years or 25 years?

Or what if the job you had . . .

. . . disappeared.

. . . didn't have anything to do with anything that really meant something to you?

Right. So these are all questions that, I don't know, I ask myself a lot, I guess, and hey, I've had an enormous amount of luck and fortune and have worked hard, but that other thing, I don't know, it never feels that far away, and I think that it's as far away as the guy next to you. It's not that far.

If you believe as you said once that people listen to your songs not to find out about you, but to find out about themselves, what do you think they'll come away from this record thinking or thinking about?
Basically, I think I tried to sit down and feel . . . I think your music always ends up being two things. One, it's probably a photograph of your own inner landscape, emotional landscape to some degree. And possibly your character in some fashion—how you perceive your life, lives around you, the place you live. And then it's a picture—I tried to reflect what the country feels like to me right now. The bottom line. America will always be judged against what the American idea was, some concept of shared burden. I guess what I was trying to do probably for myself was to put myself back in touch with those ideas, those values. I have children now. I'm a grown man. Now's not the time to *think about* what I want to be like, it's the time for me to *be* what I want to be like. So I think I was trying to really get myself back in touch . . . with my family, my children, the man you want to be and what you want the place you live in to be like. I sorta go for that first, and I assume that if it's working for me, then it'll work for my audience or whoever listens to it. I think that's probably where I'm coming from.

[*Music plays*] That was "Youngstown" from *The Ghost of Tom Joad*. Wanna talk a little bit about the inspiration for that?
That was a song that really—I go back to this book called *Journey to Nowhere*—I had written the whole record and then I read the book, and "Youngstown" and a song called "The New Timer" are really drawn from a lot of the information and the stories that were in this particular book. I guess that was something that probably out of all the things on the record maybe that connects the most directly to something—if you were a fan of "The River" or just the story of post-industrial America— what happens when your job disappears? You were able to make a good living for 20 years, and all of a sudden that's not there for you. And maybe you can find a job that pays half as much, or a quarter as much, and you're 45 years old, you're 50 years old. What happens when the craft you've learned, the skill you've learned . . . I think, hey what if I

couldn't . . . my music ability, that's all that I have. I'm not a multitalented person; I have a talent in a specific area, and I fumble around every place else. So I wanted to re-engage some of those ideas and some of those issues, and that's really where that song came out of.

How much of your present approach on this album is attributable— even if it's a small amount—to some self-doubt about whether you'd become, for whatever reasons, too mainstream? The whole idea that celebrity is the natural enemy of integrity, so you'd better deliver a counterpunch.
Oh, I don't know. I'm not sure I really . . . I don't steer myself by those particular lights. And I have a variety of different feelings about it. A lot of the things I really liked were things that were very mainstream. The stuff that moved me and changed my life were mainstream records. They were from people who came from outside of the mainstream but changed the mainstream to accommodate who they were by the force of their abilities and their talent and their ideas and their presence. Those are the artists that I admired a lot, whether it was Dylan . . . hey, before "Like a Rolling Stone" you couldn't sing like that and get on the radio. They couldn't get on the radio like that. I've also said the same thing before Nirvana came out with "Smells Like Teen Spirit." You couldn't sound like that and get on Top 40 radio. And I always believed that it was a valuable risk to take. It was a funny situation in that I think that I was essentially probably a child of Elvis Presley initially, but I grew up in the '60s and Dylan's work and later Woody Guthrie's also meant an enormous amount to me so I sorta got caught in between . . . those are some different roots in certain ways. The things that meant a lot to me when I was young were the things that came across the AM radio. I didn't live in an environment where there was a lot of cultural education. We weren't exposed to things that were outside of the mainstream, for the most part. The mainstream was what you had, and in your small town what came across the radio was . . . I found it very liberating, and I found it very meaningful.

I had my choices. Way back, way way back in 1975. I could have not have done those interviews and probably not have been on the cover of both *Time* and *Newsweek*, and I could have possibly made some different choices in '85, but I was very interested in where that road led and in finding out about who I was and what I could do or would do under those circumstances. 'Cause I thought I'd do something different, and in some ways I did and in some ways I didn't. And those are the things that interested me. I think that at this point if I had anything to say about that particular *level* of celebrity—which I don't have now, ten years ago it was different—was that at some point it felt pretty overwhelming, and I think at some point it overwhelms the story you're telling and trying to tell.

This much is also undeniable: Without everything that went before the audience would be smaller for what you're trying to say here. There's no fighting that.
Right now, there'd be almost no audience [*laughs*].

On its own merits, no matter how high those merits are, absent what went before, this is a record that only a few people hear.
You are absolutely right. And that's the facts. And that's something that I've been conscious of throughout my career. I've made one sort of record, and I'll go off and make another one. And that balance has always felt right to me. I know that an audience is hard to find. And it's easy if you've had one for a long time, it's easy to take that audience for granted and think, "Oh, hey, people just come when I play, they just buy my records when they come out." But the truth is that that audience—I was years on the circuit, years on the circuit. I studied my craft in bars since I was 14 years old, that's 32 years ago, and it happened over a long period of time. And it is something of tremendous value.

At the same time, not just necessarily any audience is of tremendous value. I think that if you subvert what you're saying, what you're doing, what you want your work or your life to be about, then you've lost yourself and the essence of what you do.

Do you feel like you ever did that?
I don't think so. I think, basically, I've made the records that I've wanted to make. I think that in the course of probably the *Born in the U.S.A.* record, the story I was living overshadowed the story I was telling, and that is the consequence of a certain amount of success and fame, and that's just something you learn. Not with everybody, not with my core audience, and I think that there's a few things on that record that are probably . . . certainly the title song, which I knew that when I wrote it that it was gonna have impact. But "My Hometown," I didn't know people were gonna respond like they did one way or the other. But I

think that it's something that I'm very, very conscious of right now, and I feel like I'm just out there checking it out. I'm trying to find . . . I want this record to be heard; at the same time, I want it to be understood.

Seems to me like *The Ghost of Tom Joad* is a record that people will have to listen to a half dozen times before they begin to form their feelings about it.
I don't know . . .

The first couple times through, I'm not so sure you're going to get it all.
I don't know. That's for the listener. I've heard it a lot of times. I haven't heard it since we finished it off. I think I can have the experience of the record, I can't quite have that initial listening experience that you're talking about. That's something I have as each song goes down, and that's slightly different because if I don't think I'm getting it, I move on to something else. Sometimes I'll go back—like "Straight Time." I played it once, I put it away, and basically, I threw it away. And Jon [Landau] came out, and he has a tendency . . . he always asks my engineer, "What's laying around that hasn't been played or I haven't heard?" I think my engineer pulled that one out, and [Jon] came back and said, "Hey, wait a minute." So sometimes you don't know; sometimes you do something that was better than you thought it was.

When people come to see you on this tour, obviously they're going to see an acoustic show, not an acoustic version of songs previously recorded . . .
It's not *Unplugged*, it's not *Unplugged* . . .

Right. So they're gonna see an acoustic show. There's an interesting contrast in that . . .
What the show is, it's a folk show, in the sense that I'm not sorta doing my favorites or their favorites, or the hits or whatever you call it. I'm concentrating very specifically on this particular record and material that feels like it complements it. It's a show that . . . it's a quiet show. There's a lot of focus in it. So it's pretty different.

I guess there is some feeling on the part of fans of an individual or a group, that when they go to see a concert, that concert should be an updated version of the catalog. We're gonna get all the classics, plus we're gonna get the handful from the new release that will join that group of classics, and that's not what's going to happen here.

I think there's a time to do that. We'd played a couple nights with the E Street Band and we played a bunch of the old songs, and it was fun to do. I enjoyed it. [This is] something where it's a departure. I really haven't done this before. I've played a few isolated shows. I've played Neil Young's Bridge Benefit a few times acoustically, and I've played a benefit for the Christic Institute acoustically with Jackson Browne. Then I started out on my own: when I got signed I was playing Max's Kansas City by myself with acoustic guitar, so in a funny way it's a throwback to what that was. But it's something I haven't really done before; it's something I've wanted to do for a long time. It really pares everything away and makes what you're about and what you're doing real clear, and that's what I'm interested in communicating right now. I'm real excited about it, and I think the fans are going to enjoy it.

Everyone wonders, no matter how much they enjoy this record, no matter how much they enjoy this tour, when will Bruce be back with the E Street Band? So now I've asked the question. I've discharged my obligation, now you discharge yours.

[*Laughs*] Oh, we had a great time doing the *Greatest Hits*, and what can I say, it's a special group of people and I'm sure at some point we'll be doing something. I hate to predict because I'm always wrong myself. I said you sort of follow your voice, and the voice of this particular record was just something I heard in my head right now. Whether you hear the world speaking to you or something inside you speaking to you that moves you in a particular direction that leads you hopefully to your most honest work, hopefully to your best work, hopefully to your honest job. But then also if you make a quiet record, you tend to want to make some noise maybe later or something. I'd want to be able to call on the guys, and if everybody felt like it . . . and if I was gonna make a rock record right now, that'd be the first thing that I'd do. Outside of my family, that's the most important relationship in my life, that and my relationship with my audience.

Do you still stand by your statement that the two best days of your life were the day you picked up the guitar and the day you learned how to put it down?
Oh, those days have been supplanted now. I guess the best days of my life were certainly the birth of my children. I think any parent always says that. And finding the thing that moves you . . . something to do . . . finding something to do is really really important. I think maybe that that's why I'm attuned to that in others. Something that is so important to me, it was so important, and it's been so rewarding. That was the American idea was that everybody would have that opportunity, that chance. That's an idea worth fighting for.

The easy, glib thing is when people say when someone gets successful and they have material wealth they get out of touch with the troubles of people on the margins. I think that's too easy, but if a person truly finds happiness—and it seems like you're happier than you've ever been for a stretch of time now in your life—if the person finds happiness, is there a danger that the artistic edge can be muted?
No, no, because . . . it depends, once again . . . any of those things you can't generalize. Life's circumstances change people in a lot of different ways. I know you can make a lot of money and be isolated, but I knew some hardcore isolated people who had nothing and who cut themselves off. I've said in the past, you can isolate yourself with a six-pack of beer. I don't buy those types of generalizations. I think it depends on the individual and the idea that happiness somehow mutes your work, I'm not so sure. It depends what drives you, it depends what you want. I still search for the big part of the meaning of my life in my work.

Gavin Martin

New Musical Express,
March 9, 1996

The Ghost of Tom Joad allowed Springsteen to give full attention to his folk, as opposed to his rock, voice, and the solo tour that followed required an adjustment on the part of his audience who were asked to be quiet and to listen to the stories of the songs. "I don't need to sell records that are going to make millions. I need to do work that I feel is central, vital," Springsteen explains.

He'll be remembered as the most unbounded performer in rock 'n' roll history. His records took you inside a world of naked honesty and passionate conviction, and his marathon shows were founded on deep audience empathy. But surely there must have been something else—some tough-bastard instinct—to get him where he wanted to be, to make him The Boss?

Bruce Springsteen laughs—partly in amusement, partly in protest. "The Boss was an idiotic nickname. It's the bane of my entire career. I've learned to live with it but I've hated it, y'know. Basically it was a casual thing. Somebody said it when the paychecks came out at the end of the month and then it ended up being this stupid thing—in my mind anyway. But, hey, so it goes.

"The thing is, I believed when I was young. I was a serious young man, I had serious ideas about rock music. I believed it was a serious thing, I believed it should also be fun—dancing, screwing, having a good time, but . . . but I also believed it was capable of conveying serious ideas and that the people who listened to it, whatever you want to call them, were looking for something.

"And maybe because it was the only culture I knew when I was 15, it succeeded as a tremendous source of inspiration for me for the entire part of my early life. It truly opened things up for me.

"I heard tremendous depth and sadness in the voice of the singer singing 'Saturday Night at the Movies,' and a sense of how the world truly was, not how it was being explained to me, but how it *truly* was and how it truly operated.

"So when it came to be my turn, I said, 'I want to try and present that and, if I can, then I'll feel like I'm doing more than taking up space, y'know?'"

He's not taking up so much space these days, not here in his modest dressing room backstage at the Rudi-Sedlmayer Halle in Munich. Not onstage, surrounded by a selection of three or four acoustic guitars and a shelf of harmonica holders on his first solo tour. Springsteen's sense of commitment to serious issues has never been tested so strongly nor proved so resolute as on this, his "Born to Stand and Sitdown" tour, aka "The Shut the F—Up and Listen" tour. A natural progression from *The Ghost of Tom Joad*—the starkest, most terrifying album of his career, released in November last year—Springsteen's solo tour is currently heading across Europe after three months in America.

He's been playing small venues, 2–4,000-seaters, many well off the normal circuit, re-establishing links with the local networks of food banks and agencies for the homeless, forged during his megastar years. But now the clamour is less frantic and the aims more focused. That's how he wants it to be; a reflection of the world-weariness and sense of fatalism that informs *Tom Joad*.

In Detroit, Bruce talked onstage about a year-long local newspaper dispute and, although he made a donation to the strikers, was careful not to make moral judgments about those forced by circumstances to cross the picket lines. Then the day he played in Austin, Texas, a city-wide ordinance which effectively made it a criminal offence to be homeless came into effect. In Atlanta, the city's relief organisations told of the pressure that local business interests were putting on police and politicians to clean the vagrants off the streets in preparation for the summer's Olympics.

And when he played in Youngstown, Ohio, the depression-hit, population-decimated steel town featured in the eponymous song that gives voice to all those deemed expendable by late 20th-century American capitalism, they say you could hear the very heartbeat of the place pulsing inside the hall when he sang their song.

Springsteen says there's no substitute for going to the town where someone lives and playing to them. He says there's nothing that can match actually being there. This is, after all, a performer who keeps in touch with his fans—and their mothers. Like the woman he met back in 1981 after going to a cinema in St. Louis.

"That particular evening was funny because I saw *Stardust Memories*, the Woody Allen film where he was knocking his fans. The kid sitting next to me said, 'Hey, is that what you think?' and I said 'No.' I was by myself, I was in St. Louis and it was 10 pm. He said, 'Come on home and meet my mother and she'll make you something to eat.'

"That to me was part of the fun of being me—people asked you to step into their lives out of nowhere. It was always fun, interesting and fascinating. I just saw this kid's mother a couple of weeks ago in St. Louis. I still see her, she's come to every show for 15 years. She comes backstage, gives you something to eat and a kiss. Her son's a lawyer now.

"I liked that. Part of what I liked about my job was that I could step out of my hotel, walk down the street and some nights you could just get lost and you'd meet somebody and they'd take you into their life and it was just sort of . . . I don't know, a way of connecting with things."

In Munich, as with every other show, there's a polite announcement before the performance, reiterating what Springsteen has already told the local press—silence is an integral part of much of the music he'll be playing, and audience co-operation is appreciated. Shortly into his set he puts it rather more bluntly: "Yes, folks, this is a community event, so if anybody near you is making too much noise why not all band together and politely tell them to SHUT THE F—UP!"

The rapt attention and reaction over two nights in Munich and Hamburg suggests that the qualities being appreciated aren't just the lyrics, but the poetic inflections in Springsteen's voice, the feel for his characters' cadences and rhythms of speech; the way each breath, sigh, pant or moan is heard and made to count.

Years ago, Springsteen told an interviewer he was "a nuts-and-bolts sort of guy," who wouldn't make his mark in a mercurial flash of brilliance, but gradually over a long "20 to 25-year" haul. The *Tom Joad* tour, allowing him to expand the artistry of his voice and the eloquence of his guitar-playing as never before, bears the fruits of this approach. But that's not to say the new shows are solely a dark ride. The ripe friskiness of a horny, middle-aged male who has become a father three times since his 40th birthday is well in evidence in introductions to "It's the Little Things That Count" and "Sell It and They Will Come"—unrecorded songs about his own "squalid little sexual fantasies."

A compelling blend of good-natured showman and dedicated artist, Springsteen is obviously aware of the value of contrast. So the jocular banter between songs just goes to highlight the depth of torment and heartbreak at the core of the show—be it a wicked Delta-blues reworking of "Born in the U.S.A.," the lost-tether confession of "Highway 29," the awesome unreleased *Joad* outtake, "Brothers Under the Bridge," or the violated innocence of the kids in "Balboa Park."

The impression of a man at ease with himself and his new, lowlier rank in the Celebrity Freak Show is apparent when we meet backstage, some 15 minutes after his final encore in Hamburg. Springsteen is short and stocky, polite and deferential. With his goatee beard and receding hair pulled back into what's not so much a ponytail as a sparrow's cock, he looks not unlike a guy who might change your oil or check your tyres in any western town.

Then, when he grins and his face creases, he reminds you of Robert De Niro—another hardworking Italian-American whose art has centred on struggles of the soul and obsessional behaviour.

In conversation, Springsteen is given to a lot of self-mocking chuckling, but just as likely he'll slip into a long, slow, deliberating drawl, restarting and revising his meanings; a painstaking approach not dissimilar to the one that has produced the bulk of his recorded output.

He puts his "limited repertoire" of poses into operation for a short photo session, with the proviso that his socks aren't showing.

"That's the only rule I have about photos and I'm very strict about it," he grins.

The photographer mentions Nick Cave and Springsteen interrupts: "Oh, he probably has great socks—he insists you show his socks, am I right?"

Photo session over, he serves up two glasses of Jack Daniel's and ice.

Undoing the belt around his pleated pants he attempts—unsuccessfully—to open a bottle of Corona. Then he opens the door and pries off the bottle top using the lock-keep, but the beer froths up over his trousers and shirt.

"That's the trouble with doing it this way," he says, navigating a quick detour into the shower room.

Finally, lager-stained but ready, Springsteen sits down, resting his drinks on the coffee table beside a silver bill-fold, holding some Deutschmarks, an expensive watch and a biker's key ring. Ninety minutes later, Bruce—who admits that he used to drink but "only for effect"—still hasn't touched either his brew or his Jack.

Have you been working up to a solo tour for a long time?
I've thought about it since *Nebraska*, but *Nebraska* sort of happened by accident. A planned kind of accident, but enough of an accident that I didn't really think that was something I was going to tour with. I thought about it again when I did *Tunnel of Love*, but *Tunnel of Love* was in between a group record and a solo record, and I still couldn't quite imagine going out onstage by myself at that point.

We did rehearsals where it was just me and a sit-down band and—I hate to use the word—an *Unplugged*-style show. That didn't feel right, if there's a band on stage, people are going to want you to go, "One, two, three, four," y'know? So we ended up putting a big tour together.

So when *Tom Joad* came about I thought, "This is the chance to do something I've been waiting to do for a while." Also, I wanted an alternative to touring with a band and all that that involves. I've done it for a long time and I felt like, at best if I got out there with a band I'd only have something half new to say, because, if you're there with a group of people, automatically you're gonna want to hear, A, B and C.

Really, the bottom line is that, through the '90s, the voice I've found, the voice that's felt the most present and vital for me, had basically been a folk voice. It really hasn't been my rock voice.

I was originally signed as a folk singer and so it's a funny sort of thing. John Hammond [the late legendary CBS talent scout who signed Billie Holiday, Bob Dylan and Bruce] would be laughing right now, because he was always saying to me, "You should make an album with just a guitar."

When Jonathan Demme [director of *Philadelphia*] asked for the song ["Streets of Philadelphia"] he focused me outward and then working with the band did the same thing because they are the living manifestation of the community I write about.

Musicians are funny. When you're home, you're never a real connected part of your own community, so you create one of your own. So I created the band and that was your family and that was the living manifestation of whatever community you imagine and sing about, and I think that's what they were to my fans. I think that's what they represented and that's why the band has power and why it is important and has been important.

That sense of friendship, loyalty, everybody's different but somehow together; that's why the whole idea of the band has always been a central idea of rock music; that's why bands keep coming. Whether it's the brothers in Oasis or whoever, everybody's fascinated because IT FEELS LIKE REAL LIFE. People trying to make it, to get together and do something together. That's why bands are powerful.

Do you follow young bands?
Not that much, I hear things in passing. Occasionally I'll go out and do a lot of curiosity-buying. Since the early '80s, my musical influences . . . they've been ultimately more . . . I sort of fought back in a way. There was Hank Williams and some of the blues guys and folk guys, but films and writers and novels have probably been the primary influences on my work.

On the album sleeve and onstage monologues, you're quite specific that it's the John Ford film, rather than the Steinbeck book of *The Grapes of Wrath* that inspired *Tom Joad*.
That's the way it happened, that's what I saw first. Then I read the novel, which is incredible. I recently re-read it, and you have that beautiful last scene. The book ends on a singular act of human kindness or compassion—the entire book leads to that point. That had a lot of meaning for me at the moment I re-read it because I was searching for a way to go beyond broad platitudes or whatever you want to call them.

I was looking for a way to make whatever light there is in the world feel real now. So I found myself turning at the end of my record to one person making one decision. I think the things I use to bring some light into the show are those types of things, that's why I play "Spare Parts" and "Galveston Bay." To me, those things are possible, those are things that . . . any individual at your show can walk out of the building and can lead the next day with that idea or that possibility.

Did therapy affect your most recent writing?
Nah, that had more affect on my life and the choices that I had; it gave me more control in the way I could live my life. Early on, when I was younger, I could only live my life in one way, it was the only way I knew. I was locked into a very specific and pretty limited mode of behaviour. It was basically the road, I had no capability for a home life or an ability to develop anything more than a glancing relationship.

Did you feel something happening to you at the time?
No, you're 25 and you don't know anything that's happening to you. All you know is that things are rushing by. At the time I felt like—this is the race.

As a rock 'n' roll athlete, Springsteen may be unique—there's never been any account of him having taken a drug, for instance.
"No, I never did."

Yet your songs suggest someone well aware of self-destructive urges.
I've had many self-destructive urges but they've never worked themselves out in the drug area. I've had a funny experience in that I didn't do any drugs; I've never done any drugs. It's not about having any moral point of view about drugs whatsoever—I know nothing about them. I didn't do them for my own reasons, which were probably . . . I didn't trust myself into putting myself that far out of control. I had a fear of my own internal life.

I lived in a house where I experienced out-of-controlness and I didn't like it. I suppose I had fears that that was going to be me if I do A, B, C, D or E.

I was 'round very many people who did many drugs and I can't particularly say I liked any of them when they were stoned or high, for the most part. Either they were being a pain in the ass or incomprehensible. That's my experience—so it didn't interest me.

Also, at a very young age, I became very focused on music and experienced a certain sort of ecstasy, actually, through playing. It was just something I loved doing.

But you did take oxygen blasts between sets during your stadium shows?
"I suppose so, if necessary," he laughs.

Those were the days when he was the Boss. A near-superhuman creation, trailing anything up to a four-hour extravaganza of euphoria, shaggy-dog monologues, stories with a bittersweet twist, clowning, death ballads and hard-won heroics. The extended victory march by the man who wanted the heart and soul of the music to rage long into the night. Can he imagine doing it ever again?

"I don't know. I can certainly imagine playing with the band again. I don't know if I'd play for that particular length of time at this point. I mean, I certainly *could*, but I believe I might want to create a more focused show if I went out.

"But it's very tricky because I had the same thought the last time I went out, probably the last five times, then all of a sudden you're looking at the clock and three hours have gone by. So y'know, I'd have to get there and see.

"As far as the other stuff goes, it was really I had a lot of fuel. I always felt the E Street powering me. We had a lot of *desperate* fun; I think that's what gave the fun, that the band presented an edge, y'know. There were always two sides to that particular band, there was a lot of dark material and yet there was this explosion of actual joy; real, real happiness— whether it was being alive or being with your friends or the audience on a given night. That was real but it was the devil-on-your-heels sort of fun—laughing and running, you know what I mean?"

Did things change when Patti Scialfa [long-time New Jersey musician and, since 1991, the second and—he's sure—last Mrs. Springsteen] joined?

"When Patti joined, I wanted the band to be more representative of my audience—I said, 'Hey, we need a woman in the band!' I saw the band as representative of myself. We were all in our mid-30s and I said, 'It's time to deal with these ideas. The band as a lost boys club is a great institution—the level of general misogyny and hostility and the concept of it as always being a place where you can hide from those things.' But I wanted to change that, I didn't want to do it."

What changed you?
Just getting older, you know, and realising, like the old days—you can run but you can't hide. At some point, if you're not trying to resolve these things then you are going to live a limited life. Maybe you're high as a kite and it doesn't matter to you, I dunno. But ultimately it is going to be a life of limited experience—at least that's what it felt like to me.

Not only did I want to experience it all—love, closeness, whatever you want to call it, or just inclusion. To create a band that felt inclusive—someone would look and say. "Hey, that's me!" That's what bands do. That's why people come and why your power is sustained: because people recognize you, themselves, and the world they live in.

You didn't really start writing about sex until the *Tunnel of Love* album. Why had you avoided it until then?
I hadn't avoided sex, but I'd avoided writing about it. It was just confusing for the first 30 or 35 years of my life. Whatever you're caught up in—you know, you're traveling round with the guys, and women are sort of on the periphery. By the time I was in my mid-30s that wasn't acceptable any more. I didn't want to be some 50-year-old guy out there with the boys. It seemed like it was going to be boring. Boring and kinda tragic."

On "Lucky Town" you sang, *"It's a sad, funny ending when you find yourself pretending/A rich man in a poor man's shirt."* On *Tom Joad* the metaphor is more explicit: you're a land-owning Californian millionaire, writing about welfare rejects, illegal immigrant drug-runners and child prostitutes—people as far removed from you on a socio-economic scale as is possible. Is that what writing is about? Making connections that aren't supposed to be possible?
The point is, take the children that are in "Balboa Park," those are your kids, that's what I'm trying to say. It's like, I've got mine, you've got yours and these are kids, too. As a writer, I've been drawn to those subjects, for personal reasons, I'm sure. I don't have some big idea. I don't feel like I have some enormous political message I'm trying to deliver. I think my work has come from the inside. I don't start from the outside—"I have a statement I want to make, ladies and gentlemen!," I don't do that. I don't like the soap-box thing, so I begin internally with things that matter to me personally and maybe were a part of my life in some fashion.

I lived in a house where there was a lot of struggle to find work, where the results of not being able to find your place in society manifested themselves with the resulting lack of self-worth, with anger, with violence.

And, as I grew up, I said, "Hey, that's my song," because, I don't know, maybe that was my experience at a very important moment in my life. And those ideas, those questions, those issues were things I've written about my entire career. I still feel very motivated by them and I still probably do my best work when I'm working inside of those things, which must be because that's where I'm connected. That's just the lights I go by.

Did you do any research to amass the material and detail that features in *Tom Joad*?
Things happen from all over the place. I met a guy in Arizona who told me a story about his brother who rode in a teenage motorcycle gang in the San Fernando Valley, called the Vagos. I just happened to meet this guy by the side of the road in this little motel. I don't know, it just stayed with me for a very long time and when I went to write it, I kept hearing his voice.

If you're in Los Angeles, there's an enormous amount of border news. Immigration and border life is a big part of the town. That's part of what I've gotten from being in California every year, for half the year, for the last five years. It's a very, very powerful place; a place where issues that are alive and confronting America are happening at this moment. It represents what the country is turning into; a place where you see the political machinations of how the issue of immigration is being used, and a lot of the bullshit that goes down with it. It's just the place that, ready or not, America is going to become.

Your reputation has always been of someone who is incredibly prolific and gives away as many good songs as you keep for yourself. Have you ever had a period when you haven't been able to write?
Well, if I was *that* prolific I'd have put out more records. I suppose there's prolific in writing a lot of songs and there's prolific in writing a lot of *good* songs! I've written plenty of songs, but to me a lot of them didn't measure up because I wrote with purpose. My idea wasn't to get the next ten songs and put out an album and get out on the road. I wrote with purpose in mind, so I edited very intensely the music I was writing. So when I felt there was a collection of songs that had a point of view, that was when I released a record. For the most part I didn't release a record until I felt like it, because I didn't think my fundamental goal was to have hit records. I had an idea, y'know, and following the thread of that idea, when I thought I had something that would be valuable to my fans, something enjoyable, something entertaining, something that wouldn't waste their time when I put a record out. I could have put out a whole lot more casual records but, at the time, you're honing an identity of some sort.

An image?
Image? Sort of, I suppose. That's part of it to some degree, but that's like the top part—the frothy stuff.

Did you ever have a big gay following?
Not to my knowledge.

There was always something very camp about that grease-monkey-baseball-hat-in-the-back-pocket look during *Born in the U.S.A.* . . .
It was probably my own fault. Who knows, I was probably working out my own insecurities, y'know? That particular image is probably the only time I look back over pictures of the band and it feels like a caricature to me.

Everything before and after that is just people, but that particular moment I always go, "Jeez," y'know? I couldn't tell you what that was about.

All I could tell you was, when I wrote "Streets of Philadelphia" and I had some contact with gay people, who the song had meant something to, I felt the image that I had at that time could have been misinterpreted, y'know? That is something that I regretted and still do regret, to some degree.

But I think, at the same time, it must have been an easy image to latch onto. Maybe it had something to do with why it was powerful or what it represented. But it was very edgy to me and very close to—if it wasn't already—over-simplification. It was certainly over-simplified if you just saw the image and didn't go to the show and get a sense of where it was coming from and what it was about. It had implications that I didn't tune into at the time and I don't really feel are a fundamental part of my work.

Is there an element of surrealism playing at the Rock and Roll Hall of Fame and finding yourself standing beside the real, living, breathing heroes you once worshipped from a distance?
Yeah, one night I was standing between George Harrison and Mick Jagger and y'know, I sat in my room with their records, I learned to play my guitar from those records. I studied every riff and the way they played it, and my initial bands were modeled on them. So there's always a little bit of, "Hey, what am I doing here?" You realise there were millions and millions of kids at that time that had that particular fantasy or whatever you want to call it.

But I'm sort of glad I have a place generationally, where I get to stand with those people onstage. It's a tremendous source of pleasure being able to back up Chuck Berry, one of the great American writers, a *great* American writer. He captured an essential part of the country in a fashion that no one has done before or since."

Are you sad that his creative life as a writer lasted for such a short period?
That's just the way it goes. I have no idea how people's creative instincts work. I'm just glad for the work he's done. It was very influential in my work in the sense that there was a lot of detail in the writing, fundamental images I carried into my own music.

That's the course of rock music. It's very unusual to be 20 or 25 years down the line and still be doing vital work. I think the reason is, it takes an enormous leap of faith at the time of your success, a leap of consciousness, and the ability to suss out what is essential and what is bullshit is very important.

Money comes in—great! We can let the good times roll, we can have fun with it. But if you start out and get caught up in the idea that these things are going to sustain you in some fashion when you get 20 years down the road, you're gonna be in for a surprise.

Right now, I don't need records that are Number One. I don't need to sell records that are going to make millions. I need to do work that I feel is central, vital, that sets me in the present, where I don't have to come out at night and depend upon my history or a song I wrote 20 years ago. What I'm interested in doing now is finding my place in the world as it stands. That to me is what is vital and sustains you and gives you the commitment and motivation to tour and stand behind your work. That's all I know, 20 or 25 years down the line.

Is there a sense of fear attached to what you do?
Of course, that's part of everything. I think if there is a fear, it's a fear of slipping out of things. By that I don't mean the mainstream of the music business. This particular record, I knew when I put it out it wasn't going to be on the radio very much, and it wasn't! Fundamentally, it wasn't going to be part of what the mainstream music business is today, in the States anyway.

We've all seen *Spinal Tap*, with the idea of an audience becoming more selective.
[*Laughs*] I guess there's the sense that you are protective over your artistic life and creative impetus, your creative instinct, your creative vitality.

That's something I've known since I was tearing the posters down in 1975 [on his first visit to Britain, Springsteen went on the rampage, tearing down posters outside Hammersmith Odeon proclaiming him "the future of rock 'n' roll"] and it's something I still feel real strongly about today.

Are there moments when you've surprised or disappointed yourself?
You're always doing that. You look back and say, "I did that well, I didn't do that, I communicated well here but not there." It's just endless, y'know? That's the idea, that's why you've always got some place to go tomorrow, something to do now. That's why this particular music is not a rock show, it's not unplugged, it's something else. I don't even know if I should call it a folk show. In a funny way, the songs are based in rock music, but I suppose it's based around the new record. It's not a night where I come out and play hits or favorite songs you wanna hear. There's no pay-off at the end of the night with those things. It is what it is and that's my intent.

Is your ongoing work a reaction and extension of the work you've done in the past?
Of course, because the artist's job, in my opinion, is to try and answer the questions that your body of work throws up, or at least pose new questions. With this record, that's what I'm trying to do.

"I felt for ten years I put a lot of those questions on hold because I was writing about other things, I was having some reaction to the *Born in the U.S.A.* experience, because I was finding my way through a new life, in some sense.

On the sleevenote to your *Hits* collection you describe "Born to Run" as your shot at the title, a 25-year-old's attempt to craft "the greatest record ever made." How do you feel about it today?
Oh, I don't know, I can't listen to it objectively, it's too caught up in my life. I don't sit around listening to my work, I'd be insane if I did, I'd be crazy. I like it as a record but, right now, it's hard for me to hear it because it's caught up with so many other things.

It's a really good song. The way I would record it now would be a lot different, probably not as good, because I would be afraid of going over the top, and there's a moment to go completely over the top and push the edge of things."

Your relationship with "Born in the U.S.A." is like Dylan's with "Like a Rolling Stone," trying to grasp back the song's real meaning rather than allowing it to become a faceless anthem. It wasn't just Ronald Reagan (who tried to claim it as an effective endorsement of his jingoistic agenda) who misinterpreted the song.
The record of it I still feel is very good and I wouldn't change it or want it to be different. I wouldn't want the version that I'm doing now to have come out at that time. At that particular moment, it was how I heard it and it happened in a couple of takes.

You put your music out and it comes back to you in a variety of different ways through your audience. But a songwriter always has the opportunity to go out and reclarify or reclaim his work; it pushes you to be inventive. I think the version I have now . . . for me, at least, it's the best version I've done of the song, I suppose it's the truest, y'know. It's got it all—everything it needs to be understood at the moment."

You write a lot about killers—people like the death-row inmate played by Sean Penn in _Dead Man Walking_ [Springsteen's title song for the Tim Robbins–directed movie has just been Oscar-nominated] and the slayer in "Nebraska." Have you ever met a real-life killer? Is it necessary, to do your job right?
No, you're not trying to re-create the experience, you're trying to re-create the emotions and the things that went into the action being taken. Those are things that everyone understands, those are things that everyone has within them. The action is the symptom, that's what happened, but the things that caused that action to happen, that's what everyone knows about—you know about it, I know about it. It's inside of every human being.

Those are the things you gotta mine, that's the well that you gotta dip into and, if you're doing that, you're going to get something central and fundamental about those characters."

So it's just coincidence that you currently look like the character Sean Penn plays in the movie?
I do? I didn't realise that. Help! I'm going home . . . I don't have as much hair as he does, for a start."

Judy Wieder
The Advocate,
April 2, 1996

In the aftermath of the success of "Streets of Philadelphia," Springsteen spoke with the editor of the *Advocate*, a national magazine devoted to gay and lesbian issues. Springsteen discusses gay rights and his attitudes toward sexual preferences and cultural conformity. As for parenting, Springsteen admits that "accepting the idea that your child has his own life is the hardest thing to do."

"The bonus I got out of writing 'Streets of Philadelphia' was that all of a sudden I could go out and meet some gay man somewhere and he wouldn't be afraid to talk to me and say, 'Hey, that song really meant something to me.' My image had always been very heterosexual, very straight. So it was a nice experience for me, a chance to clarify my own feelings about gay and lesbian civil rights," says rock's most thoughtful megastar, Bruce Springsteen. Sitting in the dimly lit living room of a West Hollywood hotel suite, the man the world calls "the Boss" is talking about his 1994 Oscar and Grammy Award–winning song from the film *Philadelphia*—a song detailing the feelings of a gay man facing the final turmoil of his struggle with AIDS.

Now, with his second Oscar-nominated song, "Dead Man Walkin'," and his stark new acoustic album, *The Ghost of Tom Joad*, the 46-year-old Springsteen seems relieved to have returned once again to the deliberately noncommercial core of his best social-commentary songwriting skills. Like "Streets of Philadelphia" and 1982's daring *Nebraska*—recorded on his home tape recorder—Springsteen's latest album and tour strip his muscular stadium rock down to a dark one-man stage show. No E Street Band, no mania-driven masses waving lighters from the balconies and shrieking "Bru-u-u-ce!" Just Springsteen, alone onstage, singing out from the shadows of all that's gone wrong between people in the world today.

For many skeptics, the idea of a hard-core rocker from the mean streets of New Jersey growing up, growing rich, and aligning himself with those who have not is pretty far-fetched. Yet that's essentially the Springsteen way. Although he has sold millions of albums, filled thousands of concert arenas, and won mantelsful of Grammy and American Music awards, over the years he's still managed to lend his support directly or indirectly to people and causes as diverse as Amnesty International, feeding the starving in Africa ("We Are the World"), the plight of immigrants, AIDS awareness, and the struggles of gays and lesbians. "After Bruce supported me by appearing on my VH1 special last year, we became friends," says out lesbian rocker Melissa Etheridge. "I think the experience of having his song in *Philadelphia* led him to meet a lot of gay people and learn a lot about our lives. My girlfriend, Julie, is always with me when we go to his house, and he always treats us as a couple. I've often talked to him about my frustration over not being able to get legally married, and he's always supportive and sympathetic."

Springsteen's own struggles with finding love and settling down have been well documented in both his songs and the press. After his herculean 11-year rise to superstardom—which began with *Greetings from Asbury Park, N.J.* in 1973 and culminated in 1984 with *Born in the U.S.A.*—he married model-actress Julianne Phillips. The marriage ended in the tabloids four years later when Springsteen fell in love with his backup singer, Patti Scialfa. They were married in 1991 and have three children.

You think you'll win another Oscar for your song "Dead Man Walkin'"?

[*Laughing*] Oh, I don't know. When those Disney pictures are out there [*Pocahontas*], you don't stand a chance. "Dead Man Walking" is another song that's pretty offbeat, so I am not really expecting one.

Still, offbeat subject matter served you well in "Streets of Philadelphia." You say you're pleased that gays and lesbians began approaching you after that song?
Oh, yeah! I had people come up to me in the streets or in restaurants and say, "I have a friend" or "I have a lover" or "I have a partner" or "I have a son."

Why do you think Jonathan Demme—the director—asked you to write a song for *Philadelphia*?
Demme told me that *Philadelphia* was a movie he was making "for the malls." I'm sure that was one of the reasons why he called me, I think he wanted to take a subject that people didn't feel safe with and were frightened by and put it together with people that they did feel safe with like Tom Hanks or me or Neil Young. I always felt that was my job.

How could you make people feel safe?
When I first started in rock, I had a big guys audience for my early records. I had a very straight image, particularly through the mid '80s.

But why could you reach them?
I knew where the fear came from. I was brought up in a small town, and I basically received nothing but negative images about homosexuality—very bad. Anybody who was different in any fashion was castigated and ostracized, if not physically threatened.

Did you have some personal inspiration for the song?
I had a very close friend who had sarcoma cancer and died right around that time. For me, it was a very devastating experience, being close to illness of that magnitude. I had never experienced what it calls on or asks of the people around the person who is so ill. Part of that experience ended up in the song.

You caught a particular isolation that many gay AIDS patients experience. When there are walls between people and there is a lack of acceptance, you can reach for that particular kind of communion: "Receive me, brother" is the lyric in the last verse.
That's all anybody's asking for—basically some sort of acceptance and to not be left alone. There was a certain spiritual stillness that I wanted

to try to capture. Then I just tried to send in a human voice, as human a voice as I possibly could. I wanted you to be in somebody's head, hearing their thoughts—somebody who was on the cusp of death but still experiencing the feeling of being very alive.

Were you surprised the song was a hit?
I would never have thought in a million years it was going to get radio airplay. But people were looking for things to assist them in making sense of the AIDS crisis, in making human connections. I think that is what film and art and music do; they can work as a map of sorts for your feelings.

Because you come from the streets of New Jersey, was there a personal journey for you in accepting and learning about homosexuality? Did it ever frighten you?
I don't know if frighten would be the right word. I was pretty much a misfit in my own town, so I didn't buy a lot of those negative attitudes. Sure, you are affected and influenced by them. But I think that your entire life is a process of sorting out some of those early messages that you got. I guess the main thing was that the gay image back then was the '50s image, the town queen or something, and that was all anyone really knew about homosexuality. Everybody's attitudes were quite brutal. It was that real ugly part of the American character.

When you said you were a misfit, what did you mean?
Basically, I was pretty ostracized in my hometown. Me and a few other guys were the town freaks—and there were many occasions when we were dodging getting beaten up ourselves. So, no, I didn't feel a part of those homophobic ideas. Also, I started to play in clubs when I was 16 or 17, and I was exposed to a lot of different lifestyles and a lot of different things. It was the '60s, and I was young, I was open-minded, and I wasn't naturally intolerant. I think the main problem was that nobody had any real experience with gay culture, so your impression of it was incredibly narrow.

So you actually met gay people?
Yeah, I had gay friends. The first thing I realized was that everybody's different, and it becomes obvious that all of the gay stereotypes are ridiculous [*laughs*]. I did pretty good with it.

Because of your macho rock image, I didn't know if you were going to tell me, "Oh, yeah, there were years when I didn't want anybody to feel that I had any sympathy for that."

No, I always felt that amongst my core fans—because there was a level of popularity that I had in the mid '80s that was sort of a bump on the scale—they fundamentally understood the values that are at work in my work. Certainly tolerance and acceptance were at the forefront of my music. If my work was about anything, it was about the search for identity, for personal recognition, for acceptance, for communion, and for a big country. I've always felt that's why people come to my shows, because they feel that big country in their hearts.

You mean a country big enough for everyone?

Yes. Unfortunately, once you get a really big audience, then people come for a lot of different reasons. And they can misunderstand the songs.

You even had to deal with President Reagan thinking "Born in the U.S.A." was about his values.

Yes, at that one point the country moved to the right, and there was a lot of nastiness, intolerance, and attitudes that gave rise to more intolerance. So I'm always in the process of trying to clarify who I am and what I do. That's why I wanted to talk to you.

On *The Ghost of Tom Joad*, you have a song, "Balboa Park," and in it you say, "Where the men in their Mercedes / Come nightly to employ . . . / The services of the border boys." Are you talking about drugs or sex or both?

I'm talking about sex, hustling.

What do you know about this subject?

I read about it in a series of articles the *Los Angeles Times* did about border life. It fit into the rest of the subject matter in the album.

It's impossible for most people to imagine the kind of fame you have. Everyone in the world knows who you are. Does it make you feel alienated?

The only thing I can say about having this type of success is that you can get yourself in trouble because basically the world is set open for you. People will say yes to anything you ask, so it's basically down to you and what you want or need. Yes, you can get isolated with an enormous amount of wealth and fame. You can get isolated with a six-pack of beer and a television set. I grew up in a community where plenty of people were isolated in that fashion.

How do you keep your personal life connected to the real world?
Over the years I think you may have to strive for some normalcy. Like you need to say, "Hey, I'm not going to lock myself up in my house tonight. I'm going to go to the movies or maybe down to a club or take my kids to Universal Studios."

What keeps you connected?
You have to want to be included. I always saw myself as the kid who got the guitar and was going to hold it for a while and play it and pass it on to somebody else. I always saw a lot of myself in my audience.

But that changed when you got so big.
True, and by anybody's measure I have an extravagant lifestyle. But I never felt that I've lost myself in it. I want to feel that essential spiritual connection that you make with your deep audience, your true audience.

So that's how you've kept it balanced?
Yeah. I just felt that what I was doing was rooted in a community—either real or imagined—and that my connection to that community was what made my writing and singing matter. I didn't feel that those connections were casual connections. I felt that they were essential connections. I was a serious young man, you know? I had serious ideas about rock music. Yeah, it was also a circus and fun and a dance party—all of those things—but still a serious thing. I believed that serious things could be done with it. It had a power; it had a voice. I still fucking believe that. I really do.

And I assume that your being here today means that you want gays and lesbians to feel they're a part of this community—this big country?
Yeah, very much so. The ongoing clarification of the way I feel, of my ideas, where I stand on different issues: That's my work now. That's why

this interview is a great opportunity for me. Hey—you write, and you want your music understood.

When you fell in love with your wife, Patti, there was a lot of negativity in the press because your marriage to Julianne Phillips was breaking up. Did your experience with this kind of intrusion into your private life give you any idea what it's like for gays and lesbians, who constantly get criticized for who they love?

It's a strange society that assumes it has the right to tell people whom they should love and whom they shouldn't. But the truth is, I basically ignored the entire thing as much as I could. I said, "Well, all I know is, this feels real, and maybe I have got a mess going on here in some fashion, but that's life."

But that's everything: This feels real.

That's it. Trust yourself in the end. Those are the only lights that can go by, and the world will catch up. But I think it would be much more difficult to be gay, particularly in the town that I grew up in. Divorce may have been difficult for me, but I don't know what it would be like to have your heart in one place and have somebody say, "Hey, you can't do that." So all anybody can do is their best. Like when President Clinton came into office, the first thing he tried to do was have gays in the military. I thought, Wow! A leader. I just felt that he was leading.

What did you feel when it all fell apart?

Initially I felt surprised at the reaction. I was surprised that it was such a big deal. But that's what the federal government is supposed to do: It is supposed to encourage tolerance. If you can't get acceptance, tolerance will have to do. Acceptance will come later. That's what the laws are for. So I was saddened by the fate of the whole thing and the beating that he took.

Were you surprised when Melissa Etheridge was able to come out and still have success in rock and roll?

It was tremendously groundbreaking. The rock world is a funny world, a world where simultaneously there is a tremendous amount of macho posturing and homophobia—a lot of it, in my experience—and yet it has as its basic rule the idea that you are supposed to be who you are.

When I first heard about Melissa, I was very happy to see that that was where some of the seeds of what I had done had fallen. I said, "Wow, a lesbian rock singer who came up through the gay bars! I don't believe it!" [*Laughing*] I felt really good about it.

I understand you and Patti and Melissa and her Julie have become friends.
We have gotten to know each other since her VH1 special. Since then, we've got a nice relationship going.

She told me she's talked with you about the fight gays and lesbians are in to have the right to be legally married. Some people, especially heterosexuals, think it isn't that important. I've had well-meaning people say, "But you know that loving is all that's important. Getting married isn't."
It does matter. It does matter. There was actually a long time when I was coming from the same place: "Hey, what's the difference? You have got the person you care about." I know that I went through a divorce, and it was really difficult and painful and I was very frightened about getting married again. So part of me said, Hey, what does it matter? But it does matter. It's very different than just living together. First of all, stepping up publicly—which is what you do: You get your license, you do all the social rituals—is part of your place in society and in some way part of society's acceptance of you.

You and Patti decided you needed that?
Yes, Patti and I both found that it did mean something. Coming out and saying whom you love, how you feel about them, in a public way was very, very important. Those are the threads of society; that's how we all live together in some fashion. There is no reason I can see why gays and lesbians shouldn't get married. It is important because those are the things that bring you in and make you feel a part of the social fabric. The idea that Melissa and Julie can't be married—that seems ridiculous to me. Ridiculous!

So you, a rock star, a symbol of counterculture earlier in your life, have come to defend the importance of traditions?
Yeah, oh, yeah. It's like, my kids are sort of little heathens at the moment [*laughs*]. They have no particular religious information. Ten years

ago I would have said, "Who cares? They'll figure it out on their own." But you are supposed to provide some direction for your children. So you look for institutions that can speak to you and that you can feel a part of and be a part of and that will allow you to feel included and be a part of the community.

What about gays and lesbians having children?
Being a good or bad parent is not something that hinges on your particular sexual preference. I think that people have some idea of what the ideal parent is. I don't know any ideal parents. I have met single mothers who are doing an incredible job of raising their kids. I don't feel sexual preference is a central issue.

You have three children. What would you do if one of them came to you and said, "I think I'm gay"?
Whatever their sexual preference might be when they grow up, I think accepting the idea that your child has his own life is the hardest thing to do. That life begins, and you can see it the minute they hit the boards. I think that when I was growing up, that was difficult for my dad to accept that I wasn't like him, I was different. Or maybe I was like him, and he didn't like that part of himself—more likely. I was gentle, and generally that was the kind of kid I was. I was a sensitive kid. I think most of the people who move into the arts are. But basically, for me, that lack of acceptance was devastating, really devastating.

Your father didn't accept you?
Yeah, and it was certainly one of the most devastating experiences. I think your job as a parent is to try to nurture and guide. If one of my kids came and said that to me—hey, you want them to find happiness, you want them to find fulfillment. So they're the ones who are going to have to decide what that is for them.

Does it get harder and harder for you, in terms of being a father, as your children define themselves more and more?
Yeah, because you are caught up with your children's identities. You try not to be rigid, but you do find out the places where you are rigid. And you do get caught up in really some of the great clichés of parenting, whether it is wanting them to excel at some particular sport—I mean, really, just some of the dumbest things.

It's hard to separate?
Yeah, it's the separation.

And then to have your child's sexuality be different from your own, that would be difficult, right?
I think that with a lot of these issues, you just don't know until they truly enter your life in some really personal way. You have your lights that you are trying to steer by, everybody has those. But then you have all that stuff that's been laid on you that you're working your way through. Sure, I can sit back and say I know how I would want to react. I know what I would want to say and how I would want to feel. But unless those things enter my life in some personal fashion, I don't know how I will act.

I think that is very honest. Do you have any family members who are gay?
No [*laughing*]. I have a very eccentric family, but, no, nobody gay in my immediate family.

In your whole career, have you ever had a man ask you out or make a pass at you?
Once or twice when I was younger. Yes [*laughs*]—I mean, no, not exactly directly—[*laughs again*] but you know how those things are.

Being gay or lesbian is a unique minority in the sense that we can pretend we're straight if we don't want to encounter homophobic feelings, including our own. Unfortunately, we'll never change the world that way. To that end it's important to identify ourselves so that people learn how many people really are gay. As always, there is a tremendous conflict going on in the gay community about pushing people to come out—especially celebrities, because of their wide visibility. Do you have any strong feelings about it?
I have to come at it from the idea of personal privacy. To me, that is a decision that each individual should be free to make. I don't know if someone should make as profoundly a personal decision as that for you. I'm not comfortable with that.

But would you encourage them?

Sure, you can say, "Hey, come on, step up to the plate" or "We need you" or "It'll make a big difference," and that would be absolutely true and valid. But in the end—hey, it's not your life.

Do you think they could get hurt professionally?

If you're in the entertainment business, it's a world of illusion, a world of symbols. So I think you're talking about somebody who may feel their livelihood is threatened. I think you've got to move the world in the right direction so that there is acceptance and tolerance, so that the laws protect everybody's civil rights, gay, straight, whatever. But then you also have got to give people the room to make their own decisions.

But on a very personal level, what would you tell somebody who asked you for advice about whether or not he or she should come out?

First of all, I can only imagine that not being able to be yourself is a painful thing. It's awful to have to wear a mask or hide yourself. So at the end of my conversation, I'd just say, "Hey, this is how the world is; these are the consequences, and these are your fundamental feelings." Because a person's sexuality is such an essential part of who he is, to not be able to express it the way that you feel it [*sighs*] has just got to be so very painful.

Will Percy
DoubleTake,
Spring 1998

Springsteen drew on many literary influences in his work, not least the writing of novelist and essayist Walker Percy—himself, it turned out, a Springsteen "admirer." Both writers' work are informed by struggles with Catholicism, and though they never met, their affinity provided occasion for one of Springsteen's most thoughtful and wide-ranging interviews. Dr. Percy's nephew, Will Percy, talked at length with Springsteen about his influences, literary and otherwise, about celebrity, alienation, and the cultural landscape of America. Bruce references Dr. Percy's essays throughout, and in a way this interview is a conversation with a ghost. Not responding to a "fan letter—of sorts" or fully appreciating his work until after Percy's death, Springsteen wrote to his widow: "It is now one of my great regrets that we didn't get to correspond."

In early 1989, Walker Percy penned a fan letter "of sorts" to Bruce Springsteen, praising the musician's "spiritual journey" and hoping to begin a correspondence between them. At the time, Springsteen hesitated in responding, but he later picked up a copy of *The Moviegoer* and began a new journey into Dr. Percy's writing. Walker Percy died in May 1990, and the two never met, but Percy's novels and essays, among other books and films, have had a most profound impact on Springsteen's songwriting. In 1995, Springsteen recorded *The Ghost of Tom Joad,* a richly lyrical album that forged a new purpose for his music, linking him in some ways to the tradition of such artist-activists as John Steinbeck (Joad is the radical hero of *The Grapes of Wrath*) and folk music icon Woody Guthrie. Springsteen's songs tell us, in their familiar narrative style, about ordinary people struggling through life's twists and turns, presenting a cast of characters that includes immigrant families, border patrolmen, Midwestern steelworkers, and America's poor and disenfranchised. The populist sensibility of Guthrie can be heard throughout: it is music competing for the public conscience.

Following an Atlanta concert promoting the album, Will Percy, Walker's nephew, met Springsteen backstage, and the two talked for hours. When Springsteen mentioned his regret at never having written back to Will's uncle, Will encouraged him to write to his aunt, Walker's widow. A few months later, Springsteen, who likes to say that "it's hard for me to write unless there's music underneath," sat down and wrote four pages—a letter years in the making.

Last fall, Will Percy and Springsteen had the chance to meet again, this time on the Springsteen farm in central New Jersey, not far from the small town where Springsteen grew up or from the Jersey Shore clubs where he first made his mark in the 1970s. With a tape running, the two explored the importance of books in Springsteen's life, most recently his discovery of Dr. Percy's essays in *The Message in the Bottle.* Like the long-in-coming letter to Mrs. Percy, perhaps this is part of the conversation that Bruce Springsteen might have had with Walker Percy.

When did books start influencing your songwriting and music? I remember as early as 1978, when I saw you in concert you mentioned Ron Kovic's *Born on the Fourth of July,* and you dedicated a song to him.

I picked up that book in a drugstore in Arizona while I was driving across the country with a friend of mine. We stopped somewhere outside of Phoenix, and there was a copy of the paperback in the rack. So I bought the book and I read it between Phoenix and Los Angeles, where I stayed in this little motel. There was a guy in a wheelchair by the poolside every day, two or three days in a row, and I guess he recognized me, and he finally came up to me and said, "Hey, I'm Ron Kovic"—it was really very strange—and I said, "Oh, Ron Kovic, gee, that's good." I thought I'd met him before somewhere. And he said, "No, I wrote a book called *Born on the Fourth of July.*" And I said, "You wouldn't believe this. I just bought your book in a drugstore in Arizona and I just read it. It's incredible." Real, real powerful book. And we talked a little bit and he got me interested in doing something for the vets. He took me to a vet center in Venice, and I met a bunch of guys along with this guy Bobby Muller who was one of the guys who started VVA, Vietnam Veterans of America.

I go through periods where I read, and I get a lot out of what I read, and that reading has affected my work since the late seventies. Films and novels and books, more so than music, are what have really been driving me since then. Your uncle once wrote that "American novels are about everything," and I was interested in writing about "everything" in some fashion in my music: how it felt to be alive now, a citizen of this country in this particular place and time and what that meant and what your possibilities were if you were born and alive now, what you could do, what you were capable of doing. Those were ideas that interested me.

The really important reading that I did began in my late twenties, with authors like Flannery O'Connor. There was something in those stories of hers that I felt captured a certain part of the American character that I was interested in writing about. They were a big, big revelation. She got to the heart of some part of meanness that she never spelled out, because if she spelled it out you wouldn't be getting it. It was always at the core of every one of her stories—the way that she'd left that hole there, that hole that's inside of everybody. There was some dark thing—a component of spirituality—that I sensed in her stories, and that set me off exploring characters of my own. She knew original sin—knew how to give it the flesh of a story. She had talent and she had ideas, and the one served the other.

I think I'd come out of a period of my own writing where I'd been writing big, sometimes operatic, and occasionally rhetorical things. I was interested in finding another way to write about those subjects, about people, another way to address what was going on around me and in the country—a more scaled-down, more personal, more restrained way of getting some of my ideas across. So right prior to the record

Nebraska [1982], I was deep into O'Connor. And then, later on, that led me to your uncle's books, and Bobbie Ann Mason's novels—I like her work.

I've also gotten a lot out of Robert Frank's photography in *The Americans*. I was twenty-four when I first saw the book—I think a friend had given me a copy—and the tone of the pictures, how he gave us a look at different kinds of people, got to me in some way. I've always wished I could write songs the way he takes pictures. I think I've got half a dozen copies of that book stashed around the house, and I pull one out once in a while to get a fresh look at the photographs.

I find it interesting that you're influenced a lot by movies—you said you're more influenced by movies and books than music. In the liner notes of *The Ghost of Tom Joad* you credited both the John Ford film and the book *The Grapes of Wrath* by Steinbeck.
I came by the film before I really came by the book. I'd read the book in high school, along with *Of Mice and Men* and a few others, and then I read it again after I saw the movie. But I didn't grow up in a community of ideas—a place where you can sit down and talk about books, and how you read through them, and how they affect you. For a year, I went to a local college a few miles up the road from here, but I didn't really get much out of that particular place. I think I'm more a product of pop culture: films and records, films and records, films and records, especially early on. And then later, more novels and reading.

Where did you draw your musical influences in your earlier writing as compared with this last album?
Up until the late seventies, when I started to write songs that had to do with class issues, I was influenced more by music like the Animals' "We Gotta Get Out of This Place" or "It's My Life (And I'll Do What I Want)"—sort of class-conscious pop records that I'd listen to—and I'd say to myself: "That's my life, that's my life!" They said something to me about my own experience of exclusion. I think that's been a theme that's run through much of my writing: the politics of exclusion. My characters aren't really antiheroes. Maybe that makes them old-fashioned in some way. They're interested in being included, and they're trying to figure out what's in their way.

I'd been really involved with country music right prior to the album *Darkness on the Edge of Town* [1978], and that had a lot of effect on my writing because I think country is a very class-conscious music. And then that interest slowly led me into Woody Guthrie and folk music. Guthrie was one of the few songwriters at the time who was aware of the political implications of the music he was writing—a real part of his consciousness. He set out intentionally to address a wide variety of issues, to have some effect, to have some impact, to be writing as a way to have some impact on things: playing his part in the way things are moving and things change.

I was always trying to shoot for the moon. I had some lofty ideas about using my own music, to give people something to think about—to think about the world, and what's right and wrong. I'd been affected that way by records, and I wanted my own music and writing to extend themselves in that way.

I notice that you talk about "writing" and not "songwriting." Do you sit down and write lyrics and then look for music?
When I'd write rock music, music with the whole band, it would some-times start out purely musically, and then I'd find my way to some lyr-ics. I haven't written like that in a while. In much of my recent writing, the lyrics have preceded the music, though the music is always in the back of my mind. In most of the recent songs, I tell violent stories very quietly. You're hearing characters' thoughts—what they're thinking after all the events that have shaped their situation have transpired. So I try to get that internal sound, like that feeling at night when you're in bed and staring at the ceiling, reflective in some fashion. I wanted the songs to have the kind of intimacy that took you inside yourself and then back out into the world.

I'll use music as a way of defining and coloring the characters, con-veying the characters' rhythm of speech and pace. The music acts as a very still surface, and the lyrics create a violent emotional life over it or under it, and I let those elements bang up against each other.

Music can seem incidental, but it ends up being very important. It allows you to suggest the passage of time in just a couple of quiet beats. Years can go by in a few bars, whereas a writer will have to come up with a clever way of saying, "And then years went by . . ." Thank God I don't have to do any of that! Songwriting allows you to cheat tremen-dously. You can present an entire life in a few minutes. And then hope-fully, at the end, you reveal something about yourself and your audience and the person in the song. It has a little in common with short-story writing in that it's character-driven. The characters are confronting the questions that everyone is trying to sort out for themselves, their moral issues, the way those issues rear their heads in the outside world.

While your previous albums might all come from personal experience—from the people and places you grew up with in New Jersey and elsewhere—you seem to have started writing more about other people and topics now, Mexican immigrants, for instance, in songs like "Sinaloa Cowboys." With that song, I remember you said in concert that it started out when you met a couple of Mexican brothers in the desert once when you were traveling.
There's no single place where any of the songs come from, of course. True, I drew a lot of my earlier material from my experience growing up, my father's experience, the experience of my immediate family and town. But there was a point in the mid-eighties when I felt like I'd said pretty much all I knew how to say about all that. I couldn't continue writing about those same things without either becoming a stereotype of myself or by twisting those themes around too much. So I spent the next ten years or so writing about men and women—their intimate personal lives. I was being introspective but not autobiographical. It wasn't until I felt like I had a stable life in that area that I was driven to write more outwardly—about social issues.

A song like "Sinaloa Cowboys" came from a lot of places. I'd met a guy in the Arizona desert when I happened to be on a trip with some friends of mine, and he had a younger brother who died in a motorcycle accident. There's something about conversations with people—people you've met once, and you'll never see again—that always stays with me. And I lived for quite a while in Los Angeles, and border reporting and immigration issues are always in the paper there. I've traveled down to the border a number of times.

Why would you travel down to the border?
With my dad, I'd take trips to Mexico a few years back. We'd take these extended road trips where we'd basically drive aimlessly. The border wasn't something I was consciously thinking about, it was just one of those places that all of a sudden starts meaning something to you. I'm always looking for ways to tell a particular story, and I just felt the connection, I can't explain what it was exactly—a connection to some of the things I'd written about in the past.

I don't think you sit down and write anything that isn't personal in some way. In the end, all your work is a result of your own psychology and experience. I never really write with a particular ideology in mind. As a writer, you're searching for ways to present different moral questions to yourself because you're not sure how you will respond, and to your audience. That's what you get paid for—from what I can tell. Part of what we call entertainment should be "food for thought." That's what I was interested in doing since I was very young, how we live in the world and how we ought to live in the world. I think politics are implicit. I'm not interested in writing rhetoric or ideology. I think it was Walt Whitman who said, "The poet's job is to know the soul!" You strive for that, assist your audience in finding and knowing theirs. That's always at the core of what you're writing, of what drives your music.

It's all really in your uncle's essay "The Man on the Train" about the "wandering spirit" and modern man—that's happened since the Industrial Revolution when people were uprooted and set out on the road into towns where they'd never been before, leaving families, leaving traditions that were hundreds of years old. In a funny way, you can even trace that story in Chuck Berry's "Johnny B. Goode!" I think that we're all trying to find what passes for a home, or creating a home of some sort while we're constantly being uprooted by technology, by factories being shut down.

I remember when my parents moved out to California—I was about eighteen. My folks decided that they were going to leave New Jersey, but they had no idea really where to go. I had a girlfriend at the time and she was sort of a hippie. She was the only person we knew who'd ever been to California. She'd been to Sausalito and suggested they go there. You can just imagine—Sausalito in the late sixties! So they went to Sausalito, three thousand miles across the country, and they probably had only three grand that they'd saved and that had to get them a place to live, and they had to go out and find work. So they got to Sausalito and realized this wasn't it. My mother said they went to a gas station and she asked the guy there, "Where do people like us live?"— that's a question that sounds like the title of a Raymond Carver story!— and the guy told her, "Oh, you live on the peninsula." And that was what they did. They drove down south of San Francisco and they've been there ever since. My father was forty-two at the time—it's funny to think that he was probably seven or eight years younger than I am

"The last morning. I had a gig in Providence, Rhode Island, that night; I was singing 'She's the One' at the same time I was mixing 'Jungleland' in another studio downstairs; at the same time I was in another studio, rehearsing the band for the gig that night. That's the truth. I almost died. There's a picture of it, this girl Barbara took a picture of it, and it's the scariest thing I've ever seen. You have to see the band. It should be on the cover of that album . . . You ain't never seen faces like that in your life. She may have it, it's something to see . . . we were there for four days, and every single minute is in everybody's face . . . and what's worse is, I can't even sing! The picture just captures that moment."
—*Bruce Springsteen on the end of the* Born to Run *sessions, 1975*

Photographer Barbara Pyle: "It was six a.m. when they went into their only rehearsal for the *Born to Run* tour. After days of windowless recording, the first rays of dawn pierced the tattered curtains of the rehearsal studio, striking the weary bodies of the band on the brink of collapse. Instinctively I grabbed my Leica M3 from my purse, as my heart skipped a beat—I knew, as I had known many nights during these sessions, that I was witnessing rock 'n' roll history in the making. With *Born to Run* finally finished, they walked out of rehearsal and onto the bus for their 'one last chance to make it real' . . ."
The Record Plant, New York, NY, July 20, 1975. © Barbara Pyle

Before soundcheck outside the Houston Music Hall on the *Born to Run* tour. Houston, TX, September 13, 1975. © Barbara Pyle

"I wouldn't trade these guys for nobody." The *Darkness*-era E Street Band [L-R]: Garry Tallent, "Miami" Steve Van Zandt, Max Weinberg, Bruce Springsteen, Clarence Clemons, Danny Federici, and Roy Bittan. New York, NY, 1978. © 1978 Lynn Goldsmith

"The audience is not brought to you or given to you, it's something that you *fight* for." Note Springsteen's photo in the newspaper article touting "SOAP: The Sound of Asbury Park." At home in Holmdel, NJ, 1977. © Eric Meola

At soundcheck on the European leg of the *River* tour, listening as the band played "Hungry Heart." Photographer Jim Marchese: "Bruce would walk all around the arenas, checking every corner of the room, so that the sound was perfect for every fan. If a slight adjustment had to be made to the PA speakers that would give a better sound to the last seat, Bruce would correct it. And then he would sit and listen as the band played." Brussels, Belgium, April 26, 1981.
© JimMarchese.com

"At the end of the *Born in the U.S.A.* tour and after we made the live album, I felt like it was the end of the first part of my journey." Shortly before the release of *Tunnel of Love*, Springsteen works at home at his writing table (which would later be displayed at the Rock and Roll Hall of Fame). Rumson, New Jersey, 1987. © Pam Springsteen

"The whole idea with the band was to get back together but move very consciously forward." At Convention Hall, on the Asbury Park boardwalk, Springsteen warmed up the newly rededicated E Street Band with a pair of intimate rehearsal shows before setting out to tour the world. Asbury Park, NJ, March 1999. © Danny Clinch

After five years playing with the reunited E Street Band, Springsteen goes it alone again with *Devils & Dust*. "With my audience, one of the things I've tried to do is retain the complexity of human life or human experience. I want to see and be seen within those parameters. That's where your freedom is, and that's where your true dialogue, a deeper dialogue with your fans, can take place." Colts Neck, NJ, 2004. © Frank Stefanko

Monmouth County, NJ, 2010. © Danny Clinch

now. It was a big trip, took a lot of nerve, a lot of courage, having grown up in my little town in New Jersey.

But that story leads back to those same questions: how do you create the kind of home you want to live in, how do you create the kind of society you want to live in, what part do you play in doing that? To me, those things are all connected, but those connections are hard to make. The pace of the modern world, industrialization, postindustrialization, have all made human connection very difficult to maintain and sustain. To bring that modern situation alive—how we live now, our hang-ups and choices—that's what music and film and art are about—that's the service you're providing, that's the function you're providing as an artist. That's what keeps me interested in writing.

What we call "art" has to do with social policy—and it has to do with how you and your wife or you and your lover are getting along on any given day. I was interested in my music covering all those bases. And how do I do that? I do that by telling stories, through characters' voices—hopefully stories about inclusion. The stories in *The Ghost of Tom Joad* were an extension of those ideas: stories about brothers, lovers, movement, exclusion—political exclusion, social exclusion—and also the responsibility of these individuals—making bad choices, or choices they've been backed up against the wall to make.

The way all those things intersect is what interests me. The way the social issues and the personal issues cross over one another. To me, that's how people live. These things cross over our lives daily. People get tangled up in them, don't know how to address them, get lost in them. My work is a map, for whatever it's worth—for both my audience and for myself—and it's the only thing of value along with, hopefully, a well-lived life that we leave to the people we care about. I was lucky that I stumbled onto this opportunity early in my life. I think that the only thing that was uncommon was that I found a language that I was able to express those ideas with. Other people all the time struggle to find the language, or don't find the language—the language of the soul—or explode into violence or indifference or numbness, just numbed out in front of TV. "The Language"—that's what William Carlos Williams kept saying, the language of live people, not dead people!

If I'm overgeneralizing just stop me. I'm not sure if I am or not, but in some fashion that's my intent: to establish a commonality by revealing our inner common humanity—by telling good stories about a lot of different kinds of people. The songs on the last album connected me up with my past, with what I'd written about in my past, and they also connected me up with what I felt was the future of my writing.

Do you think your last album, which wasn't a pop or rock-and-roll record, had the same impact on the larger public that other records of yours had?
I've made records that I knew would find a smaller audience than others that I've made. I suppose the larger question is, How do you get that type of work to be heard—despite the noise of modern society and the media, two hundred television channels? Today, people are swamped with a lot of junk, so the outlets and the avenues for any halfway introspective work tend to be marginalized. The last record might have been heard occasionally on the radio, but not very much. It's a paradox for an artist—if you go into your work with the idea of having some effect upon society, when, by the choice of the particular media, it's marginalized from the beginning. I don't know of any answer, except the hope that somehow you do get heard—and there are some publishing houses and television channels and music channels that are interested in presenting that kind of work.

I think you have to feel like there's a lot of different ways to reach people, help them think about what's really important in this one-and-only life we live. There's pop culture—that's the shotgun approach, where you throw it out and it gets interpreted in different ways and some people pick up on it. And then there's a more intimate, focused approach like I tried on *Tom Joad*. I got a lot of correspondence about the last album from a lot of different people—writers, teachers, those who have an impact in shaping other people's lives.

Do you think pop culture can still have a positive effect?
Well, it's a funny thing. When punk rock music hit in the late 1970s, it wasn't played on the radio, and nobody thought, Oh yeah, that'll be popular in 1992 for two generations of kids. But the music dug in, and now it has a tremendous impact on the music and culture of the nineties. It was powerful, profound music, and it was going to find a way to make itself heard eventually. So I think there's a lot of different ways of achieving the kind of impact that most writers and filmmakers, photographers, musicians want their work to have. It's not always something that happens right away—the "Big Bang"!

With the exception of certain moments in the history of popular culture, it's difficult to tell what has an impact anymore, and particularly now when there's so many alternatives. Now, we have the fifth *Batman* movie! I think about the part in the essay "The Man on the Train" where your uncle talks about alienation. He says the truly alienated man isn't the guy who's despairing and trying to find his place in the world. It's the guy who just finished his twentieth Erle Stanley Gardner Perry Mason novel. That is the lonely man! That is the alienated man! So you could say, similarly, the guy who just saw the fifth *Batman* picture, he's the alienated man. But as much as anyone, I still like to go out on a Saturday night and buy the popcorn and watch things explode, but when that becomes such a major part of the choices that you have, when you have sixteen cinemas and fourteen of them are playing almost exactly the same picture, you feel that something's going wrong here. And if you live outside a major metropolitan area, maybe you're lucky if there's a theater in town that's playing films that fall slightly outside of those choices.

There's an illusion of choice that's out there, but it's an illusion, it's not real choice. I think that's true in the political arena and in pop culture, and I guess there's a certain condescension and cynicism that goes along with it—the assumption that people aren't ready for something new and different.

Do you think that the culture of celebrity is a cause of some of those problems? You seem to have escaped some of the problems that go along with being a celebrity.
I don't know, it's the old story—a lot of it is how you play your role. My music was in some sense inclusive and pretty personal, maybe even friendly. I've enjoyed the trappings from time to time, but I think I like a certain type of freedom. Of course, I enjoy my work being recognized, and when you get up on stage in front of twenty thousand people and you shake your butt all around, you're asking for some sort of trouble. I hope I've kept my balance. I enjoy my privacy.

I don't think the fascination with celebrities will ever really go away. An intellectual would say that people in the Industrial Age left their farms and their towns, so they couldn't gossip with their neighbors over the fence anymore—and all of a sudden there was a rise of a celebrity culture so we could have some people in common that we could talk about.

The substantive moral concern might be that we live in a country where the only story might be who's succeeding and who's number one, and what are you doing with it. It sure does become a problem if a certain part of your life as a writer—your "celebrity," or whatever you want to call it—can blur and obscure the story that you're interested in telling. I've felt that and seen that at certain times. One of the most common questions I was asked on the last tour, even by very intelligent reviewers was "Why are you writing these songs? What are you complaining about? You've done great." That's where your uncle's essay "Notes on a Novel about the End of the World" was very helpful to me and my writing. Your uncle addresses the story behind those same comments: "The material is so depressing. The songs are so down." He explains the moral and human purpose of writing by using that analogy of the canary that goes down into the mine with the miners: when the canary starts squawking and squawking and finally keels over, the miners figure it's time to come up and think things over a little bit. That's the writer—the twentieth- century writer is the canary for the larger society.

Maybe a lot of us use the idea of "celebrity" to maintain the notion that everything is all right, that there's always someone making their million the next day. As a celebrity, you don't worry about your bills, you have an enormous freedom to write and to do what you want. You can live with it well. But if your work is involved in trying to show where the country is hurting and where people are hurting, your own success is used to knock down or undercut the questions you ask of your audience. It's tricky, because American society has a very strict idea of what success is and what failure is. We're all "born in the U.S.A." and some part of you carries that with you. But it's ironic if "celebrity" is used to reassure lots of people barely making it that "Look, someone's really making it, making it big, so everything is all right, just lose yourself and all your troubles in that big-time success!"

Do you think you're through making music videos?
I don't know. I probably am. There's nobody waiting with bated breath out there for my next video right now. I've never been much of a video artist. I was "prevideo," and I think I remain "prevideo," though maybe I'm "postvideo" now.

Music videos have had an enormous impact on the way that you receive visual images on television and in the theaters—and it sped up the entire way the music world worked, for better or for worse. When I started, you had a band, you toured two or three, four years, you did a thousand shows or five hundred shows, that's how you built your audience, and then maybe you had a hit record. I feel sorry for some of these talented young bands that come up: they have a hit record, a video or two, and then it's over. I think it might have made the music world more fickle. In some ways, it may be more expedient for some of the young acts, but I think it's harder also, because you don't have the time to build a long-standing relationship with your audience.

There was something about developing an audience slowly—you'd draw an audience that stood with you over a long period of time, and it got involved with the questions you were asking and the issues you were bringing up. It's an audience who you shared a history with. I saw the work that I was doing as my life's work. I thought I'd be playing music my whole life and writing my whole life, and I wanted to be a part of my audience's ongoing life. The way you do that is the same way your audience lives its life—you do it by attempting to answer the questions that both you and they have asked, sometimes with new questions. You find where those questions lead you to—your actions in the world. You take it out of the aesthetic and you hopefully bring it into your practical, everyday life, the moral or ethical.

"Man on the Train" helped me think about these things in some fashion, where your uncle dissects the old Western movie heroes. We have our mythic hero, Gary Cooper, who is capable of pure action, where it's either all or nothing, and he looks like he's walking over that abyss of anxiety, and he won't fail. Whereas the moviegoer, the person watching the movie, is not capable of that. There's no real abyss under Gary Cooper, but there is one under the guy watching the film! Bringing people out over that abyss, helping them and myself to realize where we all "are," helping my audience answer the questions that are there—that's what I'm interested in doing with my own work.

That's what I try to accomplish at night in a show. Presenting ideas, asking questions, trying to bring people closer to characters in the songs, closer to themselves—so that they take those ideas, those questions—fundamental moral questions about the way we live and the way we behave toward one another—and then move those questions from the aesthetic into the practical, into some sort of action, whether it's action in the community, or action in the way you treat your wife, or your kid, or speak to the guy who works with you. That is what can be done, and is done, through film and music and photography and painting.

Those are real changes I think you can make in people's lives, and that I've had made in my life through novels and films and records and people who meant something to me. Isn't that what your uncle meant by "existentialist reflection"?

And there's a lot of different ways that gets done. You don't have to be doing work that's directly socially conscious. You could make an argument that one of the most socially conscious artists in the second half of this century was Elvis Presley, even if he probably didn't start out with any set of political ideas that he wanted to accomplish. He said, "I'm all shook up and I want to shake you up," and that's what happened. He had an enormous impact on the way that people lived, how they responded to themselves, to their own physicality, to the integration of their own nature. I think that he was one of the people, in his own way, who led to the sixties and the Civil Rights movement. He began getting us "all shook up," this poor white kid from Mississippi who connected with black folks through their music, which he made his own and then gave to others. So pop culture is a funny thing—you can affect people in a lot of different ways.

Did you always try to affect the audience like that? When you first started out when you were young?
We were trying to excite people, we were trying to make people feel alive. The core of rock music was cathartic. There was some fundamental catharsis that occurred in "Louie, Louie." That lives on, that pursuit. Its very nature was to get people "in touch" with themselves and with each other in some fashion. So initially you were just trying to excite people, and make them happy, alert them to themselves, and do the same for yourself. It's a way of combating your own indifference, your own tendency to slip into alienation and isolation. That's also in "Man on the Train": we can't be alienated together. If we're all alienated together, we're really not alienated.

That's a lot of what music did for me—it provided me with a community, filled with people, and brothers and sisters who I didn't know, but who I knew were out there. We had this enormous thing in common, this "thing" that initially felt like a secret. Music always provided that home for me, a home where my spirit could wander. It performed the function that all art and film and good human relations performed—it provided me with the kind of "home" always described by those philosophers your uncle loved.

There are very real communities that were built up around that notion—the very real community of your local club on Saturday night. The importance of bar bands all across America is that they nourish and inspire that community. So there are the very real communities of people and characters, whether it's in Asbury Park or a million different towns across the land. And then there is the community that it was enabling you to imagine, but that you haven't seen yet. You don't even know it exists, but you feel that, because of what you heard or experienced, it could exist.

That was a very powerful idea because it drew you outward in search of that community—a community of ideas and values. I think as you get older and develop a political point of view, it expands out into those worlds, the worlds of others, all over America, and you realize it's just an extension of that thing that you felt in a bar on Saturday night in Asbury Park when it was a hundred and fifty people in the room.

What do you try to provide people? What do parents try to provide their children? You're supposed to be providing a hopeful presence, a decent presence, in your children's lives and your neighbors' lives. That's what I would want my children to grow up with and then to provide when they become adults. It's a big part of what you can do with song, and pictures and words. It's real and its results are physical and tangible. And if you follow its implications, it leads you both inward and outward. Some days we climb inside, and some days maybe we run out. A good day is a balance of those sort of things. When rock music was working at its best, it was doing all of those things—looking inward and reaching out to others.

To get back to where we started, it can be difficult to build those kinds of connections, to build and sustain those kinds of communities, when you're picked up and thrown away so quickly—that cult of celebrity. At your best, your most honest, your least glitzy, you shared a common history, and you attempted both to ask questions and answer them in concert with your audience. In concert. The word "concert"—people working together—that's the idea. That's what I've tried to do as I go along with my work. I'm thankful that I have a dedicated, faithful audience that's followed along with me a good part of the way. It's one of my life's great blessings—having that companionship and being able to rely on that companionship. You know, "companionship" means breaking bread with your brothers and sisters, your fellow human beings—the most important thing in the world! It's sustained my family and me and my band throughout my life.

Do you think you've extended your audience to include some of the kinds of people that you're writing about now: Mexican immigrants, homeless people? Do you feel that you're doing something for those people with your music?

There's a difference between an emotional connection with them, like I think I do have, and a more physical, tangible impact. There was a point in the mid-eighties where I wanted to turn my music into some kind of activity and action, so that there was a practical impact on the communities that I passed through while I traveled around the country. On this last tour, I would meet a lot of the people who are out there on the front line—activists, legal advocates, social workers—and the people that they're involved with. It varied from town to town, but we'd usually work with an organization that's providing immediate care for people in distress, and then also we'd find an organization that's trying to have some impact on local policy. It helped me get a sense of what was going on in those towns, and the circumstances that surround the people that I'm imagining in my songs, in the imagined community I create with my music.

I'm sure I've gotten a lot more out of my music than I've put in, but those meetings and conversations keep me connected so that I remember the actual people that I write about. But I wouldn't call myself an activist. I'm more of a concerned citizen. I think I'd say that I'm up to my knees in it, but I'm not up to my ass!

I guess I'm—rock bottom—a concerned, even aroused observer, sort of like the main character of Ralph Ellison's *Invisible Man*. Not that I'm invisible! But Ellison's character doesn't directly take on the world. He wants to see the world change, but he's mainly a witness, a witness to a lot of blindness. I recently heard two teachers, one black and one white, talking about that novel, and it sure got to them; it's what Ellison wanted it to be, it's a great American story—and in a way we're all part of it.

Mark Hagen
Mojo,
January 1999

Releasing *Tracks* in 1998, a four-CD collection of largely unreleased recordings dating back to 1972, Springsteen termed the box set an "alternate route" for his career. With a paucity of explanatory liner notes, this in-depth interview with BBC producer Mark Hagen became vital to putting the contents of the collection in context. Delving into the whats and whys of these outtakes and B-sides, Springsteen reflects on his creative process and retraces his career in light of these lost songs. On the verge of reuniting with the E Street Band, he exclaims that playing rock 'n' roll "is the greatest job in the world."

<hr>

That is definitely a deer. Fast-moving, hard to spot and not prepared to hang about and exchange pleasantries. Yes, a deer. And it's running past the front door of Bruce Springsteen's Thrill Hill Recording studios, a farmhouse on the fringes of his land deep in rural New Jersey. It's a lovely old building, combining the hi-tech Springsteen now uses to make most of his recordings with a warm homey atmosphere, artfully distressed walls, comfy sofas, a roaring log fire, a fine collection of horse prints, an impressive selection of tequilas and bourbons. Currently in residence is Patti Scialfa (otherwise known as Mrs. Springsteen), and we are discussing the finer points of *Bridget Jones's Diary*.

An engine growl signals the arrival of an immaculately restored and customised 1948 Ford pick-up truck driven by her husband. He bowls into the room, tanned and smiling, with hair trimmed back to *River* levels and no sign of the *Tom Joad* goatee. With none of the "look at me" attitude that so often comes with the turf, Bruce has the kind of natural charisma that makes a room somehow seem more alive. Relaxed and friendly, the conversation moves to the finer things in life—the delights of vintage denim and old rockabilly records; the Mavericks, the Waco Brothers, the Clash and Dave Alvin; tattoos; the sartorial requirements of the British judicial system and the short stories of William Price Fox.

We're here to talk about Springsteen's long-hidden but now (partially) revealed artistic life, the fruits of which are, after years of fan requests and vague promises, collected in the *Tracks* box set. Springsteen recording sessions are epic occasions which have been known to stretch over several years before an album emerges, inevitably leaving behind dozens of fabulous songs gathering dust on the studio shelf. It's from these that *Tracks* has been compiled. Initially a 6-CD set featuring 100 songs, it's now emerged as a 4-CD, 66-song affair focusing, according to Bruce, on "songs that were part of specific albums, things that got left off the records that came out rather than songs that were recorded without a particular project in mind." While this has meant the loss of material like "The Promise" ("I just didn't have a take of it I was happy with") and "The Fever" ("It was never one of my favourite songs anyway!"), what has emerged is a secret history of a man with a larger plan than we might have realised. Also on the horizon is *Songs*, a large collection of photos and lyrics which Springsteen has introduced, annotated and augmented with such fascinating curios as the original work sheet for "Prove It All Night" and the note to manager Jon Landau, suggesting that new song "Born in the U.S.A." might have potential.

All this retrospection and, presumably, the death of his father earlier this year has cast Bruce in a more than usually reflective mood. In the past a reluctant interviewee, on this occasion he relaxes right into it and digs candidly and deep, his voice at times cracking with emotion. Springsteen is a mesmerising speaker, often circling a subject cautiously before honing in on it full-beam. Oh, and he laughs a lot too . . .

The first voice that we hear on *Tracks* is John Hammond, introducing your audition for Columbia. What do you remember of that day?
It was a big, big day for me. I'd played a lot of bars, a lot of different shows. I was 22 and came up on the bus with an acoustic guitar with no case which I'd borrowed from the drummer from the Castiles. I was embarrassed carrying it around the city. I walked into his office and had the audition and I played a couple of songs and he said, "You've got to be on Columbia Records. But I need to see you play. And I need to hear how you sound on tape." Me and Mike Appel [his manager/publisher] walked all around the Village trying to find some place that would let somebody just get up on stage and play. We went to the Bitter End, it didn't work out. We went to another club. And finally we went to the old Gaslight on MacDougal Street and the guy says, "Yeah, we have an open night where you can come down and play for half an hour." There were about 10 people in the place and I played for about half an hour. John Hammond said, "Gee, that was great. I want you to come to the Columbia Recording Studio and make a demo tape." A demo I made at Bill Graham's studio in San Francisco in '69 was the only other time I'd ever been in a real recording studio. Columbia was very old-fashioned: everybody in ties and shirts; the engineer was in a white shirt and a tie and was probably 50, 55 years old, it was just him and John and Mike Appel there, and he just hits the button and gives you your serial number, and off you go. I was excited. I felt I'd written some good songs and this was my shot. I had nothing to lose and it was like the beginning of something.

I knew a lot about John Hammond, the work he'd done, the people he'd discovered, his importance in music and it was very exciting to feel you were worth his time. No matter what happened afterwards, even if it was just for this one night, you were worth his time. That meant a lot to me. He was very encouraging—simply being in that room with him at the board was one of my greatest recording experiences.

How did you arrive at the sound on that audition tape?
I'd been in Steel Mill, which was basically a riff-oriented hard rock thing, and we took it to San Francisco. Drove across the country in a truck older than my '48 out there, I was 19, it was 1969 and we auditioned at the Family Dogg, which was a well-known ballroom in San Francisco at the time. There was three bands, another band got the job and we thought we were robbed, blah blah, but we really weren't. They were just better than us. I'd played a lot locally, and for a long time

hadn't seen anybody better than I was, and I walked into that ballroom that afternoon, there was somebody better than we were. We played a few more shows but I knew that I was going to do something else.

We ran out of money, and scrambled our way back across the United States—I ended up in the back of this big flat-bed that we'd built a box on for two days, in the wintertime in a sleeping bag with my bass player and the equipment. We got back home and I started another band. I moved from hard rock to rhythm and blues–influenced music, and I began to write differently. We'd built a very large audience, sold out 3,000 seaters in a few places down South and in Jersey—an enormous audience for a band with no record—and we were able to live on it. A lot of that audience disappeared and I couldn't keep it going. It became the Bruce Springsteen Band—basically me, Vini Lopez, Steve Van Zandt, Davey Sancious, Garry Tallent—which played initially at a place called the Student Prince, a bar in Asbury Park. But I'd lost my audience almost completely, so the first night we played, we charged a dollar at the door and that was our pay. The first night we made 15 bucks. The next week we made 30 and then when the place was jammed you could make 150, which spread five ways, three nights a week, was enough to keep you going.

Eventually I had some personal problems with this, that and the other thing and I decided I was going to California to make a living out there playing. But I really couldn't do so—nobody really paid unknowns to play at that time. So I said, "Well, I've got to come back home because this is the only place I can really survive as a musician." My parents didn't have the kind of money where they could support you—they lived in a little apartment and you slept on the couch. I drove back to New Jersey and did some bar gigs and I started to think that I needed to approach the thing somewhat differently. I began to write music that would not have worked in a club, really. It required too much attention, too much listening, a certain kind of focus. But I felt if I was going to take a real shot at it, I was going to have to do something very distinctive and original. I wanted the independence, the individuality of a solo career, and that's when I began to write some of the initial songs for *Greetings from Asbury Park*. I was living above this little out-of-business beauty salon with an old piano in the back, and at night I'd go down amid all the hair dryers and I wrote a bunch of the songs from that album.

I'd met Mike Appel before I'd gone to California and I was thinking, "Well, I know a guy in New York who's connected to the music business." Mike was enthusiastic and talked his way into an audition with John Hammond through John's secretary, which was a miracle as it was—John Hammond invited us in off the street just on his secretary's hunch. I don't know if that happens anymore but it was pretty amazing just to get in the door.

I had to have some slightly bigger idea about the music I was going to make, some different context. I'd always had a band but I also wrote acoustically on the side quite often, and occasionally I'd play that music in local coffee houses. But I focused on it and committed to it in a way that I hadn't before. I'd stopped working in the bars and was strictly, strictly working on my writing, hoping that I was going to get somewhere, find somebody who was interested in it.

How did everybody react, then, when you started to bring the band in again?

I think the record John Hammond would have liked would have been one that the first four or five cuts from *Tracks* sound like. Maybe that exact thing, and, listening back, he may have been right. When I went back and listened through some of that music, it was a very austere presentation of those songs, probably more immediately connected to folk music. Which is really what it was—the music was an abstract expression of my direct experience where I lived in Asbury Park at the time and the kinds of characters that were around; they call them twisted autobiographies. Basically, it was street music.

The first few things on *Tracks* are really that in its rawest form. It's funny—Patti never heard any of those things, and when she heard it she said I should have made the record like that. But Mike and his partner Jimmy [Cretecos] were always very production-oriented; they were big Cat Stevens fans at the time and he had these very enhanced acoustic records—everything was limited and compressed for a slightly hyped sound, and that's the direction that *Greetings* went in. Also, I wanted a rhythm section—I wanted a *band* actually because I'd played with a group for a long time and knew that a big part of my abilities was to be able to use a band. So what we ended up doing was an acoustic record with a rhythm section, which was the compromise reached between the record company, everybody else and me.

I handed the finished record in and it was handed back. Clive Davis [Columbia Records boss] said there were no singles. So, because I'm in the music business now, I said, "OK, I'll write some." I went back home and wrote "Spirit in the Night" and "Blinded by the Light," where I

moved back a little bit into the R&B that I had been working on earlier, so I said, "Hey, all right, let me try and find that sax player . . ." I'd
met Clarence [Clemons] while I was playing in Asbury, but he was hard
to find, which wasn't that uncommon in those days. You'd see people,
then you wouldn't see them—no-one had addresses so sometimes
months would go by before you saw them again. But I got hold of him
and he came in and played on those two songs. So that's how we filled
the band out.

But listening back now, that pure, very straightforward presentation
of those initial songs sounds a little truer to me now.

Did you find yourself writing songs for live performance, for a specific function?

Yeah. All of a sudden I was doing some shows to support the first record, and you had 30 or 40 minutes to make an impression, which was
something I knew how to do because I'd been doing it for a very long
time. I began to try to incorporate the acoustic music and ideas with
what I'd learned leading a band for 10 years or so. And that's how the
second record came to be. I said, "Well I want to hold onto these characters, this point of view and this writing style, but I want to include
the physicality of rock music, or band music."

The song "Thundercrack" was something that we wrote as the show-
stopper. It ended three or four different times—you didn't know where
it was going to go. It was just a big, epic show-ender that was meant to
leave the audience gasping a little bit for their breath—"Hey, who was
that guy? That was pretty good . . ." That was "Rosalita"'s predecessor;
later on, "Rosalita" began to fill that spot in the show and held it for
many, many years, probably the best song I ever wrote for that particular job. Before that, "Thundercrack" had the same function. It was
meant to make you nuts, and that's why I wanted to get that song on
this record. It was one of the few songs that actually was finished when
I went and found it. I listened to it, and it seemed like it was so long and
the guitar didn't sound right; I just said, "This is going to be too much
work." It was meant to be played live in front of an audience and when
we plunked our way through it in the studio, at first it just didn't feel
right. But it was probably about 80 percent done—we had to shape it a
little bit, but I wanted to get that on because if you were a really early,
early fan, that was the song that was a big hallmark at shows at the time.
But I found a version which was actually pretty good, called up Vini

Lopez and I said, "Vini, I have some singing for you to do" and Vini—he's a caddy master at a golf course—he just comes by and I said, "Remember this song?" He came in and sang all his parts completely unprompted, like he remembered it exactly from 25 years ago. We put the same harmonies we used at that time and finished it up a little bit.

Do you think people will be surprised when they see all this unreleased material, this whole other Bruce Springsteen?
It depends how closely you followed what I've done. Many of the songs we played early in concert—we played "Santa Ana" all the time. When I went on the road, I took the point of view I developed on my first record and I began to just write with the band in mind, with the idea of mixing those two things. We cut them all and at the time they didn't get on, probably because there was a limited amount of time you could put on a record, only about 36 or 40 minutes tops, and so things just didn't get on because there wasn't enough room, or you didn't think you sang that one that well, or the band didn't play that one that well, or you wanted to mess around with the writing some more.

"Zero & Blind Terry" was a big song we played live all the time and "Santa Ana," "Seaside Bar Song," "Thundercrack" were from that particular period. Max [Weinberg, E Street Band drummer] came by when we were mixing the stuff, and it was fun watching Max listening to Vini's drumming. Vini was a very eccentric drummer. But when you went back and listened, he played really great. The band at that time, we were folk musicians. With the exception of Danny [Federici], who had taken accordion lessons, there wasn't any real formal training. People played very personally and very eccentrically, and if you listen to those cuts from *The Wild, The Innocent,* the band playing is very unusual. It's a little carnie band. You hear the influences which Danny had a lot to do with—the boardwalk, the accordion, the atmosphere from the lyric writing which came out of that particular environment. And then you hear people who have probably really never heard themselves play that much, and so they're just playing how they play, not playing like this guy or that guy. Garry's playing is all over the place on the bass, Vini's all over the drums. We had come out of a band that had jammed a lot, so when I put the band together as an ensemble, they had this tendency to want to play and play and play. Vini's style was quite beautiful and very responsive and just totally original. It only lasted for a very brief period. The next record was *Born to Run* and it was immediately less eccentric.

And took much longer to record?
Yeah. The first record took three weeks. My recollection was the second record and the music from that record that's on *Tracks* took two months, three months tops. And that was not recording solidly. Previously we'd played what you played on stage or in a room for John Hammond. But *Born to Run* was the first time I went in to use the studio as a tool and not in an attempt to replicate the sound of when we played.

That approach is basically what Phil Spector did. When he put that kind of snare sound together in the studio, that was the only place it existed, unless you play in a big armoury or high school gymnasium on a Saturday night. I'd gotten into the idea of production and was interested in doing that myself in some fashion. And that took a long time because no-one really knew how to get the sounds. I liked to put everything on, but then I couldn't understand why the guitar sounds so small. The guitar sounded small because there was 20 other things on there competing for space. For a really big guitar sound, you just have a guitar with not that many other things. It took about 10 years to figure this out.

So when we went in to cut *Born to Run,* writing it was very difficult, then recording it and getting a sound that approximated to what I wanted was very difficult. I was striving for something very specific that I didn't know how to get. So I had to spend time finding it. There were two outtakes from *Born to Run:* "Linda Let Me Be the One" is on *Tracks,* and there was another one called "Walking in the Street" which I would have liked to have put on but I couldn't find the master. We searched and searched. It might have been simply recorded over, because in those days, if something wasn't going to make it, you're going to need that tape so you recorded something else over the top.

The cut "Born to Run" took about six months. The rest took maybe another six. I went in and I had my eight songs; I knew these were the songs the record was going to comprise. I took each song and worked on it very, very intensely, lyrically and musically—that's all we did was shape those eight pieces of music.

By the time we got to *Darkness* the stakes had changed. They had gotten a lot higher. All of a sudden I had an audience. I hadn't really had one—just a little grassroots audience. The first record, I asked Mike, "How many did we sell?" "Well," he says, "About 23,000." He was disappointed, but I said, "We did? Wow!" It was a shock to me that there were 23,000 people I didn't know who had gone out and bought the music that we'd made. I felt that was a great success, and the second record did probably about the same. But then when the third record hit all of a sudden, we had a real audience that the record company took notice of. All of a sudden you're being watched a lot more closely; all of a sudden your actions have implications. I began to think about who I was and where I came from. It was a disorienting moment but it's also one of those moments when you either find yourself on your feet or you get lost and maybe don't find your way back. I took a very close, hard look at who I wanted to be and what I wanted to do and what was important to me. And then I got involved in a lawsuit to get the rights back to my music and control of my creative life, which went on for a long time.

So this long period went, and then when I went in to make *Darkness* I had very specific ideas of the record I wanted to make. I'd bring the band in and say, "OK, tonight we do 'Give the Girl a Kiss' " . . . or "So Young and in Love"—anything to break the tension in the studio. You're still learning how you sound and how to use the studio. So a lot of different kinds of music occurred. I edited *Darkness* very, very tightly and specifically for that particular emotional tone and a very hard focus on what I wanted to write about. So, a lot of music I put to the side.

Basically the second half of the first CD of *Tracks* were all things that occurred during the *Darkness on the Edge of Town*. There were things that might have fit but we didn't have the time, and other things that were just terrific but would have been very out of context on that particular record, like "Give the Girl a Kiss" or "So Young and in Love," which were great bar party songs. I didn't even know that "Give the Girl a Kiss" existed—wow, that's pretty, that's fun. And "So Young and in Love"—a full band, beautiful ensemble club playing, very exciting. Meant to blow your head off.

It seems to me that at about the same time your writing changed; up to *Darkness* you had characters that were going somewhere, trying to get out of this community, for whatever reason. To some degree it seems the rest of your career has been spent trying to get them back in.

Those were the questions that came up for me at that particular time. Initially you're in search of a certain freedom—you want some sense of control of the arc your life is gonna take. You grew up in a particular environment, you had a very particular place you were gonna fit into, so your initial thrust is to explode those limits for yourself. That was what music offered in general: you were the guy getting up at 11 or 12 and going to bed at three, four or five in the morning and I liked that kind of life. Then when I found I had an audience, all of a sudden I had a lot of personal freedom, I thought, "What do I want to do with this?" I had seen enough people who had come before me to know that this point was where lots of people lost track of the essential things that made their music vital and made it move forward. I always say I picked up the guitar because I wanted to speak to you. And the irony is that moment, when you have an audience, is when you are separated and isolated. How you handle it from that point on has a lot to do with the course your music takes.

I had a while to throw those ideas around because I couldn't record for a couple of years. I was living on a farm in Holmdel, New Jersey. I went out and I played in the bars at night, and we toured a little when we could to try and keep everything going. And I thought a lot about what kind of record I was gonna wanna make when I had the chance to record again. That is probably why some of these songs got let off, because they were a lot of fun but there was a moment when I said, "I need to identify myself at this particular moment." We'd had the success, then I disappeared for a couple of years. You pick up the papers and just read those "whatever-happened-to?" articles, that's not fun, ha ha. So finally, when I got to record again, I needed to identify myself and exactly what I wanted to write about: where was I going, where was I going to sit in my audience's life . . . It was the central moment when my writing took a fundamental turn—which has continued for the rest of my work.

Does that mean that to one degree or another you were actually writing about yourself the whole time?
You're always writing about yourself: not literally or specifically, but there's got to be some part of you in everything. No matter how you may choose a story or a set of characters that you may have had no experience with, the job is to connect and create understanding, to see yourself in them and have your audience do so too. You try to find that place where there's a fundamental human commonality around very basic issues of work, faith, hope, family, desperation, exuberation, joy. The song always fails unless you can find yourself in those characters in some fashion and so, like I say, I haven't written really literally about myself, maybe on some occasions, but it's a metaphor for your emotional experience. You're trying to capture a piece of the world as you see it— that's what the job is.

In another sense, none of your songs are actually about what they seem to be about; "Be True" is not really about romance.
Well, it's partly about romance. Any piece of work can be looked at through a lot of different veils. Talking about that particular song I'd say, "Yeah it seems to be a romance song"—what's this fellow doing, he's trying to say Hey, don't sell yourself cheap. It's saying be true to yourself in some fashion. He's talking to a woman he's interested in but actually that's a device to address, just how do you find yourself through the falseness of some of those things and not sell yourself short and try to get the most out of yourself? In that particular song I think there's a lot of cultural metaphors whether it's the films or whatever, but I suppose that's what that song was about.

Are you conscious of that layering in your writing?
At the time, maybe I was, "The scrapbook's filled with pictures of all your leading men, so baby don't put my picture in there with them." You're saying, Don't lock me into this particular box, I wanna reach you in a different way maybe, if I can find it within myself. It's a love song and then it's a dialogue on remaining true to the things that you think are important. Good songs work on many different levels; that's what makes them good, that's what makes them last. The other thing was I was trying to write something that was really catchy, a three-minute pop tune, that moved lyrically, that linked together in a certain way. And I was having fun using the film metaphor. To me it almost sounds like it was a hit single; it never was but it feels like one—it's accessible, the singer is open, he's revealing something about himself and he's asking the person he's addressing to do the same and trying to lay out terms for a relationship of some sort. And it all happens in about three minutes and Clarence plays the sax at the end and the glockenspiel plays that riff and it's just light and sort of sweet.

"Roulette" was the very first song you recorded for what became *The River*. It would have been a very different album had you put "Roulette" on it.
It was the first song we cut for that record and maybe later on I thought it was too specific, and the story I started to tell was more of a general one. I may have just gotten afraid—it went a little over the top, which is what's good about it. In truth it should have probably gotten put on. It would have been one of the best things on the record and it was just

a mistake at the time—you get oversensitive when you're going to release the things. That was a record where there was an enormous amount of material. There's an entire album of tracks from *The River*: "Restless Nights," "Roulette," "Dollhouse," "Where the Bands Are," "Loose Ends," "Living on the Edge of the World," "Take 'Em as They Come," "Be True," "Ricky Wants a Man," "I Wanna Be with You," "Mary Lou," all three-minute, four-minute pop songs.

It was a funny time, 'cos I'd gotten into Woody Guthrie for the first time. I'd come off *Darkness* and felt I'd really found the characters and the type of writing that I wanted to do. But one of my favourite records that summer was *The Raspberries Greatest Hits:* they were great little pop records, I loved the production, and when I went into the studio a lot of things we did were like that. Two-, three-, four-minute pop songs coming one right after another. So there was an extra album of those things that got left off, just because I wanted a record that balanced the two things that I was doing, that had a sense of continuity coming out [of] *Darkness* where you'd recognise the characters. And I wanted to infuse the record with the physicality and the excitement and the joy of the live show—Steve Van Zandt was part of the production team, and we finally learned how to capture the kind of dynamics, the explosiveness that we always felt on stage.

In some ways it was really our first successful use of the studio. We'd tune the snare way up: at the time, coming out of the '70s all the drums were too down and deep. I like the way the snare sounds on "Hound Dog": it's high, you're hearing the snare crack, you're hearing it explode. When we recorded we found a wooden studio, put Max in the middle of the room, and I said, "When you hear it, I want you to see his arm coming up and coming down and *hitting* the drum." We'd built the rest of the band around that sound and it was the first time that we really caught some of the rawness and excitement of the live show on record.

In the end I had turned in a single record that was finished, and it just wasn't good enough, it wasn't expansive enough—that was when we decided to go to the two records.

You've done that quite a lot, haven't you? Finished records and then reworked them completely.
Yeah well, it's never over until it's over. Everybody's telling you you're done and you take it home and it's just not right. It's happened many many times. It happened on *Darkness*—we had finished, I was back in

New York City, put the record on, "Promised Land" came up on the second side, it just wasn't the right mix and then I stopped the record and went back to California. I only spent it doing this, so my life at the time was extremely focused, probably to the detriment of the records. But very often these things were created amid a mess and you don't know what you're doing until you're done.

I had no intention of recording *Nebraska* in that fashion, whatsoever. It was—not a mistake—an *accident,* let's say, and, anyhow, at the same time I recorded *Nebraska* I was recording *Born in the U.S.A.* in the studio in New York, so I had these two extremely different recording experiences going. I was in my house with a little tape player about three or four times the size of a book with a couple of mics and these songs that I'd written, I wasn't sure where they came from, then I was going to the city and cutting this big studio album. I was going to put them out at the same time as a double record. I didn't know what to do.

By the time we got to *The River* adulthood was imminent, if it hadn't arrived already, so I knew I was gonna be following my characters over a long period of time. I thought it would be interesting and fun for my audience to have a certain sort of continuity, not explicit or literal or confined but just a loose continuity from record to record.

Is the Mary of "Thunder Road" the same one who crops up in *The River* and other places?
I couldn't say. Sometimes a name just comes out, I suppose there's all the interconnections that the songs make happen intentionally and unintentionally. A lot of the time you don't know a lot of what you're doing yourself.

In between recording *The River* and recording what became *Nebraska,* you went to Europe for quite a long time.
Yeah, I'd gotten my nerve up and went back, ha ha.

How did that change your perspective? On America and the subjects you were writing about?
Well, at that particular point, America in the early '80s, a sense of violence was in the air on a daily basis. It made me very sad: I was 30, having kids was on the horizon. Just the way things seemed, through television or different media, everything seemed much more aggressive and abusive. I experienced less of that in Europe—it seemed more civil, more sane.

The other thing was we really connected with the European audience. I'd been earlier in the mid-'70s and had a very disorienting experience and was simply frightened of coming back. The greatest thing that I did was to go back in the '80s and to continue to go back. It has been the centre for an intense interest in the work that I've done.

Did that experience of going overseas give you a new perspective, writing about those characters in *Nebraska*? It did seem more explicitly political . . .

I didn't think about the politics *of Nebraska* until I read in a review that it had a variety of political implications. At the time that was my most personal record—it reminded me of the way my childhood felt, the house that I grew up in. I was digging into that.

I don't know how those stories evolved, they were things I'd gotten interested in. I'd read a book about Caril Fugate and that led me to the song "Nebraska." I phoned the woman who reported on the story in the '50s—she happened to be working at the same newspaper 25 years later, so I called and they put me through to her desk. There was something about that song that was the centre of the record, but I couldn't really say specifically what it was, outside of the fact that I'd read something that moved me. Once again, you feel like you're gonna tell that story and also tell something about yourself.

I think in my own life I had reached where it felt like I was teetering on this void. I felt a deep sense of isolation, and that led me to those characters and to those stories—people I remembered growing up, my father's side of the family, a certain way they spoke, a certain way they approached life, and that resonated through that music. Along with all of a sudden trying to figure out, "Well hey, what if you don't get back *in*?" I had a lot of sorting out to do around that time. When you get older, the price for not sorting through the issues that make up your emotional life rises. The same answers and the tricks and the lies that you told yourself at 22 feel a little less comfortable at 26, 28. The older you get the more the price goes up. I was at a place where I could start to really *feel* that price: I just felt too disconnected, I just wasn't any good, right at the moment that record occurred. So that record had something to do with those things. There are things that make sense of life for people: their friends, the work they do, your community, your relationship with your partner. What if you lose those things, then what are you left with? The political aspect wasn't something that was really on my mind at the time, it was more just people struggling with those particular kinds of emotional or psychological issues.

Around the same time, Vietnam starts to creep into your work.
The late '70s and early '80s was the first time when literature and films began to be made about Vietnam. There was a subtext on a few earlier things, there was a movie called *Who'll Stop the Rain* [titled *Dog Soldiers* in the UK] with Nick Nolte, but all of a sudden it began to become very directly addressed.

It began with a strange experience when I was driving across the country and I stopped in Arizona at a drug store and I bought a book called *Born on the Fourth of July*. I drove on to Los Angeles and was at this little motel sitting at the pool and a fella came up, started talking and introduced himself: Ron Kovic. I thought, I must have met this fella, his name sounds real familiar, and he said, "I wrote a book called *Born on the Fourth of July*." I said, "Wow this is a real coincidence, I just read the book a couple of weeks ago." So Ron took me down to Venice to the Vet Centre, and I met Bobby Muller, who was the President of the VVA at the time. One thing led to another and it just began to surface in some of my music. There was a song, "Pittsburgh," which was actually written for *Born in the U.S.A.*

You hadn't been to Vietnam yourself.
No, I did the draft-dodger rag.

Did you feel guilty about not going?
No, but it was such a part of growing up at that time, it was in your home every single night. My drummer in the Castiles went—and he died. I remember a fella was the best front man in New Jersey at the time, Walter Cichone, and he joined the Marines and was posted missing in action, and on the street people were frightened and everybody was trying to figure out how to get out of the draft. Whether you were there or whether you were at home in the United States, it was a defining moment in American culture. It finds its way time and again into some of my songs. Whether you went or not, it was a big part of your life.

At the time I was 18 or 19, I didn't come out of a political household, I was part of what you'd consider the counterculture, though probably I was the conservative part. I never had any real drug experience, you know. I lived in a little town, and there were lines drawn everywhere.

Is it hard for you to arrange your records so they tell a coherent story; we have 66 songs from hundreds, is it hard to pick them?
Tracks didn't take a lot of thinking. I went in, I found pieces of music that I liked that we hadn't released. I didn't feel I had to arrange them conceptually: I based my choices on what was pretty much finished and what I felt were the best things we had done that hadn't come out. What you find to your surprise is that when you begin to sequence them, some internal logic takes over. It follows the arc of the music: in the beginning there is a young man, at the end there is a guy my age. It ends with what is basically a folk piece and begins with one, so there is a trip that's taken and you could go in and interpret it pretty easily. It's the alternate route to the road that I took on the records that I released. It tells a similar story but you are going down a different road where all the roadside markers are a little different and the sights are different.

This is really something the fans have wanted for years. What made you decide to put it out now?
A couple of years ago I had some spare time, and I said to my engineer, Toby [Scott], send me everything that you have recorded. It often takes so long between records, and I said, "Gee, if it's going to be a year or longer in between records I have all this unreleased music that I know is very good and I should release some of it." So it began just with that idea and we listened to about 250 songs, maybe more, I made quick notes in a notebook and put it away.

A year went by, more maybe, and I came off the *Tom Joad* tour and I began to write acoustically again and I wrote about half a record. Then I got stuck and said, "Well, I'm going to put this aside for a while." Then I wrote half of an electric record, and hit the same place. So I thought, instead of waiting for another year to put something out I'll put some of this music together. So once again I went back to the archives. Charlie Plotkin, who has produced many of our records, came in and we sat and listened together and we came up with about 100 things. We sequenced them pretty quickly. I said, "This is going to be great," because the mix was pretty good. Then I played it for Jon Landau and he said, "Yes it's great, but I think it needs to be mixed." I said, "Mixed, oh my God, there are 100 mixes or 80 mixes, has *anybody* ever done 80 mixes?" We had, like, two months to go. I said, "It will just screw the whole thing, let's just not bother." But when a song that came up that had been mixed, like a B-side, it just sounded a lot better, had more focus and impact so I went back and I listened some more and realised Jon was right, of course.

I called him and I said, "Well OK, how do you mix 80 songs?" Charlie came in and we had three studios going at once: we had a studio in the other room, a truck out in the yard, and we had Bob Clearmountain on the phone—there was a system where he can mix in California and it just plays out your stereo speakers just like you were sitting in the studio! That's basically how the things got mixed. There was a fella named Ed Thacker who took the rough mixes, basically remained very true to that sound picture and enhanced it greatly. So when I came in, I was not hearing something unfamiliar. For the fans who'd heard these things, it's just a very different presentation of the music, much more fully realised and powerful.

One of the pleasures is actually tracking the evolution of some of the material; "Santa Ana" has got a couple of lines that crop up in "She's the One," and "Living on the Edge of the World" is "Open All Night," effectively.
If you have a good line, you don't like to throw it—you don't write that many. If I came up with a line that I liked I always tried to use it because writing was hard and, for one reason or another, things would begin here and end up there. Bob Benjamin sent me a tape with about three songs on it, and "Iceman" was one of them. I had forgotten I had even written it and I had no idea what it was, and I went back and it was a pretty nice song. Finding some of the things you'd forgot you had done, that was fun.

Do you really forget?
Yes. There were some things that I forgot I'd done—"Give the Girl a Kiss," which was a big sort of party tune, I had forgotten; "Iceman," like "Born in the U.S.A.," was just something that I didn't get at the time that I did it. When I went back and listened I realised that the reason I left it off *Nebraska* was partly because we'd already cut the band version, and this one I felt hadn't really nailed it. But it came off pretty well, when I came back and I listened to it.

Isn't that the point of this record? That people who are familiar with *Born in the U.S.A.* suddenly find there is this other interpretation?
Yes, well, if you like that record, there is another record here waiting for

you! If you like *The River* there is an album from *The River,* if you like *Born in the U.S.A.* there is almost an entire album from *Born in the U.S.A.* You like one song over another at the time, but occasionally your choices are very, very particular. Like I don't know if this particular "Born in the U.S.A." had been on *Nebraska* whether that would have changed the record.

Two songs seem to be very you; one is "The Wish," which is clearly about your mother.
Yes, that's risky territory, ha ha. I was saying on the last tour, rock 'n' rollers don't take to singing about your mother. You can do country or even rap music and sing about your mother. There was a gospel group called the Mother Lovers. Elvis, of course, sang about his mother all the time but not directly, so it's sort of a funny song. It's probably why it didn't get on!

The other autobiographical song is "Goin' Cali"; is that you?
Yes, that's me. I was going to go out and play with a band and needed music that was going to fuel that show, but in the meantime I wrote about half a record on the bass, where you had a note and you had your idea. I wrote about half or more of a record. The only one that made it to release was "57 Channels," but on this thing there was "Over the Rise," "When the Lights Go Out," "Loose Change," "Goin' Cali," "Gave It a Name," even "My Lover Man," all these very psychological portraits of people wrestling with relationships and their own isolation. "Goin' Cali," I suppose, was just an experimental thing I laid down in the studio one day: I don't even remember recording it or how it came about but it traces, ironically, my journey at that time out West.

A classic American tradition—if you assume that America was founded on people who could not fit in where they were in the first place, so moved and kept moving . . .
Well, that isolation is a big part of the American character. Everyone wakes up on one of those mornings when you just feel like you want to walk away and start brand new. The West obviously always symbolised that possibility for a long time here in the States—it probably still symbolises the *illusion* of that possibility today. I reached a point where I wanted something different. I tried living in New York City for a while and I just was not a city boy, and I had a small place in California from the early '80s on, and it was a place where I could go and I had my cars and my

motorcycles, and I enjoyed the geography of the state; you can be out of Los Angeles in 30 minutes and hit the edge of the desert and travel for 100 miles. There is still a lot of nothing out here and I loved it. You are dwarfed in it and it puts your daily concerns in immediate perspective.

You have pared down your imagery through your career. To begin with your images were florid and very wordy.
After I'd made a few albums, those were the records that I felt uncomfortable with. But now I go back and I really like them, because they are records that I made before anybody was listening. I never heard myself singing these songs until they were recorded, didn't have a tape player at home, so you were just doing it, having fun. So I look back and it was a very free moment in my writing. I just wrote what came out and the songs work on an abstract basis, but that's what makes them fun. "Santa Ana" is just a series of images, but it works, there's a story being told. But later I turned away from that kind of writing because I received Dylan comparisons. If you go back and listen it's really not like Dylan at all, but at the time I was very sensitive about creating my own identity, and so I moved away from that kind of writing. It still comes up in "Born to Run" and "Jungleland" and a few other places but by the time you get to *Darkness* it's just about gone.

What would the 22-year-old who went to see John Hammond think of you now?
I really don't know. You hear your voice from that particular period of time, and you try to think back to what you were thinking, and who you were, and you probably tell yourself that you're the same. In some essential way you are the same, but of course you're the same person at a very different place in your life. The kid that walked in that particular night hadn't begun to imagine a life with children, a wife, and responsibilities—I was trying to *avoid* responsibilities, that was why I became a musician.

So I find myself coming to terms with those ideas that I ran from for a very long time. That's quite a change. As you get older you realise that where life's satisfactions and new freedoms reside is in making specific choices, choosing the way that your life is going to go. Those choices seem confining when you're young, because you want everything, you live in a fantasy of endless possibility. Then if you have some success there is enormous amount of real possibility that is handed to you, a dangerous amount, and if you go too far down that particular road, you realise it isn't what it appears to be. You can mistake endless choice for freedom, particularly when everybody wants to say yes to you all the time. There's plenty of fun to be had, but if you don't sort that out it's a recipe for disaster.

THE FOLLOWING MORNING dawns bright and clear, which means it's an ideal day to go to the seaside. It has to be said that if you were brought up on a steady diet of Bruce Springsteen records, then to cruise today round the sea front where so much of his early work is set is a chastening experience. The relatively modest Asbury Park boardwalk is completely deserted, and almost every surrounding building seems to be in a state of major disrepair. Madam Marie's fortune-telling booth is still there, but the only signs of the once-thriving club scene are a decidedly tatty looking Stone Pony (recently converted to dance venue Vinyl) and a dancing establishment of low repute called Club Seduction; once upon a time this was the Student Prince, where The Bruce Springsteen Band plied their trade. The Palace Amusements building, celebrated in Springsteen mythology on both *Born to Run* and *Tunnel of Love,* is a wasteland of flaking paint and collapsing brickwork, and the Circuit plays host to a bloke on a bicycle and a police car.

But let's go into the town itself, and more particularly to the Saint, a long, narrow bar with a small stage that enjoys something of a reputation, having hosted both the Fun Lovin' Criminals and the Bad Livers in recent times. It's a warm and colourful place and clearly somewhere Bruce feels at home. He arrives in the same 1963 Cadillac Coupe De Ville featured on the *Tunnel of Love* sleeve, but now sporting a fetching coffee-coloured paint job ("because of Chuck Berry's Nadine!") and settles down to business. With a glass of Newcastle Brown to one side and 12-string acoustic in hand, the mood is lighter than at Thrill Hill but no less revealing.

THIS WAS ABOUT the size of the Prince. The Prince held about 175 people and it was run by a bricklayer from Freehold, the town I grew up in. He'd bought the place and he was dying; there was nobody in there. And I couldn't get a gig because I wasn't playing the Top 40 material—it was a resort area, people came out on Fridays and Saturday nights and they wanted to hear the songs that they knew. Steve [Van Zandt] and I went down one Friday night and walked in and the place was empty, about two people at the bar. We said we had a band and would he let us play. And he says what kind of music, and I said, "Well we just play our own music." We said, "Look, this is not going to cost you anything, we'll charge a dollar at the door; try it once and if you don't like it, we'll split." So that's what we did. On Saturday night I think 15 people showed up but it was 15 more than the previous Friday night, and so he gave us another couple of weeks. Pretty quickly we built a crowd to be almost 30, then 80, and in a month or two we were close to filling the place three nights a week. We just lived off it then— you needed very little money to get by, you were a kid just living hand-to-mouth and so it worked pretty easily.

The one thing that was unique about the town at the time was a club, the Upstage, that was open from eight to five in the morning— there wasn't any booze or anything, and it was just kids. And because it was open two or three hours after the bars closed all the musicians, af-ter they finished their regular gigs, would come down. In the late '60s it was a tremendous meeting place for both local musicians and musi-cians who simply came into the area to work over the summer. I met Southside [Johnny] and Garry Tallent, Danny Federici. When I walked in the first night Vini Lopez was on drums, Danny was on organ and it was a revelation because we had good musicians and there were people playing some original music. It was a shock to me. I can remember walking in and I felt like I really discovered something. It's how I be-gan to play with many of the fellows that I played with for a long, long part of my career. It was very fundamental.

Why do they call you The Boss?
It all started with nicknames. Everybody had to have a nickname, there was no one in Asbury Park that did not have a nickname. My original nickname was The Doctor, because I had a band called Doctor Zoom & The Sonic Boom. In the local music scene there was a combination of original music and, I would hate to call it performance art because none of us had ever heard of the term, but there would be a Monopoly game going on on-stage, say, and other people engaged in disconnected activi-ties that seemed to be part of the show. So that was what I was called originally. Southside was 'cos he was into the blues, I guess, Steven was originally Miami Steven, 'cos he went to Miami once and came back and

had on an Hawaiian shirt, and he would traipse around Asbury with a Hawaiian shirt and a Russian winter hat—no one had ever been to Miami at the time. So the names came from anywhere, there was Big Tiny, Little Tiny, there was White Tiny, Black Tiny, anyone who obviously wasn't tiny got that nickname. My recollection was The Boss was a result of paying them at the end of the week . . . it was never meant for public dissemination. I personally would have preferred that it had remained private.

One of the good things about *Tracks* for me is to hear the funny songs, like "Part Man, Part Monkey," that haven't appeared before.
The best part about doing the record was that all these things that I'd taken off because they were too entertaining, I got to put back on. A lot of the things we did very spontaneously, but a lot of them fell by the wayside. *Tracks* consists of an enormous amount of material that was just out on its own. The interesting thing about the early stuff from CD 2 is that I thought I hadn't really written about men and women until *Tunnel of Love.* Then I found "Dollhouse," plus a lot of other things that began to address those issues, even in the early '80s.

I guess "Stolen Car" is really the start of a lot of that kind of thing.
Well, it was the presentation of that particular guy, of somebody who was concerned with those ideas, for the first time: that if you don't connect yourself to your family and to the world, you feel like you're disappearing, fading away. I felt like that for a very, very long time. Growing up, I felt invisible. And that feeling is an enormous source of pain for people. To make your life felt, it doesn't have to be in some big way; maybe it's just with your family and with the job, the basic things you live for. So to have somebody who could feel himself slipping away from all that, and who didn't know what to do about it, that idea was related to the heart of almost all of my music. The struggle to make some impact and to create meaning for yourself and for the people you come in touch with.

With "Stolen Car" that idea includes being able to have an intimate life, something that's essential to filling out your life. He was the guy that started the rest of that idea—the things that I wrote with the bass, whether it's the guy in "Goin' Cali" or the guy in "Loose Change" that no matter what he touches it just becomes loose change in your pocket.

That's something that everybody has to learn, to find their way through. And after that came *Tunnel of Love*.

So did music help you find that way through?
Oh sure, that was my central link, the minute I began to sing. The very first time I got up on stage, when I went down to the Elks Club and sang "Twist and Shout," I felt different, very different.

You said that at the time of *Nebraska* and then just after everything went crazy with the *Born in the U.S.A* album you felt very isolated. Did that make a difference to what you were getting back?
Well it depends. Basically, all my heroes were people who had hit records. By that time I was 33, 34, I'd already been playing for 20 years and I was interested in just what could I do. I didn't have any idea that that particular record would end up being popular as it was, but I knew when we cut that song that it was going to capture people's imagination, probably in a way that possibly I hadn't since *Born to Run*. You could just tell when you heard it in the studio that it was something. And then you just take the ride, you say, "Well, let me see what happens, and let me see where it goes."

At the time I actually did enjoy it tremendously. If I look back on it now, this enormous amount of exposure is something anyone would probably feel uncomfortable with to a certain degree. But to get out there on the tightrope and walk across, that was a great opportunity. I would have regretted terribly if I felt like I had that opportunity and hadn't made the most of it. It's not something I would particularly want to relive in the way that I did at that time, it's not something I would choose, but it was a laugh, it was at the right time for me—it was before I had my kids. I had a lot of experience and I was prepared for the things that happened.

I have never been to one of your shows, or listened to one of your LPs, without it connecting with something in me I didn't know I felt.
That's the writer's job. First of all, everybody has a memory—where do you remember, why do you remember, when you were 11 years old, and you were walking down a particular street on a certain day, there was a certain wind blowing through the trees, and the sound your feet made on the stones as you came up the drive. Everyone has memories like

that, that they carry with them for no explicable reason. And these things live within you. They are an essential part of who you are. It may be that something happened. Maybe nothing happened. But for some reason on that particular day you had some moment of experience that revealed to you what it meant to be alive. How important it is, what you can do with your life.

And your life can be brought back to you by the sound of your feet on gravel at a certain moment. That's the writer's job. The writer collects and creates those moments from out of his own experience and the world that he sees around him. Then you use your imagination and put those things together, and you present that experience to your audience, who then experience their own inner vitality, their own centre, their own questions about their own life, and their moral life. Whatever you're writing about, there's a connection made. That's what you're paid for—somebody says, "Hey, I'm not alone."

You can do it on stage at night—it can be done just through an explosion of energy at a particular moment in a particular way that makes somebody want to stand up, move themselves, go home and do whatever they feel they need to do. You're just trying to bring forth experience and get people in touch with all of those things in their world. That's the real job, the job that keeps you writing. That's what keeps you wanting to write that next song, because you can do that to people and because if I do it for you, I do it for me.

What are the parts of the job you enjoy?
It's the greatest, greatest job in the world. It was great even before I made a record. I had fun and loved my life when I was 22 and 23, and when I was making my first record and sleeping in a sleeping bag four blocks from here on my buddy's floor, I felt tremendously fortunate. I was sleeping late, I was doing what I wanted to do. You were, I guess, the local hero, the big guitarist-singer, even if it was just doing a little tune. It was a position of some prestige. It was great, it's always been great—that's the reason they don't call it working, they call it *playing*. It's a very, very fortunate existence and even when we were in the station-wagon and going 13 hours you could handle it; you felt like you weren't stuck or caught, you were seeing places you'd never seen before. I drove across the country once in three days with a buddy of mine. I was 19 years old, and we drove this big old Chevy flat-back with the equipment in the back and I didn't have my licence, hadn't driven and

it came to dark and he says, "We have to make it in three days so it's your turn." He put the truck in first and got it rolling and we switched seats and then I grinded the gears for the rest of the night and we went straight from New Jersey to the Esalen Institute in Big Sur in California. We got a gig there to play New Year's Eve; it was 1969, and it was a real adventure. I look back on it and the hard times just felt like good times too. It was just a real charmed existence, I loved every little bit of it.

Do you still get the same pleasures from it now?
Yeah I do. I think the fundamental thing remains the pleasure of simply picking up the guitar and having an opportunity to speak to people and be heard, writing a song that you haven't written before. It's still a tremendous source of inspiration for me. I connected myself to my world, to the world that was out there via music. You felt that impact whether it was 100 people or a big crowd. That feeling stays fundamentally the same—it doesn't grow incrementally with the size of the crowd or the size of the place you're playing because it's about something you're doing internally, to feel yourself, to feel your own existence and to feel the impact of that existence in your town, in your neighbourhood, in the world. I still feel that need; that's my place, that's where I fit in. I still try to do it as well as I can and hopefully better than I have done it previously. That's what I want to do.

AND THAT IS nearly that. There's a line in "The Wish," perhaps the best song on *Tracks,* which goes, "It's a funny old world, mama, where a little boy's wishes come true." Almost 25 years ago I bought *Born to Run* and it changed my life. After the interview, on our way to dinner, I find myself sitting with Bruce in the front seat of his Cadillac outside the house where he wrote "Backstreets," "Thunder Road" and all the rest, and that line pops into my head. Over the years Springsteen's music has inspired me more than any other, often seeming to parallel my own life and addressing my own concerns when I most needed it to. You can't ask more from popular culture. As we drive home, Bruce and Patti's car peels on a different route. For a second they're silhouetted, leaning towards each other in a perfect image of love and happiness. And sparks fly on E Street.

Patrick Humphries
Record Collector,
February 1999

Another important interview for parsing the immense, career-spanning *Tracks* box, from the reasons these songs weren't released sooner to the reasons "The Promise" still didn't make the cut. Asked about *Born in the U.S.A.* and its outtakes, Springsteen says, "There's an extra album of that material on *Tracks* that I actually think might have made a more interesting record," admitting that *Born in the U.S.A.* "was a record I always had some ambivalence about, perhaps because of its success." Beyond *Tracks* talk, Humphries asks wide-ranging questions and elicits revealing responses. Springsteen discusses the dualism of a career that now had him doing solo acoustic shows in support of *The Ghost of Tom Joad* as well as reconvening the E Street Band. Here on the cusp of the 1999–2000 reunion tour, Bruce says, "I got great satisfaction out of *Tom Joad*, but it wasn't something that I'd like to have been doing all along . . . The physical intensity of playing with the band, and the way you reach and touch an audience in that context, is thrilling."

It's been a long time since anyone called Bruce Springsteen "the new Bob Dylan." Over the last twenty years, an equally grim fate has befallen artists like Steve Earle, John Cougar Mellencamp and even Bryan Adams—"the new Bruce Springsteen."

But which Bruce Springsteen are those pretenders supposed to be imitating—the bar-room rocker from New Jersey, or the troubled troubadour recreating the spirit of Woody Guthrie?

The real Springsteen is more than either of those caricatures might suggest, as Patrick Humphries discovered when he recently met the man they still call the Boss. The party animal is alive and well, though these days he has to be in by ten. The social commentator is also still at home, though he's tired of the responsibility of speaking for anyone but himself.

More than anything else, Springsteen is a surprisingly reflective and thoughtful songwriter, as the upcoming publication of his lyric book *Songs* will prove. During a long, revealing interview, Patrick Humphries persuaded Bruce to explain what motivates him to make music—and how that music has changed over the last thirty years.

The first question long-term fans will want to ask you is why did *Tracks* take so long to arrive?

[*Springsteen roars with laughter. He does this a lot. He also . . . pauses a lot while answering questions.*]

I guess . . . I sort of released records very carefully and somewhat cautiously from the beginning, because I felt from my first contact with the record industry . . . The first thing that happened after I signed to Columbia, the first photo session I did was in New York City. They said, oh, you're from New York. I said No, no, no; I'm from New Jersey. But there hadn't been anyone who'd been from New Jersey since Frank Sinatra!

A lot of your music has a really strong sense of place and your name has been inextricably linked with New Jersey, right from your first album . . .

I was strolling along the boardwalk, and I pulled out that postcard that was on the cover of my first album [*Greetings from Asbury Park, N.J.*] and I brought it in and said "I wanna use this for the cover." Luckily I had an art director who thought it was great.

But I guess I felt that once you step into that arena, and enter at play with all those different forces that are in there, who you are can kind of get lost. And so I constructed myself, both through my records, and the band I put together, in what I felt I came from, and who I felt I was. And when the time came to edit the music I was going to put on those records, I was very specific about what I wanted to say, and what I wanted each specific record to be about.

Particularly after *Born to Run*: I had the first success, I had been on the cover of some big national magazines, and there was this . . . "Were you invented by the record company?" I'd been playing for 10 years by then in every bar up and down the East Coast! So I said wait a second! But I understood it. I'd seen that happening. So when I went in to make *Darkness on the Edge of Town*, I edited that record very tightly. I had two years where I hadn't recorded, and I knew that what I put out next I wanted to be centered around who I was, what I wanted my music to be about and what I wanted to say. What I was going to write about, I thought was different from what was out there at the time.

We made a lot of music at that time, in some fashion or other, I thought didn't fit on the records. And then, I didn't really release at random, I didn't feel that I needed to have a record out every year. I always felt that I needed to put out the *right* record—I wanted to put out a record that hopefully would mean something, that would deepen my relationship with my audience, that would clarify who I was and what I wanted to do.

This was the way I released my albums. I looked at them in some fashion as all of a piece. I was writing about a particular cast of characters, following their lives. Consequently, a lot of things ended up not getting on records. And when I put this record [*Tracks*] together, one of the things I did notice was gee, you know, I put on CD 2 and there's an entire album from *The River*; there's almost an entire album from *Born in the U.S.A.*

So I said, I wonder what would have happened if I'd put this album out, just a year after *The River* and before *Born in the U.S.A.*? And what if I'd put this album out in the middle of the *Born in the U.S.A.* tour? . . . I don't know if it would've made a difference or not . . . Or if it would just have been more music for people to enjoy?

With the benefit of hindsight, do you think now that perhaps you were too rigid about it, that you took it too seriously?
Looking back, I don't know if I would make those decisions differently, because basically I created the only way I knew how, and I presented my music the only way I felt I could at the time. But it meant

that later on I found myself playing catch-up: so when we put out a live album it had to span 10 years of work because we'd never released ones as we went along! And now we're putting this out—basically 25 years of work because this music didn't get out at the time . . . I think now, when I look back, that there are certain records where that focus was essential to what the record became—*Darkness on the Edge of Town*, *Nebraska*, *The Ghost of Tom Joad*—and then there were other records where I could have had more flexibility, more leeway with what I put on.

I think that a lot of the things that come from *The River* sessions on *Tracks* could have switched places with any ten things that I did put on that record and would have performed the same function. And really, at that time, the reason *The River* became a double album was that I was seeking a relief from that rigidity. *Darkness* was the record I wanted to make, but I already had some of the outtakes that are on here—some of the bar band, party music—and I felt that these things were great, and they are an essential part of what I do, and yet because I release records relatively sparely I have a difficult time squeezing them in. It didn't feel right to me. So when I went to *The River* the first thing I said was, I want to include some of this music—things that happen spontaneously, things that we use to fuel the show.

Listening to *Tracks*, what's interesting is the extraordinary quality of the music that got left off. Did you never consider releasing things like "Rendezvous," "I Wanna Be Where the Bands Are" or "Thundercrack" as singles, or as B-sides?
I think that when I put those things out I wasn't really a singles artist. This was the early '70s—unlike 10 years earlier or even six years earlier, when you waited for that Rolling Stones single to come out, and you went straight down and bought it. At that time everyone was thinking more on 45s. Albums were still unusual. It was really the Beatles, a few records in, who all of a sudden created the idea of the album as a singular piece of work that people were going to be drawn to, and then there were singles that would come off it.

Previous to that, the music scene was fundamentally singles. It was fuelled by singles cuts, and I think that here in the States it was the British

Invasion that changed that picture, and then I think Dylan coming along, and the idea that maybe you can tackle some serious ideas with this music—and all of a sudden, the extended format, the album became the thing. The album always had a serious tone . . . when I was a kid, you saw an album, you knew it was going to be classical music or jazz. When I was a child, simply by their size, albums seemed very grown up.

I wasn't ever really a singles artist. I've had hits at a particular time, for one reason or another, but there wasn't anything different about those records and the ones that I'd released four years earlier; it was just a particular moment. So I never really thought like that. From when I first began and affected people. All of those guys had internalized that, and when they went out and did what they did, which could have appeared to be something that was the polar opposite of church music, it was not necessarily so.

At the start of the '80s when I first saw you play, it struck me that the brilliance of your shows was the rollercoaster ride you gave the audience—it was like the best Saturday night you're ever going to have, but then you'd pull it back with "This Land Is Your Land" or "Independence Day" and make it much more pensive and reflective.

I thought that was what it could do . . . present ideas in a more literal fashion, but then you want people to just raise their hand at a particular moment. And when you threw all these things together on a given night, something happened, something happened . . . and it could be inspiring. I've been inspired, and I hope to inspire. When you went out on that stage at night, you yearned to inspire, and bring happiness and fun and enjoyment, and make people laugh—and think. To me that's what I had always got out of music, and that was what I wanted to return.

For me the people whose music I cared about, still care about, all had that element, an element of spirituality. The pure humanity of Woody Guthrie's writing, it just cuts through everything. It's why Dylan drifted back towards gospel, and when you hear his "Every Grain of Sand," it's rooted in those things. They made those connections, and all of those connections were things that were part, in some fashion, of everyone's life.

I think that's what I was interested in doing—talking basic, daily experiences that I had, that everyone had: being involved with family, work, their friends; the way they fitted in, or did not fit in, the town that they grew up in; the way they saw themselves as a citizen . . . These were things I felt were a constant part of people's lives. And I wanted to create music that would encompass all of those issues and be fun and entertaining and would rock you on top—inside and outside!

Watching you play on *The Ghost of Tom Joad* tour, I got the impression that that was what you really wanted to do; you'd proved you were "The Boss," you'd got the gold records, you'd got the record sales, and it was almost as if the rock 'n' roll stuff was now just like the day job.
Not necessarily. I pretty much always did what I wanted to do. To do what I did on any given evening, I needed to have that commitment; so anytime I walked onstage, I had focused and committed myself to the job in hand. But I got a great deal of satisfaction out of that tour and that record. I hadn't written about those things in a while, and I felt it connected up to my earlier music . . . there was a connection back to *Nebraska*, which I'd always felt was one of my best records. And when I finished the *Tom Joad* record, that's how I felt. I played it and I said I don't know how this is going to do, or what people are going to think about, but it's one of my best records.

But I always loved playing with a rock band too, and I wouldn't put one thing necessarily in front of the other. I got great satisfaction out of *Tom Joad* but it wasn't something that I'd like to have been doing all along . . . The physical intensity of playing with the band, and the way you reach and touch an audience in that context is thrilling . . . and it's something I've done since I was very young. I always went back and forth, almost since I started. Before I ever made records, I wrote acoustic music and played it in some local coffee houses here. I always did both things . . .

I wanted access to the physicality, the energy, the grab-you-by-your-throat intensity you get when you put on a physical performance that you can do with a group. But the *Tom Joad* tour, that's sort of where you can focus and refine your ideas and present some of the things you're thinking about, very clearly, very precisely, and with a certain sort of depth and clarity that you couldn't achieve in a big concert.

In 1982, you wrote in a note to Jon Landau: "The song is in very rough shape but is as good as I can get it at the moment. It might have potential." That song was "Born in the U.S.A.," which two years later hurled you from being a cult, blue-collar rocker into the biggest rock star on the planet. But although *Born in the U.S.A.* remains among the best-selling albums ever released, it's not an album that you seem particularly fond of . . .

It was the record I made at the time, but I wouldn't say it was the record that I wanted to make. I spent a lot of time on it, we cut a lot of music. There's an extra album of that material on *Tracks* that I actually think might have made a more interesting record—"This Hard Land," "Murder Incorporated," "Frankie." There were some really good songs that, for one reason or another, at the time just went by the wayside . . .

It was a record I always had some ambivalence about, perhaps in the end because of its success. But I look back and it was really my purest pop record, and it functioned like that. I think that when I went into the studio initially, I wanted to take what I'd done on *Nebraska* and electrify it in some fashion. And on occasion—"Born in the U.S.A.," "My Hometown," "Glory Days"—I wrote some songs I liked. But I'm not sure I wrote the entire record that I wanted to. Sometimes that happens.

Given the astonishing range of material on *Tracks*, a lot of your longtime fans are going to want to know why "The Promise" isn't on there.

Yeah, that was a song that people really liked. There were a few things over the years that fans had mentioned that they liked and I did make an effort to include them. But when I went back—and I did go back—we didn't have a particularly good recorded version of that. It was very slow, and plodding. I just felt it was . . . heavy-handed. I was never completely satisfied with the way I'd written the song. I played it out a little bit when I wrote it—and we did cut it in the studio, for *Darkness*, I think, but it just never felt right to me. I thought at some point of attempting to re-cut it, but it just didn't happen.

In concert during the late '70s, you would bounce back onstage at the end of a draining three-hour show, and scream, "I'm just a prisoner of rock 'n' roll," then play another hour's worth of material. I always believed that to be true, that you had never had a "proper" job . . .

[*Laughs indignantly*] Hey, I was a gardener. I tarred roofs. I was a house-painter. But it was pretty brief, when I was a teenager, and basically I used that work to buy my first guitar. I went to a Western Auto Store, I remember I was paid 50 cents an hour, and I saved up 18 bucks, and I went out and bought my first guitar. I studied it for about six months and then I said, "If I'm going to be able to make a living, or get a job playing, I need an electric guitar," and that leads into "The Wish."

That must be a rock 'n' roll first, a song written by a rock star to his mum!

Yeah! And after that, literally from fourteen-and-a-half on, I made money playing. I made money six months after I picked up the guitar; it wasn't a lot, maybe five dollars on a particular night. But you forget, at 15 years old, ten or twenty bucks a week was an enormous amount of money for a kid to have in the mid-'60s. I was still living at home. So it was great: I made my own money, I didn't need to go to my folks for money—they didn't really have money they could give me. And relatively quickly, in the next two or three years, I developed into a "local attraction."

From that point on, you shared a room with three or four other guys, there were times you slept on people's floors. I lived in a surfboard factory. There wasn't any rent, you could eat for three dollars a day, or less . . . If I made 20 or 30 bucks a week, I'd scoot by to the next weekend when I had a job. I focused completely on music. I guess I was single, and I was a kid, and I had living conditions that allowed me to do that.

If you went back and looked at them, you might think . . . a room with a couple of mattresses on the floor, a refrigerator in the corner, a TV on a little stand . . . and that's how you lived! But that was pretty much how everyone I knew lived at the time—Vini Lopez [original E Street Band drummer] I think lived in the bathroom at the surfboard factory. We literally lived in an industrial park. It was tough, because the resin from the surfboards really knocked you out for a while. But it allowed me to spend my time working on my music, so I really did do that from when I was very, very young.

Do you remember the first song you wrote when you really thought, "there's something here"?
My first band, the Castiles, played some original music from the very beginning. We made a record that was never put out, just a demo that had a couple of original songs on it. I don't remember the first one that I actually taught to the band, but it was probably right back at the beginning.

Your relationship with your father has been pretty well documented in your songs ("Independence Day," "Factory," "My Father's House") and I wondered exactly when your father first began to feel that perhaps you were finally beginning to amount to something?
Being on the covers of *Time* and *Newsweek* was the big one. I always remember calling him up . . . it was a time when I didn't see my folks much, from '69 probably through to the 70s, because they moved out West when I was 19, and no one had ever been on an airplane. It was inconceivable to buy a plane ticket. So I had to drive out to California to see them, which I did a few times when the opportunity arose, but we were pretty distant. I did call and tell my mother that I had a record deal, and her first question was "What did you change your name to?"

I remember when I called and said to my pop, "I'm going to be on the cover of *Time* and *Newsweek*." That must have sounded insane! I had made a few records, but they hadn't done particularly well, and I remember my dad's only comment was: "Well, better you than another picture of the President!" Obviously that was the moment they knew something was going on. They didn't know exactly what it was . . . but they did know that, miraculously, *something* had occurred.

So you're out driving around New Jersey, and you hear a Bruce Springsteen song on the radio. How does that feel?
Initially it was a great thrill. It still is, to hear your music on the radio —particularly new music. I was in a place the other day, somebody

had the radio station on, and I hear, "I Wanna Be with You," and you sit, and you're listening, even 25 years later, you're going yeah, that *is* me. The radio still can feel like it's a magical device. It's something you can hear in your room, something that was incredibly personal to you, being disseminated over the airwaves—literally over the airwaves—it's put out into the air, over thousands and thousands of miles. Some intimate thought you had on a particular night about something that was so deeply personal to you that you wrote a song about it—and all of a sudden, that song is on the radio. It's still pretty incredible.

I haven't gotten jaded about it. I can still remember the first time I heard "Spirit in the Night" [his second single] on the radio, in New York City. A car pulled up at a light, and the window was open, and I heard my record through the window. And I was shocked—it felt *so* great. But you're frightened, because you're listening and thinking, gee, did we make it right? Is it good? What does it sound like? And what does that complete stranger think? Does he even care what he's hearing?

I saw Dylan in the summer. Sometimes he does a show and it's not great, but this was, and I felt really privileged to be in the same room and hear him sing "Blowing in the Wind," even though he's sung it thousands of times before.
I think when he's singing it, he probably has a different connection to it than you do, and though the song has become iconic . . . I'm guessing, but for myself, sometimes you just go back to the original reasons and feelings and personal experience that made you write the song in the first place. And those things are all still, no matter how far you travelled or move on, they're still a deep and integral part of you. So I think you can summon up the 22-year-old that sings "Growin' Up," or the 25-year-old singing "Born to Run" or the 30-year-old who sang "The River," I think that person is always inside you, that part of you is always there to summon up and reconnect with that music.

I played behind Roy Orbison once, it could all just have been current music, the way he approached it . . . He sang everything literally exactly like it was on the record. Which I felt like was a gift he gave to his audience. In his hands, it didn't feel rigid; in his hands, it didn't feel nostalgic to me. There may have been a nostalgic element, but it wasn't fundamentally nostalgic. And he presented it to you in a way that felt incredibly fresh, and also tied in to your memories. You could tell when he stepped to the microphone, that he still had complete access to his emotions and to what those songs were about, and he didn't short-change any of the music that he'd done, whether he'd sung it a thousand times before or not. He was able to step up and make it feel real to you on that particular evening, just in the beauty of his voice, and his own respect and profound connection to what he had created.

Responsibilities

With the responsibilities of fatherhood, do you manage to get out much to see much live music these days?
I haven't lately . . . This summer I saw John Fogerty's show, but I really haven't a lot lately. Your life changes, and all of a sudden it's, "It *starts* at 10 o'clock?" So it has affected my getting out and seeing a lot of live music. Last summer I got out a bit, saw some local bands, and played a little bit myself . . . Over the last year or so, I saw Sheryl Crow, I saw Bob [Dylan] play. But I haven't gotten out as much as I would have liked.

Seeing how much work went into the drafts of the songs outlined in *Songs*, and having enjoyed the essays you wrote for the book about the creation of the music, I wondered if you'd ever considered writing on a more sustained level, maybe short stories, a screenplay or a novel?
If I had any thoughts about it, just trying to come up with the things I wrote for the book cured me forever! It's a very different process. Initially I thought: it's a lyric book, so what are we going to put in it? Maybe I could write a little bit about some of the records, yeah, that's a great idea. And I sat down to write and write and write, and then I went back a week later and said this just isn't working. And so I spent a long time even for the brief comments that are in the book . . . Writing about what you've done proved to be pretty challenging for me.

It was different from doing an interview, where *you* also bear a good deal of the responsibility. All of a sudden you're left with having a written voice on a page, and it's different. I think I find the voices in my songs through a variety of different techniques. Part of it is what sound am I making with my own voice? The written words on the page, the music I'm strumming, all becomes part of the voice that you're seeking and the voice that you find for the characters you're writing about. It's a very different process and in no way did it lead me to think I was going to pursue a writing career—I'll stick with songwriting, I think!

But as a songwriter in rock 'n' roll, everyone assumes that when you write "I did" or "I am," that really is you singing, rather than a character you've written.
That's something that is particular to music I think. I suppose if you're a film actor who plays an enormous amount of action heroes or tough guys, then somebody might come up to you in a bar and take a swing at you, maybe [*laughs*]. But I think it's less likely. I think part of it is that it is self-contained, in the sense that you are the writer, you are the performer, you are the singer—and if you've done your job very well, and brought forth a lot of real emotion, I think it calls for the listener to take a step back and realise that they're listening to a creation of some sort, a work of imagination. That what you're doing, part of your craft, is understanding—and you may be singing through the voice of another character to create that understanding.

I've written in many, many different voices—of which a listener will say well that's obviously not literally your life. But I've experienced it from time to time, where someone will come up and very literally assume that you've written very specifically about yourself—or about *them*! That's the scary ones.

Occasionally you will write something that's more autobiographical than not, but really it just goes all across the board. And I think that to over-interpret it, to overpersonalise it, is generally a mistake. As a writer you're paid to use your imagination, and your emotions, and your eyes, to create something that is real—in the sense that there's real emotion. And I think that whatever you're writing about, you have to find yourself in there in some fashion. That's what makes the song work.

But because you come out on stage and sing in that voice and tell that story, it may make the lines a little greyer than with novelists or film directors—I don't think anyone thinks Martin Scorsese is *in* the Mafia! So it is perceived a little differently in music.

How did a song like "Iceman" turn up on *Tracks*? It hasn't even appeared on bootleg before.

I didn't even know it existed myself, until a guy named Bob Benjamin sent me a tape with three songs on it, and that was one of them. When I was making the record I did sort of feel around: what did people want to hear? What do they like? I had feedback from a lot of different places. Bob sent me that tape and I'm like, "Iceman," what's that? I put it on in my car and said, wow, that's pretty good. So we had a look to see if we could dig up the 24-track, and sure enough we found it and it ended up on the record. And "Give the Girl a Kiss," the party thing from *Darkness*, I didn't know that existed either.

It seems ironic that the keenly awaited, long-overdue box set should come so soon after your appearance in court battling against the release of archive material. And it was a pretty weird sight seeing you in a suit . . .

A pretty weird sight! Yeah, it must have been, because the picture was printed in papers all over the place simply because I was wearing a tie! I mean it was news of some sort—some distorted sort! If I'd known I was going to get that sort of publicity, I'd have worn a tie years ago!

Ken Tucker
Entertainment Weekly,
February 28, 2003

The Rising found Springsteen doing more publicity than he had in years—perhaps ever. "Current reality is that you can't count on radio [to play your music] when you're my age," he tells Tucker, "that's just the way it rolls. This was a record I felt very strongly about and I wanted it to be heard; I wanted people to know that it was out there." In what may be the most sober interview ever published in *Entertainment Weekly*, Springsteen discusses the meanings of success and the political situation in America. "I'm always fighting against that feeling of helplessness," he admits. "I can be overwhelmed by ambivalence, by the despair of the day. [But] that's what people use music and film and art for; that's a light on new possibilities."

Driving to talk with Bruce Springsteen, one passes small businesses that might pop up in one of his songs: Two Men and a Truck: Movers Who Care, and the Cree Mee Freeze ice-cream stand. This is rural Monmouth County, NJ, where the Boss lives surrounded by vast cornfields cleared for the winter, and a short distance from his seminal Asbury Park. On a cold day in early February, the living room of his converted farmhouse is warmed by a glowing fireplace; three guitar cases and a keyboard sit in the hallway. Springsteen, dressed in Johnny Cash black (quilted jacket, shirt, pants, boots), has just come from his home recording studio, where his wife, Patti Scialfa, is completing her second solo album—a decade after her first. "Yeah, a bit of a gap between, but"—Springsteen pauses—"that's the way we do things in this family!" he says, laughing.

Springsteen went seven years between his last two studio albums— 1995's spare *Ghost of Tom Joad* and last year's 9/11-themed *The Rising*— and 18 years between collaborations with a fully constituted E Street Band. He seems at peace with that pace. After 30 years of hard work and harder playing, he's got a realistically skeptical view: While grateful for *The Rising*'s Grammy nominations, he scorns a music industry that seems focused solely on quick, hit-single careers; his kinship with the bedrock beliefs of his fans has grown, but he thinks the Bush administration is headed in the dead-wrong direction; and out of this troublesome world he's done his best to carve a haven for his family— wife and E Street Band member Scialfa, and their three children, Evan, 12, Jessica, 11, and Sam, 9. With all the accolades, and sales of just under 2 million copies, *The Rising* has revived his career while maturing the man. As became clear during our interview, Springsteen has worked strenuously to find a strategy for survival, and almost welcomes the notion that even if he has peaked as a mass-culture phenomenon, he can still passionately connect to an audience with shared values and concerns.

READYING HIMSELF FOR his first in-depth interview since last August's media blitz in support of *The Rising*, he plops into a rocking chair and vigorously musses his already-mussed hair. He's eager to hear what Secretary of State Colin Powell has said earlier that morning to the U.N. about possible war with Iraq. Foreign travel, among much more pressing things, is on his mind. (A new album, in case you're wondering, is not.) After the Feb. 28 airing of a CBS concert special taped recently in Barcelona, Springsteen will resume his "barnstorming tour"—the first leg of which took him and the E Street Band across America through the fall and early winter—with U.S. dates in March. Then, at least through June, he and the band head overseas, to everywhere from Australia and New Zealand to Germany. Rocker, reader, and peace-seeking road warrior, Springsteen refuses to be pinned down. He holds within him all the surprises and contradictions of an artist not just born in the USA, but now set loose in the world.

By the time most readers see this, *The Rising* may have won a Grammy for Album of the Year and Song of the Year. Are you excited to have been nominated?
I don't put a whole lot on it, 'cause I've been around a long time, and I made some pretty good records [that didn't get] an Album nomination: *Darkness* [*on the Edge of Town*], *Born to Run, The River, Nebraska....* But this is nice. It probably means a little more to me now than it would have back then, y'know?

Why?
Because maybe I would have said, "Wait a minute, maybe I'm doing something wrong." That kind of acceptance might not have fit my idea back then about whether a rock & roll rebel, or whatever I thought I was, should be winning awards [*laughs*]. But [*The Rising*] is an important record to me. It's the first record in such a long time with the band, and I wanted to make it really good, a record that could stand shoulder to shoulder with all our others. The whole idea with the band was to get back together but move very consciously forward. . . . [If you] saw the band on this tour, your older brother or dad couldn't say, "Oh man, I saw them back when they were *really* good." The band's playing as good—as committed and intense—as at any time in its history, and making a record that carried on those values and ideals was very important. So the [Grammy] recognition is nice, it's enjoyable.

Are you familiar with your Grammy competition?
Yeah, I've heard probably just about everybody. Norah Jones is terrific. Eminem, he's good: intense—intense—and committed. He's got a lot to say and says it. Vehemently.

You did a ton of publicity for *The Rising*, appearing on TV everywhere from the *Today* show to *David Letterman*.
Current reality is that you can't count on radio [to play your music] when you're my age; that's just the way it rolls. This was a record I felt very strongly about and I wanted it to be heard; I wanted people to know that it was out there. . . . So we immediately said, there are some

things I would be comfortable doing. [But] *Letterman* threw me a little. They said, "Ya wanna come over and sit on the couch?" I said, "Ahhh, ya sit on the couch ya gotta be *funny*. That's too much pressure." But *he's* funny, so you don't have to be too funny yourself.

You really thought a Springsteen album with songs about the aftermath of September 11 wouldn't sell or attract attention?
Hey, it's a big tent out there [in pop culture]. I take my kids and we buy popcorn and see the big movies. The problem is that [the marketplace] pushes to the margins things that may not be immediately accessible. . . . It's like, you're either in the mall or the little tiny theater downtown. . . . The hegemony of a certain type of movie or a certain type of music at any given time isn't a good thing.

That's the way the game is played, I understand that. But you have to fight for your place—the audience is not brought to you or given to you, it's something that you *fight* for. You can forget that, especially if you've had some success: Getting an audience is *hard*. Sustaining an audience is *hard*. It demands a consistency of thought, of purpose, and of action over a long period of time. . . . You have to be willing to roll the dice, you have to be willing to risk, to step up and enter your particular arena and stake your claim to a piece of it. That's part of what *The Rising* meant to me.

You recently toured Europe and are going back there again soon. How do you think America is perceived now?
For the best part of a decade, we've had a bigger audience overseas than in the States. Two thirds of my audience has been there; they were very connected to the *Tom Joad* record, very connected to music that was explicitly American, [so] there must be a tremendous commonality felt about the values of those songs. People continue to be very taken with America, with its bigness and its history and its drama, its myths and its values.

There's a lot of dissent about America [now], about this administration's policies. But I think those things are specific, I don't think they're something as general as a blanket anti-Americanism. Bob Herbert said in a column in *The [New York] Times* a few weeks ago that [Europeans] respond to a country that uses its power wisely abroad and dispenses its benefits fairly at home. Those are the things that are very debatable right now—the direction we're going in.

Do you think we'll go to war with Iraq?
I think we [already] are; I think the administration is just set on it. A month ago I wasn't so sure, but now I am. Those drums are being beaten really hard. I think the administration took September 11 and used it as a blank check. And like most Americans, I'm not sure the case has been made to put our sons and our daughters and innocent citizens at risk at this particular moment. But I don't think that's gonna matter, unfortunately. . . . The actual war against terrorism is extremely complicated. You try not to be cynical, but without the distraction of Iraq, [people would notice] that the economy is doing poorly, and the old-fashioned Republican tax cuts for the folks that are doin' well will seriously curtail services for people who are struggling out there. I don't think that's the kind of country that Americans really want. All the cutbacks in the environmental restrictions—it's just a game of shadows and mirrors at the moment.

Shifting gears a little: Bobbie Ann Mason, a writer I know you admire, just published a biography of someone else you admire, Elvis Presley. In the book, she theorizes that Presley, brought up poor and ill-educated, had a lifelong urge to please people, whether it was his father or Colonel Parker, and he ultimately just gave up. He said, "Okay, I'll go do this next crap movie and Vegas show."
The key to survival in the line of work he . . . *invented* is the replenishment of ideas. You can't really remain physically or mentally healthy without a leap of consciousness and a continuing, deeper investigation into who you are and what you're doing. Those are the things that will make sense of the many silly and weird things [*laughs*] that *will* happen to you [when you're a star]! [But] what keeps you from maintaining that replenishment of ideas is an insecurity about who you let in close to you. To have new ideas you usually need to have new people around, people willing to challenge your ideas in some fashion, or to simply assist you in broadening them. Which means you have to be open to the fact that your thinking isn't everything, y'know?

The performers who suffer through their success have a difficult time making those connections, because they come from a different environment. The culture of ideas is usually over here [*gestures to his left*] and you've grown up over here [*gestures to his right*]. In between is this tremendous void that, when Elvis started, was rarely bridged. Bridging that void is your ace in the hole, but to do it you've gotta be aware of the limitations of where you come from and be willing to say, "Well, I've gotta go out and seek new things."

You seem to identify with Elvis in this way.
For me, I was somebody who was a smart young guy who didn't do very well in school. The basic system of education, I didn't fit in; my intelligence was elsewhere. I found I could apply my intelligence when I started to play [music], but once you get to that point. . . . There was a moment during the [recording of] *The Wild & the Innocent* when the band was having a kind of breakdown—we couldn't make the record, the sessions weren't going well. I happened to bump into Jon Landau [then a rock critic for Boston's *Real Paper*, and Springsteen's manager since 1977] outside a club I was playing in Boston. I was reading his review, which was pasted up outside the club in a feeble attempt to lure some paying customers inside [*laughs*], and he said, "Whattya think?" I said, "It's pretty good," not realizing he had written it, and we just struck up a conversation about our love of music. I thought, This is an interesting guy and I don't know any guys like this. That was my take on him: "I don't know any guys like this."

So he came in, he had ideas about how the band should sound, about how the band should be arranged. We listened to records together and we said we like this drum sound, that guitar sound. And it became clear to me that what he was doing was *assisting me in doing what I wanted to do*. So the security for a young guy like me was suddenly there. I was like, "Hey, I'm steerin' the boat, I got some help here." And I felt comfortable. My own tolerance for outside help was limited for all the same reasons [as Presley's]—I went to just a year of college and you're self-conscious about those things, believe me. But my artistic survival at that moment depended on some fresh ideas.

So how did you spark some of those fresh ideas?
I began to look at movies differently and I began to read more intensely. It led me on my own journey through the world of ideas, which I feel has sustained the vitality of what we've done for 30 years: It is at the *essential core* of everything that happened next. I was lucky to come along when I'd seen the mistakes that my predecessors had made and I instinctively understood some of those mistakes before I was able to articulate them. [As a popular entertainer] you can culturally feel very,

very isolated. No matter how revolutionary an artist Elvis Presley was, the flip side of that is that you are singular, you are alone, and so you seek the comforts of home and of personalities that you utterly dominate. You effectively isolate yourself from the world that keeps you alive.

As you get older, the price you pay for not sorting through your [emotional] baggage increases. At 22, you can get away with a lotta slippin' and slidin', and you can get away with a good deal of that at 32, but by your early 40s, you're skiddin' *all* over the place. The pressure on you increases and I think that leads you to release this pressure, whether it's with drugs, or whatever it may be for you. Because you can't figure it out, you anesthetize yourself against it to go on livin'. And some people get dug in so deep that if the person [who could help him] was standing right in front of him it wouldn't matter. I've seen that plenty of times. It's a real tragedy because [an artist] who gave so much couldn't get it in return: the things that really matter, the things that would have brought him fulfillment and meaning and understanding of the beautiful and vital role that he played in so many people's lives. . . . You need to make that leap of consciousness. It's a self-protective mechanism that protects your gifts. Otherwise, you'll get totally spent and trashed. It's a job you can only do by yourself, assisted by—if you are very lucky—a trustworthy companion and some close friends. I've been very lucky that way. I drift, but not too far—so far [*laughs*]. There's always tomorrow!

This was how you felt even at the height of your popularity?
Yeah, sure. We were doing good, makin' a lotta dough, but when you're in the spotlight, it makes you hyperaware of what you're doing, and that can make you more self-conscious than you need be. I wrestled through all those things, and I found my own way of alleviating those pressures, partly by making an [experimental] record like *Nebraska*—that helped me feel very balanced. . . .

At the heights of success you're a little extra cautious because the level of exposure becomes wearisome. I truly don't know how some big stars do it. I could make a commitment to it for a certain amount of time, but after that I just had to get my feet back into what felt like real life. I always come back to the same thing: It's about work—the work, working, working. Write that next song and put that next record out; speak to my audience and continue to have that conversation that's been going on for so long. After a while you build up a large body of work that serves as a foundation. It's not like when you get your first record out and you wonder, Am I gonna get a chance to put another record out? Are people gonna care six months from now?

I have a lot of sympathy for some young musicians who are trying to crack it. We've gone back to the pre-FM [hit-driven days of] Top 40. It's a very different environment for young, thoughtful musicians. If I was just coming up, I wouldn't want to be stuck playing by the particular rules of the music business right now.

So you're unimpressed by the opportunities to be found for young talent on *American Idol*?
Ah, the great, terrible Darwinian spectacle! I haven't seen it, but it's the theater of cruelty that has everybody fascinated at the moment.

Speaking of embarrassment, do you ever hear one of your old songs and wonder, Where the hell did that come from?
Yeah, and it's a feeling of, I wouldn't write that now but I'm glad I wrote it then! [*Laughs*] Those first two records [1973's *Greetings from Asbury Park, N.J.* and *The Wild, the Innocent & the E Street Shuffle*] were very freeing because I didn't have an audience and I wasn't reacting to something I'd done previously. I just had this explosion of youthful creativity and exuberance. Those records were filled with exuberance and enormous energy. . . . I had heroes I was emulating, but I also had my own little world that I was trying to give life to. Those records always bring me back to the street life of my early 20s and the boardwalk.

Then came *Born to Run*.
Yeah, with that one I was shootin' for the moon. I said, "I don't wanna make a good record, I wanna make The Greatest Record Somebody's Ever Heard." I was filled with arrogance and thought, I can *do* that, y'know? It was fun, it was a great time, but if I had to measure it all up I don't think I've ever been as satisfied as I am right now. The combination of this particular record coming at this particular time, and the band being present and everybody being alive and accounted for—only a few bands can say that. We go to Europe and the front of the stage is filled with 15-, 16-, 17-year-olds—they see [the E Street Band],

who stood there 30 years ago. And not only are my guys *still* there, they still *mean* it.

Born in the U.S.A. **was by far your most commercially successful record. I have a friend who, remembering the album's cover, wanted to know what it was like to have had, for a time, the most famous ass in America.**
[*Laughs heartily and turns red*] That's funny because Annie Leibovitz would tell you she shot hundreds of pictures. [But] I kept looking at that one picture and said, "Well, I dunno, there's something about *this*." It had a certain laconic iconography that I liked. And I remember Annie yelling, "Oh no! It's out of focus!" It was just a kind of instinctive thing, what can I say?

Got a current cultural hero, someone whose work continues to evolve in a way you'd like yours to?
I tell ya, those three [recent] books by Philip Roth—*American Pastoral*, *I Married a Communist, The Human Stain*—just knocked me on my ass. To be [in his 60s] making work that strong and so full of revelations about love and emotional pain—man, that's the way to live your artistic life: Sustain, sustain, *sustain*.

You once said that part of entertainment is to provide food for thought. For you, that seems to be very much about resisting complacency; the battle to not become cynical.
A certain amount of skepticism is necessary to survive in today's environment. You don't want to be taking everything at face value. But for that [questioning] to be worth something it has to be connected to an element of energy and creative thought—that's the thing that's gonna have some impact. . . . So that's my approach: Try to be wise about the way the world works. But at the same time, you need to find some way to turn those insights about what's real and what's true into some creative process, creative action. That's what we try to pass on to our audience so [they] don't feel powerless. . . . Tommy Morello, the guitarist from Rage Against the Machine, said in an interview that history is made in people's kitchens, in living rooms, at night; it's made by people talking and thinking things through. That, I think, is true: You should throw your two cents in as best you can.

So much information comes from the top down. What do you say to people who feel like they don't have much say in what goes on in the world?

I'm always fighting against that feeling of helplessness. I can be overwhelmed by ambivalence, by the despair of the day. [But] that's what people use music and film and art for; that's its purpose. Its purpose is to pull you up out of that despair, to shine a light on new possibilities. And I think if you look at it pretty hard-eyed, it helps. That's where the living is, that's where life is. Regardless of what's going on externally, those are the powers that you find within yourself to keep going and change things. To try to make some place for yourself in the world.

Christopher Phillips
Backstreets,
August 1, 2004

Backstreets began in 1980 and over 30 years has become the premier international magazine and online resource devoted to Springsteen and related New Jersey artists. Phillips joined the staff in 1993 and became editor and publisher in 1998. But until 2004, 24 years burning down the road, Springsteen had never spoken directly with *Backstreets*. The interview itself captures Springsteen at the moment he was about to support publicly John Kerry's run for president—a move that proved too controversial among a portion of his politically broad fanbase—and launch Vote for Change, a series of concerts intended to, in Bruce's words, "mobilize the progressive voters . . . to change the direction of the government, to add our voices to the folks who are trying to make a change at the top."

Bruce Springsteen has directly entered the political fray of this fall's election, leading a coalition of artists through the so-called swing states to call for the election of John Kerry on November 2. One year after the *Rising* tour wrapped at Shea Stadium, Springsteen will be bringing the E Street Band together for five arena dates in early October (with a potential sixth date in Miami pending as this issue goes to press).

Joining them for concerts in Pennsylvania, Ohio, Michigan, Minnesota, and Florida (with nary a show in Springsteen's New Jersey stronghold) will be R.E.M., John Fogerty, and Bright Eyes, making this the first Springsteen tour with an opening act since John Wesley Harding opened the Berkeley shows of the *Tom Joad* solo-acoustic tour in 1995.

Along with additional artists such as Pearl Jam, Dave Matthews Band, Jurassic 5, and Bonnie Raitt, Springsteen has thrown his considerable artistic and commercial power behind this Vote for Change series of concerts—presented by MoveOn (www.moveonpac.org), benefitting America Coming Together (www.actforvictory.org)—to rally support for change in the coming election. It's a twist that, predictably, brought a few shouts, with conservative politicians, pundits, and more than a few Springsteen fans decrying his "sudden" political activism. Why has Citizen Bruce, after decades of expressing social commentary through his art, decided to speak out loud and clear?

We thought we'd ask him.

In his first-ever *Backstreets* interview, Springsteen spoke with editor Christopher Phillips in the days leading up to the August 4 Vote for Change tour announcement. Making clear what has long been expressed through his body of work, Springsteen discussed the motivation behind his involvement: "This is probably the most important election of my lifetime . . . given what I've written about, the things that I've wanted our band to stand for over the years, it's just too big a battle to lay out of."

Springsteen spoke in unambiguous terms about his hopes for this country, his convictions about the role of the artist in society, his perspective on the relationship between music and politics, and the complexities of his responsibility to his audience.

You've supported a lot of causes over the years, but as political and socially conscious as a lot of your work has been, this is the first time you've really weighed in on electoral politics. So I guess the big question is, why now?

Basically, this is probably the most important election of my lifetime. I think that the government has drifted too far from American values.

After 9/11, I was like everybody else—I supported going into Afghanistan, and I felt tremendous unity in the country that I don't think I've ever felt exactly like that before. It was a moment of great sadness, but also tremendous possibility. And I think that was dashed when we jumped headlong into the Iraq war, which I never understood, and I talked about that on the road. I never understood how or why we really ended up there. We offered up the lives of the best of our young people under circumstances that have been discredited. I had to live through that when I was young myself, and for any of us that lived through the Vietnam War, it was just very devastating.

Along with that, the deficits, the squeezing of services like the after-school services for the kids who need it the most, the big windfall tax cuts, the division of wealth that has threatened our connection to one another over the past 20 years that is increasing . . . these are things that as the election time neared—I couldn't really keep true to the ideas that I'd written about for 30 years without weighing in on this one.

I don't think I've seen anything like it before in my lifetime. I think that the freedoms that we've taken for granted—I spoke about this on the road a little bit, too—they are slowly being eroded. In the past I've gotten involved in a lot of grassroots organizations that sort of expressed my views, and where I thought I could be of some small help. I guess I've been doing that for about 20 years, and that was a way that I was very happy to work. I always believed that it was good for the artist to remain distant from the seat of power, to retain your independent voice, and that was the way I liked to conduct my work. But the stakes in this one are just too high. I felt like, given what I've written about, the things that I've wanted our band to stand for over the years, it's just too big a battle to lay out of.

A lot of great, unique artists are coming together for these shows— R.E.M., Pearl Jam, Jurassic 5, Bonnie Raitt—so I'm guessing that even with the unity of at least one common goal, there will be some different viewpoints. How much expression of that do you think there will be? Will we get different perspectives from different artists?

I would imagine so—as different as all the artists involved. I think we've all come together with one goal in mind, but I think everybody's idea of where it goes from there could very well be different. Myself, I like John

Kerry a lot. I don't think he has all the answers, or that John Edwards has all the answers, but I think they have the experience, the life experience, and I think they have the sincerity to ask the hard questions about America and to try to search for honest solutions. I believe they're going to do that. And I don't feel that way about the guys who are in there right now. I feel that trust has been broken, and there's no going back.

What did you think of Kerry's speech [at the Democratic National Convention]?
I thought it was fantastic—the best one I've heard him give.

And using "No Surrender" for his entrance music—is that something the campaign clears with you in advance?
No—somebody mentioned to me that they'd heard it at different rallies here and there, around the country . . . but it was a nice call.

You've focused a whole lot more on issues than labels or parties over the years—whether that's Democrat, Republican, Independent, Reform, Green, or anything else. That has appeared to be a very conscious decision, so in this case was it just that things reached a tipping point?
Yeah, I would say. I mean, I grew up in a Democratic house. The only political discussion I ever remember in my house was when I came home from school when I was little—I think someone asked me at school what we were, it must have been during an election season at some point, and I was probably around my son's age, eight or nine. And I came home and said, "Mom, what are we?" And she said, "Oh, we're Democrats. We're Democrats because they're for the working people." And that was it—that was the political discussion that went on in my house over about 18 years.

So I've always held progressive beliefs, or liberal beliefs. I think that when I went to write—you're shaped by your background, fundamentally, there's no getting around it. I lived in a household that was caught in the squeeze, endlessly trying to make ends meet. My mother running down to the finance company, borrowing money to have a Christmas, and then paying it back all year until the next Christmas and borrowing some more. So I know what that's like. This time out, there just wasn't really any way I could sit on the sidelines.

That makes me think about that "criticism" you always seem to get: how can a millionaire still write about blue collar concerns? Something similar gets leveled at Edwards: he's the son of a mill worker, and yet he turned into a millionaire lawyer, as if one negates the other. But clearly those formative experiences help shape how you see the world.

That criticism is also a tremendously muddled idea of how writers write. First of all, have you ever been to Mark Twain's house?

No, I never have.

It's *really nice* [*laughs*]. The room he wrote in is beautiful.

It wasn't a whitewashed shack with a bunch of frogs hopping around outside?

No, it's a really beautiful Victorian home. So it's been done before! [*laughs*] . . . It seems to me that particular criticism gets aimed at musicians rather than, say, filmmakers. Nobody complains that Marty Scorsese isn't actually in the Mafia. It always comes up—I've settled into the fact that I'll be answering that question for the rest of my working life. But it's a muddled understanding of the way that things get written.

Well, I hear you've been writing up a storm these days.

People say that all the time. I wish that were true!

Just wondering if we should be looking for any new material on the tour, if you've written anything for it specifically?

I'm always trying . . . I don't have anything until I have it, you know? Actually, I took a lot of time off—Patti was working on her record, and so I've been spending time with the kids, and I enjoyed watching her work. I'm always writing, I'm always trying to come up with something, but until I have it, I don't have it. So I can't predict.

You've said that "a writer writes to be understood." And there's been so much misinterpretation of your songs over the years, the obvious ones being "Born in the U.S.A." and "American Skin (41 Shots)." For the most part, you've let your songs do the talking, but I'm wondering, in addition to the changes these shows are trying

to effect in the country, if you think this will give your audience more clarity as far as the meaning and intent of your writing?

I don't know, it's possible. Basically, I have faith in the songs. And I also surrender to the reality that once your songs are out there, that you're simply another voice in the ongoing discussion to define them. That's just the way it plays. And that's okay—I think they're out there to be debated, some of them. It's funny with "American Skin," I do run into people who thoroughly believed the *New York Post*'s interpretation of that piece of music! But I've also run into a lot of people who completely understood what I was trying to say. And that's the way that it goes. When those songs go out there, then you add your voice to the chorus of people fighting for their definition and what they stand for. I have an edge, because I've still got the guitar in my hand.

But it's possible—it's not something I thought about, but it may.

In the past when you've felt the need to define something more clearly—I'm thinking right now of "Empty Sky" at the [2003] Atlantic City show, when you made it very clear what you intended "an eye for an eye" to mean—what goes through your head when you decide to clarify things like that?

I have no compunction about stopping and telling someone what I mean. There's a moment to do that. And so, hey, I had the stage at the moment [*laughs*], and generally if I feel any sort of recurring misunderstanding that's occurred more than a few nights running, I'll say, "Okay, there's *a few* people. . . ." Maybe there's 100, maybe there's ten. Maybe there's two. Maybe I'm just hearing the guy who's making the noise at that moment. But in the end, I am speaking to you. I'm speaking to you individually.

And so I don't have a problem stopping at a particular moment and making clear my intentions. And now with the fabulous help of the Internet [*laughs*], those intentions are instantaneously around the world, and it helps clear things up even faster.

Well, hey, happy we could be of service!

Or muddle things even quicker, I suppose. . . . But when you have an audience the size of mine, that audience is broad. And when I spoke about the Iraq war during this past tour, before the truth came out, there were people who cheered, and there were people who booed. And that's the way it rolls. I tended to keep my comments down to approximately two minutes at the end of the night, which I felt was a pretty good balance to the three hours that we'd spent playing, you know?

I do believe that you serve at the behest of the audience. But, at the same time, I believe that my ideas and the beliefs that our band has stood for over the years are an integral part of our work, and we have a *duty* to make those ideas as clear as possible. To make our stand at different moments as clear as possible. I think that's part of what people look to us for, that's a part of what we have provided to a portion of our audience. And I think on any given night I'm playing to many of my audiences out there. There's the *Tom Joad* audience, there's the "Dancing in the Dark" audience, but hey, they're all there at that particular moment. So I look at it as a part of our process. You also figure, these are the times we're working in. And I think you've got to take your stand in them.

When some conservative fans bristled at some of that stuff last summer, like your mention of the Al Franken book, I think some people felt that it was a contradiction of your welcome to fans of all political persuasions. I guess I always just took that as, "Everybody is welcome here, but that doesn't mean that I won't speak my mind or challenge you on occasion."

That's right. It's pretty simple. I don't need people cheering everything I'm doing—I don't go out expecting that, and we've done enough that I've seen both sides of the coin. And that's all right. The show is a forum of ideas. That's one of the things that we try to provide over the course of the evening. And as such, that's part of what you're getting when you walk through the doors.

Which shouldn't come as a surprise to anybody who has been following you for any decent length of time. Some fans seem to have been taken aback by the posting of Al Gore's speech on your website, or the impeachment jokes onstage, but it seems to me that your political stance and your social concerns have been consistent for a long time.

Yeah, I would be surprised if there are *longtime* fans who were surprised. I could see somebody who casually comes in and out depending on what you're doing, or on a particular song, but I think if you followed us over the past 30 years, our positions on most social issues have been consistent and straightforward.

Some people may have blinders on and just choose not to see it, or choose to take the "good parts" and leave the rest.
That's true—I think that part of the audience/artist relationship is one of intense identification. "You're me, I'm you." That is a big part of the deal. And I think part of what we do is say, "Well, yeah, we *are* one. But we are not the *same* one."

I love John Wayne's work like crazy. I've found great inspiration and soul in it my whole life. I'm not a fan of John Wayne's *politics*. But I love John Wayne, and I love the work he's done. And so that's how it bounces sometimes.

So who inspires you not just artistically but politically as well? It looks like John Fogerty is going to be on the bill, and his songs seem to be a touchstone for you in that way.
Really, if I go back to it, when I was really young, even with Steel Mill, we did the local benefits, marches down to Washington in the late '60s. So the truth of it is, if you're in my generation and if you grew up in any part of the alternative culture, that was just a part of your birthright. Whether you want to call it activism, or concerned citizenry, that came as a part of those times. I find it unusual when I meet people who did *not* have that experience from my generation. They are out there, you know? But for me and most of my friends, those were things that were just a part of growing up when we did. And the people who we admired and emulated—which for me obviously begins with Dylan— had a very clear political voice. John [Fogerty] did it more subtly, but fabulously also.

And so I took my own spin on it. I couldn't exactly tell you why I started writing in that direction. It's funny, Steve [Van Zandt] went on to be one of the most political songwriters, but back in the early times, he was like, "I don't know if those should mix" [*laughs*]. That's classic Steve—when he goes, he *goes*! There's no coming back! That's Steve Van Zandt [*laughs*].

But yeah, when I was very young, maybe it was because of my background, or because of the music that I liked—I was interested in the class-conscious music of the Animals—these are things that spoke to me and that I also wanted to address in my own music. That was really the way I came to it. I didn't have a political education when I was young, as I said, I didn't really grow up in a political family. The politics in my town were small-town politics. So it was something that, in truth, I really came to through popular music. Through a combination of the times and popular music.

As political awakenings go, I've always had the impression that the time around *The River* was big for both you and Steve, as far as getting out of the States and seeing our country through other eyes.
I know for Steve it was a tremendous awakening, that tour. More so for him maybe than for me, because I had kind of started to write about it on *Darkness on the Edge of Town* and *The River* already, really before we went overseas. But I know for Steve it was tremendous. We went to East Berlin together, and it was quite an experience, East Berlin at that time. It was real noticeable, what that does to you. And also, when you spend a good amount of time over there, you do have a moment to step out of the United States and look back with a critical eye.

If there was one single thing I'd like to give every high school kid in the United States, it would be a two-month trip through Europe at some point during the formative years. Because it's very difficult to conjure up a real worldview from within our borders. It's *hard*. It's hard because we're so big, and the hegemony of American culture is so weighty and so heavy that it's very difficult without stepping outside and realizing what it's like to have the next country just a two-hour drive away, to have a certain kind of interdependence that is different than what we have here. It's just a certain view of the way the world works that is different. So if I could give every young kid one thing, that would be it—because it would broaden what we listen to, the way we perceive ourselves, the types of leaders we choose. It would change the nation dramatically.

I always remember going down to South America on the Amnesty tour and hearing *incredible* music, or going into Africa and seeing some amazing acts that opened up for us on that tour, and realizing that only a minuscule amount of people are going to hear this music back in the United States. Meanwhile, a six- or seven-piece rock band from Central Jersey is playing the Ivory Coast, and people who have barely heard our music before are going crazy. And we're speaking English, you know? The openness I've found outside the United States contrasted a bit to some of the closedness that we have here. And it's not intentional—it's cultural. And it comes from a lack of exposure to other things.

What opened your eyes to some of those things initially? On the
River* tour you talked about the Joe Klein book, *Woody Guthrie: A
***Life*. Was that book pivotal for you?**
That's a big book, a very powerful book. I was looking for ways that
other people went about creating work that spoke to all of these things—
emotional, and social, and political, the environment of the day. How
did other people do that? How did they balance their creative instincts
and their political instincts? I was a very different creature in that, hey,
I was a successful pop musician, and that changes the cards to some
degree. But at the same time, what's at the heart of it is still the same
sort of questing after the country that you're carrying in your heart, the
country that you want your kids to grow up in. So I studied all of my
forefathers very intently along the way. And I just put together something that felt right for us, and for me.

One of the purposes of art is to reflect our world back to us. And
there's so much animosity and fear surrounding that right now—a
lot of people, the whole "shut up and sing" faction, seem to think
that's not what an artist should be doing. But considering the folk
tradition you're a part of, thinking about Woody Guthrie, "shut up
and sing" is a real oxymoron.
First of all, there's a long tradition of artist involvement in the nation's
social and political life. Woody Guthrie, Bob Dylan, James Brown, Curtis Mayfield, Public Enemy . . . not only was their music joyous and ex-
hilarating, but it was *timely*. And it was essential, for me, to understanding
some of the events of the day. When they spoke, I heard myself speaking.
I felt a connectedness. So I think that any time somebody in this country
is telling somebody else to shut up, they're going in the wrong direction.
No, no, no, you're supposed to be *promoting* speech. You may like it, you
may not like it—I hear a lot of things I don't like, either, but hey [*laughs*].

Also, if you listen to the airwaves and the level of discussion out there,
we can't screw it up. It's already broke! It's screwed already [*laughs*]. So it's
not like the musicians are going to come in and screw all this up now,
you know? That's not going to happen.

It's amazing how violent some of the reactions have been—like
what happened to Linda Rondstadt last week in Vegas.
A tragicomedy . . . [*laughs*] The description of it was hilarious, you know?
The idea that people actually got worked up enough to throw drinks,

pull down concert posters, and storm the lobby or whatever, and that they felt the need to escort her *off the premises*—for mentioning a *film*. That's scary. Or even the Dixie Chicks, who were pounded so relentlessly. So it's kind of crazy. But right now we live in very divided times; people's feelings about these issues are very intense, and people are going to have strong responses to anybody coming out and moving toward one side or the other. Particularly if it's somebody who you like, or whose music you admire. I think for a lot of people it severs a part of that artist/audience bond. But that bond is a little more complicated than that. It's just a little more complicated. I know what you're saying: I think we're waiting for the drums to start.

Considering how divided things are, ideally, what's your goal on this tour? What's the message, or the result that you're looking for? Well, the best thing is that we have a very simple result in mind—and that result is to change the administration in November. So at its core, it's a very direct goal. At the same time, working with MoveOn and America Coming Together, we're trying to get voters registered, trying to get people mobilized to vote, trying to get people out on the street to mobilize the progressive voters, to get people involved in the democratic process. That's the means to the end. But the end is very clear for this short tour: we're out trying to change the direction of the government, to add our voices to the folks who are trying to make a change at the top.

Nick Hornby
The Guardian,
July 17, 2005

The novelist Nick Hornby has always been a fan of Springsteen, and his essay on "Thunder Road," in *Songbook*, is one of the most penetrating meditations written about the song. Hornby interviewed Springsteen, who was on tour for *Devils & Dust*, and asked some probing questions about stage presence, writing style, and musical tastes.

Earlier on in the week that I met Bruce Springsteen, and before I knew I was going to meet him, I'd decided I was going to send him a copy of my new book. I got his home address off a mutual friend, and signed it to him, and the book was lying around in my office in an unstamped Jiffy bag when the editor of this magazine asked if I'd like to do this interview. So I took the book with me.

I wasn't expecting him to read the bloody thing, nor even to keep it, and yet even so it seemed like something I needed to do. *A Long Way Down* was fuelled by coffee, Silk Cuts and Bruce (specifically, a 1978 live bootleg recording of "Prove It All Night," which I listened to a lot on the walk to my office as I was finishing the book). And Springsteen is one of the people who made me want to write in the first place, and one of the people who has, through words and deeds, helped me to think about the career I have had since that initial impulse. It seems to me that his ability to keep his working life fresh and compelling while working within the mainstream is an object lesson to just about anyone whose work has any sort of popular audience.

The first time I met him was after his Friday night show at the Royal Albert Hall, at a party in an upmarket West End hotel. He talked with an impressive ferocity and fluency to a little group of us about why he demanded restraint from his fans during the solo shows. The following afternoon I went to the soundcheck for the Saturday show, and sat on my own in the auditorium while he played "My Father's House," from *Nebraska*. It wasn't the sort of experience you forget in a hurry. I interviewed him in his dressing room, and I was nervous: I have, in transcribing the questions, made them seem more cogent than they actually were.

He looked younger than the last time I saw him, and he's clearly incredibly fit; he changed his shirt for the photographer, and I could tell that he does a lot more two-and-a-half-hour shows than I do. He was pleasant and friendly, but though he asked after a couple of younger musicians who both he and I know, there wasn't much small talk; his answers came in unbroken yet very carefully considered streams. He is one of the few artists I've met who is able to talk cogently about what he does without sounding either arrogant or defensively self-deprecating.

I gave him the book, and he thanked me. I have no idea whether the cleaner took it home, but it didn't matter much to me either way.

I was thinking when I was watching the show last night that maybe when you play with the band you can at least say to yourself, "I know why people are coming to see us. We're good at what we do, and there's this dynamic between us." But when it's you on your own, you can't tell yourself that anymore. How does that feel? Have you got to a stage in life where it doesn't feel weird that so many people come to see only you?

I performed like this in different periods of most of my playing life before I made records.[1] It just so happens that I didn't do it on the *Nebraska* tour, maybe I was feeling unsure about . . . I hadn't performed by myself in a while. It feels very natural to me, and I assume people come for the very same reasons as they do when I'm with the band: to be moved, for something to happen to them. So I think the same things that make people plunk down their hard-earned bucks for the tickets, it works both ways. You're looking for an experience and something that contextualises, as best as possible, a piece of the world. I'm just taking a different road to it out there at night. It's the same thing, you know?

It's always struck me that you work very hard on the stage side of things, that you have a theory of stagecraft. Is that right?
Well, I don't know if I've worked hard at it. It's always felt natural, because I'm generally very comfortable with people. That's probably genetic in some fashion [*laughs*]. There is a presentation and I think being aware of the fact that there's a show going on is a good idea [*laughs*].[2] I think it fell into some disrepute when the idea of the show became linked to falseness in some fashion, which is a superficial way to look at it. It's actually a bridge when used appropriately. It's simply a bridge for your ideas to reach the audience. It assists the music in connecting and that's what you're out there for. I think if you do it wrong, you can diminish your work, but if you do it right you can lightly assist what you're doing. It can be an enormous asset in reaching people with what might be otherwise difficult material. I have a large audience coming to see this kind of music, an audience which in other circumstances would not be there. The audiences are there as a result of my history with the band but also as a result of my being able to reach people with a tune. I have my ideas, I have my music and I also just enjoy showing off [*laughs*], so that's a big part of it. Also, I like to get up onstage and behave insanely or express myself physically, and the band can get pretty silly. But even in the course of an evening like this there's a way that you sort of attenuate the evening. Your spoken voice is a part of it—not a big part of it, but it's something. It puts people at ease, and once again kind of reaches out and makes a bridge for what's otherwise difficult music.

I think that's right. Those shows where you borrowed things from James Brown . . . I think some people did find it troubling that this music is supposed to be real and authentic and yet there's this stagecraft, this messing around, at the same time.[3] I think the people who get the shows always see that there's not a contradiction.
Plus, you know, when I was young, there was a lot of respect for clowning in rock music—look at Little Richard. It was a part of the whole

thing, and I always also believed that it released the audience. And it was also a way that you shrunk yourself down to a certain sort of life-size (*laughs*) but I also enjoyed it, I had fun with it, and I never thought that seriousness and clowning were exclusive, so I've approached my work and my stagecraft with the idea that they're not exclusive. You can go from doing something quite silly to something dead serious in the blink of an eye, and if you're making those connections with your audience then they're going to go right along with it.

What have you been listening to the past couple of years?
I listen to all kinds of things, you know? Take your choice. [*He reaches into a bag and pulls out a whole heap of home-made CDs.*] I've made all this music for walking . . . A lot of this is a little acoustic-oriented but I hear everything. I hear all the Britpop stuff, the Stone Roses and Oasis, and I go on to Suede and Pulp. I'm generally interested in almost everything.

For the benefit of the tape I'm looking at CDs which feature Dylan and Sleater-Kinney and the Beach Boys and Jimmy Cliff and Sam Cooke and Bobby Bland and Joe Strummer; pretty much the whole history of recorded music.
I left a lot of my more rock things off, because this is my walking music. But I listen to old music; some Louis Armstrong stuff recently. And then I'll listen to, I don't know, Four Tet or something. I do a lot of curiosity buying; I buy it if I like the album cover, I buy it if I like the name of the band, anything that sparks my imagination. I still like to go to record stores, I like to just wander around and I'll buy whatever catches my attention . . . Maybe I'll read a good review of something or even an interesting review. But then I go through long periods where I don't listen to things, usually when I'm working. In between the records and in between the writing I suck up books and music and movies and anything I can find.

And is that part of the process of writing for you?
I don't think it has to be. I tend to be a subscriber to the idea that you have everything you need by the time you're 12 years old to do interesting writing for most of the rest of your life—certainly by the time you're 18. But I do find it helps me with form, in that something may just inspire me, may give me an idea as to the form I'm going to create

something in, or maybe the setting. Ten or 12 years ago, nature writing struck my imagination and it's seeped into my work a little bit here and there ever since. It's all kinds of things. I heard this live version of "Too Much Monkey Business" by Chuck Berry and it sounds so close to punk music. So when you go to record with your band, you have all those sounds, you've created a bank. I like to stay as awake and as alert as I can. And I enjoy it too, I have a lot of interest in it . . . I like not being sealed off from what's going on culturally.

Have you got to the stage where your kids are introducing you to things?
Yeah, my son likes a lot of guitar bands. He gave me something the other day which was really good. He'll burn a CD for me full of things that he has, so he's a pretty good call if I want to check some of that stuff out . . . The other two aren't quite into that yet. My daughter's 12, 13, and she likes the Top 40. So I end up at the Z100 Christmas show, sitting in the audience with my daughter and her friends watching every Top 40 act . . . I'm all over the place.

How did that Suicide thing come about?[4]
I met Alan [Vega] in the late '70s. I was just a fan. I liked them, they were unique. They're very dreamy, they have a dreamy quality, and they were also incredibly atmospheric and were going where others weren't. I just enjoyed them a lot. I happened to hear that song recently, I came across a compilation that it was on and it's very different at the end of the night. It's just those few phrases repeated, very mantra-like.

It's especially striking in a show that's built almost exclusively on narrative.
Right, but it's the fundamental idea behind all of the songs anyway [*laughs*].[5] It's just a different moment at the end of the night, where you go to some of the same places with virtually very few words. I like narrative storytelling as being part of a tradition, a folk tradition. But this envelops the night. It's interesting watching people's faces. They look very different while that's happening. It's a look of some surprise, and that's part of what I set the night up for—unconventional pieces at the top to surprise the audience and to also make them aware that it's not going to be a regular night. It's going to be a night of all different

things and the ritualistic aspect of the night is dispelled. As long as it's not something that I've done before . . .

How do you think of your relationship with your own material? Because when you were here with the band a couple of years ago, you were playing stuff from the first three albums and some of those you were doing solo as well. And yet last night I think there was one song from the first four albums . . .

Is that right? On certain nights I'll play more. I think I played "For You" for a while . . . It depends. My only general rule was to steer away from things I played with the band over the past couple of tours. I was interested in re-shaping the *Rising* material for live shows, so people could hear the bare bones of that. And the new material and [*The Ghost of*] *Tom Joad* and *Nebraska* gets a nod, and I think "Tunnel of Love" comes up. I play "Racing in the Street" . . . I haven't played much off *Born to Run*. It's predicated on anything that doesn't have a formulated response built in.

Does it feel like young man's music to you now, the first three, four records?

I would say that it is, you know, because a lot of young people actually mention those records to me. I remember I was playing over here a while back and I was staring down and there was a kid, he couldn't have been more than 14, 15, he was mouthing every word to us, *Greetings from Asbury Park*, literally word for word and this kid—forget about it, his parents were the glimmer in somebody's eye [*laughs*]. In some ways I suppose it is, but also a good song takes years to find itself. When I go back and play "Thunder Road" or something, I can sing very comfortably from my vantage point because a lot of the music was about a loss of innocence, there's innocence contained in you but there's also innocence in the process of being lost [*laughs*]. And that was the country at the time I wrote that music. I wrote that music immediately preceding the end of the Vietnam War, when that feeling swept the country. A part of me was interested in music which contained that innocence, the Spector stuff, a lot of the Fifties and Sixties rock 'n' roll, but I myself wasn't one of those people. I realized I wasn't one of my heroes, I was something else and I had to take that into consideration. So when I wrote that music and incorporated a lot of the things I loved from those particular years, I was also aware that I had to set in place something that acknowledged what had happened to me and everybody else where I lived.

I presume that's where the emotional connection with your music came for so many people at the time. Because all those people had grown up loving that music, but it wasn't doing the job any more.
I think we were a funny amalgam of things at that moment. There was so much familiarity in the music that for a lot of people it felt like home; it touched either your real memories or just your imaginary home, the place that you think of when you think of your home town, or who you were, or who you might have been. And the music collected those things, so there was an element that made you feel comfortable. And yet at the same time we were in the process of moving some place else, and that was acknowledged in my music also, and that's why I think people felt deeply about it.

I think that it made some people comfortable, and there were stylistic things that caught people's ears, that they were used to hearing . . . but that alone wouldn't have made people feel very deeply, it was the other stuff. That's why "Born to Run" resonates and "Thunder Road"; people took that music and they really made it theirs. I think I worked hard for that to happen. I am providing a service and it's one that I like to think is needed. It's at the core of trying to do it right, from year to year. It's the motive when you go out there. You want that reaction: "Hey, I know that kid. That's me!" Because I still remember that my needs were very great, and they were addressed by things that people at the time thought were trash, popular music and B-movies . . . But I found a real self in them that helped me make sense of the self that I grew up with—the person I actually was.

Notes:

[1]A few years ago, a friend gave me a DVD of early Springsteen performances, bootleg stuff taken from the Internet, and on it there's shaky black-and-white film of Bruce performing solo at some folk club, probably in 1970/71. And, of course, there's a difference between performing solo as an unknown artist and performing solo when you're one of the biggest acts in the world. Back then, it would have been very hard for Bruce to kid himself that anyone in the crowd had come to see him; they'd come to see the headline act, or they'd come for a

drink. And if in those circumstances you can delay one person's retreat to the bar, then you're doing well. At the Royal Albert Hall, people had paid £50–£60 to watch Springsteen's every move, for over two hours. That must focus the mind.

[2]This sounds like a throwaway remark, but how many shows have you been to where the band pretend to be unaware that there's a show going on? All that tuning up and talking to each other, while the audience waits for something to happen. Springsteen's simple recognition of the fact that people pay for every onstage second separates him from almost every single other act I've seen.

[3]Every now and then, *No Nukes*, the film of a big 1979 anti-nuclear concert in Madison Square Garden, turns up in the middle of the night on Sky Movies. Springsteen is one of the artists featured: he sings "The River," "Thunder Road" and then "Quarter to Three," the old Gary U.S. Bonds hit that he used to play as an encore. In "Quarter to Three," he does the whole hammy James Brown thing; he collapses on the stage, the band attempts to lead him off, he suddenly pulls away from them and does another couple of verses, stripped to the waist. It's electrifying, and funny; but what's remarkable, looking at it now, is that Springsteen's uncomplicated showbiz gestures seem way more "authentic" than all the smiley, gleaming-teeth sincerity that James Taylor, Carly Simon and the rest of the performers are trying to project. What, after all, could be more sincere than a performer performing—and acknowledging that he's performing?

[4]Springsteen closed the Royal Albert Hall shows with an extraordinary cover of "Dream Baby Dream," an old song by the scary punk-era experimental duo Suicide. He got some kind of echoed loop going out of his pump-organ and strolled around the stage singing the song's disconnected phrases; there were no beats, of course, but it was as hypnotic and as hymnal as Underworld's "Born Slippy."

[5]"All art constantly aspires towards the condition of music," said the critic Walter Pater. As it turns out, even musicians aspire towards the condition of music—something less wordy, less structured, more visceral.

Phil Sutcliffe
Mojo,
January 2006

In this interview conducted on tour for *Devils & Dust* Springsteen talks about his earlier albums, and he defends the work that many considered his weakest—the songs on *Human Touch* and *Lucky Town*. He also reminds readers that for all he talks about himself and his experiences, "trust the art, be suspicious of the artist. He's generally untrustworthy."

Chicago United Center is home to the Bulls, the NBA basketball team who used to win everything back when Michael Jordan was king. It's the usual big, dark cave. But when, for the soundcheck, *Mojo* takes a solitary spot in the semi-darkness among the 9,000 empty seats, the place bears a strangely private air. Bruce Springsteen is alone on-stage at the piano talking through the mike to a soundman in a remote location, marked only by a reading lamp. Nobody else is visible except when a tech walks on with the next instrument to check.

Springsteen's wearing a sartorial hodgepodge of suit jacket, blue jeans and baseball cap—reversed part way through, the only whimsical moment in the entire process. He sings a verse or two of each song— "Saint in the City," "You Can Look (But You Better Not Touch)," "Jesus

Was an Only Son"—working briskly through piano, electric piano, pump-organ, various acoustic and electric guitars, harmonica, a ukulele (given to him by Eddie Vedder) and finally autoharp. He checks out the "bullet" mike, beloved of Tom Waits, which twists his voice into a deranged howl for "Johnny 99." Everything's in good order and requires no comment beyond "OK" and muttered thanks as each new instrument is handed over.

When he's done he picks up some papers, shoves them in a battered black briefcase, walks off on his own like some slightly bohemian clerk on his way to the office, and goes straight to his dressing room.

It's a prime year for Springsteen, one that's drawn the threads of his past and present together. In the spring, he released *Devils & Dust*, the third of his powerful solo-ish and mainly acoustic albums following *Nebraska* (1982) and *The Ghost of Tom Joad* (1995). In November it was the plush 30th anniversary reissue, with bonus DVDs, of *Born to Run*, the album that made his career. The two records could hardly better represent the extremes of his appeal down the years, from the big adrenaline thrill of youth to the dark knowledge and doubts of middle age (he was 56 in September).

Born to Run was uninhibited: the appassionato vocals like a street-rough Roy Orbison, the almighty rockin' R&B grunt and Spector-tinselled grandeur of the E Street Band with Clarence Clemons' sax in excelsis and Roy Bittan's piano hinting at dirty concertos. His third album and breakthrough after his first two failed to nail it, it teemed with all-but-doomed youth living it large in a small world, wheeling and dealing, fighting and romancing, chasing a dream of nobody-knew-but-what-the-hell. And it was the last album like that Springsteen ever made.

As a songwriter and musician he moved on into the big world. The broad picture is that, while he never invented a genre nor even experimented much within the idiom, he did bring the whole history of rock 'n' roll together with love and verve and imagination and a protean attention to detail. The music was kind of taken care of in the blood, and the soul was right there—anyone who heard what he did when a wordless howl or holler was called for knew what he had inside. But, chiefly, he pulled off his translation from excitable boy to rock 'n' roller for the ages by becoming a great storyteller. In fact, that process of development did start on *Born to Run* with "Meeting Across the River," the one slow track, murky with melancholy piano and lonesome trumpet. The stroke that hinted at Springsteen's narrative gift was that he chose to write the lyric as just one side of a conversation. "Hey Eddie, can you lend me a few bucks / And tonight can you get us a ride," asks first-person unnamed. From those opening lines all his fears, failures and serial delusions of grandeur hang out there in the empty air, unanswered and exposed, until this poor dope who's "planning" a stick-up without a car or a gun has finished his fantasy about impressing his wife—"I'm just gonna throw that money on the bed / She'll see this time I wasn't just talking."

By the following album, *Darkness on the Edge of Town* (1978), he was committed to developing this craft. It included a crucial stepping-stone in "Racing in the Street." Perhaps deliberately confronting the "cars-and-girls" line of criticism that dogged his early years, it started out with a car-obsessed hotrodder in barroom braggadocio mode: "I got a '69 Chevy with a 396 / Fuelie heads and a Hurst on the floor." After a bit of boasting about all the races he's won, he suddenly finds himself thinking about his girl, her love, her ageing, her loneliness, the ways his neglect has worn her down until "She stares off alone into the night / With the eyes of one who hates for just being born."

The stories operate in a political landscape—working-class people struggling to make ends meet, financially and morally—against a backdrop of religious language that rarely suggests true belief. And some of them absolutely rut with sex, from "I'm on Fire" (*Born in the U.S.A.*, 1984), through "Highway 29" (*The Ghost of Tom Joad*) to "Reno" (*Devils & Dust*). Bruce really delivers, somewhere between Aretha's version of "The Night Time Is the Right Time" and the kitchen table in James M. Cain's *The Postman Always Rings Twice*.

Springsteen is a relentless thinker about what he does and, in recent years, writing carefully about the craft and the craftsman, he's offered two very different approaches. The first, in *Songs*, his lyrics book, is seriously analytical: "When you get the music and the lyrics right, your voice disappears into the voices of those you've chosen to write about . . . But all the telling detail in the world doesn't matter if the song lacks an emotional centre. That's something you have to pull out of yourself from the commonality you feel with the man or woman you're writing about." So the egos of artist and listener are set aside and they meet in the fictional characters and their stories. But that was 1998. Now Springsteen has turned seriously satirical on the subject, having grown far more interested in uncertainties, especially his own identity and how that relates to his fans. Or doesn't. When *Mojo* saw him recording his *VH1 Storytellers* show back in April, he raised the topic in comic vein while discussing "Brilliant Disguise"—a song from *Tunnel of Love* (1987) in which our narrator, who sounds closer to an autobiographical Springsteen than usual, wonders who he is, who his wife is, and how far both of them are faking it.

Springsteen discoursed on how "We all have multiple selves" and began a yarn about how, a while back, he was spending the afternoon at a favourite strip club out on the highway—"that holier-than-thou bastard Bruce Springsteen" having left him to his "simple pleasures" for once. However, when he left, trouble lurked out in the parking lot: "A woman and a man spied me and said, 'Bruce, you aren't supposed to be here.' I could see where they were going with this so I said, I'm not. I am simply an errant figment of one of Bruce's many selves. I drift in the ether over the highways and byways of the Garden State, often touching down in image-incongruous but fun places. Bruce does not even know I am missing. He is at home right now doing good deeds."

He wound up with his psycho-philosophical QED, "So the self is a mysterious thing." And as we will discover, with Bruce it is.

BACKSTAGE IS SPARSELY populated: three or four crew, management and the local promoter pad about a brick and concrete corridor wide enough for army manoeuvres.

After a few minutes' wait, at the appointed time, 6 p.m., Springsteen appears in the dressing-room doorway and waves *Mojo* in. He's smiling, with a note of reserve you might almost call English.

The room is bare except for a scattering of his possessions on a large glass-topped table—more papers, a personal stereo (he's not taken to the i-Pod yet), a paperback copy of his lyrics book, *Songs*. There's a small electric table clock, Woolworths maybe, which faces away from him as he takes a seat. Nothing at all purports to make the place feel "like home."

He sticks one leg straight out on the table and leans back in the black moquette and chrome chair. The seams at the crotch of his jeans are worn white and about to go. He speaks slowly, carefully, pausing often to gather the exact words he's seeking. An odd aspect of his presence close up is that he looks average height, average build when standing, and broad to the point of massive when sitting down. Maybe it's a trick of the blue plaid shirt which, someone says, was a gift from Tom Hanks.

It's strange to think that such a solid looking man, at a middle-years artistic peak, should talk and sing so much about ambivalence and doubt. Back in 1987 he was wrestling with the divided soul behind his "Two Faces" One that does things I don't understand / makes me feel like half a man." Three years ago, on *The Rising*, he was imagining himself into the traumatised, blank soul of the Nothing Man: "Darlin' with this kiss / Say you understand / I am the nothing man." But maybe now his life and work have arrived at one of those realistic-but-positive spots he made over into romance for "All the Way Home" on *Devils & Dust*: "I know what it's like to have failed, baby / With the whole world lookin' on / . . . Now you got no reason to trust me / My confidence is a little rusty / But if you don't like bein' alone / Baby, I could walk you all the way home."

He sits ready, gazing at *Mojo* with a small frown.

At *Storytellers*, a fan describing herself as "a person of colour" asked how you "managed to capture the minority experience." You said, "I think it comes from that feeling of being invisible. For the first 16 or 17 years of my life I had that feeling of being not there." Was that one of the foundations of *Born to Run*?
Oh, it's one of the building blocks of all rock 'n' roll music. Or blues or jazz. It's at the core of songwriting and performance and . . . almost any creative expression. It all comes from a will and a desire to have some impact—to feel your connection to the world and other people and to experience it. To experience your own vitality and your own life force. Go back through any creative expression and you're trying to pull something out of thin air and make it tangible and visible. That's why you're the magician.

But you also told that woman how painful and unpleasant your experience of invisibility was.
Yeah, uh . . . [*hesitates*]

It reminded me of the story about you as an eight-year-old boy in Catholic school; you got your Latin wrong and the nun who taught you stood you in the wastebasket because "that's what you were worth."
[*Laughs hoarsely and heartily.*] I suppose that was about as symbolic as you could get. So, yeah, the idea of struggling against the wasted life

has always been behind my songwriting. And obviously class and race play an enormous part in that here in the United States.

If you saw the shock expressed when, during Hurricane Katrina, suddenly all these people who had been marginalised were on television and visible. And people's shock . . . was shocking to me. Those people who had been marginalized—who you're normally seeing on the nightly news in handcuffs being arrested, that's basically all you ever see of them—suddenly there they are with their kids, their families, and the country reacted with a sad sort of shock, and that's just part of the history of class and race and it's a permanent connection to the heart and the birth of blues and jazz and R&B and rock 'n' roll music.

That music is one of the tools by which the invisible, the people who were born on the margins, have made themselves visible. It's crucial and critical to making that kind of music. And I wanted to make a big noise. You want to let people know that you're here and you're alive.

Did coming from New Jersey play a part in the sense of being disregarded that fuelled *Born to Run*?

Maybe the thing that was different back then was I'd never met anybody who'd made an album. You were much further out of the mainstream, particularly before localism in pop music became accepted. I mean, one hour out of New York City and you were in the nether world. Nobody came to New Jersey looking for bands to sign. That didn't happen and the sense of being further away from those things was very pronounced. I did shows in my late teens and early twenties when I was playing to thousands of kids, but nobody really knew about that. We were acting independently of the record business and the concert business; they were just local events. And we were guys who had never been on an airplane until the record company flew us to Los Angeles.

Today I hardly know a band without a CD. Any local band, I go to their show and they're selling a CD. But that wasn't the case in the '60s and early '70s. The machinery, the technology, to make records was not in your hands. So when I got a record contract I was the only person I had ever known who had been signed, that was the big change, and then we made a couple of records and they didn't sell that well but still it was miraculous. And then *Born to Run* came along and [*breaks off, with a tilt of the head at everything that followed*].

In terms of your standing then, something unprecedented happened: you got the covers of *Time* and *Newsweek* in the same week (October, 1975). But then you seemed to hate it when they came out. Why?

That was the big decision I made. A moment came along when I said, "Gee, I'm not going to do these interviews." So I wouldn't have been on those covers. But then I was like, "Why wouldn't I do that?!" This is my . . . [*halts a rush of words to consider*]. I had tremendous apprehension and a good deal of ambivalence about success and fame—although it was for something that I had pursued very intensely. But it was: "I'm never gonna know unless I do this." You know? You're never gonna know what you're worth or what your music is worth or what you had to say or what kind of a position you could play in the music community . . . er, unless you did it. So I said, "Well, this is my shot and I'm gonna take this."

You were talking about rock 'n' roll springing from political and social issues. How was your political consciousness when you recorded *Born to Run*?

It didn't exist. That was the last thing in the world that I was . . .

Even though you grew up in the '60s?

No, you're right, I don't mean it to that degree. In the '60s, the United States felt more like South America or Central America when I went on the Amnesty tour there [1988, with Sting, Peter Gabriel, Tracy Chapman]. At the press conferences it was all very intense political questions and everybody was involved in these tumultuous events in Argentina and then we played right next to Chile where they'd just gotten Pinochet tottering and so everybody was imbued with political consciousness. In the States in the late '60s, if you weren't involved in protesting against the Vietnam War and what the government was doing and the way the culture was changing, people thought there was something wrong with you. So that was bred into you and I carried that along with me and at times it came forth and at other times it would recede, but in the early '70s I wasn't particularly aware of it. After the end of the Vietnam War people felt at loose ends and there was a lot of instability. Look at *Born to Run* and it would be one of my least political records, certainly on its surface. I was motivated by records that I loved, by the sound I wanted to make and the feeling that I wanted to bring forth. A feeling of enormous exhilaration and aliveness. That was what I was pursuing. A cathartic, almost orgasmic experience.

But then, in 1978, you made *Darkness on the Edge of Town* and that "darkness" became a prevailing metaphor in your lyrics.
Mmm. With *Born to Run* there was a certain degree of your-dream-came-true. You'd found an audience and you've had that impact. So it was just part of my nature for better and for worse to go, "Well, what does this mean? What is its personal meaning? What is its political meaning? What does this mean not just to me but to other people?" There's the concern about the fame, which is interesting because it makes you very present and you have a lot of impact and you have force, but it also separates you and makes you very, uh, singular.

You're now having an experience that not many other people you know are having. Its irony is that it carries its own type of loneliness. And a whole series of new questions. So I said, for me, really the rest of my work life will be to pursue those answers. *Born to Run* was a pivotal album in that, after that, my writing took a turn that it might not have in other circumstances. *Darkness on the Edge of Town* was an immediate and very natural response to, uh, "How do I stay connected to all these things?"

It was in the *Darkness* period that you started your campaign of self-education and particularly studying American history.
Well, *Born to Run* did have those big themes on it. I was interested in who I was and where I came from, the things I thought gave my music value and meaning, so I pursued that information. Also I was just naturally inquisitive. High school was just so boring and I never went to college so I missed out on a moment when I may have been—and I say "may have been" more susceptible to learning things. So in my mid-twenties I pursued a lot of things that I found inspired me. History inspired me. I guess I was aware of wanting to write about the place where I lived, the people I knew. You wanna get everything you can get out of it and you wanna give all that you can give. You wanna explore the self, you know.

***The Grapes of Wrath* became very important to you—the John Ford film, the novel and Woody Guthrie's Dustbowl songs. What got to you about the 1930s and 1940s?**
A lot of the blessings and the curses were closer to the surface. Look at the movies. From the John Ford film of *Grapes of Wrath* I got that ele-

giac view of history—warmth, fidelity, duty—the good soldier's qualities. But film noir came out of those periods too and they were popular
films. I think you see that again through the early '70s, big films like
Taxi Driver. People had interest in the undercurrents, the underbelly,
an interest in peering behind the veil of what you're shown every day.
There was a sense that there was more than what you are seeing and
what was being presented to you, and that was pervasive in the country
at large, I think, not just in the progressive elements of society. I mean,
the Vietnam War didn't end with the hippies being against it or the pro-
gressives being against it, it ended when the truck drivers were against it.
The '30s and '40s, the early '70s again, those were times when things
were in great relief. People were willing to look past society's mask.
That was compelling to me.

Looking past that mask, what did you see?
Just that people were . . . I do kind of touch on it in some of my early
things—"Lost in the Flood" (from *Greetings from Asbury Park*, 1973). I
was trying to get a feeling for what was actually going on, what were
the forces that affected my parents' lives. I suppose you would have to
say it all goes back to your immediate personal experience. Those are
the things that shape you. The whole thing of the wasted life, it was
very powerful to me.

**Did you go on to read political books like the Communist Mani-
festo?**
No, I didn't read that. But I went through a lot of what was out there it
seemed, bits and pieces of a lot of different philosophers. But a book
that had an enormous effect on me was *America* by Henry Steele Com-
mager [and Allan Nevins], a very powerful history of the USA. It went
back to that core set of democratic values that the country guided itself
by sometimes and sometimes not. It was the first thing I read that
made me feel part of a historic continuum—feel our daily participation
and collusion in the chain of events. As if this was my historical moment. In the course of your lifetime how your country steers itself is
under your stewardship. So what did you do? That was an interesting
idea to me in terms of how to look at your life, your work and your
place.

That was very tangible for the first time and it directed some of my writing—along with you want to rock and have fun. You see the effects in *Darkness*, *The River* and *Nebraska*. It's certainly in the song "Born in the U.S.A."; that's a Vietnam veteran who's on fire because he's colliding with the forces of history. But this guy has accepted that personal and historical weight—it's angry, there's a social element, there's a lot less innocence.

With *Born in the U.S.A.* were you deliberately commenting on Reagan's America—with him in the middle of his first term when you wrote it—or was it post-Vietnam issues that stirred you up, the problems the veterans were having 10 years on?
I was moved a lot by the veterans I'd met. I'd become close to some of them. Vietnam wasn't written about almost at all until a decade after it stopped—earlier, all I remember is *The Deer Hunter* and a great Nick Nolte movie which hardly got shown called *Who'll Stop the Rain* (both 1978). But in the early '80s there was the birth of the Vietnam Veterans of America. My friend Bob Muller was heading it up and we did a benefit for them on the *River* tour (1981). I remember going to see *The Deer Hunter* with Ron Kovic, who wrote *Born on the Fourth of July*, and he was looking for things that reflected his experience. The song came out of all that. Bob Muller was the first guy I played it to. That was something.

Apart from reading, you explored America more literally by just driving around the country.
Well I travelled a lot from the time I was 18 or 19. My parents were gone [factory worker Doug and legal secretary Adele moved from Freehold, New Jersey, to California in 1969] and they didn't have any money to buy me a bus ticket much less an airplane ticket so I'd drive out to the West Coast maybe once a year to see them. We'd take these big country trips, three or four or five of us—and a dog—jammed into the cab of a truck and you're driving three days straight without stopping. Just the stuff you did when you were a kid.

COME THE '80s, though, Springsteen really wasn't a kid anymore. Pictures of America as seen through a car window were still important to him—that's the point of view in "Wreck on the Highway" (*The River*, 1980), "Mansion on the Hill" (*Nebraska*) and "My Hometown" (*Born in the U.S.A.*), as well as the cover picture of *Nebraska* (from the bottom in monochrome: dashboard, snow on a windscreen wiper, road and empty land, cloudy sky). But it wasn't a matter of grabbing unfocused snapshots on the move. With diligently, deepened knowledge and wider awareness added to instinctive, passionate insight, he developed and extended the charmed life of success and public esteem begun by *Born to Run*.

This period reached a wildly disproportionate crescendo though, with *Born in the U.S.A.* The title track blitzkrieg kicked open the door to a whole new audience with the E Street Band playing more widescreen than ever and Springsteen in character as the crazed Vietman Veteran "burning down the road / Nowhere to run, ain't got nowhere to go." But these agonies of ecstatic self-destructiveness were often misunderstood—in the 1984 US Presidential election, Ronald Reagan first tried to co-opt the song as a patriotic anthem (his advisors only heard the hook-line) and then his Democrat opponent Walter Mondale did the same. Springsteen forbade both sides to use the song, but the politicians weren't the only ones whistling but not listening. With more pop-inflected singles "Dancing in the Dark" and "Cover Me" hurrying it along, the album sold out more than 15 million worldwide, which was about three times the core audience he'd previously reached.

In Springsteen, this experience of hyper-fame snagged many of the same nerves as the *Time* and *Newsweek* covers had back in 1975. As he noted in *Songs*, "A songwriter writes to be understood," and he hadn't been, or not by a large proportion of this new audience. What's more, he called the album a "grab bag," lacking the coherence he always strove for and which he had found in the plain and slow-selling *Nebraska*. Yet with its broad-push appeal and seemingly anthemic feel, *Born in the U.S.A.* brought Springsteen a host of fans who took him for a rock god and worshipped him, revered him, as a hero who could do no wrong.

Springsteen enjoyed the response on-stage, no doubt, but felt a fundamental unease that much of this huge audience was "transient" and, if courted further, could distort "what you do and who you are." Seeking to reestablish control of his career—and to express himself both more subtly and more clearly—he recorded the subdued album *Tunnel of Love*. At its heart were the identity-challenging "Two Faces," "Cautious Man," "One Step Up" and the song that's been so much on his mind again of late, "Brilliant Disguise." He found his own (smaller) audience again, all right, with many of those core fans still regarding it as his best ever.

But, by then, "control" was exactly what he didn't have, not in any area of his life. The spell had broken.

The first flicker came in 1985, when he hit trouble with two former senior roadies. Mike Batlan (who'd recorded *Nebraska* on a 4-track Teac) and Doug Sutphin quit their jobs and sued their ex-boss for $6 million in punitive damages. When a judge threw that out, they lodged further suits against Springsteen for hundreds of thousands in alleged unpaid overtime and—trivial yet resonant—docking their wages for loss of his canoe in a storm. The Springsteen camp fought it all the way for six years, creating bad publicity all the while, through to an out-of-court settlement—which meant the publicly aired issues were never publicly resolved.

Then in 1988, his first marriage fell apart. Worse, the story broke messily in the tabloids on a European tour via paparazzi pictures of Springsteen keeping company with backing singer Patti Scialfa. Separation and divorce from Julianne Phillips, his wife of three years, followed in short order.

Finally, in November 1989, he parted with the faithful, beloved E Street Band—albeit after personal explanations to each member (Clarence Clemons told *Mojo* years ago "I was shocked, hurt, angry all at once") and offers of severance pay which, it was reported, may have totaled $2 million a man.

Although he married Scialfa and they started a family—they have three children now—the music went off the boil when, in 1992, after a long hiatus, he released two separate albums, *Human Touch* and *Lucky Town*, on the same day. They were reviewed at the time (and are generally remembered) as his least satisfying since his debut.

Moving onto your late-'80s emotional turmoils: your first marriage ending, the roadies case, breaking up the E Street Band. Time for some self-examination?

[Laughs, stands up and walks across the room to get some water, talking en route.]

I'm always doing that! Soon as I get up in the morning. It'd be nice to get away from it, but it's one of those things I'm stuck with. It's been good for my music and my work, I think, and ultimately it's been good for my life but, uh, I've never been . . . I think on-stage is about as care-free as I get, that's when things switch off and you're just living, you know. Most of the rest of the time it was always my nature to analyse and so, uh, I can't say there was any particular period when . . .

OK, specifically the strange case of the roadies, why did you pursue it for so long and make it such a big event?
It was very intense because it was a divorce case. In general, the things I've been, uh, involved with have been divorce cases. With Mike [Batlan] it was very similar where you have people you've known for a while and relationships go sour and in the end that's what it is. That's what that was.

Did the parting from the E Street Band come under the same heading?
That was just a moment when I didn't quite know where to go next and it needed to stop for a while. We needed a moment of discontinuity. It sent people out into the world on their own—me too—and it ended up being really healthy. I think if you talk to most of the guys they would agree with that. I didn't know what I wanted to do, I didn't know what I was going to do with the band, so I said, "Well, I'll see what happens."

Now, playing with them again over the last five years I know, well, I'm with these people till it's over. That 10 years apart, it's not that people change so much, but, as I said when I inducted U2 into the Rock and Roll Hall of Fame, one of the rules of rock 'n' roll is, "Hey, asshole, the other guy's more important than you think he is!" [*Snorts and laughs.*] It can take time away from people to get a view on that. But we've had long deep relationships and it's gonna go until it's done.

When you talked about "Brilliant Disguise" on *Storytellers* you said the song questions the difference between appearance and reality in everybody. Then you pointed at yourself and said, "So this is my public self" and somebody applauded . . .
Sure.

And, clapping sarcastically, you turned to that person and said, "What, you think I worked well on that lying, cheating public face . . . ?"
[*Giggles startlingly, maybe half pleased he was so direct, half worried he went too far in giving a fan such a hard time.*] It's just . . . the reason I talked

about "Brilliant Disguise" is it's about identity. And your identity is so multi-faceted and diffuse it's amazing that every part of you is in the same place at one time! That's the way that I experience it. So part of what I was talking about was that there's an act of presentation. That's daily life. If there are two people in a room there's a play of some sort going on. That's human interaction. And me talking about it is a way of dispelling some of the myths that build up around you and which tend to box you in. I don't like that. That song is asking, "Is it me or a brilliant disguise?" And the answer is it's almost always both. You know, you've gotta put out an enormous amount of your real self for it to feel real. You can't . . . it's not something . . . for it to feel real, it has to be real. At least, that's the way that I operate. But it doesn't have to be all, it's not all, you know?

Not the whole of you, you mean?
Exactly. It can sometimes be just a very specific slice that may be very deep but . . . We forget that every adult was brought up on fairy tales so it's natural to go on and, politically for example, want to believe that your President is an honest, nice man. The inability to turn to an adult perspective once you get to the age where you have some political weight is a great tragedy, and this is a period of history when it seems the most obvious type of disguise is on display to the entire world and yet those are the people who are still in power.

You're thinking of the "war on terrorism"?
Well, although elements of that are real and true, it was basically co-opted. But to go back to the question of my identity when I'm on-stage: it's not a face that's dishonest, it's a face that's incomplete and a couple of things I did that *Storytellers* night were . . . What happens is when you have a lot of success your complexity tends to be whittled down into a very simple presentation, not necessarily by the artist or musician, it's just the way that people want one-sentence explanations for everything and everybody; he's the nice guy, he's the nasty guy. And so, with my audience, one of the things I've tried to do is retain the complexity of human life or human experience. I want to see and be seen within those parameters. That's where your freedom is and that's where your true dialogue, a deeper dialogue with your fans, can take place. So I was taking . . . a kick at that.

Given the events of the late '80s, did you feel that your fans' opinion of your integrity had been blemished—that people were thinking less of you?

Well . . . I don't have a problem with that [*laughs*]. That's the way I would put it. Life is a messy business. Just as much for me as, I imagine, anybody else. My feeling at that moment was my . . . I was worried about my real life, not how my image was. Here I was trying to do things that were really hard for me to do; I was trying to connect with somebody [Scialfa] and get a family started and for somebody like me that was probably the hardest thing I ever had to do.

I had a grasp that those were the things that were going to matter to me as I moved forward. As to people's perceptions of me, I didn't have and I don't have complete control over that and it goes up and down and in and out and that's OK. By then I had 20 years of work behind me and I thought, "I'll stand on that." If people see you making a mess or stumbling around, well that's life too. You don't do everything right, you know. You make bad decisions or wrong decisions or misguided ones and as far as I know that's how everybody's living out there, so I didn't have a problem with people seeing me do the same.

OK, but maybe that attitude didn't work with the fans who feel the kind of reverence that made it hard for them to see you as that fallible human being.

I'd say in general those things are always a good deal of your own making, you have to take some responsibility for it, and when I was younger I probably felt differently about it. But certainly as I got into my middle age, how people felt about me . . . wasn't quite as important to me. I was trying to find integrity within my own experience, my own life and, uh, I'm always going to trust the art and be suspicious of the artist because he's generally untrustworthy flimflam, a stumbling clown like everybody else. That aspect, the reverence I attracted, dispelling it is important because it hinders your communication and diminishes the complexity of the dialogue you're trying to have with your fans.

There's quite a transition from the early '90s albums to *The Ghost of Tom Joad*.

Yeah, but people talk about the records from the early '90s . . . I joke about it on stage, "I'm told this is my weakest record." But if you go back to the songs from *Lucky Town* and *Human Touch*, I play a lot of them on this tour. The production on *Human Touch* we didn't quite get right, I think, but I look at those records, *Tunnel of Love*, *Human Touch* and *Lucky Town*, and it was me writing personally, looking at relationships and how they were playing. I was also interested in not being "the other guy" at that moment. I wasn't writing like that for a time, I didn't have those good songs in me, and the moment you're trying to write something that conforms to a particular . . . [*trails off*]

But then I did move back in that other direction. "Streets of Philadelphia" probably started it. Then *Tom Joad*. I was living in California at the time and there was a lot of border reporting in the media. California had become very multicultural, a big Hispanic population. Go back to Freehold now, central New Jersey, 10 years later that's happened there [the latest census shows his hometown's 11,000 population is 28 percent Hispanic]. I did have a feeling it was what the country was going to look like and feel like in another decade or so and it gave me a new perspective.

I remember writing *Tom Joad* very quickly. I'd gotten into my midforties and when you're younger you feel, "This is gonna stop, it's gonna get fixed" [the social ills he was addressing] and then by the time you're in your forties and fifties, oh, you've seen it cycle around a few times under a lot of different guises.

It's cliché, but when you're writing passionately it . . . What people are experiencing with *Born to Run*, what makes music different from the other arts is it conveys pure emotion.

Given what you've seen, what are your political beliefs now and, presuming you're somewhere on the left doesn't having great wealth present a conundrum?
I don't know how to describe my political views in left/right terms. I started out following my instincts and it seemed the country was best when it stuck to that democratic thread of good ideas and good values. The past 20 years or so have been rough. A large number of people have been marginalised, generation after generation. So what I think is it's a reasonable expectation to have full employment, health care and education for all, decent housing, er, day care for children from an early age, a reasonably transparent government . . . Big money in politics is dangerous and antidemocratic. Well, to me these are all conservative ideas.

Do you see it like that? Really?
Economic stability. Health. That's not remotely radical. All these things are in Jesus's teaching. All part of a humane life. But we have failed in almost all of these civil ideals. It all seems common sense to me. These points are not a political philosophy, but good things I wanted my music to advocate. I find that vision in Woody Guthrie . . . well, even in the Animals' records, back before I heard Woody. Working-class music, that's part of pop history—natural politics. I didn't go to college, I'm not a socialist economist, but these are things the guy on the street can understand.

But what about the personal wealth issue?
I'm a child of Woody and Elvis. They may not be opposite ends of the spectrum. Elvis was an instrument of revolutionary change. Elvis drove a pink Cadillac and Woody wrote a song about a Cadillac, he was not dismissive of those pleasures. What you do with the conundrums, you try to deal with it as thoughtfully and responsibly as you can. I don't know if there's a clear answer. You live with the contradictions.

On _Born to Run_'s thirtieth anniversary, having worked so much on the re-release material, how do you see the album now?
I look back with a lot of amusement on the band at that particular moment, the audacity and insecurity that was all right above the surface. When I came back off the _Rising_ tour [2002] I was excited about the band and I both reflected on the present and took a look in the rear-view mirror, kind of saying, "Where do I go now?" And I'll tell you what, the finiteness of your experience is real once you're in your late fifties. This [_he gestures at his life, pointing both hands hard at the ground_] is finite. There's x amount of years left in what we're doing. I don't know how many. I hope there's a lot. I feel like there's plenty to do, plenty of songs to write, I feel about that the same as I did when I was 24 years old. But part of taking your place in the world is letting that clock tick. Letting that clock tick and being willing to listen to it tick and understand that your mortal self is present and walking alongside of you all the time now.

NOTHING LIKE INTIMATIONS of mortality to draw an interview to a close . . . Springsteen's due on stage in less than an hour. Standing up, shaking hands, he says, "I hope I was helpful," and offers more time on the phone. As *Mojo* leaves he's unhurriedly poking about among the bits and bobs scattered across the table, muttering, "Right, let me see what I'm doing here . . ."

Until showtime he's alone again in his dressing-room, apart from a visit from long-time, Zen-calm tour manager George Travis. Usually, team members say, in the last hour or so before a gig he spends some time handwriting a setlist for photocopying to the crew. This changes substantially show to show—here in Chicago a dozen different songs from the previous night when *Mojo* saw him in Minneapolis. Even when he's on-stage it's more a basis for negotiation than a promissory note.

List complete, he'll sit and play guitar a bit, gathering himself in. No conspicuous signs of nerves except, just when he's due on, he might suddenly decide to change his shirt. When he's set and he starts his walk towards the stage that's one time nobody ever talks to him. And from then on, he's told them, he doesn't see anyone, not a face, only feels a crowd and a place, he's so deep inside himself.

Though that's not how it looks and feels tonight out in the audience. It feels intimate as he ranges over his 35-year songbook and a testament's worth of stories and characters, and gets right down into the guts of all the emotional/sensual details—pungent aromas of the *Devils & Dust* battlefield as the day heats up and "the smell began to rise" or of the Reno motel room where the prostitute's offering "Two hundred dollars straight in, two-fifty up the ass." The songs scale the big hall down to a room. The listeners are engrossed in these people, what happens to them, what it means, engrossed in themselves.

When, in "Long Time Comin'," he sings for the weathered and back-sliding husband and father who watches his wife and children sleeping around a campfire and vows to "bury my old soul and dance on its grave" and that he's "not gonna fuck it up this time," people cheer and "Yeah!" Springsteen picks it up before the next song, musing about how that line should have been "I'm not gonna fuck it up this time if I can help it but given the range of my own behavior which is completely dysfunctional I wouldn't expect too much" and swears he could have made it fit the music back in the days of "Blinded by the Light."

He's been a dab hand at these intensity-easing moments of yarning rumination since the Jersey Shore club days. "Ain't Got You" he introduces with, "People often ask me, 'What's it like to be The Boss?' I usually say something humble like, Those are the breaks . . . But honestly, it's very sexy. Sometimes I wish I was Bruce myself . . ." For "Jesus Was an Only Son"—apart from a familiar speculation on Christ as a would-be Galilee publican if only he didn't have to go be the Saviour—it's reminiscence about his Catholic childhood and the non-stop schedule of Irish and Italian family wedding which meant they had to collect up the rice they threw so they had some ready for the next one, and "I think we even threw it at funerals. We did throw shitloads of rice." On the politics front, he plugs the Greater Chicago Food Depository who have a stall in the foyer and, introducing the *Devils & Dust* border tragedy "Matamoros Banks," calls for "a humane immigration or guest-worker policy."

It's quite something, then, that after all the writing and rewriting and fucking it up anyway and starting again—and all his "interminable bullshit" of self-examination and puzzling over identity and disguise—Springsteen closes his set every night with "Dream Baby Dream" from Suicide's self-titled 1980 album.

Springsteen sits at the pump organ, starts pushing out the broad sustained chords and singing, round and round, "Dream, baby, dream . . . / Come on dream on, dream, baby dream . . . / Keep the fire burning . . . / Open up your eyes . . ." He sings this for some minutes, then he stands up, the organ chords looped now and louder and more churchy, and sings on and on, heart and soul, dream on, open up your eyes, swaying down to the front of the stage, one man singing in the big hall, and it's overwhelming, jaws drop, tears gather, everyone swimming in the same heavy sea, nobody knows what's up, we're just taken for everything we've got.

Earlier in the dressing-room, as the interview concluded *Mojo* had asked about "Dream Baby Dream."

"I've liked Suicide for a long time," he said. "I met the guys late in the '70s in New York City when we were in the studio at the same time. You know, if Elvis came back from the dead I think he would sound like Alan Vega. He gets a lot of emotional purity. I came across 'Dream Baby Dream' again because Michael Stipe included it on a compilation and I thought maybe I could do it.

"It's a mantra and it works because the night is filled with so much narrative and detail and then at the end there's just those few phrases repeated and they are the essence of everything else I'm saying and doing in the course of the evening. The night opens and opens and then, at the end, when you think it can't open any more it does and it's completely embracing. It's yeah, I guess . . . I have, an eye for a lot of detail and this is a lesson in uh, "What is a song?" It's so purely musical, that's what's beautiful about it, it's so simple and so purely musical."

A COUPLE OF weeks later, Springsteen calls as promised. He's in cheery form, having finished filming the show in Boston. He clears up a few points from our last meeting before asking for a final question.

Well, we've done politics, work, money, sex, time, death and the divided self OK. Religion. You've described yourself as "a runaway Catholic" and said that, although you use religious imagery in your songs for its resonance, you don't need to know The Truth. Does that mean you've definitely decided you don't know?
Yeah, the spiritual life is going to be a life of mystery," he says. "Why would you not be humble in the face of that mystery? Why would you assume that the answers can be handed down to you, A to Z, no room for doubt? That's child-like, that desire for answers. Adult life is dealing with an enormous amount of questions that don't have answers. So I let the mystery settle into my music. I don't deny anything, I don't advocate anything, I just live with it. We live in a tragic world, but there's grace all around you. That's tangible. So you try to attend to the grace. That's how I try to guide myself—and our house, the kids."

What do you mean by "grace"?
Grace to me, it's just the events of the day. The living breath of our lives . . . Woody Allen once said he found himself happiest when he was standing in the kitchen in the morning buttering his toast. So you're chauffeuring your kids somewhere and you think it's a burden and something happens . . . it's there."

And the strip-club denizen, unholy Bruce, is he still around?
Unholy Bruce is alive and well," he laughs. "Narcissistic, sexually obsessed, talks a good game then runs off in the other direction. Likes a good drink, let's the good times roll. I'll tell him you asked after him."

Dave Marsh
Backstreets,
Spring 2006

In 2006, Springsteen released *We Shall Overcome: The Seeger Sessions,* an often raucous collection of folk songs originally popularized by Pete Seeger. Springsteen went back to the roots of American music and explored a number of traditional forms, from bluegrass to gospel to New Orleans second line—sometimes in the same song. He also toured with a full band that sometimes reached as many as twenty members. "I was just looking for what stories enthrall me right now, and what do I think I can bring to life," he tells Marsh of this major departure from E Street. Conducted in Asbury Park as Bruce prepared for his new band's live debut, this interview originally aired on Marsh's Sirius Satellite Radio program, *Kick Out the Jams.*

On April 20, in the midst of preparations for that night's Seeger Sessions Band debut on the Asbury Park boardwalk, Bruce Springsteen sat down for a long talk with his old friend Dave Marsh. Good thing for us, Marsh has a radio show. Airing a few days later on Marsh's Kick Out the Jams *program, on Sunday, April 23, the interview found Springsteen speaking expansively about the Seeger Sessions project, taking the listener through its*

*genesis session by session, as well as tracing his folk roots—and his
aspirations—back to a circle of strummers on the beach.*

JUST BEFORE BRUCE arrived on the mezzanine of the Paramount Theater for our interview, Thorn Zimny, who was going to film it, placed a
guitar next to the little round table where the microphones were set up.
"Maybe he'll use it, maybe not," he mused.

By the time I sat down across from him, Bruce already held and
strummed the guitar, which he continued to do throughout the discussion. Since what we always talk about, when we talk, starts with music,
it added immensely to what got said and how. When we got around to
"Eyes on the Prize," the radio version became a virtual seminar in how
he constructs meaning. It's what he does at the beginning of *Storytellers*
with "Devils and Dust," with the difference that the issue was not what
the lyrics might mean but the way that performing a song determines
meaning.

The Seeger Sessions provides the best opportunity in many years for
Bruce to talk about such things, because music is what it's about, from
the time he crashes into "Old Dan Tucker" to the last line, when he de-
clares "If you want any more, you can sing it yourself," an act of encouragement 180 degrees from the silence he's commanded for his other
"folk" projects. For someone like me, who values a truly original performance even more highly than an original song, that spirit places *Seeger
Sessions* in the top rank of what he's accomplished.

I'd first heard what was already being called "the Seeger project" in
late December 2005 and immediately fell for its energy, the swinging
drumming, the relaxed way in which he and the group delved into
frenzy. Bruce and I had a couple of talks about it before the album came
out, which sort of grew into the "liner notes" on his website. I remember
telling him about Sis Cunningham, who wrote "My Oklahoma Home,"
after he said he was sure that Woody Guthrie had written it. (I can imagine someone in another half-century insisting that Bruce did. I sort of
came to the conclusion that it's all true.)

That, the research for the notes, and seeing an early rehearsal (about
a week before the public ones) constituted my preparation. Well, if you
don't count being immersed in some of these songs since I was a teenager. Bruce's circle on the beach had very broad boundaries, and somewhere even further on the fringe, they made room for me, too.

Once we started, we had an hour (the raw tape is 64 minutes). We stayed focused on music, and all the other topics flowed from that. The guitar and the freer state of mind Bruce seems to have been in since the *Devils & Dust* tour took off into the deepest realms of his song catalogue made this the easiest interview of the many we've done since the first one, 32 years ago. I came away from it thinking that I knew something new about my old friend and where he came from. I learned a long time ago, that you can never figure out where he's going next.

Well, Bruce, first of all I would like to congratulate you on once again confounding everyone else's expectations.
[*Laughs*] Including my own, I think.

Well, I have never seen you excited in quite the way you are by this music right now.
It's fun—it's just exciting stuff to play, and the band is exciting. It's an exciting group of musicians, and also it's very freeing in the sense that the nature of the music, and not having to write it, kind of opened me up to be just purely musical.

Kinda like the way you can brag on something if it isn't yours?
[*Laughs*] So it opened the whole thing up to just this purely musical experience. A lot of the rhythms that were used—the only rule I had was if it was something I did with the guys, with the E Street Band . . . whatever this is, it has to be not that.

You're talking about stuff that's not on the record, but for your show.
Yeah, for the show—straight down the line, really, from the record to the show, just the different rhythms. The main thing, my only sort of line, was that everything felt rhythmically different. And we were drawing directly from a different—there's some crossover, but mainly from a lot of different influences.

Actually, the first note I have here is "beats." And that they're rowdy and participatory beats.
Yeah, it's interesting—there are bluegrass grooves, there's country grooves, there's gospel grooves, there's a lot of New Orleans in it.

And swamps further back than New Orleans, too.

Yeah . . . we have a version of "My Father's Place" that's very field chant. And it just goes a lot of places I haven't really gone before.

It's your most syncopated recording ever.

Yeah, and that really came from the different rhythms [of] the music that I chose, but then also came from the musicians themselves. There's a spot in "Pay Me My Money Down" when you can hear the band—there was a series of steps that we took that happened very naturally. When I first went in, it was obviously just to find a song for Pete's record [Appleseed Recordings' 1998 tribute, *Where Have All the Flowers Gone: The Songs of Pete Seeger*]. And so I listened to a lot of his music and picked out a bunch of things that I thought I could sing and would sound right interpreting.

This was way back in '97.

This was in '97. I think the first thing we played was "Jesse James." [*Plays and sings*]: Jesse James was a lad / That killed many a man / He robbed the Glendale train . . . So that [sound is] already something—I don't play that with the E Street Band. That's a very different feeling. So it started there. And these guys, who I had met at my farm, through Soozie Tyrell, came down from the city; they were playing sort of a zydeco and Cajun feeling, it just clicked. I think, literally, the take on the record is the second thing we ever played together—the second take. So just right from the beginning, just *bang*, it was it fired up right from the start. So it started there, just with a little bluegrass [feel], and then . . . I'm trying to think what else we cut that day, the initial day that we recorded. You might know better than me . . .

I actually don't.

No? Okay, the things we cut from the first session were "Jesse James," "My Oklahoma Home" . . .

"Oklahoma Home," which is the least-recorded song, one of the newest songs . . .

That's interesting, I didn't know that.

There are only two other versions recorded: Sis Cunningham, who wrote it, and Pete.

That shocks me. I didn't know that at all.

It hadn't been recorded in 40 years!
Strange. Because it's such a fabulous story, and the guy tells such a tragic story with so much wit, and strength, and humor, and the verses are just—

Well, when they get to that Smokey Robinson internal rhyme, with "mister" and "kissed her" . . .
[*Laughs*] [*Plays and sings*]: Got picked up by a twister . . . . And I guess what caught me was the chorus, it's got that great [*sings*]: blowed away (blowed away!), she's blowed away (blowed away!), I said yeah, that'll be fun to sing! So we cut that the first day, and that turned into almost a—we sort of combined a little of the bluegrass rhythm with some Texas swing. So all of a sudden, we started out with that beat, and then some Texas swing kind of slipped in.

A little Bob Wills—because you've got the horn section in there . . .
Bob Wills, right. And the bizarre thing, I don't know why I did it, was why I had the horns come at all! I got a letter from Pete, and Pete said, "Wow, horns on 'Jesse James'! Who would have thunk?" [*Laughs*] And I knew what he was talking about, because I don't know why I had the horn section come. And really, for the first session it was only Richie "La Bamba" [Rosenberg] and Eddie Manion, so we had just a trombone and a saxophone, because I think Mark [Pender] was doing something. But I must have heard something, some of the '20s influence coming from somewhere, because I had the guys come down. I had no idea what to tell them to play, so I didn't tell them to play anything. I put them in the hall, and I said, "just sort of play along," y'know? [*Laughs*] And I think it was at the end of "Jesse James," where Richie starts to move into that Dixieland solo on the trombone. It's player's music, also: it's music where there's a lot of soloing.

A different kind of soloing than you'd get in a rock band.
Yeah—literally, it's jamming, you know? [*Laughs*] So there's a lot of soloing, and at some point I said, "Well, the fiddle played, the accordion played . . . all right, Richie!" And Richie went into that Dixieland feeling, and so that entered into the picture. I think that same day we covered "Stand at Every Door," which we had a nice version of but didn't end up on the record. We also cut "Pretty Boy Floyd" and "We Shall Overcome."

And the one track that comes out, of course, is "We Shall Overcome." You would not have guessed that all those people were there, because that really just feels like you and Patti [Scialfa]. I don't know who else is on it.

That was just a step up from people sitting in their living rooms singing. When we approached the background vocals, we approached it like that. There was very little rehearsing of the voices, and Patti's worked incredibly hard—there's a lot of singing in the show, just an enormous amount of singing, and she really arranged and put all the singers and the chorus together that we have. But at the initial session, I wanted to keep it very, very much like parlor singing, very loose and unstructured. So basically we got parts very quick, and we rushed through everything, and that was the sound that I liked. We played the track, and then everybody came in and sang it. Patti's voice is very prominent, as it is on a lot of the things on the record—"Shenandoah," she's got that beautiful "high country" sound.

And as people get to the bonus side, on "How Can I Keep from Singing"—which actually, to tell you the truth, I was thinking gee, maybe this belonged on a Patti solo record! Because she owns that.

Yeah, and she just did a beautiful job. So it was exciting, because when you can get a lot of people singing together, that choral sound of human voices is always something. It always ends up very personal, very human. There's all kinds of choral music . . . there was a lot of different kinds of singing on there: "Shenandoah," and "We Shall Overcome" and then obviously the stuff that veers closer towards gospel singing, like "Jacob's Ladder." But that came third session—we're still on the first session! The first session, we're running through those, and . . . We need a songlist. Can somebody dig up a list of songs from the album?

There's an album here . . .

You got an album? Let's look at it, because it'll jog my memory. All right: "Old Dan Tucker," first session.

So the first thing you're hearing on the album is something from the first session.

The first thing we did was "Jesse James"; "Old Dan Tucker" was one of the first things.

Well let's talk about that for a minute, because those two songs— "Jesse James" is a song that people associate with Woody Guthrie, because he rewrote it. And "Old Dan Tucker" is actually written by Bob Dylan a hundred years before Bob Dylan was born, right? [*Laughs*]
That's really strange. . . . the surrealism and the lyrics are so modern.

"Washed his face in a frying pan," "died of a toothache in his heel . . ."
[*Starts to play*] The surrealism. The only thing we could use is if anybody has the lyrics, which I assume are in this . . .

Yeah, they probably are, but we'd need a magnifying glass.
I don't know, my eyes still might be—might be, and I say might . . .

Might be good enough for the task? I have bifocal contact lenses, so I get away with it sometimes.
I'll tell you in a minute. [*Long pause*] I can't read 'em [*both laugh*]. My apologies to my fans with fading eyesight [*laughs*].

There's a few of us out here.
But yeah, the surrealism in the lyrics is just fabulous.
     You know what I need? If somebody could get me—is Terry here? My bag, I actually have glasses in there. Shh! Edit that part out! [*Laughs*] Yeah, there's a bag somewhere that's got 'em.

Anyway, we end up with "Froggie Went a Courtin'," which is surreal in another way.
Yeah, and I read your essay about it—I want to hear all those verses! That was the only version I knew, and you said there was like a hundred . . . I want to see all the verses. We may add them as we go along.

May the tour last that long! [*Both laugh*] Well, you've got to do "Here's to Cheshire, here's to cheese" once, that's one of Pete's great little moments. Now, Pete Seeger did three different "Froggies." I don't know if you heard all three of them.
I don't think so, no.

So you heard one or two, but you didn't—and now we're moving toward the second and third sessions—you didn't restrict yourself to the versions that Pete did. You went and did some—you had Terry Magovern, your assistant, and you guys sort of did some research, right? Picked and chose? In a proper folkloric manner?

No, not really. I'm trying to think if I might have tried to dig up some extra lyrics on some things, but for the most part . . . no, I didn't hear a lot of other versions of that.

No? I thought we talked about that earlier. But the thing you did do, to really change several songs, is you changed keys.

The changes I made, a lot of it was musical. I changed "O Mary," which is generally done in a major key, I just heard it in a minor key for some reason. It made it darker, and it sort of brought out its apocalyptic side. There were a lot of things I did like that. I don't really remember the musical changes I made now, but I was throwing in chords and just trying to fit things to how I heard them, resetting lyrics.

Okay, we've got a session in '97, you don't do another session until 2005. In between, what's happening to this stuff?

It's just sitting around, like a lot of my things do! [*Laughs*] And I'm off doing other things. After I did the session, I was really excited about it, and I got really excited about it over the next seven years, probably four or five times. But there was always something else coming up. I had it there, and I'd go back to it, say, "Let me hear that stuff we cut at the house. . . ." Toby [Scott] would send me over the tape, and all I knew was that I enjoyed listening to it a lot. It was so listenable.

Especially because your last three records have been tragedies.

Yeah . . . I mean I hadn't thought of it in that way, but they were pretty dark. . . . and the main difference is just whether you're writing, or just singing and playing. I find that when I'm writing, I'm on my way to try to find a setting for the lyrics. And if I'm writing for the [E Street] Band, I'm trying to find a setting for the lyrics that fits with a lot of what we do in the band. If I'm writing my narratives and short story kinds of songs I write, I think like that a little bit more, and the music tends to be—certainly in the narrative things, I use very basic and very simple [music], because the lyrics are so dense. So I think what you get with this particular music is, when all this music was written, the sense of struggle is in it, but there's also the strange brightness of the twisted American spirit that keeps pushing its way through.

Well, how "John Henry" becomes an uplifting song . . .
The music is just vital—it's simply vital. That's what pours out. And you hear it—you know, there's the most beautiful music that comes out of Africa. The struggle songs are all—you know, the bubbling rhythms, bubbling rhythms, dance music, dance rhythms, things that are so transcendent. Bob Marley: incredible lyrics of struggle, and yet dance rhythms, and bright. That's a powerful combination, when those things come together. And so, in a funny way on a lot of these songs, you get a similar kind of experience.

Even "Mrs. McGrath," which is very downtempo, yet . . .
It's got that big chorus. [*Plays and sings*]: *Too-ri-aa, fol-did-dle-di-aa . . .* It's the sound of determination.

It's interesting, because that's the only song on the record that's really, truly what you'd think of as a topical or protest song. It's the only song that addresses an issue. Even "We Shall Overcome" and "Eyes on the Prize"—"Eyes on the Prize" says "the day I started to fight" and that's a freedom song addition, but for the most part, this is a record that is in another world than that.
Once again, I think you're choosing things that you think you can make "of the moment" and so you're connected to this present world. I didn't choose anything as a historical piece.

Well, you're not approaching this as historical music, because nobody would put a brass band on "O Mary Don't You Weep." It's been done 200 times; nobody ever did it that way.
It was: how do I make this very, very present? How do I make these characters leap off the record and make them sit, or dance, or sing in your living room? Right now. That's the key—you have to make it very, very present. I didn't have a lot of interest in the music as a historian. That's sort of somebody else's job, you know?

Yeah, me! [*Both laugh*]
And so my main thing was, what's gonna be exciting to play, and fun to sing and to hear people cut loose on, you know? That was my main

criteria. The stuff that passed the bar, that was the stuff we used. So that was my approach to the whole thing. Pete wrote me a letter about the history of a lot of the songs and talked to me on the phone about it once I told him what I was up to, and then you researched the stuff quite a bit, and that's where most of my information about the music is from.

If you'd known more, you wouldn't have done what you did. I don't think you would have felt free to do what you did, if you'd gone and done that kind of research.
Basically, like I say, I was just looking for what stories enthrall me right now, and what do I think I can bring to life right now and do something with—and what can I add my two cents on as an interpreter. Which is something that I've done only very rarely in the past, because I never saw myself primarily as an interpreter of other people's music or of other songs.

But these aren't other people's songs, because they're everybody's songs. Most of them.
Yeah, and I think the idea that these are songs, many of them, that have been roundly sung, and passed around, and handed down, I found some element of . . . there was a lack of self-consciousness. This is there to go to, and that was very freeing.

And at the same time now, if you look back on it (because I know you do that periodically when we make you), it does fit in with your other stuff. The themes . . .
Oh yeah. It all fits with the story that we've been telling for a long time, and it's just another stop along the way, really. I think if you followed my music, bottom line, "Dan Tucker" could have come off *Greetings from Asbury Park*, you know? [*Laughs*]

And "My Oklahoma Home" could have come off any record from *Born in the U.S.A.* to *Devils & Dust*.
And now I have my glasses . . . [*Plays and sings first verse of "Old Dan Tucker."*] So that's like off of *Highway 61*, or . . .

Oh yeah! And sort of bleeding into your first two albums. "Mrs. McGrath" could have been on *The Wild, the Innocent & the E

Street Shuffle **pretty easily. The other thing is that part of that story you've been telling all this time is about a kind of participation that sometimes hasn't been readily available, or it hasn't been real obvious how people could participate. And on this one it's really obvious—I mean, some of these are sing-alongs.**

Oh, I think probably most of them. Most of them are. Like I've said, it's tavern music, it's living room music, and the collectiveness of it is part of its essence.

In the documentary that comes with the album, one of the things you talk about [is] your cousin, Frank Jr., and his dad, your cousin Frank, how this is one of the places where your guitar playing first came in. You never told this story before, so I was dumbfounded.

Frank—who is playing in this band, Frank Jr.—is my cousin, and his dad is a few years older than me. I remember when I was probably around . . . when I was 14 he must have been like 16 or 17, and you know how it is when there's somebody a few years older in the family. . . . And Frankie played the accordion, in the classic sort of Ted Mack *Amateur Hour* style. I'd go over to his house all the time, and he'd bust out the big box, and he'd play the accordion. Well, one day I go over, these were family functions, and he's playing the guitar. Had to be around '64, I guess, and he had an acoustic guitar, and he was playing a lot of folk songs.

This was the height of the folk boom, '63 and '64, and *Hootenanny* was on television. And you'd go to the beach on Sunday, and one of the things that used to inspire me was there was about 20 guys that used to meet at the beach on Sunday, and they would sit in this big circle on a Sunday afternoon. And they would draw 100 people around them, playing "Twist and Shout," and folk music, you know, "If I Had a Hammer." And this would go on all afternoon at the beach—for hours, three or four hours, they'd all. . . . I said, *man*, if I could just get a guitar, I'd love to just find my place in the sand, and . . .

In the circle.

That's it—I just wanted to find my place . . .

This is exactly the same thing we talked about when we talked about *Born to Run*.

Yeah, I wanted to find my place in that circle of guys. And you know, they were just kind of strummers and shouters, but hey, the girls in the bikinis were there, standing all around. So I said [*laughs*], man, I just want to find my place, you know, I just want to learn a few chords and squeak in there on a Sunday afternoon, sit in the back and strum along.

And so, Frank had started to play the guitar. And I remember I went over one night, and I was enthralled. I had gotten a guitar, but I had not learned how to tune it or how to read any chord charts. Basically, I brought it home, it was all out of tune, and I was making up songs, just plunking away on what I had. I don't know if I brought it with me or what, but he taught me how to tune the guitar, and then he had a folk songbook with the chord charts in it, and he said, "Look, see where these black dots are? That's where you put your fingers. You put your fingers on those spots [*laughs*], and you're on your way!"

I remember I went home that night—he gave me the book, I went home that night, and it was "Greensleeves" or something, and I saw it was E minor, because it only takes two fingers [*laughs*]. So I said, "I'll start there!" And E minor was my first big success. And the interesting thing was, see, I started off in a minor key, and that led me down that road ever since.

So his son picked up a guitar quite a few years back and wrote some songs and has made some music, and so I said, gee, you know, I wonder what Frank is doing? So I said, let me call Frank, and I had Frank come in. Because the idea was, yeah, it's sort of this family thing: everybody sits around and sings. And so I said, "Frank, come on up and play!" And so he came up, and he plays well, and he covers all my guitar parts when I'm simply hamming. It gives me a lot of hamming room, because someone else will actually be playing while I'm clowning.

That guy Steve used to do that.
Yes! Yes [*laughs*]. So that was the actual, initial thing that got me down the road to learning actually how to play. [*Strums*]: E minor, A minor, those were the first two; they're close to each other. And I never made it to that circle on the beach. I don't know what happened.

I think the circle dispersed—and joined rock bands and played at night.
That's what happened! By '65, when I was ready, it was over. I think I spent about the first six months—I did work on some folk things, and then immediately, you know: [*plays "Twist and Shout" intro*] I

immediately picked up "Twist and Shout." "Twist and Shout" was the first thing I learned. And I tried to move along to some Beatles songs, and Stones songs and things.

So yeah, it's nice having Frank up there with us.

And actually, the other person who's sort of renewed with your crew here is Patti. Because you've got not only Soozie, who was on the *Rising* tour, but you've got Lisa Lowell, and they were sort of a busking trio on the streets of New York at one point.

The interesting thing about the group is that it's kind of half people who've played together for a really long time, informally, and half people that just kind of happened by the house one day [*laughs*].

And then people that I've met in sort of other unusual . . . like, once I put the horn section on, the only thing we overdubbed on a few tunes was the tuba. Because, man, I have a *brass band* going, and part of the sound of that particular brass sound, on some of these things I need the tuba.

It's the humor, and the drama.

It's the humor—and so I met this fellow Art [Baron], from the City, and also I went up and saw the *Nebraska* [Project] . . .

That's right, the [New York] Guitar Festival did a tribute to *Nebraska*.

And I went up and I met Marc [Anthony Thompson], the guitarist, who played "Johnny 99" that night. I'd seen him on television with Marc Ribot. [Thompson] records as Chocolate Genius and, by the way, has made two fabulous records—I think one is *Godmusic* and one is *Black Music*—you should rush out and get those, they're really beautiful records. And so we kind of met there, and I forgot about it, but Art the tuba player said "Hey, you know, I know this guy Marc . . ." and I said "Oh yeah, we've met." And he said he'd be interested in doing some singing, doing some background singing. I said "Well, great, come on down!" And he came down, and it was like, bang!, it was just perfect right away. And so the whole thing is just a happy accident, it was the nicest way for music to get made—completely unplanned.

But Patti and Lisa and Soozie sang together, busking in New York City, when they were in their late teens and early 20s, so they've sung and played together for a *really* long time.

I'm glad you didn't put a number to it [*both laugh*]—save us both a lot of grief!
So it's nice to have the three of them together. And the horn section, obviously, with Southside from 1975.

And your bass player, your drummer, and Sam Bardfeld, the one fiddle player, those guys play together all the time. So it's interlocking circles.
Yeah, exactly. It's a circle that slips over the edge of another circle, that slips over the edge of another circle . . . and it really, I believe, has something to do with why they play so well together. Because it's all a bunch of people who've played really well together for a really long time, slipping one over another. The horn guys have played together, so I can just say, "I want something that feels like this." "I want these kinds of harmonies."

And everything that's on the record happened while the music was being played; I may have sung a little riff or something.

And then you've got Cindy Mizelle and Curtis King. And they sing together in the studio all the time, don't they?
Yeah. It's interesting because it wasn't a group of disparate musicians who then had to learn how to play together. It's people who knew how to play together when they walked into my house. And the shocking thing was, I didn't know anything about them other than I liked how they sounded playing at my bash.

Well, they were probably playing outdoors, right?
Yeah, it was just an old squeaky sound system. So the guys came 'round, and the level of musicianship once we started—of course, Charlie Giordano, incredible accordionist and keyboard player—once we got into it, things really started to happen.

And the other thing was, they were experienced musicians; they understood the whole art of listening while the music is being played. And that's why I said, in the record, that people get a chance to hear music being made as it's happening, as it's occurring. Everything you're hearing on the record is something—it is probably the livest live record I've ever made. It had the things that I've done with the E Street Band that are similar, like "Born in the U.S.A." The same things: there's a riff, there's a count-off, and it's the second take, and that's it—it's done.

That's pretty much the way the guys describe it. And that's why it feels like, I think, like it's in continuity with your other records, because the energy level is up there.

And as we went session to session, things started to change and happen. By the time we got to the second session. . . .

Well, had you been in touch with those guys in that whole intervening period?

No [*laughs*]. So we played, and like seven years went by, and I don't know, maybe they played at my house again a few times, I'm not sure! [*Laughs*] But for the most part, not really. And so 2005 comes along, and after one of my listenings, I said gee, that was a lot of fun, I think I'll do another session of that. Because if I do another session, I'll have enough for an actual album. And I don't know if I'll ever put it out or what I'll do with it, but I'll have enough songs. And so the second session comes along—and where's our cover here?—and I think we did "Mrs. McGrath," "John Henry," "Erie Canal," "Shenandoah," "Pay Me My Money Down," maybe "Froggie." A lot of things came out of that second session.

So for that second session, were you going back to Pete records? Where were you going for material that time?

At some point, I said I'm going to do this drawing off of Pete's records, because I've said in a few interviews that as far as a library of music and just the sheer archival size of it, it's unmatched. I don't know any other single performer who has put his hands on so many disparate kinds of music.

People think of Pete as this "folk singer" but they have no idea what that means, musically.

Yeah, and so everything that happens on our record is implied in something that Pete was doing. The band, there's a great banjo player, there's a great 12-string player—they're all things that I heard after hearing those records and hearing the things that those musicians brought.

So that was a big session. Once again, the session would last an afternoon, and then we would, sing in the early evening. So the record was cut in two-and-a-half days—shortest record I ever made. That was a big session, because I started to move away from [*strums "Jesse James" opening riff*]. That's where I started, and "We Shall Overcome." And I said well, geez, there's a lot of other—[*plays "Erie Canal" riff*] "Erie Canal," that minor thing, it feels very '20s or '30s to me. There's a lot of ragtime elements in it, you know? And early jazz elements.

Now, there's a case where—I've got the horns on "Erie Canal," and they're playing in sort of that very "brass band" style, and so okay, the solo is coming up, and I'm going, well, our horns . . . you may even hear me say it on the record, because if you listen to the record, there's a lot of me going: "Horns!" "Intro!" "Sam!" You know, I'm yelling out people's names, and calling solos.

That feels appropriate to the genre somehow. I mean, that's how it happens.

Yeah, that's actually how it's supposed to be played [*laughs*]. So the horns come along, and all of a sudden, bang, they burst into that Dixieland thing, New Orleans/Dixieland, which is the first time it actually occurs during the sessions. So we've got the trumpet, we've got the three-piece horn section, and people are really playing. And I'm going, wow, that sounded really great. And so now, all of a sudden, we've moved into some other . . . we've pulled in this other genre that feels like it's fitting very naturally, and it happened on the spot.

So when we came back for the following session and we're doing "Eyes on the Prize," now I've got in my mind: okay, well, this is gospel, and jazz, and we're getting the church, and we're getting sort of the gutter, and that's the kind of ground I want the music to cover. So on "Jacob's Ladder," the gospel thing bursts into that real dirty horn, and same thing with "Eyes on the Prize." So once again, as we played together more, things just started to happen.

And the New Orleans thing, you can hear it happen on "Pay Me My Money Down." [*Plays and sings*]: *I thought I heard the captain say / Pay me my money down / Tomorrow . . .* That's your basic folk rhythm. The song starts, and that's what I'm thinking—that's where the thing is sitting. But then Larry comes in on the drums, and somewhere, I don't know exactly what verse it happens, but it starts to pick up that "jump" [*demonstrates rhythm*] that's sort of zydeco and Cajun. That starts to happen, and all of a sudden we've gone there. And I don't know if it's a quarter of the way through the song or halfway through, but you can feel it. You can feel the rhythm shift slightly, and all of a sudden we're there. Now we're someplace else—we've gone to some other part of the country.

The process is fascinating, because that song, which began in the Sea Islands off Georgia, ends up being done quite often by West Indians in sort of the Calypso rhythm that you were just doing.
Really? So you know, that was something that these guys just—it was there, and it had to come out! So all of a sudden I'm hearing that, and Charlie's got the accordion going, and they play that stuff real, real well. When they came down and played for us, that's the kind of grooves and feels they were playing. And so now we're there, and now we have this whole other place to go, you know?

Yeah, you sort of moved your music from the one to the two and the four.
It just moves, so we're kind of taking a trip around the country itself, geographically, as the sessions are going along. We're visiting different places: Appalachian places, and we're moving down south . . .

One of the things about your singing on this record, and "Pay Me My Money Down" is one of the places, is you sound more New Jersey than ever. I noticed this on the last tour . . .
[*Laughs*] I'm not sure that's something I'm aspiring to! But go ahead.

Well, no [*laughs*], it was a little bit on the last tour I noticed it, too. There's a very distinct accent in central and southern New Jersey.
And see, not being in central and southern New Jersey, I do not know what that might be!

But being married to somebody whose whole family is from Trenton, I hear it.
I know there's a north Jersey accent . . .

Nope, this is different. Yours is more . . . it's almost Elizabethan in some strange way. It's nasal . . .
Nasal, that I got covered! [*Both laugh*] That's one of my specialties!

But I hear it, anyway. We'll see if anybody else does.
I don't know, I mean, your voice shifts in response to the music you're playing and singing instinctively, and the only thing I knew when I went in to sing on these things is, well, I'm going to sing a way I haven't sung before, I thought. Which I thought is what I was doing! [*Laughs*]

Well, it may be as simple as that—that you just felt comfortable with other intonations.

And I'm singing from a different place in my throat. If you go from, say, the early music—*Born to Run* is a lot of chest. And as I've gone along over the years, I've found a falsetto, and I also move my voice up very often into a somewhat higher place. And then on this particular music I think I might have moved it up even higher into my throat. I was looking for something that was frayed, really just ragged around the edges. Because that's what all these characters are.

On stuff like—very different tracks, but "Old Dan Tucker" and "My Oklahoma Home," that kind of thing?

Even "Eyes on the Prize." I found I wanted to sing it . . . they didn't want to be *sung* out, and I don't know why, but the way I approached the freedom songs particularly was: it's surreptitious. There are secrets being told at the beginning of all those songs. And so the idea was, yeah, I'm gonna start out, there's a secret being told. That you're not supposed to know about, really. But that you *need* to know about. You *need* to know about.

And so the singer starts off, well, he's whispering. [*Plays and sings*]: *Paul and Silas bound in jail / Had no money to go their bail / Keep your eyes on the prize / Hold on.* So this guy he's in the shadows. You're walking down the street, and you're thinking everything is fine, and it's not too early in the evening but not too late, either, and all of a sudden somebody collars you and pulls you into the alley and says, "Wait a minute." [*Laughs*] "You don't know what's happening here, my friend." And starts to tell you that story. And he starts to: "Man, you better keep your eyes on the prize, because it's coming down." And so that was the way I approached that.

The line you really brought out in that song for me, which I hadn't really thought about, I guess, is "I wouldn't take nothing for my journey now." Which felt very personal.

Well, you're making all those connections. To do it right, you are understanding the journey the song's taking, and you're acknowledging its history; but you're acknowledging your own history, too. That's what makes things work, creatively. Those are the two things that I try to connect together. [*Plays and sings first verse again.*] And now it opens up with *Hold on, hold on . . .* a few more people are in on the secret now . . . *Keep your eyes on the prize / Hold on.* . . . That's a personal statement, or a political one. And this guy's thinking, how am I gonna save my ass, right now? [*Laughs*]

I got my hand on the gospel plow / Wouldn't take nothing for my journey now—and then it opens up again—*Hold on.* I continue sort of telling this secret story, right up through *Only chain that a man can stand / Is that chain o' hand on hand / Keep your eyes on the prize . . . I'm gonna board that big Greyhound / Carry the love from town to town*—that sounds sinister, and it's supposed to. It's a threat [*laughs*]. That's a threat, you know? It's meant to be read as both a promise and a threat. So *Hold on* . . .

And the guy keeps telling his story: *The only thing I did was wrong / Stayed in the wilderness too long* . . . He's just talking about himself. Then, it moves, and the background singers enter: *The only thing we*—bang! the song expands and opens up—*we did was right / Was the day we started to fight.* Suddenly the guy in the alley is in the street. He's in the street, and he's not alone, he's not by himself. He's surrounded by other people. And other people are picking this secret up, and it's turning into not such a secret anymore. That bursts wide open after the next chorus, after the horns hit and play a real guttural Dixieland, and all the singers [*intensely*]: *The only thing we did was wrong / Stayed in the wilderness too long.* . . .

Now you're singing out.

And you're testifying.
Right. And you're shoutin' at somebody, and it's a promise, and it's a threat, and now the guy's not in the alley, now everybody—people are out there. And that's where the song moves, right up to its very end [*softly*]: *Ain't been to heaven, but / I been told / Streets up there are paved with gold.* And you get a little refrain of your original singer again.

So that's the way I approached those songs particularly, was they had to go from the deeply, deeply personal, to the political, to the gospel.

From the frightened, isolated man to the empowered? Is that the idea?
The frightened man. Yeah. They had to go from that very—you know, the running man. And they had to start there. The doubting man. The guy who, whoa, he's not sure about the next step he's gonna take. And

move out into the other stories. And really, I approached the freedom songs . . .

Are the freedom songs, for you, "We Shall Overcome" and "Eyes on the Prize"? Do you include "O Mary Don't You Weep" in that?
Yeah, you would, you would. That starts out, the same thing—most of the stuff, it's that I've got to find . . . you, the singer, you have to find your individual place in it. Where's the story?

Did you read the *New Yorker* story about Pete Seeger?
I haven't seen it yet, no.

Well, it's very interesting, because that writer makes an interesting contrast—I don't even know if he intended to, it was just sort of laying there on the page. I think he intended to. It's a very good story for anybody out there who hasn't read it. But he talks about Pete almost trying to become transparent in these songs—I don't mean anonymous, I mean to let the song come through him, that that was his approach.
    And of course, you're in here, you and the writer are talking, and you talk about finding *yourself* in the song. And that's a different approach. And I think that's why, if you listen to, say, your version of "Oklahoma Home" and Pete's version of "Oklahoma Home," Pete's trying to let that guy come through. You're *being* the guy.
Well, I think that whenever I say sort of "finding myself," it's not quite as simple as that. Because really, you're trying to find your voice in that music, so that the character can come forth and tell his story again. All valuable stories need to be told over and over and over again. And at the same time, yeah, obviously, it's that big collective "we" you're always on the lookout for, and so [it might be] misleading when I say . . .

I understood what you meant, and that's what I mean about finding yourself in the song is a way to give that character a life.
Yeah, and I do it with all the songs—on *Tom Joad* and *Nebraska*, everything I write, if it works, those mechanics have to be in place. Because it's the thing that connects the singer to the singers, and to the audience . . . and makes those walls as porous as can be. So those are the elements, whether it's *The Rising* or anything else, I'm always on the lookout for.
    But the way to get to it, once again, is you've gotta—there's no cheap

way to get to it! You gotta pay. The way you pay your dues on every song is by digging up the piece of you that has felt that frightened, that uncomfortable, that disempowered, that scared, that lonely, and that angry. That's the price of admission if you want things to fly. And then everybody starts singin' and talkin', and the song comes to life, and the character emerges and comes to life.

Well, this is making me think about "John Henry" because I've heard—well, *everybody* has heard "John Henry," since *they* were a little baby. This one's different. That's the triumph, when Polly picks up the hammer at the end, it's different, because it's a personal triumph.
Yeah, his story keeps being told, the hammer keeps being swung [*laughs*].

That's the one song, when I was researching, I could never believe, it seems unquestioned: this *really* happened. Well, I don't know about the Polly part, obviously, but it really happened—some guy took this on! It's one of the most amazing things in American history to me, that somebody did that. To try to save his job [*laughs*].
The version I read—which is funny, this is a song I heard many other times in different guises, but I didn't remember the verse about Polly. I said, that's a cool verse! [*Laughs*] And it does lift the song to a different place, because the hammer continues to be swung.

And anybody can swing it.
Yeah—who's next? Anybody can. And that's the beauty of folk music, and the stuff that Pete has handed down. And obviously Bob Dylan and everybody else.

Well, Bob sort of hovers around the fringes of this thing, doesn't he? You've got the one song, "Froggie," that you and he have both done now.
Bob is the father of my country, so . . . [*Laughs*]

The old, weird America.
And the one that I know! The one that I recognize. He was the guy who really first gave me a vision of my country that I recognized. Wasn't the one I got in history books in school; it wasn't the one that I was hearing

completely on pop radio. Bob was the guy that really laid out the first map of America that was, I think, understandable and felt real and true. And so, a lot of us are running to this day on that inspiration. And so he's just always there.

But I think, for another generation, so are you. Not because you made this record, but because in a lot of ways you describe an America for people now that—you know, *The Rising* is part of that. *Devils & Dust* is part of that.
That was something that the guys that I loved—you know, Frank Sinatra did it. Hank Williams did it. Woody Guthrie did it. Bob Dylan did it. Elvis did it. James Brown did it, big time!

Maybe that's the circle on the beach where you belong, Bruce!
Curtis Mayfield. Marvin Gaye. Public Enemy. So, you have those seminal musicians that come along that—the Band, obviously—that for one reason or another want to tell that story. Those are the guys that I admired, and those are the things that I aspired to. And they still really are, you know? I just want to tell my part of that story—I want to be part of that story, I want to be a part of that circle on the beach [*laughs*].

Well, I think you are, and it's a big beach that runs the length of the country, so, we're all lucky to share it with you.

Christopher Phillips
Backstreets,
August 24, 2007

In his second interview with Phillips, Springsteen was in the midst of rehearsing with the E Street Band for their first outing since *The Rising*, as they prepared for the *Magic* tour. He discusses songs he hasn't played live in decades, like "The Price You Pay" and "Crush on You," as well as the then-impending *Magic* album: "We've got a record that's gonna play really great live. It's just built for it." Approaching 60, Springsteen is acutely aware of the passage of time—though he promises he will never do a farewell tour—and deeply appreciative of the long run he has had with the same band members. Sadly, it would be Danny Federici's final tour. The organist of the E Street Band would succumb to melanoma on April 17, 2008.

———————————

So—the E Street Band is back!
Yeah—it's pretty exciting. We've been having fun.

Gearing up for the tour now, how much of a vision do you have in advance? When you go in to rehearse, do you have things planned out in your head?

No, I don't, really. What do we do—we kind of pick up a little bit where we left off. First of all, we start playing just to feel the machine again [*laughs*]. You've gotta drive it a little bit before you push the envelope on it.

So you take a few laps.
Yeah. You know, we'll get in, and we may run through a few things we know, just to reacquaint ourselves with the sound and the power of the band. How it moves underneath you, and everything. That's sort of the first thing I do, is I refit myself into that bucket seat, you know? "*Oh* yeah, okay, now I remember . . ." And that takes all of about 15 minutes.

And then you just start. I'll probably go in with a general idea: maybe I'll have a general list of some songs I know I want to play, maybe there will be some things I'm not thinking of playing. But we leave the door very open, because over the course of a long tour, we end up playing so many songs . . . I don't know, I think there were 120 or something we played on the last tour? [149!—Ed.] So it's a very open door.

I think the initial thing you try to do is, you try to place your new work, to find a place for a lot of your new work. Obviously, you're excited about that. I'm excited about it. We have some stuff—not *some* stuff, we've got a *record* that's gonna play really great live. It's just built for it. I wrote with a lot of melody, and with a lot of hooks, and there's a lot of band power behind the stuff that I wrote this time out. So I'm excited to hear that come straight off the band.

I'll begin by just starting to play some things, and once you get comfortable with the playing of them, then you search for their context. You start making connections between the songs you have from your past work and some of the new songs. You're in search of *the show*. So once we start playing the things really well, then we go in search of how we're going to present it this time out. You go searching for the show: what collection of songs, what's feeling right, the balance between [old and new].

I like to play a lot of new stuff. We played a lot of *The Rising* on the [2002–2003] tour, that was pretty consistent. Because once again, it was stuff that just played really well live. We've got that again in spades on this record.

And would you say it's wall-to-wall that way? I remember on the *Rising* tour, there were a few songs like "Paradise" that took a while to come out. Do you think this whole record is going to play pretty initially?

There are always the things that draw you in more than come out and grab you, I suppose, I always have some of that. And then you've got to see what people respond to. I have a *good* idea, but it's still a conversation with your audience. And when they start listening, and talking back, then different things come to the front.

And that's one thing that's been pretty consistent with your tours over the years, is that you seem to come out with something in mind, and there's always the evolution that occurs as you continue.

Yeah, we'll come up with a show, and we may play that pretty steadily for the first series of gigs, because we're getting our feet underneath us. And then somewhere along the way, things start to loosen up—it's a pretty natural progression. Until we get to the end, where it gets . . . I still try to keep a schematic that remains centered around our newest material, but also you start to open up to your whole body of work. And that's always fun to do, too.

On the last few tours, at a certain point a lot of the experience really became about the songbook—I was thrilled on the *Devils & Dust* tour when you wound up playing every song from *Tunnel of Love*, and I think a lot of other people were, too. Were there some discoveries there that you think you'll bring to this tour?

That *Tunnel of Love* record had a lot of good songs on it! [*Laughs*] And I think we only touched on it on the *Rising* tour. Toward the end of it, we started to play "Tunnel of Love" and some other things from it—I remember it was fun bringing some of that stuff back. But it's hard to say until we get into it. I don't know, I don't like to go in with any rigid ideas; these days I try to remain as fluid as possible. I'm interested in seeing where the music is going to take us, and where the band feels best. And that shifts slightly as the tour goes on, and obviously we try to make the shows unique, and it all falls into place. But I've got a lot of songs, obviously, that I'm carrying around at this point, and it's fun to get to them as the tour passes.

I think back to '88, when you came out on the *Tunnel* tour and kind of chucked a lot of the stuff that had become rote. And since then, you've tended to start off some tours with some resolutions, like "We're not playing 'Rosalita,'" or on *Devils & Dust*, "I won't be playing 'Thunder Road.'" Anything on your mind that you're *not* going to play this time?

It depends on what feels right. I mean, those are songs I'm sure we're not going to be playing every night. But I wouldn't go into the tour saying I'm never going to play anything at this particular point. I mean, stuff comes up, and if something feels right for a stretch of shows . . . we played "Rosalita" over that last piece of the *Rising* tour, we played it during the summer. And that was fun, bringing that back. It's fun to bring it back, but the band is currently making too much good music to sort of lock yourself into anything. And particularly something like that . . . yeah, it's got some miles on it! [*Laughs*] A lot of those songs, they have some miles on them, so I tend to treat them like that: Like, "Oh, no, this song has served its purpose and done its job well." So it's a horse I'll call in every once in a while.

Well, one horse you haven't called in for a while is "The Price You Pay"—I know a lot of people have been hoping to hear that one.

Yeah, I have no idea why—it's become a thing just because I *haven't* played it. If I had played it, nobody would give much of a damn if they heard it or not! [*Laughs*] Just because it *hasn't been played*.

So you kind of keep that going, don't you?

Well, you start to get into that thing, which I don't like very much, like: "Oh, man, I'm gonna be there the night . . ." you know, "I was there the night he played . . ." [*Laughs*] I don't run by those rules very much. If I haven't played something, it's usually because I don't *want* to.

But no particular reason for not bringing that one back?

No specific reason—I'm sure if you searched the catalog, maybe there's other things that we haven't played, too. You know, my recollection is that it's been a while since we've played "Crush on You" [*laughs*]. And I'm not sure that one's going to be popping up in the set any time soon, either, you know?

Your last two tours were about as far removed from E Street as you could get. One thing you said about the *Sessions* tour was, "During the course of the evening we play all the music that *leads* to rock music, but we don't play rock music."
Yeah—I'll be playing the *rock music* this time. In case anybody's wondering!

Once you get in that mode of performing in a whole new way, as you did on those last two tours, is it difficult to come back to the band setting at all?
You usually think it will be when you're in it, because you're *so* in it—it's like everything else, for it to be really great, you've got to be 100 percent committed at the moment. So when you're in it, that's all there is. And I think that's what it takes to be really good. So I'll just lose myself in whatever form I'm working in at any given moment. And the other things seem distant: "Oh yeah, I like to do that too, and I like to do that too . . ."

But really, I'm very comfortable moving between all the different formats that I play in now. And I love them all, and I plan to continue doing them all—or variations thereof—in one form or another. I enjoy making acoustic records and writing those sorts of story songs; the Sessions Band was a tremendous discovery, and just such an amazing group of musicians that—I mean, those are some of the best shows that I feel that I've put on. So that was really just a great discovery, and it's something I look forward to finding another outlet for at some point.

And then the Band is the *Band*, you know? It's fabulous, and it's the only place where I really do the thing that I suppose that I'm most known for, which is . . . it's a *peak experience*. And so it's very easy—I enjoy doing them all, and I'll probably continue doing so.

You know, I always have a variety of records in the works. I wrote most of this E Street Band record while I was touring with the Sessions Band. So it's not hard for me. I'll go home and just—*boop!*—and I'll switch over. And I've probably written some story songs already for *that* type of record. I'll be working one thing, and when I go home at night sometimes I'll already be slipping into another way of writing and performing. At this point, what I do enjoy is playing regularly and getting a good amount of music out to my audience. Which is really something that, in my early years, I had a difficult time doing.

And you've really managed to do it—it's amazing, you've toured more in the last five years than you have since the late '70s.
Well, it was a promise I sort of made to myself, a decade or more ago. I just wanted to be more productive. And luckily—you have your muses, you're always dependent upon your muses, but I've had a lot of songs to write, and records to make, and I've just found a lot of different ways of making music that's allowed me to stay in contact with my fans on . . . I guess it's been almost a yearly basis. So I like doing that a lot. I mean, that's how I remember the bands that *I* liked: you know, every six or eight months there was something going.

The only thing that we've missed so far, because of the release schedule, was a film of the *Devils & Dust* tour. Which we have, and we've been in the process of working on, it's just we had so much going on, it was one of the things that just—you know, the Sessions Band kind of came up quick, and we didn't have the slot to get it out.

Plus you had the *Born to Run* 30th Anniversary set in there, too.
Yeah, there were a lot of things that just took precedence.

But that DVD is still in the works, that could still happen?
Yeah, I have a real nice film—I think it's a collection o f several nights that we played, I think there was some stuff from the last few shows in Trenton, which were some of my favorite shows of that whole tour, and some things from Boston when we shot there. It's a blend of a series of shows. I formatted it a little different than the actual show, because I found that it plays better a little shorter, when it's just me with a guitar on screen.

Yeah, I could see that being a struggle, bringing that to the TV screen. But it's great to hear it's still in the pipeline, we kind of thought that one was lost to the sands of time. Any idea when we might see it?
Well, I've had something for a while, we just haven't kind of put the finishing touches on it and found a way to get it out. So hopefully, at some point—I'd like to even just sell it at the shows, or find some other way of getting it to people, because at this point, if I do something, I like to document it, and I like to be able to get it to the fans.

And we're loving that. If I can help in any way, getting things out there [*laughs*], let me know!
Okay, great!

Back in '99, when you were heading out for the reunion tour, you talked a lot about being grateful that the whole band was still around, and still alive, that no one was a rock 'n' roll casualty. And here we are eight years later, and you're still able to do it again.
Yeah. That's something that you become for grateful for as time passes. You know, I just lost Terry, my great friend of 23 years.

Which I was very sorry to hear.
Yeah, that was a big loss. And you're so aware that things are finite. I've always said, it's like, "Hey, I've got my guys out there," and the band really did take care of one another over the years. Like I've always said, it's one of the things I'm proudest of, and I continue to be.

I mean, there are a lot of ways that life can take you, and you never know what tomorrow brings. And so to have that kind of stability . . . and not only that, but also just the personal relationships remain so thoroughly enjoyable, it's a great gift.

Does it enter your mind that this could be the last time out? A "farewell tour"?
Oh, I'll never do that, man [*laughs*]. You're only gonna know that when you don't see me no more.

Not for *you*, I can't picture that . . . but for the E Street Band as we know it?
Oh, hell, I don't know [*laughs*]. There ain't gonna be any farewell tour. That's the only thing I know for sure. I envision the band carrying on for many, many, many, many, many, many more years.

Scott Pelley
60 Minutes,
October 7, 2007

On October 2, 2007, Springsteen and the E Street Band began their world tour in support of the new album, *Magic,* a tour that would extend, albeit with a short break, through the release of *Working on a Dream* in 2009. In the interview, Springsteen develops his American vision.

Tonight, a rare look behind the scenes with Bruce Springsteen. It's hard to picture, but Springsteen turned 58 last month. His breakout hit, "Born to Run," is 32 years old. While most rock stars his age are content to tour with their greatest hits, Springsteen launched last week what may become his most controversial work ever as a songwriter. Even now, Springsteen is an artist in progress, having moved from stories about girls and cars to populist ballads that echo the dust bowl days of Woody Guthrie. Springsteen's put all that together now in his first tour with the E Street Band in four years. He's returned to full throated rock 'n' roll, and a message that is sharper than ever, damning the war in Iraq and questioning whether America has lost its way at home.

*   *   *

[Springsteen's voiceover] You're the shaman, you're the storyteller, you're the magician. The idea is that whatever the ticket price, we're supposed to be there to deliver something that can't be paid for. That's our job.

You have got to be, wild guess, worth somewhere north of $100 million. Why are you still touring? You don't have to do this.
What else would I do? Give me—you got any clues? Got any suggestions? I mean, am I going to garden? Why would you stop? I mean, you know, you play the music and grown men cry and women dance, and, you know, like and that's, you know, that's why you do it.

It's good to be a rock star.
I would say that, yes, it is, you know? But the star thing I can live with; the music I can't live without. You know, and that's how it—how it lays out for me. You know? And I'm as—I got as big an ego and enjoy the attention. My son has a word, he calls it "attention whore." You have to be one of those, or else why would you be up in front of thousands of people, you know, shaking your butt? But at the same time, when it comes down to it, it's the way it makes you feel. I do it because of the way it makes it me feel and the way that I can make you feel when I do it. And I like making you feel a certain way when I do it. It thrills me, it excites me. It gives me meaning, it gives me purpose. You know?

Some of the pieces in the new record are going to be considered controversial. Give me a sense of what you think has to be said. Why are you still writing?
I'm interested in what it means to be an American. I'm interested in what it means to live in America. I'm interested in the kind of country that we live in and leave to our kids. I'm interested in trying to define what that country is. I got the chutzpah or whatever you want to say to believe that if I write a really good song about it, it's going to make a difference. It's going to matter to somebody, you know?

[*Voiceover*] E Street keyboardist Roy Bittan and guitarist Steve van Zandt go back with Springsteen more than 30 years.

You have got to hate "Born to Run." Right? Come on.
Roy Bittan: That's funny you say that.

Come on, when it's time to . . .
Bittan: You know, we play it, it's good, you know?

. . . comes up on the list, and it's "Come on, boys, play it like you've never played it before." Here we go.
Bittan: It's funny—it's funny you said that because I was watching something on TV, and it was Tony Bennett. And they asked Tony Bennett, "Aren't you tired of singing 'I Left My Heart in San Francisco'?" And his answer was, "It gave me the keys to the world." So, a lot of times we play that song, sometimes, you take it for granted and other times you go, "Well, there it is, you know?"
Steve Van Zandt: Exactly.
Bittan: That's it.
Van Zandt: You know, I figure if we do a few more tours, I might actually learn it. So, you know. I mean, we live and hope, right? I mean, he thinks I'm kidding.

Humor helps if you're an E Streeter. Because in the 1980s, Springsteen walked away from the band after more than 15 years together. He wanted to play with other musicians, and sometimes with none at all.

How was the news broken? Did Bruce tell the band himself? Tell me about it.
Bittan: I think Bruce picked up the phone and called everybody. And I think everybody was shocked and hurt and just felt really abandoned.

Was that hard? Was it heartbreaking? And you say, "Look, I'm going on. I'm leaving you behind."
Well, I didn't exactly put it like that.

So, how did—how did you put it? How did you put it?
I soft soaped it somehow. And, you know, everybody had different feelings. I mean, people were mad or angry, and some of them said, "OK." But at the time, I wasn't going to be any good to them at that moment. I think what happens is sometimes you've got to break your own narrative. You—we all have stories we're living and telling ourselves. And there's a time when that narrative has to be broken because you've run out of freedom in it. You've run out of places to go.

What'd you learn about the band tonight?

We made fewer screw-ups than I thought we might. You know? The main thing you learn is not so much the band, because the band will just play better from tonight on out, you know? But you learn a lot about the set, the set that you're creating. You're trying to work your new things and you're trying to say what you're trying to say, you're trying to get people just to rock, you know, to go crazy and have fun.

Pretty good for 58.

Oh, that's nothing. That's—I'm still a chiseled hunk of muscle. So, I guess I'll keep going for a while.

You know, I was probably one of the smartest kids in my class at the time, except for you would've never known it. You know, you would have never known it just because where my intelligence lay was not—wasn't able to be tapped within that particular system. And I didn't know how to do it myself until music came along and opened me up, not just to the world of music, but to the world, period: to the events of the day, to the connection between culture and society. And those were things that riveted me, engaged me in life, gave me a sense of purpose, what I wanted to do, who I wanted to be, the way that I wanted to do it. What I thought I could accomplish through singing songs.

It's not just the singing, it's the writing, isn't it, for you?

Of course. You wrote about what you were—what interested you. And every good writer or filmmaker has something eating at them, right, that they can't quite get off their back. And so your job is to make your audience care about your obsessions.

His recurring obsession is the life that he knew as a boy, the harsh relationship with his working-class dad who didn't think much of a rock 'n' roll son.

You know, hey, it was a tough, struggling household. People struggled emotionally. People struggled financially to get through the day. A small town, a small-town world which I continue to return to. It's like when I went to write, though, I put my father's clothes on. You know, the immersion in that world through my parents and my own experience as a child and the need to tell a story that maybe was partially his, or maybe a lot his.

Your dad wasn't all that proud of you as a young man?
Oh, he was later. When I came home with the Oscar and I put it on the kitchen table, and he just looked at it and said, "Bruce, I'll never tell anybody what to do ever again." It was like—that was his comment. Oh, that's OK, you know?

[*Voiceover*] **The music that emerged from his upbringing was a blue collar ballad set to rock 'n' roll. Elvis meets Dylan, uniquely Springsteen.**
   Much of the new music is a protest, some of it blunt, as in the song that asks, "Who will be the last to die for a mistake?" But most of it is subtle, like the story of a man who returns to his all-American small town but doesn't recognize it anymore.

[*Voiceover*] "It's gonna be a long walk home."

What's on your mind? What are you writing about?
I would say that what I do is try to chart the distance between American ideals and American reality. That's how my music is laid out. It's like we reached a point where we're so intent on protecting ourselves that we're willing to destroy the best parts of ourselves to do so.

What do you mean?
Well, I think that we've seen things happen over the past six years that I don't think anybody ever thought they'd see in the United States. When people think of the American identity, they don't think of torture, they don't think of illegal wiretapping, they don't think of voter suppression, they don't think of no habeas corpus, no right to a lawyer to—you know? Those are things that are anti-American.

You know, I think this record is going to be seen as anti-war. And you know there are people watching this interview who are going to say to themselves, "Bruce Springsteen is no patriot."
Well, that's the—that's just the language of the day, you know? The modus operandi for anybody who doesn't like somebody, you know, criticizing where we've been or where we're going, you know. It's unpatriotic at any given moment to sit back and let things pass that are— that are damaging to someplace that you love so dearly and that's given

me so much, and that I believe in. I still feel and see it as a beacon of hope and possibility.

[*Voiceover*] Springsteen sees himself following a long American tradition that reaches back through Vietnam and on to the Great Depression, from Dylan to Guthrie.

There's a part of the singer going way back in American history that is, of course, the canary in the coal mine. When it gets dark, you're supposed to be singing. It's dark right now. The American idea is a beautiful idea. It needs to be preserved, served, protected and sung out. Sung out.

Mark Hagen
The Guardian,
January 18, 2009

Springsteen discusses the songs of *Working on a Dream* and the passing of his dear friend and E Street bandmate Danny Federici: "He's the first guy we ever lost. The thing I've been proudest about for a long time was that, unlike many other bands, our band members, they lived. They lived, and that was something that was a group effort; it was something that we did together, the surviving part."

It's a cold winter's day, and I'm driving through snowy fields on my way to meet Bruce Springsteen. Towards the end of the 18th century, a Scottish émigré came to this part of northern New Jersey in search of a new world. He bought land, built a house for his family and settled down to the life of a farmer. The ducks and chickens are still here, but the current owner lives a very different life.

Bruce Springsteen and I struck up a friendship 10 years ago when I came to this same farm to make a film for the BBC. It's a warm, familiar place, the wood and slate of the kitchen giving way to a small recording studio and a front room decorated with photographs of Elvis Presley, Bob Dylan and the Band; the room, in fact, where Springsteen made 2006's *The Seeger Sessions* album, the musicians setting up around the sofas and on the stairs. In the parlour some of the photographs for *Devils & Dust* were taken in 2005 and just out the back is the swimming pool from which he emerged, dripping, in the dead of night for the video of "A Night with the Jersey Devil," a spectral blues number based on a sample of Gene Vincent's 1958 single "Baby Blue" and given away as a web-based Hallowe'en surprise last year.

I've been back regularly, sometimes to revisit old ground, sometimes to talk about new projects, but always to drink beer, swap musical discoveries and speculate on life's great mysteries, like how exactly Elvis got his hair to do that quiff thing. Today I'm here as Springsteen prepares to release his 16th studio album, *Working on a Dream*, a collection of intimate songs about long-term relationships, meditations on the effects of time that come wrapped in lush, layered arrangements rooted in the 1960s of the Beach Boys, the Turtles and the Byrds.

Springsteen has seldom shied away from big themes—think back to 1975 and the way a worried post-Vietnam, post-Watergate America responded to *Born to Run*'s romantic vision of escape, or how the small-town dramas of 1984's *Born in the U.S.A.* found resonance as the Reagan era deepened the divide between have and have not. In recent years that has continued to be the case; he famously began to make 2002's *The Rising* in the wake of 9/11 after a passing stranger wound down his car window and told the singer: "We need you now." *Magic*, released two years ago, was in large part a railing against the Bush era, and in November last year, Barack Obama came to see him play live and confessed to his wife that he was only running for president because he couldn't be Bruce Springsteen. He has often referred to his work as a long conversation with his audience, and it's the ability to keep that exchange going—and it is most definitely a two-way thing—that has kept him relevant, timely and firmly in place alongside Dylan, Presley and Johnny Cash on the Mount Rushmore of American popular music.

With that in mind, plus the fact that he plays at the Super Bowl—that most American of events—on 1 February, the week after its release, it's something of a surprise that *Working on a Dream* isn't a state of the nation address, but something more personal, and a departure from his usual sound. Springsteen himself recognises this when he says: "You'll hear pieces of it in all my other records, but if you have all my other records, you don't have this—it takes it to some different place."

The Springsteen who greets me with a warm hug is in typical form, however, laughing wheezily as he recalls the time he saw the New York Dolls at Max's Kansas City in 1972, stranded in Manhattan after missing his last bus home. He asks me what I'm listening to at the moment, and carefully notes down the names of Kate Rusby and Girls Aloud for further investigation. Svelte in a black shirt over a black skull and crossbones T-shirt, he's never been the world's most eager interviewee, but he goes about it with a good grace, refining and honing his answers as meticulously as one suspects he writes his songs. Which isn't to say that he's guarded or in any way circumspect, nor does he steer clear of politics. In fact, the next couple of hours reveal a man prepared to open up about his life and work to a quite remarkable degree.

Working on a Dream starts with "Outlaw Pete," which is a very American story: a fable about a character who can't escape his past.
The past is never the past. It is always present. And you better reckon with it in your life and in your daily experience, or it will get you. It will get you really bad. It will come and it will devour you, it will remove you from the present. It will steal your future and this happens every day.

We've lived through a nightmare like that in the past eight years here. We had a historically blind administration who didn't take consideration of the past; thousands and thousands of people died, lives were ruined and terrible, terrible things occurred because is there was no sense of history, no sense that the past is living and real.

So the song is about this happening to this character. He moves ahead. He tries to make the right moves. He awakes from a vision of his death, and realises: life is finite. Time is with me always. And I'm frightened. And he rides west where he settles down. But the past comes back in the form of this bounty hunter, whose mind is also quickened and burdened by the need to get his man. And these possessed creatures meet along the shores of this river where the bounty hunter of course is killed, and his last words are: "We can't undo the things we've done."

In other words, your past is your past. You carry it with you always. These are your sins. You carry them with you always. You better learn how to live with them, learn the story that they're telling you. Because they're whispering your future in your ear, and if you don't listen, it will be contaminated by the toxicity of your past.

So do you think that kind of nightmare is going to change? That to an extent America has now taken account of that?
Yes, because, you know . . . the whole place practically has come crashing down [*laughs*]. Yes, there is severe accounting being taken of it right now. We're going through something that we haven't gone through in my life. Foreign policy, domestic policy—driven to its breaking point. Everything got broken.

And the philosophy that was at the base of the last administration has ruined many, many people's lives. The deregulation, the idea of the unfettered, free market, the blind foreign policy. This was a very radical group of people who pushed things in a very radical direction, had great success at moving things in that direction, and we are suffering the consequences.

And are you optimistic?
It's like this. You go out. You spend 35 years singing your songs about a place. And you see that place in things that people are doing in their communities from city to city on a local basis. But you don't see it on a national level. Matter of fact, you see the opposite. You see the country drifting further from democratic values, drifting further from any fair sense of economic justice.

So you work under the assumption that you have some small thing that you can do about it. You proceed under the assumption that you can have some limited impact in the marketplace of ideas about the kind of place you live in, its values and the things that make it special to you. But you don't see it. And then something happens that you didn't think you might see in your lifetime, which is that that country actually shows its face one night, on election night.

A MAN WHOSE political beliefs had generally been implied rather than stated, Springsteen finally broke cover with his public support for Democratic presidential candidate John Kerry in 2004. This time he came out for Obama early, declaring him "head and shoulders above the rest" in April 2008. In October he headlined a fundraiser alongside Billy Joel and John Legend, then hit the road to play four rallies; the last of these, in Cleveland, Ohio, on 2 November, saw him debuting the title track of Working on a Dream *before bringing his entire family out on stage to stand alongside Obama's wife and daughters.*

You said you had to be "peeled off the wall" after Kerry lost; what was this year like?
Well, it was an exhilaration I've never seen after an election. And it was rooted, I think, in a recognition that this country, that so often seems buried beneath missteps and mistakes, had suddenly shown its real face.

And what about Obama himself?
Obama's a unique figure in history. The fundamental American-ness of his story and the fact that he represents for many, many people an image and a view of the country that felt like it was so long missing in action.

His election was an incredible moment for someone who seemed to carry, both seriously, and . . . not, not lightly but without great burden, enormous parts of American history with him. Enormous and painful parts.

Somebody who can reckon with the past, who can live with the past in the present, and move towards the future—that's fabulous. And for the country to recognise that was a wonderful moment. This place we've been talking about, singing about . . . it's alive. It isn't dead. It exists.

That dynamic in my life has been a big part of staying alive. Staying present. Not fucking it up too bad at any given time. But it's a day-to-day experience. There's always tomorrow and, hopefully, you can use the word "hopefully" now. You can live here, and use the word "hopefully." So that's pretty nice.

WITH THE ELECTION *won, it would seem that other things are on Springsteen's mind. Now approaching 60, his personal world is changing too. Much of that has been constant: he's lived in this same part of Jersey for most of his life. His professional career has predominantly been spent with the same group of musicians, the E Street Band, and this in a world where the Beatles barely lasted a decade. He's been with wife Patti Scialfa—herself a member of the band—for 20 years, and they have three teenage children.*

Now those children are growing up and leaving home, with eldest son Evan just starting college, and in the past 18 months he's had to endure the deaths of two close friends: personal assistant Terry Magovern and then, in April, E Street keyboardist Danny Federici, who had played with Springsteen for more than 40 years. Little surprise, then, that when talking about the themes of this new album he quotes Martin Scorsese—"The artist's job is

*to make people care about your obsessions and see them and experience them
as their own"—although some of those obsessions come from unlikely sources.*

**There's a song on this album—"Queen of the Supermarket"—
about a guy who has a terrible crush on a check-out girl. Where on
earth did that spring from?**
They opened up this big, beautiful supermarket near where we lived.
Patti and I would go down, and I remember walking through the
aisles—I hadn't been in one in a while—and I thought this place is spec-
tacular. This place is . . . it's a fantasy land! And then I started to get
into it. I started looking around and hmmm—the subtext in here is so
heavy! It's like, "Do people really want to shop in this store or do they
just want to screw on the floor?" [*Laughs*]

Sometimes it's about buying groceries, you know . . .
But maybe . . . [*laughs*] maybe there's this other thing going on. In the
States they're sort of shameless, the bounty in them is overflowing. So
the sexual subtext in the supermarket; well, perhaps, it's just twisted me.

It must be really hard to go shopping with you.
I'm telling you, it's there! So I came home, said: "Wow, the supermarket is fantastic, it's my new favourite place. And I'm going to write a
song about it!" If there's a supermarket and all these things are there,
well, there has to be a queen. And if you go there, of course there is.
There's millions of them, so it's kind of a song about finding beauty
where it's ignored or where it's passed by.

And does Patti still take you shopping?
Yeah, she does [*laughs*]. Says, "Hey—what's this one about?"

I wouldn't tell her if I were you . . . you've got to keep some mystery.
It's funny—all those great old records always seem to trail off into
mystery. You always wonder, "What was the room like that these guys
made that record in? Where they made those Sun records, what did it
feel like?" They're surrounded with so much mystery. These days a lot
of the mystery has been drained from popular music, but it still comes
forth.

HE FIRST BECAME enthralled by that mystery in the small town of Free-hold in Jersey's Monmouth County where he grew up the son of a bus driver and a legal secretary. By all accounts blindsided by Elvis, and an awkward youth who could only make sense of his world through music, he chuckles when he mentions he's recently been listening to tapes of his first band, the Castiles, and his face lights up at the memory:

ALL THE MUSIC I loved as a child, people thought it was junk. People were unaware of the subtext in so many of those records but if you were a kid you were just completely tuned in, even though you didn't always say—you wouldn't dare say it was beautiful. You would just say, "I like it. No, Dad, I like this," or it's great, or it's fun, or it's exciting me. And those records, some of them sustained their beauty. If you listen to the great Beatle records, the earliest ones where the lyrics are incredibly simple. Why are they still beautiful? Well, they're beautifully sung, beautifully played, and the mathematics in them is elegant. They retain their elegance. So you're trying to write elegantly also. I was interested in that kind of a creative pull, and that's not the stream that runs on top through your farm, it's the stream where it disappears underground.

"Kingdom of Days" has the best line on the record—"I don't see the summer as it wanes, just the subtle change of light upon your face."
It's a line about time and I'm old enough to worry about that a little bit. Not too much but a little bit [*laughs*]. And at certain moments time is obliterated in the presence of somebody you love; there seems to be a transcendence of time in love. Or I believe that there is. I carry a lot of people with me that aren't here any more. And so love transcends time. The normal markers of the day, the month, the year, as you get older those very fearsome markers . . . in the presence of love—they lose some of their power.

That's true . . .
But it also deals with the deterioration of your physical body. It drifts away, it's just a part of your life. But beauty remains. It's about two people and you visit that place in each other's face. Not just the past

and today, but you visit the tomorrows in that person's face now. And everybody knows what that holds.

And recently that's the thing that you've had to deal with that you haven't really had to deal with before, which is the death of people your age that have been close to you . . .
It's in most great rock music, you know. Because the impact of so many great records, immediately tells you, "Oh, there's something else, my friend!" The desperate presentness of so much great rock music, the life force in it, it's a ranting against the other thing.

The mythology is always mixed. The skulls, crossbones, death's head. It's ever-present. I hear death in all those early Elvis records, in all those early, spooky blues records. And in records made by young kids—it's in "Thunder Road." A sense of time and the passage of time, the passage of innocence. It cuts through all popular music but in this record, it comes more to the surface.

Well, "The Last Carnival" is obviously for, if not about, Danny Federici . . .
It started out as a way of making sense of his passing. He was a part of that sound of the boardwalk the band grew up with and that's something that's going to be missing now.

Does writing something like that help you process it yourself?
Maybe. I don't know. You know, uh . . . on one hand it's just a song.

It's never just a song, Bruce . . .
You know, he's the first guy we ever lost. The thing I've been proudest about for a long time was that unlike many other bands, our band members, they lived. They lived and that was something that was a group effort; it was something that we did together. The surviving part. People did watch the other person. And it was a testament to the life force that I think was at the core of our music—that nobody gave up on you. And that lasted a long time. People got pulled out of a lot of holes. And I would include myself, in different ways over many, many different years.

IF NOTHING ELSE, time tells us that a lot of rock stars struggle with the age-ing process. One of the tragedies of Presley's life was that he was the first of those stars and back then the job didn't come with a road map. Thirty-six years after he released his first album, it's obvious that Springsteen does have a map, one he drew himself and studied carefully. He has a clear vision of the future, saying: "All I'm trying to do now is get music to my audience that is relevant to the times we're living in and to the times in their lives," and in difficult times his thoughts are on what endures.

That sense of survival—or maybe not—is also in the title song you wrote for the film *The Wrestler*, where your friend Mickey Rourke plays a man who's washed up, whose career is ending. How do you write something like that?

It's the old job of putting yourself in somebody else's shoes, while you've got a foot in your own shoe. And that's how it works. I'm grounding this song in something I've experienced myself, that I believe I can write about.

Everybody understands damage by the time they're 12 years old. Most of what you write comes from that point in time, and before. Your life narrative, the inner geography that you are going to have to make your way through is quite firmly set pretty early on.

And that was a song about damage, about what it does to somebody with the inability to get in to normal life. The inability to stand the things that nurture you. Because much of our life is spent running. We're running, we're on the run; one of my specialties.

You can find your identity in the damage that's been done to you. Very, very dangerous. You find your identity in your wounds, in your scars, in the places where you've been beat up and you turn them into a medal. We all wear the things we've survived with some honour, but the real honour is in also transcending them.

Everybody has experience with those things, but if you live in them, it's a very dangerous life, and it's going to be a very hard and unsatisfying one. And that's a daily choice. In my own life I've built a lot, but . . . I don't kid myself.

Do you still feel like that 12-year-old?

Of course. There is no part of yourself that you leave behind; it can't be done. You can't remove any part of yourself, you can only manage the different parts of yourself. There's a car, it's filled with people. The 12-year-old kid's in the back. So's the 22-year-old. So is the

40-year-old. So is the 50-year-old guy that's done pretty well, so's the 40-year-old guy that likes to screw up. So's the 30-year-old guy that wants to get his hands on his wheel and put the pedal to the metal, and drive you into a tree.

That's never going to change. Nobody's leaving. Nobody's getting thrown out by the roadside. The doors are shut, locked and sealed, until you go into your box. But who's driving makes a really big difference about where the car is going. And if the wrong guy's at the wheel, it's crash time. You want the latest model of yourself at the wheel, the part of you that's sussed some of this out and can drive you someplace where you want to go.

The artists people are interested in have something eating at them. Those are the guys they're interested in. Elvis. What was eating at that guy? Why did he have to sing like that and move like that? Jerry Lee Lewis, what was eating at him, what was eating at Hank Williams? Johnny Lydon. Something was.

So the idea is: how do you manage that thing that's eating at you, without letting it eat you? 'Cause that's what it wants to do. The thing that's eating at you, wants to eat you. And so your life is . . . how do you keep that from happening? That's a pretty interesting story too, and that's what a lot of my records are about, maybe all of them. So now, you know—my records and the music and everything are me attempting to keep from being eaten [*laughs*]. As best as I can.

Elvis Costello
Spectacle,
September 25, 2009, and January 27, 2010

Spectacle was a UK/Canadian television show hosted by Elvis Costello that ran for two seasons between 2008 and 2010 and appeared on the Sundance channel in the United States. Costello and his guests engaged in extended conversation and musical performances; Bruce's two-part appearance, filmed in one night and edited down from a four-hour event, ended the second season. What makes the interview special—aside from the fact that it is a rare Q & A before a live audience at the historic Apollo theater in Harlem—is that Bruce sits down to discuss his career with a friend and peer. With an easy rapport, Springsteen and Costello discuss musical influences and relationships. "The greatest rock 'n' roll musicians are desperate men," Bruce states. "You've got to have something bothering you all the time." Despite his success, it is clear that Springsteen continues to be driven because he has not lost that sense of desperation.

Part I

In my introduction I attempted to bring you out on the stage here in a manner that befits the Apollo Theater . . .
[*Laughs*] You did.

When I heard your records . . . I had never been to America so I had no idea of what the place that you were singing about was like. There must have been some advantage to it being somewhere kind of obscure even to a lot of American people.
I think people forget, there were still a lot of very local scenes and if you grew up an hour south of New York like we did along the Jersey Shore . . . I mean most of the people in my town had never been to New York City. And there was no one who came along the Jersey Shore to find talent or songwriters or bands. It just didn't happen then . . . this was the late '60s and early '70s. You were left in a bit of your wilderness, you know, but it also created a very specific group of influences and a very specific sound. And primarily of course, Asbury Park was kind of low-rent Fort Lauderdale at the time in the '50s and '60s . . . and so what it was, it was bars, cars, girls, it was the things I ended up writing about, you know. But, I lived locally most of my life . . . part of the reason is it was sort of the most quiet local life I could find and we're still there, we've stayed there. I looked at my heroes, a lot of my heroes, the people that came before me seemed to lose something when they lost a little sense of, I hate to say the roots because you can go any place and take it with you anywhere you go, it's not necessarily being in a physical place so that may help somewhat. But it's just that sense of your own history, what your initial motivations were, what the point was. What was, in the beginning . . . I think . . . and so I was very, very paranoid . . . I think the benefit we had coming up when we did was you were paranoid about stardom and that was a good thing. It didn't mean you didn't necessarily pursue it with everything you had, but you kept a very, very watchful eye to protect your music, your band, your internal life and I thought it was a very healthy paranoia because it was the nature of the business to suck those things out of you. That's just the rules.

I was in London when you came to play your first show in London around the time of *Born to Run* and they were saying the future,

it's the future of rock and roll. And I'm thinking, there's so much in this, people might not get how rich it is.

I think the problem is when that first hits you, you sort of half-agree . . . you go, hmmm, future of rock and roll, I kind of like the way that sounds. But then you go, but it also sounds like a shitload of trouble man [*laughs*]. But you know, it goes the way it goes.

But also, I don't think London had seen a show that was informed by the things you were talking about first . . . the bar thing and everything from R&B. They had you on record but they didn't know what you did live, so when Bruce came out it was like we were seeing the Stax/Volt Revue from 1965. It was very informed. The songs were these rich songs but the way you presented 'em it was not, there was nobody doing that.

The music, it was romantic, because I grew up on the great romanticism of the Drifters and Spector records and Benny King and that whole generation of beautiful romance that was in those songs. And then we were brought up because we played in bars night after night, you know, you had to have something that caught people immediately and it was, the idea was soul bands, soul bands, soul bands. That was a huge part of the Jersey Shore and so that was a very natural thing to absorb. And also, it was the music that I admired because I used to go out and see Sam and Dave . . . and man, they put on a show and all of those devices, the use of dynamics, the use of the way long songs that built, and built, and built, and built . . . really came out of a lot of those soul reviews. And we remain a sort of bar band so . . .

But the songwriting that was on those first two records that came before I saw you perform for the first time . . . there was a scope to some of those songs that when I heard them . . . what I dug about them so much was I thought, well maybe this is a guy that likes the same records, lots of words, images tumbling out. And I thought, here's the guy that spent some time listening to *Astral Weeks* and *Bringing It All Back Home* . . . and all those R&B records you talk about and that's a great combination.

It was kind of pragmatic because we played in bars as long as we could but really because we played original music and we weren't your local Jersey Shore Top 40 band, it was very difficult for us to get work. We worked, the way we did it, Steve and I . . . one night we canvassed the entire town from north to south . . . it was a Saturday night in the middle of the summer. And the idea was to find the emptiest dump in the whole town and try to get the guy who was running the joint to hire us. And we went bar, to bar, to bar, to bar . . . and Asbury was jumping those days, the circuit was filled with cars and college kids. And we finally found one, it was a place called the Student Prince . . . it was run by a bricklayer from Freehold and the place was empty. And Steve and I talked him into letting us play for one dollar at the door. And we started, and we played to 20 people or something . . . and next week, we played to 30 or 40 people. We worked our way into kind of a small group of local hipsters who would come down and see us. In the end, that kind of ran out. And I got to a place where I said I gotta make do with just the guitar and my voice at some point. And now, I was a good guitar player, accompanying myself alright . . . my voice was, my first band I was in wouldn't let me sing at all. And so I said, the words better be good, the songs better be good. And that kind of set me off on the path of trying to be able to sit down with something and come up with something that was kind of electric just with the voice and the guitar.

And I've heard you revisit songs that you wrote in that era in recent times . . . and it isn't with any sense of like, they're a different language. I mean the songs I'm thinking of are things like "New York City Serenade" and "Incident on 57th Street." They're multi-parted and if I say operatic . . . I don't mean like Puccini, I mean like *West Side Story*. They're like a whole story going on and it's a way you wrote for a while and then you only recently went back to it . . . songs like "For You" and "Growin' Up" are really favorites . . . tumbling words really about real experiences. They serve all that but at some point you decide less is more enduring maybe, less words is more enduring.

Initially, I think I wrote a lot of that music once I wanted it to be lyrically electric. I had to hit you with something. Then there was a lot of initially, the Dylan comparisons. So after that, I said well maybe I'll try to sing more colloquially, the way that people speak, move back from some of the imagery . . . which really looking back on it, at that age you're oversensitive to every sort of criticism.

And it was so early . . . I don't know why people thought they needed a new Dylan. The old one was still really young at the time. And he's still incredible! But it was just, I think he invented a language that didn't exist in popular song before, so when you came along and you built on that language, you were just immediately connected to it. Part of it was flattering and part of it was well, I better figure something out. [After the] first two records, the third record I moved back off a lot of the wild imagery and stuff.

Well, there's one song I'd really like to just ask you a moment about, because it is one that has a lot of fantastic images—but they're completely appropriate because the location of the song is the circus. And you have images from it and you have the character Billy in the song and you've returned to him throughout your career, you've made references, passing references. Did you ever just want to ever run away to the circus and did that thought ever occur to you?
The circus came to Freehold. It was a Clyde Beatty–Cole Brothers Circus, they do it every summer. It's an old-school travelling circus, they pitch the tent in your local fairgrounds . . . or they pitch the tent near a local racetrack in Freehold. And I used to go with my mother and I think when you're a kid, the things you notice about the circus aren't the things you're meant to notice. But those are the things that are fascinating to you. You know what you're watching, that right underneath it . . . you'd walk down the midway, but I was always interested in what's going on down that side alley back by that trailer. And then late at night, if you happened to be stranded there at 11:30, midnight, after it had shut down, it was the province of local hoodlums at the time and it was really scary for a little boy.

It was magic and dread . . . and a little bit of illicit stuff going on. It's the fabulous stuff of songs and of dreams, of childhood dreams and you turned it into this beautiful song, "Wild Billy's Circus Story."
We can't possibly go through every stage of your career. People know so many things about you. And I mentioned seeing you on the occasion you came to London to play *Born to Run*. And the next time we met, I think you really would have been forgiven for not recognizing me, because it was in 1978 in Nashville and I had gone on a shopping expedition while I was there. And for reasons I

don't know why I went to Bruce's show dressed in a 10-gallon hat, red lizard skin boots and a Western shirt with horses on it.
A full cowboy suit [*laughs*].

Yeah, I had everything but the holster and the pistol. The show was just a knockout because *Darkness on the Edge of Town* had just come out. And this is Nashville now, it's 1978 and the word had not reached Nashville that your songs were not exclusively about cars and girls. So you opened with I think "Promised Land," you did "Badlands," remember . . . and I'd heard the record, but the way they sounded live was like the way they sound today, they just took off.
It was funny, we were talking . . . if you were around at the time you might remember, when the record came out, it got a lot of nice reviews. But the fans weren't . . . people didn't take to it right away. I think because it had been three years since *Born to Run*. So that was a long time between records. And you had read all those "whatever happened to" articles in the newspaper and we finally got the record made and it was different. And one of the reasons it was different was because there was some young English songwriter at the time who said the songs in *Born to Run* were too romantic.

It wasn't me I hope.
I can't remember his name right now . . .

It wasn't me. Was it me?
I've been waiting 30 years for this moment, what do you think? Of course it was [*laughs*]!

I was clearly in a different relationship with the idea of romance then. But really, the serious point of telling the story about coming to see you was, one, it is an amazing record. The way you played the songs live they had . . . it was like something was really coming out. There was a change of tone in your writing and watching it—I mean you've got to remember I was a fan of yours before I got started. So I'm taking cues like you described—you take your cues from the best people. I'm watching you play. We'd made three records in a two and a half years, me and the Attractions . . .
Elvis's first three records were hurricane. He made great ones since, all of 'em, but you had the perfect storm of first three records going. *Whoa.*

Songwriting is like, you're watching everybody that is out there. You're looking over your shoulder the whole time. It sort of never stops but those [albums] were like wow, they were scary.

Well thank you, that's too kind. But of course, I'm watching you in the opposite direction disappearing into the distance, and I'm going . . . if Bruce, if they're going to resist this change, how in the world am I going to do that?
I think at the time, it had been a long time in between records and we knew the record was a different kind of record. That was the idea . . . it had been written to be tougher. There was influence from the punk scene and your stuff and there was a lot of tough music that came out of England in those years. I loved those early Buzzcocks records, all the Clash records, the singles—because you couldn't get the records you had to try to go and get the singles. And that stuff found its way into the subtext of *Darkness on the Edge of Town* along with sort of a cinematic-ness that was sort of growing up on all the Westerns . . . and so, the record ended up being a blend of those things in a funny way. There was an element of what you'd absorb from John Ford westerns, also you'd travelled yourself now. And we travelled through the west now and we'd seen some of it firsthand and we'd been out in it firsthand. Those things all kind of connected for me when I was writing in my room. And also wanting to be about something. I think that was important to me. I said well, the people that I liked sort of . . . they gathered their times in and found a way to contextualize it in a language to speak about the events of the day. That's what I want to do if I can do it.

There's a choice that you made after you had a degree of success to change your language. I mean, it's not like a theoretical thing, you just did it. It was an instinctive thing obviously but if Wild Billy is some kind of carnival colors, these songs are in black and white.
The three years from say when you're 25 to 28, those are big years. They take up a lot bigger percentage of your life than now. So you change a lot. And also the position you're in . . . I was both elated and embarrassed by my good fortune. It was like whoa . . . and I knew I had worked hard for all that stuff. And part of *Darkness* was me trying to sift through a lot of those issues and in the end my music was always about identity, identity, identity. Who am I? Where do I be-

long? What's the code I'm trying to live by? All of these things that are all about identity issues and so *Darkness on the Edge of Town* was sort of inspired by that search for . . . alright, I've been through, I had that first type of success but what does that make me, what does that make me now. And the only thing I knew to do was to stand very hard and connect with the things, the few things I was sure of . . . which was I suppose where I come from and all those things. It wasn't a result of any social consciousness really, it was purely a matter of my own inner-psychological life and search for who do I want to be, who am I gonna be?

But contained in your relationship with the audience, because you'd become popular, and because the songs even when they're about dark issues are played with such fervor . . . people, they kind of feel they're your buddy. This they said about George Bush the lesser as well, you know, they said that people wanted to have a beer with him and that was part of his appeal. And that's the weird conundrum as a writer, because sometimes when you're writing songs and examining identity and even when you start writing character voices . . . you are not portraying you the good-hearted man. It could be a conflicted man, the conflict in it . . . and there's a real balance to be struck between showman and artist in this moment.
I think theater is drama. I think filmmakers, songwriters, artists, you're drawn to conflict. It's one of the things that people go to music for, and any kind of art for . . . it's, okay, we're all conflicted inside so how do you begin to contextualize some of that conflict, how do you begin to make sense out of it, how do you build something out of it? Instead of letting it destroy you, how do you make something out of it?

I know when I moved into *Darkness* I was interested in a few things . . . one was adulthood. I didn't feel particularly young at 27 or 28 years old. And I had gotten into country music, I had begun to get into some Woody Guthrie and I wanted my songs, I wanted to write something that I could sing when I'm the ripe old age of 40, please. And that will feel real and connected to me. And I remember thinking about that very consciously at the time. So I wanted to move into adult issues.

And the second thing you're doing is, you're playing with a certain level of ferocity for your own survival. And for one reason I've always believed the greatest rock 'n' roll musicians are desperate men. You've got to have something bothering you all the time.

You can't always be a nice guy in the songs is what it is.
Why songs are good is, it's like an art . . . one and one makes three. In music, if it makes two you failed, my friend. If you're painting and all you've got is the paint and the canvas, you failed. If all you got is your notes, you failed. You've got to find that third thing that you don't completely understand but is coming up from inside of you. And you can put it, you can set it any place, you can choose any type of character, but if you don't reach down and touch that thing, then you're just not going to have anything to say and it's not going to feel like it has life and breath in it. You're not gonna create something real and it's not gonna feel authentic. I worked hard on those things.

Yes, indeed. Throughout those slower songs on what you'd do next—which is *The River*, the huge record—the narrative aspect in these songs, it puts me in mind of great character writers who you might have admired.
You roll along and you sort of stumble on some part of your talent that you're good at, that you didn't know you were good at. I think I stumbled into that sort of writing through writing *The River*. It's the sort of writing where it's just "I," you're not outside the character, you're basically the voice of the character's internal life and you're really, all the songs are what someone's thinking. It's like being able to overhear someone's thoughts. And originally, I guess the first song I wrote was really "The River" where it had that [*sings lyrics*]. . . . And that came about from just . . . it was a song I actually wrote about my sister and brother-in-law. It was the late '70s, New Jersey, there was a recession. My brother-in-law was a construction worker, building stopped, lost the job, struggled very hard. My sister, I have a sister a year younger than me, became a mother very, very young and struggled through a life similar to my parents. And so, for some reason and I don't know, I remember sitting at my table one night and those opening lines came out. Then when the record came out, there was some folks who mentioned that particular song and that particular kind of point of view as a writer. Said oh gee, well the record's really great when somebody comes in and they tell their story and they kind of leave. I think my

friend Greil Marcus wrote something about it and I said I like writing like that.

The idea of the moral conflict of the characters you're describing within people, is a lot again about class, a lot about social justice, although not spoken about in any kind of way that could ever be said to be a sermon. It was always about somebody's predicament that they're in . . . moving more and more into that, the territory of writing in character, while really rocking the fuck out as well.
That really was important to us on that record. We realized you don't want to be Mr. Glum, either. I said no, that's sort of our bar band record. I wrote some songs that were, defined the characters I was writing about, the part of me I was writing about . . . and I wrote a lot of songs that might be songs that they're listening to in a bar on a Friday or Saturday night. And, because we were a show band and remain a show band, I was trying to write things that would be exciting live.

I call them mobile songs. You can be writing a story and have connections between the songs and even a narrative thread between songs that you want to develop sometimes when you're writing and then sometimes, like you say, you want to write the song that's playing on the radio in the corner of the room when those things are happening.
A lot of the songwriting that I grew up on—and I know you grew up on, too—was music that performed that function. And I was very interested in us sort of as a band also making that kind of music. I wanted to make pop music. When we wrote "Hungry Heart" . . . it was originally when I met the Ramones in Asbury Park, and I wrote "Hungry Heart."

For the Ramones?
Yes, and then Jon Landau heard it and said we can't give that one away.

I would have loved to have heard . . . did they ever cut it?
No, I don't think so.

Oh, what a shame.
I was interested in just writing—"Girls in Their Summer Clothes" or "Waitin' on a Sunny Day," they're meant to be sparkling pop records.

The flip side of that is . . . the craft that you have as a writer gives you choices and certain moments you can use those things to make explicit statements, unambiguous statements. I'm thinking in terms of a song like "41 Shots," the impact of something like that. Have you ever had a sense of any risk in your abilities to say such things when moved to write them?

Nah. "41 Shots" I wrote, I didn't think a lot about it, just thought it was a part of my body of work like "Promised Land" or anything else. Played it in Atlanta. I could tell it went over well, people listened to it. But then Steve came running into rehearsal and said man, did you see the front page of the newspaper? I said no. We're on the front page. I said really. And I think I was referred to as both a "dirtbag" and a "floating fag" at the time. "Dirtbag," I knew what it meant, I had to go to the dictionary for the "floating fag", though, and it wasn't in there.

So, that was really drummed up. I was getting letters from people asking me not to play it. We did play it at Madison Square Garden and Amadou Diallo's parents came . . . and there was some booing, there was some booing. There was flaunting of the New Jersey state bird [*laughs*]. At one point, I said, hey, this is what our band, this is what we're built for. This is what we do. But the only thing unusual at the time was I didn't understand . . . it's reported on the news, it's written in the newspapers, but if a guy writes a song about it, it may show that people take music very personally. There's something about music, and I think you used the phrase, it puts its fingerprints on your imagination. I'll sing a little bit of it . . . [*sings*]

You mentioned when you were in the bars in New Jersey that you had the R&B repertoire, and that the E Street Band is an R&B band. There's a difference between a R&B band and a rock 'n' roll band. And a rock band and certainly an R&B band. Like you said, shows came to town, did you see like great guys who came up? Who did you see?

There was a place called the Satellite Lounge at Fort Dix, New Jersey . . . I know you have not been there. And actually a place called the Fast Lane. I saw Sam and Dave at those places. And this was probably late '70s and they were incredible. And I stood in the Fast Lane one night with probably a hundred people and maybe half, a third full or something and watched them just blow the roof off the place. But Sam—there was a tradition of great bandleaders, great band leaders came out of soul music. There's a beauty in watching a guy like Sam

Moore lead his band while he sang. Sam was the heavens. His voice was almost not human in that he had as incredible tenor. And he was gospel . . . he had a little of the Sam Cooke thing. But Dave rooted their music in the dirt and in the Earth. That's why Sam and Dave were great because Sam was up here in the clouds and Dave was down here scrapping, scrapping on the Earth. And there was, that's why it worked, that's why they were so fabulous. Dave's voice was so gritty, so earthy, so much pain in it, and so connected to the Earth . . . while Sam's was incredibly powerful but it also went up, up, up, up, up. And look, that's what you aspire to. You try to have your music rooted and at the same time flying. That's what they had. That's why they were so great.

We've got a decision to make. Who's going to go to the heavens and who's going to go to the dirt?
I'm singing the Sam part.

OK that's sorted out and I'm glad I can tell ya!

We're back with Bruce Springsteen. Part two. The middle years [*laughs*].
I think we're past that part already [*laughs*].

We shared the stage in the tribute to Joe Strummer after Joe passed. That's right. You sang the hell out of "London Calling." At the height of the *Born in the U.S.A.* success, you came out in the greatest way for the *Black & White Night* [Roy Orbison television special] I don't know about you, I get asked about that show than any single thing I've done on TV.
Me too.

Is it true?
Yah!

Like once a week.
Somebody comes up and goes . . . that thing was played constantly. But I think I was asked more about that show than anything that was put on in my life. It's incredible.

More than even this show. But we're gonna fix that. But it was so great . . . one of my favorite memories of that night was coming in the dressing room. And we'd rehearsed and this band is just incredible. We had Elvis Presley's band, we had the TCB band.
That was fun.

We had Jerry Scheff, Glen Hardin, James Burton . . . and the singers, the background singers alone were K.D. Lang, Jackson Browne, J. D. Souther, Bonnie Raitt. And Bruce turns up with his Walkman on, checking out that he's not going to mess up any Roy Orbison songs, doing his homework to the last minute.
They were hard. They had a lot of chords in 'em. ·

I mentioned family, Bruce, and there's a curious thing that I think happens. As somebody said, the author Philip Roth could be as savage as he was because he didn't have children. On the other hand, the joy of it in itself and the beauty of it is inspiring and then, they, those children, they grow up and start telling you about records you never heard.
I have that happen all the time. My kids, they'll listen to music. My daughter listens to a lot of Top 40, so I hear a lot of current Top 40 music from her. My youngest son, he started out as a total classic rocker. He was big reggae, 12-year-old reggae freak. Bob Marley, you know.

He's got a big sound system?
Then he got into acoustic Dylan stuff. That was fascinating, he was very young when he got into it. He came in one night and I was watching Dylan at Newport, the DVD. What's that Dad? That's cool. I said, yeah, that is cool. I went out and I got him all the records . . . and it was great, you see your child sort of connecting with something that has meant so much to you. Went to his door one night and I listened, he's got "Chimes of Freedom" on, and he's probably about 12 or 13, and I said what do you think? He said epic, Dad, it's epic. I said, that's right, that's what it is, it's epic. And it was one of those great, sort of, wow, ya know? My older boy he was into a lot of political punk music, Rage Against the Machine, Against Me! . . . [*laughs*] . . . he's against a lot. But and then a lot of, recently he's gotten into a lot of alternative singer-songwriters, Bright Eyes . . .

Any names that have really struck you that you've heard as a consequence?
Oh yeah, he turned me on to Gaslight Anthem. They're actually guys from Red Bank. It's fun to see the kids at a point where, hey, they go out and they find their own heroes. I was happy that my kids sort of found their own home in music because it's kind of the family business. And so you're worried, it's like whoa, that's something to keep away from. But it's so essential. I watched them . . . they found their own way, they weren't interested in "listen to this and listen to that" . . . they were interested in "no, *you* listen to *this*, or you check this out or you check that out. And it became a big part of my relationship, particularly with my oldest son.

That's a wonderful moment. To hear records, it's like looking through a photograph album and seeing your life through the eyes of your child or when you fall in love and you share those memories . . . I mean, Patti and you come from the same kind of background, so presumably you have the same kind of jukebox in your head.
Patti and I, we really came from the same area so there was a lot of cultural similarity. I didn't have to tell her anything about the Crystals. She was steeped in all that stuff, she was steeped in the great soul music, Dusty Springfield, the great songwriters. And it's always like a connection like I have . . . you hear something and you go, oh there that is.

It's not a nostalgic thing because it's the moment you're living in now. You carry the memory of the record as you heard it, you share it and it's like a language that, as you said, it's just a look when the record comes on.
It is a language. I think the nice thing is, the whole thing that songwriting is about is you're a storyteller, you're trying to, you hope to become a part of the fabric of someone's life—beyond the fact that you want to make people dance and laugh and be entertained and have something to vacuum the floor to. I think your grandest aspirations, I know when I was young was wow, I wanted to do something that I felt had been done for me. Music, certain artists, became such an important part of my life experience. I always go, well, Dylan, he's the father of the country that I recognize. He's the father of my country in the sense that he was the first

place I went where I heard an America that I felt and believed to be true, that felt unvarnished and real, it felt like what I was experiencing. It was really my first true vision of the country I felt come out of those '60s records of his, you know *Highway 61*. And it opened up your vision in a way that, for me at the time, the school didn't do and other things didn't do. And it allowed you to dream and have possibilities about what you might be able to do with yourself, what you could do you with your life . . . and just about the intensity of living that was available. And don't, sort of . . . it's just so easy to step back. Those records were so intense.

And they continue to be as well. Obviously, I had the real pleasure and honor really to be on the Bob Dylan show for about five weeks a couple of years ago. I watched the show most nights to hear what he would do, he changed it every night. There was always something fascinating in it. And the really striking thing about it was these younger people—and I suppose some of them are only a little older than your older son—were responding with this same kind of fervor to his newer songs. And there is in the people that inspired me to start, and we've spoken about so many of them already, there is this combination of vigor in the writing of words and then there is this transfiguring kind of element of performance. I mean Van Morrison is somebody that I couldn't sing like if you held several guns to my head, but when I heard his records, I felt as if this is somebody who can abandon himself to something.

We were both brought up Catholic, I believe, and in my case the Catholic guilt part . . . I used a lot more of the guilt than the Catholic bit, you know?

You did well with that, though.

Yeah, I worked that angle for a while. I mean, I've got to say for a Protestant from East Belfast, Van Morrison has a lot of the Holy Ghost in him [*laughs*]. He can just go. I've seen him sing his own songs. I've seen him turn into the kind of abandon that you only see in the great R&B singers, the great blues singers.

There is the religious element of, I need to be transformed—that for some reason you need to be transformed into something other than what you are. Catholicism is good for shooting at you, straight into you. It's a funny thing . . . I look back and I've got a lot of harsh memories of my childhood. It was very strict religion at the time and blah, blah, blah. But at the same time, it was an epic canvas and it gave you a sense of revelation, retribution, perdition, bliss, ecstasy. When you think that that was being presented to you as a five- or six-year-old child . . . I think I've been trying to write my way out of it ever since.

I'm completely with you.
And it ain't gonna happen.

You've written songs with humor and they're some of the toughest things to do. But are there any kind of—and I mention actors a lot not because I think you are one—but are there any comic actors that have ever been an influence or . . .
Well Steve and I are high on Dean Martin and Jerry Lewis.

Which one is he?
That's a good question.

I was the guy walking around in 1977 called Elvis . . . [*Laughs*]
And then Costello . . . you had to be aware of the comedy team in the States.

Well, I was aware of them, but I never thought it'd make such good comedy, you know?
They were huge.

I never knew I'd grow to resemble them so much.
But it was perfect because it was like the ultimate sobriquet and then this absurd thing. That's kind of our business, and it worked so great.

I have to tell a story just for a moment, I'm going to make a total fool of myself doing this. You and Patti are the only people that have ever been able to persuade me onto horseback. It's not an image that you want to carry in your mind late in the night, I know. I went out to visit Bruce and Patti at their place and they were kind enough to take me out. They took me out to the stable. You took me, thankfully, past the stable that contained Lightning and Thunder Bolt.
Acid Trip. Widow Maker. Just don't get on a horse with those names and you'll be alright.

What was the name of the one you put me on, Slow Poke? Trotted me around the ring until it looked like I might be able to cling on with my knees.
You did pretty good.

I've been singing Gene Autry songs since.
And I had photographic evidence of that at one time. That was the only thing I lost.

You haven't got it with you?
No.

You lost the picture. My secret is safe with you and your lovely wife.
Very strange. You looked pretty good, though.

I've never once been back on a horse since. But it was a thrill to ride with you, I can say I rode with Bruce Springsteen. All of this really is a convoluted way of mentioning Patti and she is just the loveliest person and she's a member of your band. She talks to my wife about children, she gives us advice. It's a balance that's difficult to achieve—working life, family life, musical life and she's an incredible singer, songwriter. I mean, she's made great records, I really would love to try to sing one of her songs. [*sings*]
　　It must have been a really extraordinary experience, quite apart from everything else . . . from a musician point of view, to be up on those steps on Inauguration Day [2009] and I think it was an experience that a lot of people shared, that a lot of witnesses to so many things, so many struggles were there. You sing for these reasons. I'm not trying to compress a lot of thoughts into one, but I was really struck that you were standing side by side with this man [Pete Seeger] who is now in his 90s.
It's incredible. 90 years old. I thought hey I was a teenager in the '60s, you lived through the Civil Rights movement, you realize you go from the Voting Act to the first African-American president. In really, historically, a relatively compressed, short period of time. So, it was amazing to have lived to be there really. And also [there were] the ideas you have of the country you live in and you want your kids to grow up in.

　　Steve said to me—he was doing some research for one of his garage shows, and he said, you know, I found the greatest thing ever said about rock 'n' roll in this little ten-cent paperback. He said it was a quote from one of the go-go dancers on *Shindig*. Right? He said it's about the greatest thing I ever heard. I said, what is it? Well, that rock 'n' roll was always something coming. It creates an energy that pushes you toward the future. And it did do that. It's a developmental force for some reason in that way. I always believed that Elvis sort of presaged a certain type of modern citizen that was a decade away. Gender lines dropped, racial lines dropped. He crossed all those boundaries. And there is some forward energy in it.

I think in everything you write, there's two things. One, is I think to live fully and you can find it in music, you need—there's the ever-present now that's a part of grabbing life by the horns that you know people come to rock shows for. But there's also a forward energy that it's always for tomorrow, it's always for tomorrow, it's always for tomorrow. In a sense, I think you're right. I think in a lot of songs that I've written, it's the idea that it's for now but it's for tomorrow too because what I see isn't here now. It doesn't exist now. But I have some sort of faith that it can exist . . . whether it's social justice, economic justice, you get out there and go well, it's for tomorrow, it's for tomorrow, it's for tomorrow, while constantly trying to pull it into the present.

So I think that for me that day, it was a day when I said well maybe my songs are going to ring a little truer the next time I sing 'em . . . whether it's "Promised Land" or something else. So it was big and I think a lot of people experienced that particular day like that. It was like, hard to believe.

It was beautiful to see . . . and obviously they try to do these things with the appropriate gestures and the right people were there, the right people were up there saying the right things.
So for Pete, 90 years . . . the administration before sort of forgot the past, screwing up the future, and the present was pretty ugly. So, for him, it was fun being part of his excitement on that particular day. It was a lovely privilege.

Your willingness to stand and be unambiguous in the face of very, very catastrophic circumstances is something that . . . I suppose you just get to a time in your life when you can't be told you have

no right to say this. We do live in a democracy. You're up on the stage. My view is yeah, we can all say what we want, we're all talking at once, but right now this is the way I feel. But you can write your song and disagree with me. But when big things happened, you turned your talents to speaking.

I just think that was part of growing up in the '60s. I think when you grew up in the '60s, you grew up with that being part of your daily existence. The idea that we were teenagers and doing concerts to send anti-war protestors down to Washington. And it was just part of growing up at that time, it became an integrated part of what you do, I don't think for me anymore than anybody else. But it was also something I wanted as a part of my music. Once again it felt like it was a part of the basic story of identity that was a part of what I was trying to write. Because what's it about? OK. Who am I? Where is my home? How am I going to live? Where and how do I want to raise my children? All of these things ultimately lead you outward and lead you into an area of whether it's political activism or social activism of some sort . . . identity questions that ultimately lead you inward but they also lead you outward. And so, the fullness of the picture I wanted it to be part of my music and really that was the sole motivation. It was just a natural part of writing about the things I wanted to be about.

And over the course of your career and the course of this evening, you've illustrated more than I can ever thank you for, the way that you've developed the craft that allowed you to do this with eloquence.

I think you're always just trying to make sense of your own life and what's happening around you. And it leads you down . . . I always feel your internal motivations are so much stronger than whatever else might motivate you to write a song like that. I always find I'm trying to figure something out. I'm just trying to figure something out. And if I figure it out a little bit for me, maybe I'll figure it out for you. I can't claim much more credit as far as what moves me to write this song or that song, in that I'm just trying to figure out how to make sense of sometimes the unsensible. Things that are very difficult to make sense of. With a lot of that music, you're always—there's something internal that's pushing you forward and pushing you in those directions. Otherwise, I think that's what makes them good songs.

Any time I've tried to write about something, this is important, it never just sounded real.

I always denied there was even a political song, there was just an emotional reaction to events or a trend in our society or our world that we all share in. This is the version of it that moves you into song.

James Henke

Backstreets,
Summer 2010

In conjunction with "From Asbury Park to the Promised Land: The Life and Music of Bruce Springsteen," an exhibition at the Rock and Roll Hall of Fame, Springsteen gave one of the most comprehensive interviews of his long career. Sitting down with the Rock Hall's Jim Henke, previously a writer and editor at *Rolling Stone*, Springsteen enthusiastically went all the way back to the beginning, when he was 14 and joined the Castiles. As curator of the exhibit, Henke used the artifacts on display—from motel keys to guitars to *the* guitar—as jumping-off points to take Bruce through his entire professional history.

So, why now? Why did you decide to do the exhibit at this point in your life?
I thought you guys decided it [*laughs*]. I didn't know I decided it, I thought it was decided!

Well, it seems like you've kept a lot of things from your career over the years: your songwriting notebooks, guitars, posters, all that

stuff. Is that a conscious thing? You just wanted to save a lot of this stuff?

No—the pack rat is Max, Max Weinberg. And I think Danny kept a few things. But I didn't keep much. I was sort of superstitious about hoarding all that stuff, and I tended to let everything pass with the exception of only the things I needed to work. So I never collected guitars, anything. I only collected guitars that I played, you know? Until probably the early '90s, when Patti and I got a real house and said, gee, it would be nice to have a guitar in this room, or that room . . . Until then, I was into the sort of idea that it was all about what I could carry into your town—literally. And so I didn't collect. I saved my notebooks, because they had all my songs in them. And that was really it.

When we started to look around, we found pictures and posters and stuff that got basically put to the wayside—not with any collecting idea in mind, just, you know, stuff that you have [*laughs*].

So the exhibit starts with the Castiles, and then comes up to the present. You were 14 when you joined the Castiles?

Yeah, now the Castiles . . . that notebook was from a woman named Marion Vinyard. My mother didn't make those notebooks, it was Tex Vinyard's wife—and Tex Vinyard was, of course, a factory worker in Freehold and the manager of the Castiles. We rehearsed in his little shotgun-style house, which was right across the street from Caiazzo Music—where we slobbered over the window on a regular basis—and about 25 yards from the rug mill, where my dad and an enormous part of the town at one time worked, in a part of town called Texas.

So I was about 14. I was in a band; I got thrown out of my first band because they told me my guitar was too cheap—and it *was* pretty cheap, but it wasn't that bad. So I literally got thrown out because my guitar wasn't good enough.

What was that band called?

I think we were called the Rogues at the time. So it kinda pissed me off, and I went home that night and I remember I put on "It's All Over Now" by the Rolling Stones, and I forced myself to learn the lead. I just sat there for hours until I learned that very rudimentary lead that [Keith Richards] plays on "It's All Over Now." It was the beginning of my lead guitar career.

A few months later, George Thiess—who was dating my sister, Virginia—knocked on my door, told me he had a band, wanted to know if I played lead guitar. I told him that I did (which I barely did), and he took me over to Tex's house, and I met the other guys in the Castiles. There was a bass player, who we thought of as being elderly, who was probably in his late 20s at the time. He began to teach me some more rudimentary things on the guitar, and it was sort of the beginning of my guitar playing career and the Castiles, which for a teenage band lasted quite a while. I think we lasted '65, '66, and '67, it was pretty longstanding. We played in Greenwich Village in the Café Wha?; for one of your first bands, we got around pretty good.

Back then, was that when you were playing the Kent Guitar?
The Kent guitar, yes. Mine disappeared, and about two or three years ago I was thumbing through a vintage guitar magazine, and lo and behold they had a small article on Kent guitars. And there was mine! It seemed to be one of the remaining two in the world. And I immediately said "Kevin [Buell, guitar tech], call this guy up right now and get me that guitar!" I think we paid about the same that I paid for it when I bought it, which was something like $60. And the funny thing was, when I got it again, it played really well. I was surprised at how well it played.

And then there was another fellow—Kevin could tell you exactly who, I think he worked for Boston at one time—and he was kind enough to send me another one. So for a while I had two. I had one in each of my sons' rooms. It's nice to have that piece back, because that was really the piece that turned me into a lead guitarist, that single-pickup Kent guitar.

What kind of guitar did you get after the Kent, do you remember?
After the Kent guitar, I went way, way upscale, and I had a blue solid body Epiphone. Ray Cichone—there were two Cichone brothers, they were in a band called the Motifs, they were incredibly influential. They were older than us, amazingly influential musicians in the area at the time. First of all, they were the first band that sang. You have to understand there was a *before* and *after* the Beatles. Before the Beatles and the British Invasion, no one sang. All local bands were instrumental and based on the Ventures, "Pipeline" . . . it was all instrumental music. When you went to the high school dance and the local band played, it was instrumental music all night long. Finally these guys came in, and they had this guy, Walter Cichone, and he was a wild-looking . . . he

was a real rock star. A real, true-to-life, local—and probably could have been bigger—rock star. He just had it all, man: he looked great, sang great, scared people, very sexual. And he had a taller brother, Ray, who worked in the shoe store [*laughs*] in Asbury Park, I think, in the Florsheim Shoe Store. Except he was *huge*. He was like 6'5" or something, and he was a little gawky, and he kinda hunched over his guitar, which he held way up high on his chest. But he played incredibly. And he was kind enough to show me a lot—over the years he would show me anything I asked—and he would hand me down his guitars as he got better ones. I would pay him a little money.

And so from the Kent I went to a blue solid body Epiphone—which I have one of, actually, and I should give you that one, because there are a lot of pictures of me playing that thing in the Castiles.

Then I went to a Fender Stratocaster, which was also Ray's—which I didn't think sounded as good as the blue Epiphone, but it looked better, and I just decided I was gonna play it.

We also have the copy of the Castiles recording, the two songs you guys recorded. What was that like when you went into those sessions?
It was a tiny little room, maybe half the size of this living room, which is not that big, and they couldn't stand any volume whatsoever going into the microphones. We had to turn all our amps to the wall and literally put covers over them. And the guitars sounded real klinky, because we had the volume turned down to "one"—we couldn't get any distortion or speaker sound out of it. The recording studio was not set up in those days for any kind of overdrive; they just simply weren't ready to record rock bands in Bricktown, New Jersey, in 1965.

But it was a big deal. We saved up—I think it cost us, I don't know, $300 or $100, some enormous amount, what we thought was an enormous amount of money. We saved it up, did a session where we cut those two songs. Of course, they give you your two-track, which we recently found, and they give you the acetates, the little tiny 45-sized acetates. And some of those survived, also.

We also have a lot of stuff from various clubs you played back then. What was the Upstage Club like?
The Upstage Club was an anomaly. It was a bit of a freak because it was on Cookman Avenue in downtown Asbury Park, and they served no

booze. It was open from eight until *five in the morning*. I'm not sure how they did it! I mean, they simply allowed teenagers to be out 'til five a.m. I don't know if they paid the cops off or what the story was. But it was closed between twelve and one. The guy was sort of an old-school bohemian, Tom Potter, and his wife played the guitar. He would throw everyone out for one hour and then let everybody back in.

Its importance was because it was open so late, and because it had a bit of a hip vibe, and bands, when they came down to the Shore to play—it was a place where bands came from Long Island, from Pennsylvania, all over, in the summertime—at the end of their gigs, they would go to the Upstage. And so you had a moment when every musician in the immediate area would show up there at some point, and the thing to do was, of course, to play. So you saw everybody get up and play, just people from all over. And everyone was waiting for the next— who was gonna be the gunslinger? Everyone was waiting for the gunslingers to come in.

I came in from Freehold one night, by that time I had quite a bit of playing experience, and I got up on stage one night. There were no amps; the amplifiers were *in the walls*. So imagine, you're standing in front of a huge wall, and behind you is just, I don't know, 50 or 100 ten- or twelve-inch speakers. And in front of you there's a little deck where you plug in. There are no amplifiers in sight. You would plug in, basically, to the wall, and this huge sound would come roaring out. It was a pretty creative idea—I've never seen it done again [*laughs*], and I don't think I will!

But anyway, no one had to bring any equipment. That was the point: all you brought was your guitar. And you plugged straight in, and you gathered a group of musicians—"In a half-hour I'm gonna . . ." and you had somebody [say], "Yeah, man, I'll play the drums," or "I'll play . . ." you know, you picked up whoever was there, and played, and demonstrated your wares for whoever was around. That's the way a lot of musicians met. I met most of the E Street Band there, and Southside Johnny. So it was a very pivotal place.

What was the Sunshine Inn like?
The Sunshine Inn was a huge, empty garage which had originally been a Hullabaloo Club. When *Hullabaloo* was on television, they franchised the clubs and these clubs swept the nation—or at least the East Coast at that time—and every down-on-your-luck supermarket or

parking garage become a Hullabaloo Club. The Hullabaloo Club was
in a supermarket in Freehold. In Asbury Park it was in a big old parking garage. And basically they went in and put up a lot of black lights—
which no one had ever seen then. I remember the first time my buddy
and I went in at Asbury Park, we went in and our shirt lit up, we went,
". . . Whoa!" [*Laughs*] "Wow! . . . This is, like . . . This is special!"

The first band I saw in the Hullabaloo Club was Sonny and the
Starfires—Sonny [Kenn] still plays in the area—and so on the drums
was "Mad Dog" Vincent Lopez. Sonny was this great R & B player:
fabulous blond hair, handsome guy, hair slicked back, just a stone-cold
rocker. Just really something to see. And they were very big in the area
at the time; to us, we thought they were gods.

After the Hullabaloo Clubs all, of course, tanked after two or three
years or however long it took for that to run its course, then all of a sudden this place became the Sunshine Inn. Run by a guy I believe named
Mr. Fisher, who was really strange and kind of funny—classic New Jersey small-town shyster. Once again, because I played, I became friends
with everybody, and I saw quite a few acts there. They had quite a few
national acts: Allman Brothers, Humble Pie, Black Sabbath . . . I first
saw Peter Wolf and the J. Geils Band there, and we opened for some of
these acts from time to time.

I think we have a poster for you guys opening for Humble Pie.
Yeah, we opened for Humble Pie. That was usually with Steel Mill, and
I had this band Dr. Zoom, we opened for somebody.

**I was gonna ask about them, because it sounds like those shows
were really interesting and different with the Monopoly players ad
all that.**
It was just weird—I have no idea what it was about. We might have
gotten the idea from, like *Mad Dogs and Englishmen* or something at
the time. But it was just this huge band of all local musicians. And the
people we liked but who didn't play anything, we just found something
for them to do, like play Monopoly, or some sort of stunt on stage. It
was really just a result of boredom [*laughs*], and people hanging around
with nothing to do and no band at the time, I guess. It was fun. We
had a big chorus, people's wives and girlfriends sang, and it was just an
outgrowth of the little local scene.

We have a poster for a benefit you did for George McGovern in '72. Between seeing that and knowing what you did this year for Barack . . .
I started early! [*Laughs*]

I was going to say, did you always know rock 'n' roll was going to influence politics?
Yeah, even as early as those days. Because you forget, we were products of the '60s, and even as a young person, that brought with it a good deal of social consciousness even in Freehold, New Jersey, and in our little town. And so we searched for ways to be involved. I know we did a benefit to bus protesters to Washington to protest against the Vietnam War. We did the thing for McGovern. Here and there we just sort of found ways. And I wrote some political music back in those days with Steel Mill—it was very much a natural part of the rock 'n' roll scene.

We have the John Hammond audition tapes—what do you remember about those sessions?
Last of the old-school recording sessions: the people working were all in suits. I probably caught the very last of the '50s/'60s-style recording business. John would be there, and he always had a suit on, and the engineers and everybody else—my recollection, they were still dressed for work. It was very probably the last of the '60s style of recording sessions where you came in, and there's a mic set up, and you got in front of it, you played your songs, and played the piano. I listened to what John had to say, which was just general encouragement, and it happened in an evening, and that was it.

One of the other audio things we have is the audio from the show at the Harvard Square Theater, the one that Jon Landau ended up writing about . . . Do you remember anything about that show?
I remember that Bonnie Raitt was kind enough to allow us to open up for her in those days, which we were (and remain) deeply thankful for. Because very few people would. It was hard to get on the bill with someone—we had a natural tendency to play longer than we should, and the band was very, very good. She was great, and Jackson Browne let me open up for him. We opened up for Sha Na Na; we opened up

for Brownsville Station, Black Oak Arkansas. We were on a lot of unusual bills, just because they sent you wherever somebody would let
you on. In those days there was no discernment between genre. You
know, there wasn't a heavy metal show—everything was all mixed up
together. We opened up for the Eagles one time. Mountain, Chambers
Brothers . . . you did a lot of unusual gigs like that in the early days.

But the Harvard Square Theater, my main memory of it was that it
was a really good show, people liked us a lot. I think we really shook
the house down—it was just a good night. I didn't meet Jon that night;
it was just a good night in Boston.

**And we have the audio from the 1978 show at the Agora in Cleve-
land, which was WMMS's tenth anniversary. Since this is in Cleveland, maybe you'd want to talk about Cleveland and what it's
meant to you, the support early on in your career.**
There were places that were pockets of support. And my parents did a
strange thing, which was they moved away from me in 1969 [*laughs*].
Usually you leave home—my parents left home! My sister and I remained in Freehold. My sister was 17 and just had a baby and married
a local guy in Lakewood, and so she stayed behind. And I stayed behind for a couple of reasons. One is that I was financially independent
at the time, to the tune of 20 or 30 bucks a week, which was all you
needed in those days as a 19-year-old kid to live on. My parents had
nothing. When they left for California, they had 3,000 dollars—every
cent they had; they had all their stuff piled on top the car (I might have
sent you the picture; if not, I'll send it to you). They didn't have enough
money to stay in motels when they crossed country. They slept in the
car very often. They literally slept a night in a motel and then a night or
two in the car.

I tried to go out there at one time, and I couldn't make it. Once I got
to California, my value was zero—I was worthless in California, because I had no reputation. But in New Jersey I could make that 20 dollars down at the Upstage on a Friday night, or the Student Prince, or
someplace where it was just enough to get me by through the next week.
We had the band, so we all lived together and pooled our resources for
rent. And, at 19, I was independent, if that's what you could call it.

So we had certain places that supported us. In the beginning there
was New Jersey, in this immediate area; and Richmond, Virginia, and
that was with Steel Mill. We literally wouldn't have survived otherwise.

Then when the band started playing and touring—in the beginning, they don't pay you any money. Very often you play for free. So Cleveland became a place, because it was such a big rock 'n' roll town, where we developed an audience very early. Cleveland, Philadelphia . . . Texas, believe it or not: Austin, Houston . . . There were a few cities where we developed strong early audiences, and Cleveland was a *big* one that kept us going for quite a few years.

The radio station WMMS really got behind you guys too.
Right, a lot of it had to do with the stations backing you. In Philadelphia, there was a guy called David Dye, he came down—it was in the strange days when a guy could come down from the radio station, just the DJ could come down. He could see you play to 15 or 20 people—nobody. You could *be* nobody, and that night on your way out of town you could turn on the radio and hear this guy play your record if he liked you. And the next time you came into town, there were 40 people there instead of 15. And so, the support of the old-school radio stations was enormous and incredibly important. It was where the band's live experience paid off. Because when we came into town initially, we played to nobody. *Nobody* came to see us—ten, 15 people. No one knew who you were. So when the DJs came down, and with the free format that still existed at that time, they went back and they began to play your records, then next time you came out there were more people there.

It was a very organic, grassroots growth that you were able to get going in those days. It was a combination of the bands' excellence in live performance and a system that could *respond* to that excellence. [These days], a guy could come down, love you, and say "You're great! I'll never *play* you, but you're fabulous." [*Laughs*] "You're never gonna get on the radio, but you're a genius!" I've heard people say that.

So it was a combination of a place in time when our power live was able to affect one person, who was then able to go out and affect his community through the ability to simply play your records on the air. It was a very different day and age. The music business was much smaller, there was no entertainment media, there was no entertainment culture, there was no coverage of rock music on television—very little, you had *American Bandstand*, and *Midnight Special* or something. It was still a novelty in your daily newspapers, major newspapers, it was still consigned to a little space. It was a very different kind of business. The upside was you had quite a bit of room to grow, experiment, and get your act together before the big spotlight hit you—if it was ever going to.

One part of the exhibit is devoted to *Born to Run*, and I read in one of the books that you weren't happy with the album when you first delivered it.
No, but I don't know if I would have been happy with anything, because I was just generally not that happy. My expectations—the sound I heard in my head was not one that was physically reproducible [*laughs*]. Of course, I wasn't aware of this at the time. I had no record-making knowledge. We had around us people who had *some*. The record probably wouldn't have gotten made without Jon Landau stepping in at the time, so that was enormous. Because we got stuck in the studio. I just worked on it for a long time, and I just couldn't hear it by the time it was done. I've had that happen with other records. Doesn't happen now, because we make them quickly. But in those days we made them very slow because I was hyper-conscious, a very self-conscious young kid. I hadn't gotten used to hearing the sound of my own voice, so it disturbed me; I hadn't gotten used to the use of the studio to get the most out of it that I wanted.

But I'll tell you, the amazing thing was: hey, we made that *Born to Run*. That was us scrubbing away in 914 Studio up in Rye, NY. And it still sounds pretty good today. It was nice when they did the 30th anniversary [reissue], I sort of got to re-experience it the way I should have when I was 24 or 25. And I was just like, whoa, yeah, this was really good!

What was it like when that album took off and you wound up on the cover of *Time* and *Newsweek* and all of that?
It was exciting . . . disturbing . . . sometimes enjoyable . . . horrifying . . . embarrassing . . . also, it was my dream come true.

It was so much more complicated than I thought it was going to be. I mean, when anybody imagines something wonderful, they only imagine the wonderful parts [*laughs*]. That's why you're imagining something wonderful! You only imagine the wonderful parts!

It's like if you see that girl walking down the street and you say, "Oh my god, life would be ecstasy if she was just my girlfriend." You're only thinking of the wonderful parts, you're not thinking . . . who knows. It's sort of like that. Success is like that girl: if only I had that, I wouldn't have a worry in the world. And then you get it, or you get in a relationship, and then you realize that there are some things I'm not good at, and she's telling me what she doesn't like about me . . . And so all of a sudden you're in the real world where it's really happening, and it's a complicated experience.

I don't have any complaints, because I wouldn't have had it any other way, no matter what it was like, because that was what I had my sights set on, and I was just gonna push on through until I figured out what to do. Because I wanted to play, I wanted an audience, I was cocky enough to think I was something special—along with, of course, thinking you're a fraud and worthless, but that's part of the artistic experience [*laughs*]. I had both sides. I had the other thing too: Hey, I'm the greatest. And I want my audience, I deserve your ears!

Steve had a lot of fun with it, because of course it wasn't *him* on the cover. But it was the band, so he bought all the magazines and passed them out around the pool at the Sunset Marquis, and I ran upstairs to my room. There was a lot of tough stuff that went with it, and it's all sort of been talked about over the years. But for a young kid . . . success is hard for any young person. I feel for the young people today when I see them out struggling, whether it's Britney Spears or somebody; it takes an enormous leap of consciousness to handle yourself well under that kind of spotlight. And most kids don't have the guidance or the facility to be able to do that at 22 or 23 years old.

I only asked one guy about it, *ever*. I happened to be in L.A. in 1975, which was right when we were exploding, and Jack Nicholson came to the show. Jack Nicholson from Neptune, New Jersey, next door to Asbury Park. He came to the show, we spent some time after the show, and he had just become quite successful himself. So I said, you know, "What was the deal, what did you think about it?"

And he said, "Well, I was older. I had been around quite a while, and I was older. And so when that happened, I was really ready for that to happen."

I was pretty young. I was 24 years old, 25, and so you make your way through it. Luckily I had the band and good people around me. The people who you see end up failing are the people who just don't have the people around them—or they simply don't and won't listen and learn. And there are a lot of folks like that out there, too.

The way the exhibit is set up, the first floor starts with the Castiles and goes up through *Born to Run*, and it's basically chronological. On the second floor, it's more thematic. There are four walls, so one wall is all of your guitars and on the other walls your songwriting stuff. Let's talk about some of the guitars for a second. The Esquire: first off, thank you so much . . .

The Esquire was purchased for 180 dollars—maybe 185 dollars. It was my official just-signed-a-record-deal-you-get-a-guitar. I got it after I signed my record deal. Previous to that, you would not have 180 dollars at any single moment. So I think my earlier guitars—good guitars I got, a Les Paul and a few other things—I had Tex co-sign for me and I paid them off week-by-week, month-by-month. For quite a few years all I did was pay off guitars.

But for the Esquire—and Mike Appel might have been with me—we went down to Phil Petillo's guitar shop in Belmar, New Jersey, on Highway 34, I believe. I went in, and I wanted a Telecaster, because I'd played a Telecaster previously when I was younger, I'd picked one up somewhere along the way. Jeff Beck was one of my great guitar heroes, and I think Pete Townshend played one in the Who also for a while. It was a guitar that was a good mixture for playing soul music, à la Steve Cropper and James Burton, and also good for rock music like Jeff Beck. So it was a versatile instrument, it was a light instrument. I wasn't playing heavy rock 'n' roll anymore, I was playing something that tilted closer to soul music, and so I wanted a guitar that could handle the funk and that feeling. And that guitar was hanging there, and I didn't ask anything about it—I just bought it.

Later on I found out—I knew a couple guys who had it before me—it's a bastard. It's not one guitar. The reason the neck says *Esquire* is because it came from another guitar, and it was a Telecaster body. And a couple of guys who had it before me—maybe Billy Ryan had that guitar, he was a very good local guitar player, played with James Cotton for a while. He might have had that guitar for a while, and I know another guy, and they kinda futzed around with it, and it ended up being what it is.

It also ended up having a very distinctive sound, and it still is unique amongst all my guitars for the way it sounds. I played it at the Super Bowl. So I still play it occasionally on stage. I have my pickup set a little different now, so I don't play as often as I did. But it is, for me . . . when I put it on, I don't feel like I have a guitar on. It's such an integral part of me. It's the only instrument that when I put it on, I can't feel anything on me. It's an extension of my body. Everything else, I'm putting a guitar on. That thing is just an extension of who I am. It literally was the receptor of all my hopes and dreams, the symbol of my ambitions and desires. I've held it aloft to the audience on thousands and thousands of nights, I suppose with the idea that it says something about the power of rock 'n' roll and the power of us.

Are there any recordings that you think that guitar is an essential part of?
I would say "Kitty's Back," I played that lead on "Kitty's Back" on it. All of the stuff from Hammersmith Odeon, the guitar sounded *so good* on that, at that show that we put out with the *Born to Run* [30th Anniversary] package. It's just very distinctive—and I had a couple of great Fender amplifiers, old Bassmans that I used, also. It was just a very warm, very old-school sound, and yet I was able to get clean funk and country playing like James Burton out of it, along with Jeff Beck-style leads.

I was going to ask you about the amps—we have two Fender Bassmans that you sent us. And one has four Fender ten-inch speakers, and the other has four Jensen ten-inchers. Any stories behind those two amps? Were they used in the studio or touring?
I don't remember—generally those Bassmans, what I used to do is wire them together and play them in stereo on either side of the drum kit. If somebody finds old photos of our stage setup, they may find two of those out there. As far as the speaker setups, you just blew them up and other ones were put in—whatever were considered to be the good speakers of the day, I suppose.

Another thing we have is the tape machine you used for *Nebraska*. Do you want to talk about those sessions?
They were pretty basic. What happened was, I got tired of spending every single penny I had making records. In 1980 when we went to go on the *River* tour, I was just broke. After almost 10 years in the music business, I had about 20 grand to my name. And this was after million-selling records and the cover of *Time* and *Newsweek*.

Now, I had gotten into a lot of trouble and made some bad deals and had to hire a lot of lawyers. And then nobody in the band had ever paid any taxes, because nobody in *New Jersey* pays any taxes [*laughs*]. At least, not amongst our crowd. I didn't know anyone who paid taxes—I didn't know anyone who had an honest job, barely. And if they *did* have a job, they were taking the money under the table. This is how everyone lived here. As a matter of fact, some of the guys who first worked for me out of New Jersey were shocked when I said that we had to pay taxes. It was like, "Hey, you trying to scam me, man?" [*Laughs*] "You're ripping me off!"

So it was a bizarre thing, I believe some enterprising young man at the IRS must have looked at the *Time* and *Newsweek* covers and asked, "Who is this guy?" and when they looked into it: "I don't know who he is, but I know one thing: he isn't paying any taxes." And so we got chased after for an enormous amount of back taxes, not one cent of which had ever been paid. So between 1974 and 1980, I paid lawyers, the tax man, tried to keep the band afloat (which I barely could), and spent money in the recording studio. The result being, in 1980, I had no money after playing for quite a while in the professional music business. And so when I came back from the *River* tour, it was the first time I had a little money in the bank, and I said, this time I'm not gonna go in and break myself again. Because the record company paid up to a certain point, but after that if you were scrubbing away in the studio learning your craft, it was on your dime, my friend. You *paid*. You just had to pay. And I was spending a lot of time learning what to do in the studio. An enormous amount: the *River* record went on for a year or two.

So I told my roadie, go out and get me some little tape player. I don't care what you get, just get me a little tape player I can sing some songs into and throw another track on, and I can tell if I have anything before I waste time and money in the studio with the band. So he came back with a little four track Teac. Set it up in my bedroom, exactly five minutes from here, right up the road. And I sat down, and in about three days I sang all the songs from *Nebraska*. I had them written, and I think there were maybe two or three takes of each; I think there's one take of "Highway Patrolman" or something, not much.

You actually could mix—you recorded to a cassette, four track to a cassette, and then you mixed it to another cassette. I mixed it through a Gibson Echoplex, which is the sound of the echo on that record—just a separate unit, an old '60s guitar Gibson Echoplex unit—onto another boombox. So the final mix came off, like, the boombox you would take to the beach.

Now the problem is, all those boomboxes are not finely honed recording equipment [*laughs*]. They're meant to suck in the sand and keep playing! Consequently, the speed of them are all different. In those days, your cassette was being played at a variety of speeds that the artists never intended. So I did the whole record, carried it around, went into the studio, blah blah blah, tried to get the band to play it, didn't sound right; tried to play it again myself, recorded it all myself, didn't sound right; tried to take the tracks that we did and remix them, didn't sound right. The better it got, the worse it got. And I also realized the tape . . . the sound we were hearing back was slightly slowed down, because the tape had been going slightly fast.

So all of these strange accidents occurred and [combined with] this junky equipment at the time to unintentionally make this very low-fi, spooky . . . I mean, I knew the mood I was going after, but a lot of it was just an accident. I was just trying to hear some songs I had written.

Another section of the second floor is about your songwriting. One of the things we have is that table you sent us, where you said you've written most of your songs.

I think I sent you the chair too? Yeah, I've written at that table since the '70s. Many, many songs have come across that table, starting with maybe the *Darkness on the Edge of Town* record. I bought it with Anthony Rioli, who was a local antique dealer and general wild man. I had a little house, and I was looking for something to write on, and we found that somewhere. But I've kept it ever since, and I think I've written as late as . . . was there anything from *Magic* written on there? Certainly *The Rising* was written there.

In general, what is your songwriting process like?

It's very relaxed. You just get an idea, and I sit down with a guitar, and it's a meditative state. Songwriting is fundamentally a meditation. It's the exercise of your craft, your intelligence. But it's primarily meditative, in that it works best when you go into a light trance-like situation. Where you just sort of start to . . . you're scraping the top of your subconscious, like with a knife. And the shavings, sometimes they turn into a song [*laughs*]. And then occasionally, the knife plummets deeply in.

It would be like having a shapeless piece of clay or something in front of you, and you just start running your fingers over it. You're just sitting there with clay. You don't have an idea of what that clay is going to be yet, you just start running your fingers over the clay. And as you're running your fingers over the clay, your emotions, who you are, the issues that are on your mind, the sounds you may want to hear, the shapes you may want to see, your relationship to the world itself begins to define itself in the images, music, and lyrics that are just kind of flowing out of you.

Then there's a point where your studied craft comes into play. In other words: okay, you've plummeted a certain amount, you've got your basic story, you've plummeted into some of your unconscious and you've come up with something that feels like life. It feels like it has some breath and some blood in it. But now you've got to call on your craft to refine it, to write well, to make good choruses, or verses.

And so your craft comes in, but you're still listening. The main thing you're doing if you have your clay in front of you, you're seeing all the time. What is assisting you in moving forward? Your eyes: you're seeing, you're seeing. If you're a musician, what is assisting you in moving forward with a song? Your ears. Every time you strum the chord, you're listening. What is the song telling you? What is the character telling you about his fate? And if you listen hard enough, and if you yourself are a seeker—in other words, your motivation is that you are in search of whatever it is you might want to call it: truth, experience, reflection of the world as it is, you want to sing your blues away, you want to sing about your gal, your friends your town, your country, your day at the beach, whatever it feel like—these things come forth and begin to sort of give shape and refinement to your thoughts and emotions.

So it's a magic act. Basically, you're in the process of . . . nothing exists in this room when I walk in, and you literally pull something from thin air and give it physical properties, and by the end someone out in the world holds it in their hand. You've taken something, you've literally, *boom*, you know, zoom, there it is. Abracadabra. But it begins in the air. It begins as ideas and emotions, and it begins as something that has no physical property whatsoever.

So it's a lot of *fun* to do, and I get great excitement, exhilaration, enjoyment out of it—and of course, occasionally it's very, very frustrating. In the old days your percentage is about 95 percent failure to about 5 percent success. But hey, if part of your 5 percent success is "Born in the U.S.A." or "Born to Run," once those things are there, you forget about the 95. It's like coming home from the dentist: you forget about the pain, and you're happy about how good your teeth look [*laughs*]. It's the same thing. It's like, once it's played, all you're thinking about is *wow, that was great.*

Do you just start with the music first? Or the words? Or is it a combination?

I don't have any rules. The only record I started words-first was my first record, because I imagined myself as being some sort of poet at the time. I would sit there with a rhyming dictionary or just by myself and pour forth with whatever the images were in my head. Later on, almost immediately—and even on that record—the music is so evocative that you use it.

Like on this record, *Working on a Dream*, I had a very specific idea of what I wanted the music on the record to be like. I wanted a very big, orchestral kind of rock music.

Your inner world is a mine, and there are many, many different veins. And if you work one vein a lot, it may go dry. *The Ghost of Tom Joad* and *Devils & Dust*, okay, I don't have any more of these songs in me right now. But then you may, if you turn around and your eyes are open so you can see, you may go *oh, what's that over there?* Chip chip boom, a vein of a certain kind of music may come bursting forth and music will pour out of you. The minute you finish a record, sometimes.

This was something I didn't allow myself to do in the early days. I only looked at one vein—the vein I was very concerned about defining myself with—and ignored everything else. And that's what's on *Tracks*; I ignored a lot of good music! But now I don't do that. Now, I'm open to whatever feels like it's going to come through my creative system at a given moment. So at the end of *Magic*: wow, "Girls in Their Summer Clothes," that was fun. I like that big production style, I haven't done that in a long, long time. That brings you to come up with another song. And then you go home that night and think, man, I'd really like to make something big, and rich, and romantic, but that carries with it the concerns of somebody at my age. Innocent and kind of knowing at the same time. And take that sound—the sound of which is basically the sound of innocence in those days of the Beach Boys and [Phil] Spector—and take that sound and combine it with my 60 years of experience on the planet Earth. And so you have *Working on a Dream*.

"Outlaw Pete"—people said I was ripping off a Kiss song, actually I thought I was ripping off [Van Dyke Parks and Brian Wilson's] "Heroes and Villains" [*laughs*]. There was a vein that just comes rushing out. And these days I'm able to listen to it, and work on it, and I'm able to get more music to my fans.

Is there one guitar you normally use to write with?
Nope. I pick up anything that is around. If I have something nice around—I have some just beautiful-*looking* guitars. A guitar is a fetish object. That's why people love them, that's why they're used in fashion ads—they're fetish objects. The design of the guitar is incredible. I mean, they're shaped like women, number one; and they look like circus implements [*laughs*]. They may be sparkly, they may be metal flaked, but they're beautiful things simply to look upon. So a guitar can be inspiring, just picking it up and feeling the wood and smelling it. The smell of a guitar is a wonderful thing: put your nose to the strings and smell the inside, the wood. It's a very . . . dreaming sort of object. So I have a few nice ones in my room. But otherwise, I'll just pick up anything that's around, whatever happens to be available. And if you're gonna write, you're gonna write.

We also have a lot of your songwriting notebooks, and I noticed that you filled them up from cover to cover, and that there'll be several drafts of one song.
Sure. I did a lot of rewriting; I suppose I still do a reasonable amount. Probably less than I did at the time, because at the time I was trying to shape who I was and what I wanted to be about, and what I wanted to write about, and how I wanted the world to see me, and how I wanted to see myself. And also, the kind of writing I was interested in doing, which was using very classic rock 'n' roll archetypes—cars, girls, Saturday night, the job, the end of the day, all things that had long been written about in popular music and blues music—you're either going to turn them into something that are archetypes or clichés. And so, you start out usually with clichés. And I did a lot of shaving away to turn them into something more than that, to turn them into sort of classic images that I was able to use to express my own life experience.

So in the beginning, I knew enough to go, *if I get this wrong, it isn't going to be any good*. And so on *Born to Run*, I took a lot of time trying to find that place, trying to find *me* in those images, me and my world, the world in 1974 post-Vietnam America.

And okay, if Brian Wilson was . . . "Racing in the Street" I always thought was like a sequel to "Don't Worry Baby." You put ten to 15 years on the guy in "Don't Worry Baby," and he's the guy in "Racing in the Street."

That was how I was thinking about things, and so there was a good amount of rewriting. Those were the days I'd second-guess, third-guess, fourth-guess, fifth-guess and sixth-guess myself constantly, until I got exhausted and then finally decide on something and put it out.

It seems like there are a lot of drafts from the *Born in the U.S.A.* period, too.
There were just a lot of drafts from a lot of the stuff. *Bon in the U.S.A.*, I wrote I don't know how many songs for that record. Many, many, many. Look at the outtakes that are on *Tracks*, and that's probably just a part of them. I did a lot of writing before I felt comfortable putting something out.

So one of the other sections of the exhibit focuses on your tours, and one of the things I like is the set of the hotel room keys from one of the early tours.
Yeah, I wanted to remember where I'd been. And so what I started to do was just keep the keys. And I had a piece of rawhide or something, and as we traveled I'd just slip each key on that piece of rawhide. And in those days you either stayed in a Holiday Inn—that was when we hit it *big*. When we knew we were going to a Holiday Inn, we were like "Oh thank God, we will sleep well tonight!" But there were a lot of [others] . . . they gave you a key on a big piece of plastic that said the town, the city, the hotel. And I just started to keep them, just as a way of knowing, like, I've been here, I've been there, I've been everywhere [*laughs*].

It's funny, Tim Schmit of the Eagles, one of the things he gave us—he did the same thing on one of the tours, and his are just thrown in like a gym bag or whatever. It's in the L.A. section where we have stuff for the Eagles.
It was a reminder that you were *somewhere* . . . That you've been someplace. It's such a rootless existence, it's so transitory, you're moving around so much.

We have the keys to various cities like Youngstown and Freehold. How does it feel to be awarded those things?
I didn't put a lot of stock in it [*laughs*]. It's kind of nice, it's okay, people come out to the show and come backstage and say, "Here's the key to the city, my friend!" and you go, "Thank you, sir, thank you!"

I always just thought that it meant that any time when you truly fucked it up badly and screwed everything up in your life, that you could then come back to that city, and you have the *key* to that city. So you will then be able to eat, survive, and somehow be accepted at your lowest. I don't think that's what they actually mean, but that was my fantasy. My fantasy was once you got the key to the city, son, you always have a home; no matter how the world treats you or how terrible things may get, or how badly you may screw up your entire life, you can always come back to Freehold or Youngstown, Ohio, and someone will buy you a beer here. I'm not sure if that's what it means, but that was always kind of my take on it.

We also have the Blistex Beautiful Lips award, too.
That's incredible [*laughs*].

In terms of people coming to the exhibit, is there anything you hope people take away from it?
Generally, because I'm really not its creator—I guess that's you guys—my take on it is that you're providing people who've been interested in your work a little extra information about where you come from. I was always interested in, like, gee, I'd like to see Elvis's shoe rack [*laughs*]. "Is that Elvis's shoe rack? Is that *really* Elvis's shoe rack?" It's like, "Man, I saw Elvis's shoe rack!"

So, it's fun to go see, like Elvis's Cadillac. I went to the Country Hall of Fame and they had, I forget who has the Cadillac with all the silver dollars in it. They're just funny totems of people's lives, and it gives you a little more of a tactile sense . . . you know, I think the hardest thing to believe when you're a rock fan is that these things are real. In other words, I will occasionally run into someone from some gorgeous part of the globe—Stockholm, Paris, Barcelona—who tell me they just came back from a wonderful vacation in Asbury Park, New Jersey [*laughs*]. And not only that, but while they were there they saw Freehold. And I always go, "Whoa, you're telling me that you had two weeks off and you spent it . . ." you know [*laughs*]. It's funny in a sense, but I understand it also, because I've driven through Memphis. I've driven past Sun Studios. I just wanted to know it was there, that it was real. That all of that stuff *really* happened. That there was a moment and a place in time when some kid stood in that room, that tiny little room right there. That room has its physical properties—it's only x by x wide, it's got these four walls, it's an actual place on earth—and something otherworldly occurred, something that touched me so fundamentally in my soul that it changed my life, and it came out of this actual place. And if it came out of this actual place, that means that where *I* am is real, too, and who knows what can come out of *my* town.

So I think that the *things*, if they have any value whatsoever beyond pure curiosity items, are tangible evidence that the things that meant a lot to you—the people, the group of musicians—have a town just like yours. And it's still there. It's still physically there, you can drive through it, you can put your feet on its streets. And there's something about that, because I meet a lot of people who do make their pilgrimages for one reason or another to this place or another. So the *stuff* is important in that sense.

Like I said, I was never much of a collector. I have a few things from other artists that were gifts that mean a lot to me, but I don't have much. But they are talismans. They're talismans of the connection between the emotional world—the world of people's dreams, hopes, fears, desires, ambitions—and the real physical world, the one that we live in and we drive through in a very mundane way on a daily basis. There's something about that physical-ness of things that a) it's fun to see, but b) it also brings it into the realm of the real for your fan.

If I see one of Elvis's guitars, or one of Roy Orbison's . . . "Wow. There it is." That's part of the magic trick, right? That's the magician's tools. And those things. . . . if somebody did a nice magic trick, those things are always fun to see and be around.

International Press Conference in Paris, February 2012

At a Paris press conference held at the Théatre Marigny, Springsteen spent an hour fielding numerous questions about the new record *Wrecking Ball*, the psychology of anger, the state of America, Clarence Clemons, his autobiography, his falsetto, and much more. "My work," he reiterated, "has always been about judging the distance between American reality and the American dream."

––––––––––––

Ladies and gentlemen, it's time for me to fulfill a lifetime dream, to share a stage with Bruce Springsteen. A few introductory questions about *Wrecking Ball*. I'm curious to know why you've changed your producer, after working with Brendan O'Brien for so many years, and I'd like to know more about the process of recording.

The guy who produced this record is a fellow named Ron Aniello. I assisted him, and Jon [Landau] executive produced. Ron had worked on a few of Patti [Scialfa]'s records previously, and I was actually working on another record before this record. I spent on-and-off about a year on that one before I threw it out, which is something I do every once in a while. He came in to help me finish that one, and as we went along, a few of the songs started to come up for this record; he had a lot of fresh ideas about the way the music could sound, and he had a large library of sounds—alternative and hip-hop elements—and we used quite a bit of different looping techniques. It was just a very different experience, really, with the two of us in the studio when we started out.

You were in your hometown in New Jersey for these recording sessions?
Yeah, we were in our own studio, and each one of the songs started off as kind of a folk song, with just me and the acoustic guitar. And then everything else got slipped on.

And you had special guests, like Tom Morello . . .
Tommy Morello from Rage Against the Machine, he came in and played the guitar on "This Depression" and on "Jack of All Trades." Patti and Soozie sang; Max plays on a cut; Clarence is on "Land of Hope and Dreams."

As we have all heard, it's a very powerful record that could have been written by both a wise old dog and a very young, brilliant man. Would you say you write more strongly when you're pissed off?
You can never go wrong pissed off in rock 'n' roll. The first half of it, particularly, is very angry. The genesis of the record was after 2008, when we had the huge financial crisis in the States, and there was really no accountability for years and years. People lost their homes, and I had friends who were losing their homes, and nobody went to jail. Nobody was responsible. People lost enormous amounts of their net worth. Previous to Occupy Wall Street, there was no pushback: there was no movement, there was no voice that was saying just how outrageous—that a basic theft had occurred that struck at the heart of what the entire American idea was about. It was a complete disregard of history, of context, of community; it was all about "what can I get today." It was just an enormous fault line that cracked the American system wide open. And I think its repercussions are just beginning to really, really be felt.

So I think I wrote "We Take Care of Our Own" somewhere around 2009 or 2010, and I put it away in my book. And the idea behind that song was that's what's *supposed* to happen, but was not happening. My work has always been about judging the distance between American reality and the American dream—how far is that at any given moment. If you go back to the work that I did beginning certainly in the late '70s, I'm always measuring that distance: how close are we, how far are we, how close are we? Everything from *Darkness on the Edge of Town, The River,* to *Nebraska, Born in the U.S.A., The Ghost of Tom Joad,* those are all records that were always taking the measure of that distance.

That song, "We Take Care of Our Own," it asks the question that the rest of the record tries to answer. Which is, of course: Do we? Do we take care of our own? And we often don't. We don't provide an equal playing field for all our citizens. And at the same time, it doesn't cede what would be patriotism or images like the flag to just the right. I claim those, as I've done in a lot of my work throughout the years. The rest of the record tries to answer the questions that come up in the last verse of that song: Where are the merciful hearts? Where is the work that I need? Where is the spirit that reigns over me? Where are the eyes that see? Those are the questions the rest of the record tries to answer and that are embedded in the *question* that the title of that song is, "We Take Care of Our Own."

Concerning patriotism, aren't you afraid that a song like this, "We Take Care of Our Own," might be misunderstood like "Born in the U.S.A."?
You can't be afraid of those images. I mean, I write carefully and precisely, and I believe clearly. And then you put it out there, and people hear it, and then it's up to them. And if you're missing it, you're not quite thinking hard enough; you know, you need to go back and take a second look sometimes. But I don't want to cede those feelings to just the right side of the street. I don't like to do that. Which is why my work is often claimed by different political groups, because there is a feeling of patriotism underneath. That's something I've had in "Land of Hope and Dreams," and in my best music. But at the same time, it's a very critical, questioning, often angry sort of patriotism. That's not something I'm prepared to give up for fear that somebody might simplify what I'm saying.

I have many questions, but I'm not supposed to be the only one to ask.
Okay. I know: how did I get this good looking? I can't tell you. All right, next? [*Laughs*] Genes. Next?
    [*Moderator opens questions to the floor*]

On this record, you include songs that aren't exactly new, with "Land of Hope and Dreams" and "Wrecking Ball" having been performed before. But they fit in the moment, right?

"Wrecking Ball" seemed like a metaphor for what had occurred—it's an image where something is destroyed to build something new, and it was also an image [suggesting] just the flat destruction of some fundamental American values and ideas that occurred over the past 30 years. It was a 30-year process of deregulation and different things that added up to the inequality that we're experiencing in the States right now. So, it seemed like a good metaphor.

With "Land of Hope and Dreams," I needed a song that was very spiritual, because the record moves from guys who are really very angry to guys who are angry but constructive. To me there's always a spiritual element in that, and a religious element to some degree. Maybe that's just my Catholic upbringing, but that's how I write about it. So that song was *big* enough.

The trouble with a record, if you write a really big song at the beginning, the record demands to gain size as it goes along—or else you blew your wad at the top, my friend [*laughs*]. That's why, how many records do you put on where it's like, hey, that first song! . . . That second song's good . . . [*snores*]. You're out by number seven or eight.

But on our records, I try to build them so there's a question asked, and there are scenarios where those questions are played out. If you look at this record, there's a question asked: *Do we* take care of our own? I don't think so, a lot of times. So then there are scenarios where you meet the characters who have been impacted by the failure of those ideas and values. You get to the guy on "Easy Money," he's going out for a robbing spree—which is really just what's occurred at the top of the pyramid. He's imitating your guys on Wall Street the only way he knows how: I'm going out tonight for easy money.

If you trace it along, every song introduces you to a slightly different character. Then at the end, I've got to find some way to meld their stories together so it all makes sense to you. I've got to try to find some way not necessarily to *answer* the question that I asked, but to move the question forward, to move the ideas forward, to move forward in the search for a new day. "A new day" comes up a lot in the record, which is really just, okay, how do you move forward? I'm interested in that.

So the record has to build, and it has to expand emotionally and spiritually, and it's also supposed to be throwing you a good time in the mix. You know, it's got to sound good and play great. That's always a challenge, but "Land of Hope and Dreams" was a song of such size and spiritual dimension that by the time the end of the record came around, it fit really well.

Also, those are voices from history and other sides of the grave. If you listen to the record, I use a lot of folk music. There's some Civil War music. There's gospel music. There are '30s horns in "Jack of All Trades." That's the way I used the music—the idea was that the music was going to contextualize historically that this has happened before: it happened in the 1970s, it happened in the '30s, it happened in the 1800s . . . it's cyclical. Over, and over, and over, and over again. So I try to pick up some of the continuity and the historical resonance through the music.

In the past, you've committed yourself to play for presidential candidates, and of course the presidential election is coming up this year in the U.S. Are you planning to sing or do some concerts for Barack Obama?
I got into that sort of by accident. What it was, the Bush years were so horrific that you couldn't just sit around. I never campaigned for a politician previous to John Kerry. But at that moment it was such a blatant disaster occurring at the top of government that you felt if you had any cachet whatsoever, you had to cash it in, because you couldn't sit around and watch it. So I campaigned for John Kerry, and Obama last time—and I'm glad that I did—but I'm not a professional campaigner, and every four years I don't think I'm gonna pick a guy and go out for him. I'd prefer to stay on the sidelines. I generally believe an artist is supposed to be the canary in the coalmine, and you're better off with a certain distance from the seat of power.

In 2008, you came out very strongly for President Obama. Are you still in the same mood today?
I think he did a lot of good things: he kept GM alive, which was incredibly important to Detroit, Michigan. He got the healthcare law passed, though I wish there had been a public option and that it didn't leave citizens the victims of the insurance companies. He killed Osama bin Laden, which I think was extremely important. He brought some sanity to the top level of government.

He's more friendly to corporations than I thought he would be, and there aren't as many middle class or working class voices heard in the administration as I thought there would be. I would have liked to see more active job creation sooner than it came, and I'd like to have seen some of these foreclosures stopped or somehow mitigated. The banks have had some kind of a settlement, a partial settlement, but really, there's a lot of people it's not going to assist. I still support the president, but there are plenty of things—I thought Guantanamo would have been closed by now. On the other hand, we're out of Iraq, and hopefully we'll be out of Afghanistan soon.

So many people after 9/11, and so many people these past couple years, look to you for your interpretation of events. Does that make you feel any kind of a burden? That so many people care? Look at us: when we were waiting for you earlier, so many people care about what you think, and what you feel about what is happening in the world.
Actually, I'm terribly burdened, and at night when I'm sleeping in my big house, it's killing me [*laughs*]. It's a rough life, it's a *brutal* life! The rock music business: brutal, brutal, brutal. Don't believe what anybody tells you.

No, it's a *blessed* life. And these are just things I'm interested in, and things I've been interested in having a conversation with my audience about.

I enjoyed artists when I was young who tried to, one way or another, take on the world—for better or for worse—and who were involved in the events of the day as well as just entertaining people. I have a big audience: I have Democrats, I have plenty of Republicans, I have people who just come to dance and enjoy themselves, and people who are interested in the social aspects of what I'm writing about. And I've really just enjoyed it all.

So I just enjoy having that conversation. If I have something to say or if I can write a song about it at a given time, I do. And if I don't, then I don't. I write to process my own experiences. I always figured that if I do that for me, then I do that for you. You write for yourself initially, just trying to understand the world you live in. And if you do that well enough, then it projects to your audience. But I'm not in elective office where I have to come up with a plan every day. I don't experience it as a burden. It's not like that. It's pretty much a charmed life, I would say, if you're a musician. That's why they call it *playing*.

On this record, more than ever, we have spiritual references, biblical quotes, things like that. Is it because you feel your own mortality now?
No, I think I just got completely brainwashed as a child with Catholicism. Once you're in . . . it's like that Al Pacino line, *I keep trying to get out, they keep pulling me back!* Once you're a Catholic, you're always a Catholic. You get involved in these things in your very, very formative years. I took religious education for the first eight years of school; I lived next to a church, a convent, a rectory, and the Catholic school. I saw every wedding, every funeral, every Mass. Your life was filled with the smell of incense and priests and nuns coming and going, so it's given me a very active sense of spiritual life, and made it very difficult sexually, but that's all right [*laughs*].

On another subject, could you say a few words about the transition from Clarence Clemons to Jake? There's a great portion of your eulogy where you say, "Clarence doesn't leave the E Street Band when *he* dies. He leaves when *we* die."
I met Clarence when I was 22. That's my son's age. I look at my son, and he's still a child, you know? Twenty-two is . . . you're just a kid. And I guess Clarence might have been 30 at the time, so it goes back to the beginning of my adult life. And we had a relationship that was, I would say, *elemental*, from the very beginning. It wasn't about anything we necessarily said to one another, it was just about what happened when we got close. Something happened. It fired people's imaginations; it fired my own imagination and my own dreams. It made me want to write songs for that saxophone sound.

Losing Clarence is like losing something elemental. It's like losing the rain, or air. And that's a part of life. The currents of life affect even the dream world of popular music; there's no escape. And so that is just something that's going to be missing.

We're lucky in that we have people around: we have Eddie Manion, who had played with the Sessions Band, Southside Johnny, and our band previously; and Clarence's brother had a son who, in 1988, came and saw his uncle play the saxophone. Clarence mentioned Jake to me quite a few years ago, and he was on the road with us a bit during the last tour, and he plays very well. He's also been around the band and understands what our band is about. We were together with Clarence the week he passed away, and there's a good musical and spiritual connection to Jake. So I'm excited about it. I think it's going to add to the new conversation about these things that we're going to have with the audience when we come out on stage.

I heard that you're going to have a complete horn section on tour—it takes a full horn section to replace Clarence.
It does—it takes a *village* to replace the Big Man! It takes many men! [*laughs*] So, we'll do the best we can.

Do you think it's going to change something in your stage personality?
I don't know. It will change everything a little bit—or a lot. The thrust of the music will still be what it is, but it's a big loss. Any time you lose . . . you know, we lost Danny [Federici], and these are guys that you've been with for 35 or 40 years, and you just enjoyed them being there, you know? But you move on. Life doesn't wait.

So Clarence has to be replaced, you replaced Max at a few concerts with his son . . .
Right. I'm working on replacing myself now, and I'm gonna stay home. I will be home, and somebody else can do it [*laughs*].

On the last tour, you paid tribute to Joe Strummer, and you showed some support for Gaslight Anthem, and it seems you're still a huge, huge music fan. I was wondering, as you look back at your music fandom, what four or five bands would you start and end with?
My own music fandom? Oh gosh . . . I hate to speak them aloud [*laughs*]. Because in truth, there were so many. I'd say one of the greatest things about music fandom is if you have one other person who is as fanatic about it as you are. That would be Steve [Van Zandt] for me. Steve and I have shared an insane and intense love affair with rock 'n' roll music since we were teenagers. If a guy changed the way he combed his hair, if they changed their outfits . . . pop is all about obsession with detail. It's a world of symbolism, and you live and die by that sword, for better or worse. But it's also a lot of fun, and fun to argue about and fun to debate about.

So one of the great things was my connection with Steve in that area, and also with Jon. Jon was another freak who just was—it was all about the music. That's the most important thing. You've got to have a friend or a pal who is sort of alongside of you in your *insanity* and knows why you can spend three hours debating these things. I remember Steve and I on the bus to New York City, battling who was supreme at the time, Led Zeppelin or the Jeff Beck Group. Old Elvis, young Elvis. It goes on forever. It still goes on to this day. So that's a great blessing. I wish all of you a good rock 'n' roll partner.

When you were younger, you could spend a full year agonizing about a drum sound in the studio. Now you release a record every two years.
Now I just agonize. It's not over anything special [*laughs*]. That's the adult. When you're an adult, you don't have to worry about it as much . . .

Does that mean you're not trying to write "the great American novel," with every record as one chapter?
Mainly, you're trying to make a good record. You're trying to make a record that won't waste people's time. You're trying to be an honest broker with your fans—if I'm asking them to listen to it, I've got to know that it's everything I have, at least at that moment. That's why I think my relationship with my audience remains so vital and so present.

You're always out there shooting for the moon, but in different ways. That hasn't really changed. Our intentions on this album were no more nor less than our intentions on *Born to Run* or *Nebraska*. My intention is to do what, say, Bob Dylan did for me, which is to sort of kick open the door to your mind and your body, and make you want to move and think and experience and get angry and fall in love and reach for something higher than yourself and grovel around in something lower than that, also [*laughs*]. That's the job description. That's what people are paying you the money for: they're paying you the money for something that can't be bought. That's the trick. And that's what you're supposed to deliver. You're being paid for something that can't be bought; it can only be *manifested* and *shared*. That's when you're doing a good job.

Can I ask you about anger? About the anger you might feel, the anger there seems to be so much of in America in the last four to five years, that anger that surfaced in the Tea Party . . . Does that anger get to you? And what do you see as its source?
I think our politics come out of psychology, whether we like to think so or not. And psychology, of course, comes out of your formative years. So my experience growing up—between when I was born to when I was 18,

I grew up in a house where my mother was the primary breadwinner, and she worked very hard every day. My father struggled to find work, and I saw that it was deeply painful and created a crisis of masculinity, and that it was something that was irreparable at the end of the day.

Those conditions are present in the United States right now, where you have a service economy overtaking a manufacturing economy. You've got a lot of guys who worked in manufacturing whose jobs have disappeared, and who are not necessarily coming out of those manufacturing jobs with the skills to move into a service economy. It's a very, very different world. And so you have quite a few homes where the man is no longer the primary breadwinner.

I think that the lack of work creates a loss of self. Work creates an enormous sense of self, as I saw in my mother. My mother was an inspiring, towering figure to me in the best possible way, and I picked up a lot of the way that I work from her. She was my working example: just steadfast, just relentless. But I also picked up a lot of the fallout. When your father doesn't have those things, it results in a house that turns into quite a bit like a minefield. And it can be abusive in different ways—just tremendous emotional turmoil.

So, I kind of lost him, and I think a lot of the anger that surfaced in my music from day one comes out of that particular scene. And as I got older, I looked toward not just the psychological reasons in our house, but the social forces that played upon our home and made life more difficult. And that led me into a lot of the writing that I've done.

I'm motivated *circumstantially* by the events of the day: that's unfair; that's theft; that's against what we believe in; that's not what America is about. But the deepest motivation—and the reasons to ask those questions, ultimately—comes out of the house that I grew up in and the circumstances that were there, which is mirrored around the United States with the level of unemployment we have right now. It's devastating. People have to work. The country should strive for full employment. It's the single thing that brings a sense of self and self-esteem, and a sense of place, a sense of belonging.

There are times in the new songs when you come close to calling for an uprising. Can you really foresee that kind of response in America?
Well, the thing that has happened that's good in the States: there's no doubt that the Occupy Wall Street movement in the United States was powerful about changing the national conversation, which has been

stuck for decades primarily coming from the right. The Tea Party set it for quite a while, and if you saw the initial years of the Obama presidency, he was kind of working under the national tone that the Tea Party set.

The minute Occupy Wall Street occurred, suddenly people were talking about economic inequality. *No one* has gotten *anybody* in the States to talk about economic inequality for the past two decades. You had politicians who tried—John Edwards tried with his "two Americas"—but they couldn't get any traction. The labor movement wasn't successful bringing that up as a current issue. But people in the street do it, and it works. It works. And if you look now, suddenly you've got Newt Gingrich calling Mitt Romney a vulture capitalist [*laughs*]. I mean, that's impossible! That would never have occurred in ten million years without Occupy Wall Street. Where they go from here? I don't know, and they've got to be careful; it's a very delicate dance, and you don't want to alienate the people who you're speaking to. You can go off the edges with it. But it was without a doubt very important in changing the tenor of the national conversation. If you go to the United States right now, there's discussion about the 1 percent and the 99 percent; you have people talking about economic inequality, and what to do about that, for the first time in a very, very, very long time.

I'd like to talk about your version of American patriotism, which has always been inclusive and generalist: it doesn't matter where you come from, you can get on the train. And then you look at America and the way that the Tea Party is polarizing one side, and there are people who don't even believe that Obama is an American. Do you think that the political system is actually irreparably damaged? Can you actually have a "United" States?
I don't know. I think this is the issue: we've destroyed the idea of an equal playing field. They've had some recent studies that say, depending on where you come from, no, you *can't* get on the train. There was a study recently that said that people were locked into the strata under which they were born. If you were born at the top, your chances for progress were great, and if you were born struggling, more often than not that's where you were going to remain. So that's a big promise that's been broken.

There's a critical mass point where a society collapses. You can't have a civilization where the society is so factionalized—you just can't have it. People have got to be connected; everyone's welfare has got to be connected. So, that's a huge, huge challenge. The unemployment level is dropping a little now, which is good, but it's going to take a long time to even remotely get back to the employment level we were at just a few years ago. Is it irreparable? I don't know the answer to your question.

I read somewhere that you were working on your autobiography. Is that true? And how's it going?
I wrote a little bit, and then I stopped for a couple of years. I haven't looked at it in quite a while. It's one of those things . . . I wrote a little bit at one time, but then I see in the newspaper that everybody else is writing them, and so you don't want to be just another goldfish in a bowl. It's like: hey, Pete Townshend! He's got one coming! Neil Young! He's got one coming . . . ahhhh, fuck it, the hell with it [*laughs*].

What would you call it?
The . . . Handsomest Man in Show Business [*laughs*]. No, I have no idea. *My Story! . . . I Believe!* I may call it that. *According to Me* [*laughs*].

I was just curious, how, throughout the years, throughout all your albums, how are you still keeping in touch with the public concern? I mean, practically, are you involved in your local community?
Well, there's an idea that it would be hard to do, but I don't think that it is; I think you can *make* it hard. We have organizations we've worked with for 25 or 30 years, in every city and also in my local area. But really, I think the answer to what you're asking, and I get asked this a lot, is that you have to remain interested and awake. You have to remain alert. You have to be constantly listening—and interested in listening—to what's going on every day. You have to remain interested in life and in the way the world's moving. You have to be awake and listening—that would be the best way that I would put it. As a writer, the way that I write, it's like you're hungry for food. That's the writing impulse. The writing impulse is the same as one for hunger or for sex—it's like that. It's not something that's related to your commercial fortunes. I mean, I'd do it for free. I'm glad that they're paying me, but it was something I did for free before they were paying me.

And so I'm constantly looking—the writer looks for something to

push up against. Tom Stoppard, the playwright, once said he was envi-
ous of Vaclav Havel because he had so much to push up against, and he
wrote so beautifully about it. I'd prefer to stay out of prison if I can, but
I knew what he was talking about. You need something pushing, pushing back at you, and you tend to do your best work when there's something that you can really, really push up against. And there has been in
the States over the past—certainly for me, over the past 30 years, but
that's come to a head over the past four years now. So this record, there
was quite a bit to write about.

**I want to ask a question about your singing. You have a wide range
now—you can go from a very high falsetto to a strong and deep
voice. Do you feel you're still improving?**
[*Sings falsetto*]: Yes, I do! I do, I do, I do . . . [*sings deep*]: I do. [*Laughs*]
For some reason when I got around 40, I was able to sing high all of a
sudden. I'm not sure why. I used to have a harder time when I was
younger; I have a little bit of a falsetto now that I didn't have. Look at
Tony Bennett: Tony Bennett's 85 and he's still singing. He still sings
great. So I think you need a little bit of luck, and then you have to have
something you're dying to sing about.

**Do you feel more powerful as a musician than you would be if you
were a politician?**
A politician? No, I could never be a politician. I just don't have the
skills. Everything that I've studied was about learning how to do my job
as a musician better, and also trying to understand the arc of my own
life and my family's life—an immigrant family that came to the United
States. I thought that there was something common in that, that if I
understood that about me, I might be able to illuminate something
about your life. That's all I do. I have no interest in any other job, really,
and I have no other skills whatsoever. So I'm hoping to continue to remain "powerful" as a musician [*laughs*] as best as I can.

**I know you've spoken about Clarence a bit already, but I just
wanted to ask, with respect to the actual making of this album, did
the passing of Clarence have any effect on that?**
Well, most of the record was made; 95 percent of it was made, and it
wasn't an E Street Band record. It was basically a solo project. So that
didn't immediately impact the record. This record took quite a different

musical tilt. We were lucky to get him on "Land of Hope and Dreams," which was essential—really essential. When he comes up, it's just a lovely moment for me.

Two years ago, onstage in Glastonbury, you joined a small band from New Jersey called the Gaslight Anthem. Is it true that your sons make you listen to new bands?
Yeah! You know, music is a family business. Of course, you're always concerned that your kids might . . . I mean, it's what Mom and Dad do, how cool can it be? I always say, kids wouldn't mind coming out to see 60,000 people boo you, but who wants to see 60,000 people cheer their parents? Nobody really wants to see that—I don't care how great a kid you are, you don't want to see that. Booing, *that's* interesting.

But he ended up with tremendous musical taste and a great musical appetite, and he just began, "Hey Dad, come here. Check it out." So I actually heard a lot of music that way: Gaslight Anthem, Dropkick Murphys, Bad Religion, Against Me! . . . a lot of young musicians through his guidance. I've gone to quite a few shows with him, and we've had some great times, so it's a nice thing to share.

I want to ask about your songwriting process. Do you set aside time each day to write? And can you talk about how inspiration comes?
I don't set aside any time in the day. I write when the fire gets lit, and then I do it in spare time. I work at home, so there's always something going on—somebody needs to be picked up from school, somebody needs to be dropped off at school. But it doesn't take me long, like it used to. These songs were all written . . . "We Take Care of Our Own," "Shackled and Drawn," and "Rocky Ground" came along for almost a gospel album package I was thinking about. And then the other things came very quickly, one after another, as soon as I found the voice that I was going to use. "Easy Money," and then the rest of the songs came pretty quickly, one day at a time.

The main thing writing is about, a lot of it is *waiting*. You may wait a year to write something good. So you have to be pretty good at waiting. And I may write a lot in the meantime—I wrote 30 or 40 songs before these songs, just to sort of keep everything going.

The inspiration thing, if that's what you'd call it, it's like a visitation. Something happens where suddenly, it's like the planets aligning: the times, what's in the air, what's inside of you, there's your craft, your skills . . . and suddenly they go *click*. And zoom. If they don't align, nothing happens. When it clicks—when the times, you, your story, the story that is alive out there at the moment, what's going on in the world, your craft, your skills align like that—then bang, it comes out, and then good things happen. Hopefully. You sort of wait for that moment a lot.

One last question. Should they ever start filming *The Sopranos* again, would you join Stevie in that? What would be a part for you? I have no acting skills whatsoever. This is all the acting I can do, and I'm doing it right now. So you see, it would be very dull. But Steve, on the other hand, is naturally hilarious, as he has been since the day I met him. He was quite a natural. I'm going to stick to music for now.

Before we go, just a personal favor . . . can you do that falsetto again? I'm not gonna be as good as Obama. Obama can *sing*. Did you see that? [*Sings falsetto*]: "Let's stay together." I can't do it [*laughs*]. He's better than me!

Robert Santelli
Grammy.com,
February 7, 2013

Robert Santelli is the executive director of the GRAMMY Museum. His books include *Greetings from E Street: The Story of Bruce Springsteen and the E Street Band*. This interview was posted just before the 2013 GRAMMY award ceremony, to mark Springsteen being honored as the 2013 MusiCares Person of the Year.

Perhaps more than any other recording artist today, Bruce Springsteen celebrates the power and glory of the gospel of rock and roll. After more than 40 years of strapping on a guitar and fronting a band, Springsteen has reached a point in his career where he could rest on his laurels and few would blame him. Only he hasn't. And won't. Not now. Not tomorrow. Probably not ever.

Here's proof: Instead of slowing down, he's sped up. Instead of playing less, he's playing more. Instead of becoming soft and more forgiving, he's become hard and more pressing. Springsteen used to play three-hour-plus shows—with an intermission. Now he plays four hours—with no intermission.

Given a long, distinguished career that includes world tours, sold-out stadium shows, No. 1 albums, 20 GRAMMY Awards, a Rock and Roll Hall of Fame induction, and a Kennedy Center Honor, Springsteen could write safe and secure albums that cater to modern pop sensibilities and the charts. But *Wrecking Ball*, his latest effort, is a masterpiece of intensity and fury. It pokes a finger in the chest of our national leaders and demands answers as to why we've come to a place where the American dream is in jeopardy of losing its soul and promise.

Recently, I met up with Springsteen in Portland, Oregon, at the Rose Quarter, where he and the E Street Band were to perform. He had just finished soundcheck, which, after finalizing sound levels and lighting cues, turned into a playful romp through the catalog of Paul Revere and The Raiders, a Pacific Northwest group from the '60s particularly popular in Portland.

I first interviewed Springsteen in 1973 when I was a budding music journalist for the *Asbury Park Press* on the Jersey Shore. Back then he was hoping to make an impression beyond the bars and boardwalk of the Shore with his debut album, *Greetings from Asbury Park, N.J.* To say he's come a long way is an understatement. Now, he participates in presidential campaigns and owns a body of work that tells us as much about America as reading John Steinbeck or listening to Woody Guthrie.

Thoughtful and certainly aware of his musical and cultural importance, Springsteen takes his role as one of our greatest music treasures quite seriously. Giving back is something that he's most concerned with, be it through his charitable endeavors, his benefit concerts, or his committed care for people who have been dealt a lesser hand. It's the main reason why Springsteen is the 2013 MusiCares Person of the Year.

What does it mean to be honored as MusiCares' 2013 Person of the Year? You're joining an impressive list of honorees.
It's really nice, really an honor. I remember I was a part of the program when MusiCares honored James Taylor. As a music event, it was very enjoyable. It's a great organization. I'm glad to be a part of it.

Over the years you've supported many causes and charities, but none seem closer to your heart than feeding the hungry. How did this act of philanthropy get to the top of your list?
In the early 1980s, at the start of the *Born in the U.S.A.* tour, I went to Pittsburgh and met a labor organizer there who told me about how the area had been affected by deindustrialization and widespread unem-

ployment. He had set up a food bank for steel workers who were having problems feeding their families. The whole food bank program was just beginning to form back then. I was looking for some way to put my music to some service on a nightly basis. You go into a town, you play a little music, you leave something behind. That idea connected us to the local community. It was a very simple idea, but it really resonated with me.

More recently, you've been very involved with relief efforts for the victims of Hurricane Sandy. Being from the Jersey Shore, where so much damage has occurred, must make this a very important project for you.

Anyone who's grown up or lived on the Jersey Shore knows the place is unique. I've watched Asbury Park try to get back up on its feet for 25 years. It's hard to see any setback at all. The Jersey Shore is the kind of place where the policeman has a little cottage that might have been in the family for years and many other people call home. The destruction was unimaginable. It's going to take years to overcome. I'm trying to do whatever I can to help my neighbors get back to some sort of normal life.

In 2012 the United States celebrated the centennial of the birth of Woody Guthrie, one of our greatest songwriters. Can you describe his influence on your music as well as your life?

I was in my late 20s, in the process of shaping my musical outlook and what I wanted it to be about, when I first encountered Woody Guthrie. I had made my way through rock music and then turned to country music. But I still hadn't quite found something that addressed the issues I was interested in at the time. Woody was like a path to a full and active musical citizenship. With him, there was a deep awareness of the social forces at work in people's lives. I was interested in addressing those ideas and having them become a part of the music I made.

Many of your songs, like Guthrie's, reach out to people who don't necessarily have a voice in our democracy. The songs echo their fears and frustrations and perhaps their diminished belief in the American dream.

In a way, I guess you could say that. You could hear someone sing the blues. You could hear frustration and anger in rock music. But you couldn't quite experience or hear a broader human thoughtfulness about where you could go with those feelings. Where do you put that energy? Woody was the first guy that showed me what to do with it.

Bob Dylan has also been an influence, especially early in your career.
That's true. After Bob, I went, more or less backwards, to pop music's antecedents. The thing about Bob's music is that it was beautiful—beautifully written, kind of wry and tough-minded, and I liked that. It was direct and quite colloquial and I liked that too. He was writing about a whole number of broader issues that were touched upon in rock music at the time, but not directly addressed.

You had the opportunity to sing Woody Guthrie's "This Land Is Your Land" with Pete Seeger at President Barack Obama's first inauguration in 2009. I imagine that was a memorable event for you.
Yeah, that was quite a moment. Pete's bottom line was that we sing all verses—including the politically charged ones—and that we get all the kids in the choir who backed us up to sing them as well. It was a lovely moment, you know, a very lovely moment.

A few months ago, you were active in the president's re-election campaign, squeezing in appearances at rallies between tour dates.
For the past three presidential election cycles, I have been a part of a political campaign. This time it was different because it was for the *president,* not just a candidate who wanted to be president. For me, the choices were particularly stark this time around. I was really glad to be there. I'd been a supporter of President Obama all along.

How is playing for a campaign audience different from playing for a Bruce Springsteen concert audience?
Well, the campaign audiences are incredibly broad. I go to Ohio with Jay-Z, so Jay-Z's audience is there, my audience is there, and then there is a purely political audience that's there. So you're playing to an enormous cross section of people, including children. On tour, I don't quite have an opportunity to reach this varied audience when I'm playing just to my fans. Basically, you walk onstage and you're looking at this broad spectrum of America. The people may or may not know some of your music. So you're depending on how good your language is. You need to communicate in a very fresh and direct way. For all three times I've helped out on a campaign, that's what I enjoyed the most.

You've never held back from inserting political messages in your own concerts.

If you come to one of our shows, the political is usually a subtext. On the campaign trail, that reverses itself. The subtext becomes the main text, because that's how everyone is hearing it. Every line and every bit of your language is shaded towards the things people are fighting for and caring about. It's wonderful to hear your music come to life in that context. It's been an honor to have that experience. If you're lucky, you get the chance to just nudge the country in this direction, or that. It was the reason why I wrote a lot of those songs.

You come from working-class roots. You've obviously gone well beyond them. How do you stay connected to where you came from?

People always ask that question like there's some trick to it [*laughs*]. Really, that was something that came very natural to me from the beginning. I could look back and see that there were a lot of my heroes who came before me that got distracted or lost in the confusing life that came with their success. So, I had a deep sense of where my power source was coming from, you know. It came from memory and experience, rooted in geography, locality, a sense of place, a certain people. These are the things that are at the heart of the engine on a nightly basis. Maintaining a connection to those things, to me, was always a survival instinct. It was necessary. The things that pulled you away from that, I viewed with some suspicion. I've certainly enjoyed the life and privilege that I've had because of my success. But there's been a fundamental focus on those things that we carried over the years with the E Street Band. I'm lucky I've had the band I've had, one that was surrounded by those things and believed in those things as well.

You say that you were suspicious of success. How so?

I was suspicious of the easy things that your talent brought you, you know. You have to be wary to survive. I think it was something that was natural to my character, so I don't take too much credit for it.

Your most recent album, *Wrecking Ball*, has been described as one of your angriest. Is that an accurate description?

Yeah, I suppose it is. There's a lot to be angry about, you know. The distortion and corruption of the American dream and a certain way of life, the loss of the full meaning of community. To me, those things felt under attack. My concern was that this all added up to a nation in decline. Like other people, I know folks who were affected by the financial crisis, who lost their homes, lost their retirement savings. So it was all very, very real for me. You can have these feelings of frustration and not be able to write about it. That happened to me before. But in this particular case, I was working on another record that wasn't about those things at all. Then I wrote a song that moved in that direction and the rest came very quickly.

Aside from simply being a concerned American citizen, as an artist how do you negotiate the waters of politically motivated music?
I'd been thinking and reading a lot about what's been going on in the country in the past 30 years, back to the Carter recession, the Reagan deregulations, and you see this long historical arc that was moving the country in one direction. On *Wrecking Ball* you hear rebel music, gospel music. I wanted both a current and historical sweep, musically speaking. In the end, it was hard to stand by and see what was happening in the last seven or eight years. The record was a response to that.

When I had the privilege to help you with your book, *Songs,* back in the late '90s, I remember going to your house and being amazed at the books in your study that were about American history, politics, art, and music. You really seemed to be immersing yourself in the American experience.
Reading those books and listening to that music, to me it was always a tool, a part of seeking out your truest identity. It was all part of trying to find out who I was, where I came from, and I was always interested in writing about what I found. So, yeah, I did become quite a student, and still am.

Speaking of books, this seems to be the era of the music memoir. Everyone from Neil Young and Gregg Allman to Pete Townshend and Clive Davis has written one. I read that you, too, were working on one, and then I read that you've given up on it.
I don't ever give up on anything, really. I do something for a while and then I put it aside, you know. I'm always returning to what I have, the raw material. A while back, I recorded a country record and put it aside. I returned to it a couple of months ago and thought, "What am I

going to do next?" As for the memoirs, I got some stuff I've worked on, but I don't have anything fixed. I worked on it for a while, then the music came along and the tour came along. There doesn't seem to be an urgency to return to it at the moment. It'll present itself and I'll see what happens. Like you said, there's plenty of others to read at the moment.

I know you're a big reader. What have you read lately that has stuck with you?
One of the things I've done recently was read all the Western stories of Elmore Leonard. If you're interested in character study, he's just the master of nailing someone in a few lines. He's good for songwriters because that's about all the time you have. And what else? Let's see. [*Springsteen goes to his iPad for his book list.*] I've also read Christopher Hitchen's collection of essays, and *Why Does the World Exist?* by Jim Holt to get my existential buzz [*laughs*]. Another book I read was *Matterhorn* [Karl Marlantes' Vietnam War novel].That was great along with *Stoned* by Andrew Loog Oldam and the follow-up, *2Stoned*. Very, very good books on the music industry. Then some baseball books. Finally, I have quite a fixation on the Apollo astronauts, so I read a few books on them. Basically, I'll get on a topic and read two or three books in a row, and then I'll move on to something else.

At the GRAMMYs last year, you had the opportunity to perform onstage with Paul McCartney. What was that like for you?
When I was 15, back in Freehold, N.J., his music spoke directly to me. This was that man. This was the man that got me to pick up a guitar early in my life and go down a particular road. I think it's important to maintain your sense of being a fan, even when you've experienced success of your own. I go onstage every night as a performer, but I also go onstage as a fan, which is what I was on GRAMMY night.

What was the first real concert you attended as a kid?
It was in Asbury Park at Convention Hall. Here's the lineup: the Who, the Blues Magoos and Herman's Hermits. I remember with the Who, people in the audience were semishocked at the destruction of perfectly good instruments [*laughs*]. That was the first concert, outside of my mother taking me to see Chubby Checker and Anita Bryant in Atlantic City [*laughs*].

I've seen many of your concerts over the years, but never one in Italy—until this summer. Your show in Trieste was amazing. In fact, it ranks as one of the best I've ever seen. How do you explain the Italians' love of your music, and your ability to so deeply connect to them?

I don't know. Every night is an opportunity. For me, it's a pathological opportunity [*laughs*]. You come out onstage and you're in the presence of some like-minded people, you know. You're also in the presence of some people that had never seen the band live before. Last night in Vancouver, probably 20 percent of the audience had never seen the band with Clarence Clemons before. Amazing. So, there's this ongoing . . . I guess you would call it a conversation with your fans that's always renewing itself. I've been dedicated to that my whole life. Why? We can talk about that all night. There's good reasons, bad reasons, straight-up reasons, convoluted ones, sane ones, insane ones. I think the best way to look at it is this way: onstage, it's me and it's this person in the audience, right now, not later, not tomorrow, right *now*. Our fans are immersed in a world that we've created. It's the one place where people go to forget about their troubles. They let themselves go and trust someone. They come into the arena or concert hall and they feel safe and they reveal by their actions their hopes, their dreams, their fears, what's hurt them, what's given them joy. You get an opportunity to witness that on a nightly basis. I have an opportunity—and an honor—to witness that on a nightly basis. And I don't take that lightly.

Acknowledgments

In gathering these interviews, we have benefited from the expertise, kindness, and encouragement of Bob Crane, Charles R. Cross, Dave DiMartino, Whitney Ferguson, Erik Flannigan, Mark Hagen, Clinton Heylin, Dave Marsh, Eric Meola, Robert Santelli, Frank Stefanko, Margaret Thresher and the Rock and Roll Hall of Fame. Photographers Barbara Pyle, Lynn Goldsmith, Pam Springsteen, Jim Marchese, and Danny Clinch were also enthusiastic and generous with their images. We are grateful to each of those whose conversations are collected here, as well as journalists (such as Nicholas Dawidoff, Mikal Gilmore, Edna Gundersen, Gary Graff, Peter Knobler, Kurt Loder, the late Paul Nelson, and Steve Pond) who are not represented in these pages but whose interviews have enriched our understanding of Springsteen over the years. Thanks to Danny Breslauer for providing transcriptions of audio interviews. This volume would not have been possible without the assistance of Jon Landau Management (thank you Barbara Carr, Jon Landau, Alison Oscar, and Jan Stabile). At Bloomsbury Press, publisher Peter Ginna enthusiastically supported the project and our editor Pete Beatty never blanched when we asked, "How about just one more interview?" He has been as much our collaborator as our editor. Nate Knaebel was a real champ throughout production. We offer our thanks as well to our agent Zoe Pagnamenta. And measureless thanks to Bruce Springsteen for the 40 years (and counting) of conversation.

In addition, Christopher Phillips thanks Jonathan Pont, Charley, Erik, Bob, and the extended *Backstreets* family for the warmest of welcomes into the fold 20 years ago, and their friendship and support ever since. *Backstreets* has long been an international effort, with literally hundreds of fellow fans who warrant a hat tip; particular thanks to Rene van Diemen, Todd Draper, Jimmy Guterman, Lisa Iannucci, Josh Jacobson, Phil and Steve Jump, Magnus Lauglo, Shawn Poole, Glenn Radecki, Bernie Ranellone, Caryn Rose, Rich Russo Tony Saddler, John Schlicher, Salvador Trepat, Richard Wolkoff, and Bob Zimmerman, longtime brothers- and sisters-in-arms all. Brandon Herndon, Harrison Howe, and John Howie Jr. provided invaluable support at the Backstreets Towers during the course of this project. Thanks to the E Street Band, Greg Linn, Marilyn Laverty, Thom Zimny, and everyone in the "Springsteen camp" who've met us with benevolence while keeping separate church and state. Constant companions of the road from Phillips Central and Phillips West (I'm including you, Ma), I wouldn't want to do it without you. Especially when you pay for dinner. Thanks most of all to my wife and daughter: Laura, I'd say that two hearts are better than one, but we know that three's even better than that.

Lou Masur expresses his gratitude to Jim Goodman, Doug Greenberg, Dave Masur, Mark Richman, Jeff Roderman, Bruce Rossky, and Tom Slaughter. Thanks go to his students at Rutgers University, for their work on "Springsteen's American Vision," as well as to his colleagues in the American Studies and History Departments. Jani, Ben, and Sophie: once again, thank you for your boundless love, forever wild and forever real.

Credits

Ray Coleman, "Springsteen Crazy," *Melody Maker*, November 1975. Used by permission of IPC Media.

Dave DiMartino, "Bruce Springsteen Takes It To the River: So Don't Call Him Boss, OK?," *Creem*, January 1981, full interview published in *Backstreets*. Used by permission of Dave DiMartino.

Robert Duncan, "Springsteen is Not God (and Doesn't Want to Be)," *Creem*, January 1976. Used by permission.

Mark Hagen, "The Midnight Cowboy," *Mojo*, January 1999. Copyright Bauer Media Group.

Mark Hagen, "Meet the New Boss," *The Guardian*, January 17, 2009. Used by permission of Guardian News and Media Ltd.

James Henke, interview, *Rolling Stone*, August 6, 1992. Used by permission. Copyright *Rolling Stone* LLC 1992.

James Henke, "The Magician's Tools," *Backstreets* 89 (Summer 2010). Used by permission of *Backstreets*.

Robert Hilburn, "New York Serenade," *Melody Maker*, August 24, 1974. Used by permission of IPC Media.

Nick Hornby, "A Fan's Eye View," *The Guardian*, July 17, 2005. Used by permission of Guardian News and Media Ltd.

Patrick Humphries, "Springsteen," *Record Collector*, February 1999. Used by permission.

"Lost Interviews," excerpted in *Backstreets* 57 (Winter 1997) and *Backstreets* 58 (Spring 1998). Used by permission of Charles Cross and Christopher Phillips.

Dave Marsh, "Springsteen," *Musician*, February 1981. Used by permission of Dave Marsh.

Dave Marsh, interview, SiriusXM, transcribed and reprinted as "Will It Go Round in Circles," *Backstreets* 84 (Summer/Fall 2006). Used by permission of Dave Marsh and *Backstreets*.

Gavin Martin, "Hey Joad, Don't Make It Sad (Oh, Go On Then)," *New Musical Express* March 9, 1996. Used by permission of IPC Media.

Scott Pelley, interview, *60 Minutes*, October 7, 2007. Used by permission of CBS News Archives.

Will Percy, interview, *DoubleTake*, Spring 1998. Used by permission.

Christopher Phillips, "Citizen Bruce," *Backstreets* 80 (Summer/Fall 2004). Used by permission of Christopher Phillips and *Backstreets*. All rights reserved.

Christopher Phillips, "This Is What Will Be," *Backstreets* 87 (Spring 2008). Used by permission of Christopher Phillips and *Backstreets*. All rights reserved.

Index

A Note on the Editors

Christopher Phillips has been covering the career of Bruce Springsteen for 20 years as the editor and publisher of *Backstreets*, the premier Springsteen magazine. He also created and maintains Backstreets.com, the primary web destination for Springsteen fans. He lives in Chapel Hill, North Carolina.

Louis P. Masur is a professor of American studies and history at Rutgers University and the author of many books, including *Runaway Dream: Born to Run and Bruce Springsteen's American Vision*. He has appeared on E Street Radio with Dave Marsh and on WFUV with Dennis Elsas, and has written about Springsteen for *Slate*, *Salon*, and other publications. He lives in New Jersey.